Abigail Adams

Abigail Adams at the time of her marriage

FROM A PASTEL DRAWING BY BENJAMIN BLYTHE

1764

Contents

Abigail Adams

by

JANET WHITNEY

With Illustrations

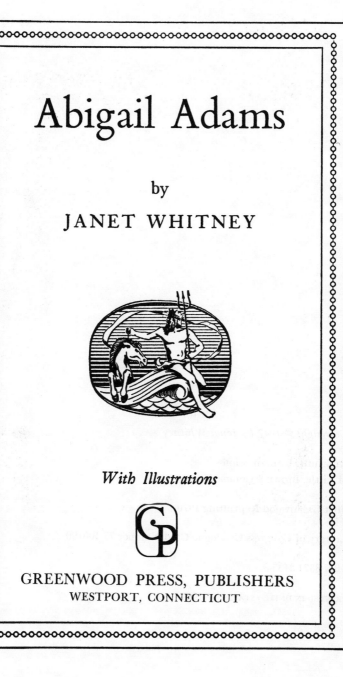

GREENWOOD PRESS, PUBLISHERS
WESTPORT, CONNECTICUT

To
Abigail Adams Homans

Acknowledgments

I OWE a deep debt of gratitude to two direct descendants of Abigail Adams without whose help this book would not have been possible. Mr. Henry Adams has lent me books, genealogical records, and other manuscript notes compiled by himself, and has allowed me access to relevant portions of the collection of Adams papers known as the Adams Manuscript (Massachusetts Historical Society). In addition he has answered my questions and has taken me personally to the places and houses connected with the Adams, Quincy, and Smith families. Mrs. Robert Homans, to whom I have dedicated this book, has also taken me to the family places, has lent me reproductions of pictures, and has accompanied me through long hours of poring over private family manuscripts.

Perhaps this is the place to say that neither Mrs. Homans nor Mr. Adams nor any other member of the Adams family had any part in the instigation of this book, or read as much as a line of it before it appeared in print. For this generous confidence I am also grateful.

I wish to thank the Massachusetts Historical Society, the Boston Public Library, the American Antiquarian Society, the Philadelphia Library Company, the Boston Athenaeum, the Pennsylvania Historical Society, the Westtown School Library, and the Widener and the Houghton Library, Harvard, for every kind of cooperation; and especially Mr. Brigham for allowing me access to the, at that time, unused and unpublished collection recently acquired by the American Antiquarian Society, and filed by them as the Adams Letters. (I have referred to this collection throughout my book as the Cranch Manuscript.)

Among numerous others who have given me help of various

kinds, I must add my friends Mr. and Mrs. Arthur Perry of Boston, Dr. and Mrs. Henry J. Cadbury of Harvard, and Mr. and Mrs. Carroll T. Brown of Westtown; Mr. Zoltan Haraszti, for allowing me the use of the unpublished letters in his care referred to herein as the Thaxter Manuscript; and, for his important co-operation at critical moments, the late Mr. Allyn Bailey Forbes.

Dr. Thomas S. Drake, Professor of American History of Haverford College, and Mrs. Helen G. Hole read a large part of the manuscript. And my husband, George Gillett Whitney, gave me, as always, a combined interest and criticism which is truly invaluable.

J. P. W.

Foreword

THIS is the story of the American Revolution as it seemed to a woman. Hundreds of her letters, carefully preserved by their recipients, bear witness to her close observation of current events, and her independent judgment. Members of her family were actors on the great stage. There were cousins in South Carolina, cousins who became pro-British refugees in England, cousins who lived in Boston and were a vital part of its mercantile and political life. All carried on voluminous correspondence, letters written not for the public but for the intimate eyes of relatives. Abigail Adams always had inside and advance information. So her eyes might be as clear as any through which to take a look at the turning point of American history, her times, and observe their close parallels with our own.

Her husband, John Adams, was the greatest orator, and perhaps the greatest intellect, in the First American Congress, and was called by his fellow members the Atlas of the Revolution. He was the first shaper of American foreign policy, the chairman of the Peace Commission, the first Ambassador to Great Britain after the peace, the first Vice-President of the new United States of America and the second President. His wife therefore had to play a prominent part in Boston, London, New York, Philadelphia, and finally Washington, D. C.

Not only her husband but her eldest son kept her finger on the pulse of public affairs. She lived to see her son John Quincy Adams appointed Ambassador to Russia, Ambassador to Great Britain, and then Secretary of State. Abigail Adams is the only woman so far to be both wife and mother of a President.

She saw, then, a lot more than most women. The great historical names — George Washington, Thomas Jefferson, Alexander Hamilton, John Jay, Samuel Adams, Benjamin Franklin — were guests at her table, daily associates and friends. To enter her life is to see the back of the stage, the personal and intimate side of what from the front was the finished dignity of history.

JANET WHITNEY

Westtown, Pennsylvania

Illustrations

Abigail Adams

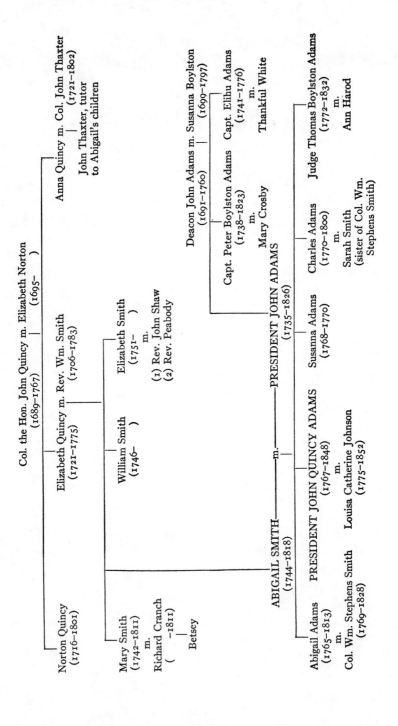

I

Abigail Smith Has an Admirer

ABIGAIL SMITH sharpened her quill pen and wrote in her flowing, rapid hand to her new-married dearest friend that she
hadn't any sparks — what an idea, were they supposed to be as
plenty as herrings? But her sister Mary, whose room she shared,
was sitting with her needle at the window, and presently crying,
"Here they come!" Mary flew down the stairs. Two young men
were riding up to the door, their horses' hoofbeats muffled in the
thick fallen maple leaves which spread a carpet of gold before the
Weymouth Parsonage. When they had dismounted and hitched
their horses to the post, the elder and taller took Mary in his arms
with the privilege of an accepted bridegroom.

The younger man, thick-set, vigorous, said, "Your servant,
Mistress Polly — soon to be Mrs. Cranch! Is Miss Nabby at home
today?"

Nabby at the top of the stairs heard him well, and stole softly
back into the room again, seized with that unaccountable shyness
which John Adams often caused in her. He had been coming to
the house a great deal of late, as companion to Richard Cranch
during Cranch's courtship of Mary, and of necessity he had been
thrown into Abigail's society. For eighteen-year-old * Abigail it
had not been unmixed pleasure. This lawyer of twenty-seven, already a rising man of affairs, noted and feared for his sharp tongue
as well as respected and loved for his honesty and good nature,
made the parson's daughter feel her youth painfully. To be sure he
was no stranger. He was the friend and classmate at Harvard
College of her cousin Sam Quincy. Sam and he had both been

* Abigail Smith was born Nov. 11, 1744. John Adams was born Oct. 19,
1735.

called to the bar in Boston, introduced by the same sponsor, Mr. Gridley, on the same day. He was an intimate in the houses of her mother's cousins, Lawyer Edmund Quincy and Colonel Josiah Quincy, at Braintree, and known well to her grandfather, old Colonel John. Her cousins Esther and Hannah had flirted with him. And Abigail had seen him in company, especially the company of men, talking vigorously, laughing heartily — deep bass gales of laughter — easy and friendly.

But accustomed as she was to queen it in her little circle, to be the liveliest person in the house, admitted by her usual companions to be a clever and brilliant girl, no sooner did John Adams approach her than she was tongue-tied. His keen appraising glance, catching hers across a room, could make her blush and become confused. Yet — did he *have* to come so regularly with his friend? Did he *have* to pass so much time at Weymouth? Was his asking immediately for Mistress Nabby purely perfunctory?

She admired and feared him. Yet she sometimes thought his interest in her was real and deep. They had had some good talks — about life and philosophy and books, and politics and the place of woman, and education, and the high manners of the Greeks and Romans. . . . She had felt her ignorance beside his erudition. Like Portia, she had confessed that before him she was but an "unlessoned girl." Yet she had been keenly aware of the unfeigned respect with which he had listened to her opinions, and it had made her talk more brilliantly than ever before. Yes, he had seen her at her best moments. And they were so because of him. But surely he had seen her at her worst as well, gauche, silent, and dull. That, too, because of him. He could create a forbidding silence in which her self-confidence died.

So she hesitated in her room. She looked in the glass, pushed her hair back over her ear, twined a ringlet around her finger. The glass did not reassure her. Her dark eyes, fine complexion, regular features, all lacked that sparkle of animation or the seriousness of thought to give them their true charm. The face in the glass looked blankly back at her, as it was to look blankly back at portrait painters. It was drained of her soul. She went down at last because she must. She greeted John Adams with the stately correctness drilled into her by Grandmother Quincy, and tried to join in the discussion of wedding plans that was going briskly forward between her mother, her sister and the bridegroom. But it was one of the bad times. Adams was haughty, cold, withdrawn. She felt the pressure of his critical attention to every word, and she felt herself becoming wooden and stiff with constraint. Her father entered, and they all rose to greet him respectfully.

He was as certain of that attention in any room he entered as if he had been born a king, and his confident, authoritative manner showed it. A parson was indeed a king in his little kingdom, anywhere in New England. And since he was seldom rich, his dignity was a counterbalance to the more mundane dignity of wealth. Vehement, salty, Reverend William Smith was sometimes a rough monarch, but there were none to gainsay it, especially in his own household where his wife was fifteen years his junior.

"And how prospers your career, Mr. Adams, now you are in full swing as a Boston lawyer?" he asked, when greetings had been exchanged.

"Oh, finely, sir!" answered John Adams. "Don't you teach 'woe unto you when all men shall speak well of you'? I am creating enemies in every quarter of the town!"

Their harsh laughter rang out in unison. But Mrs. Smith, who had been born a Quincy, turned up her aristocratic nose a little, and looked the other way.

Presently John Adams found himself — by accident or intention — close to Abigail, who sat miserable and paralyzed in a corner.

"Well, Miss Nabby, why do you sit and hang down your head like a bulrush, and let the company lose the bright sparkles of those eyes?" *

She lifted her eyes, luminous and wide-open. Her face, young and unguarded, told him much. His eyes answered hers with a sudden glow, an admiring passion. Her constraint melted and she felt freed and gay.

"I've heard, sir," she said, "that two apparitions were seen one evening this week hovering about this house which very much resembled you and a cousin of yours! How it should ever enter

* Quotations in this chapter are from letters in the Adams manuscript.

into the head of an apparition to asume a form like yours I cannot devise!"

"Come out and stroll around the garden with me," said John, "and I promise to convince you that I am not a ghost!"

That night the Reverend William Smith was asked for permission to court his second daughter. Two daughters of marriageable age; two suitors. All very fine and dandy. Two very different men though, as Mrs. Smith was particular to point out. Yet — thought the Reverend Smith — good stuff in both, though Cranch, settled, better balanced, maturer, was obviously the greater catch. He was a partner with Mr. Palmer in the glassworks at Braintree. Colonel Josiah Quincy had recently joined the firm.

In November 1762 Mary was married to Richard Cranch. Her father preached the wedding sermon on the text — "And Mary hath chosen that good part." His three remaining children sat in the square white pew and listened to him decorously — Abigail, eighteen; William, sixteen; and little Elizabeth, eleven. The Reverend William Smith did well with daughters but he was not so skilled with sons.*

But if Abigail, like others present, found a hidden meaning in her father's text, less than complimentary to her suitor, she could afford not to mind. She was certain his future would be distinguished. Her admiration for him was so complete that she could afford to laugh and be saucy.

If parents were to study the secret history of other parents it might diminish their self-confidence even dangerously. For young people rather like their parents to be positive, and would prefer to have them wrong than spinelessly unopinioned. Yet Mrs. Elizabeth Quincy Smith, anxiously observing her daughter's girlish infatuation, and setting against it the coolness of her mature experience, her belittling judgment, her knowledge of men and manners, was wrong, and Abigail's young and eager enthusiasm was right be-

---

* Young William, now apprenticed in Boston, was a disappointment to himself and to others and faded out of the family annals.

yond compare. There were no indicating circumstances which would make it possible for the Reverend and Mrs. Smith to foresee that this stocky, energetic, magnetic man, with his keen mind, his power with words, and his carelessness of making enemies, was to make their little daughter the equal of queens.

And who was John Adams anyway? At Harvard College where students were still, under the lingering influence of the Old Country, seated in class according to their rank by birth,* Charles Cushing was first, John Adams fourteenth in a class of twenty-four, and he wouldn't have got that high but for his mother's having been a Boylston.†

When they were listed academically, however, John Adams was among the first three. His part in the Commencement Day Exercises drew attention to him and got him a job as schoolmaster at Worcester.¹ While at Worcester he had had entree to the best society the town afforded. There he had qualified himself in the evenings, and in his spare time, for the law — for it had long been clear to him that he could not put his mind into the strait-waistcoat of orthodoxy required by the ministry. At his father's house in Braintree some years before he had witnessed a heresy trial. The boy's sympathy had been with the young minister. If he had not admired Mr. Bryant, if Mr. Bryant's theology had not been attacked by narrow-minded bigotry, ‡ John Adams might have chosen the ministry, and the course of history have been diverted. But already Destiny had marked him for its own.

When Mr. Gridley presented Sam Quincy and John Adams to the Boston Bar, one or two of the established lawyers h'mmed and ha'd and said well of course, they all knew Sam Quincy — he had read law with so-and-so, he was Josiah Quincy's son and the Honorable John Quincy's grandson and all that — but who was this

---

* Until 1769, when alphabetical order was substituted.

† "And what," said the recent Prince of Wales innocently, visiting Philadelphia in the nineteen-twenties, "is a biddle?"

‡ Bryant won his case, and his liberty of conscience was maintained both by John Adams's father and by the Honorable John Quincy. But the trial had been disagreeable.

John Adams? Who was *he?* And Mr. Gridley gave his personal
guarantee for John Adams, based on a single searching interview.

John Adams was not so-and-so's son, or so-and-so's pupil, he
was himself. He stood on his own merit.

It would not be true to say that he noticed nothing remarkable
in himself, because, like every young man of ambition, indeed he
did; he hoped, he feared. But he expected nothing more of himself
than to succeed at the law, to make money, and to own land.

These ambitions were enough to take care of his time, because
he had to start from scratch. His father, a respectable citizen and a
solid farmer, had sent his eldest son to Harvard. From then on,
his career was his own business.

John's youthful diary is full of exhortations to himself to make
better use of his day. To stick to his books and let nothing decoy
him — "no girl, no gun, no cards," in descending order of temptation.

But though he would read passionately for days on end — Latin,
history, law — he could not make himself a bookworm. His enjoyment of the present, his zest for life, would not be denied. Some
girl, some gun, was always getting the better of him. "Friday,
Saturday, Sunday, Monday," he would record with disgust, "all
spent in absolute idleness, or what is worse, gallanting the girls." [2]

And he would swing himself again fiercely toward his mark,
reputation, reputation, the bubble reputation. Yet the struggle
kept his balance. He compared himself with other young men.
Here is Bob Paine * saying, at about Adams's age — twenty-two —
"I have ruined myself by a too eager pursuit of wisdom." And
Sam Quincy early throwing up the sponge — "We shall never
make your great fellows." Depression and lack of courage, diag-
nosed young Adams; "Quincy's soul is afraid to aim at great ac-
quisition."

Adams's soul had no such fear. Yet when he rode into Boston to
the law court, Bob Paine and Sam Quincy had it all over him. "I
felt shy, under awe and concern. The other lawyers present
'looked sour at me,' I had no acquaintance with anybody but Paine

* Robert Treat Paine.

and Quincy, and they took but little notice." [8] However, after attending court stubbornly all day, he went in the evening to a party with Sam Quincy — "the most spacious and elegant room, the gayest company of gentlemen and the finest row of ladies that ever I saw." And he learned, he persevered, he made his way.

Shyness might make him awkward, but it did not make him silent. He was quick to make his mark in any company. Men with brains particularly sought his friendship. A letter written by him to one man was shown to another, and the second sought his correspondence.[4] He was provocative, irritating, some said conceited, but he was incurably interesting. He took the trouble to think, and he spoke his real thought, with apparently no reserve. It had the effect of startling originality, and sometimes it was. But it was too honest, too sober to be flashy. He did not deal in the epigram or the paradox. Like his contemporary Dr. Johnson in England, he took out and showed you the contents of his mind and heart, and they were genuine and various.

He was very much of a man's man, but women fell for him. They liked his vitality and they liked his susceptibility to their charms. But he always disentangled himself before he had gone too far. His narrowest squeak was with Sam Quincy's sister Hannah. John Adams was often at their house, to drink tea or to spend the evening; and Hannah and her pretty cousin Esther gave him good practice in gallanting. Esther was safe company because she was being courted every week end by Jonathan Sewall — a friend of John Adams's from Worcester days. But she combined with Hannah to provoke John to dangerous flirtation. Destiny made haste and interrupted them just in time.

A too early marriage clips a young man's wings. Mr. Gridley had impressed this upon his protégé; and John Adams, having to earn his way as he went, could read the lesson also plainly in his circumstances. Unmarried, he could afford to reserve himself time for study and so lay a foundation for future success. Married, he must give all his time and energy to earning a living, and turn into a pettifogging attorney, grinding along with the small beer of his profession. So he thanked his stars that accident "delivered me from very dangerous shackles, and left me at liberty, if I will but mind my studies, of making a character and a fortune." [5] Hannah quickly consoled herself with another suitor. Adams always boasted that, with all his affairs of the heart, he had never done harm to any woman.

A young man might well be grateful to have experienced such a liberal education as could be provided by women like Hannah Quincy and Esther Quincy; a training in manners, feeling, softer repartee, and in the ups and downs and intricacies of a woman's character. For one thing, it took away forever his fear of the bluestocking. A thinking, reading woman was a better companion than another.

But all this time Abigail was present in the background, a delicate, observant girl. She had not yet risen to the surface of his attention, because her elder cousins held the floor. When John Adams graduated from Harvard, Abigail Smith — who might have been at the Commencement exercises, a great and popular social occasion for all the good families in and around Boston — was eleven. When he so narrowly escaped getting engaged to her cousin Hannah, she was fifteen.

And how did she manage, when she was seventeen, to throw her net over this large and slippery fish?

Abigail was brought up in three homes. First, her own home in Weymouth, eight miles south of Boston, with her father, Parson Smith, and her mother, Elizabeth Quincy, and her two sisters and brother. Then, the house called Mount Wollaston at Braintree, four miles farther along the shore road, the home of her distinguished grandfather the Honorable John Quincy and his wife, Elizabeth Norton; and then the house in Boston of her father's brother, Isaac Smith, and his wife, Elizabeth Storer. In all of these homes she was exceedingly happy, and the variety of going from one to the other enlivened her mind and polished her manners. Bernard Shaw makes play with a man that had two fathers. Abigail Smith had three fathers, and what was more to the purpose in her case, three mothers. Outside her own home, which had, after all, her earliest years, it was her Grandmother Quincy and her Aunt Elizabeth Smith who meant the most in her development.

Abigail was a delicate child, and for that reason was never sent to school. Change of air was a favorite specific for health, and this added to care for her education, was the basis of her variety of domicile. But beside that, she was a favorite grandchild and a favorite niece. She was *en rapport* with grandmother and aunt; her childish company and quick response increased their pleasure in life. They invited her for long visits. As she was a welcome guest at Boston and at Braintree, so when she got home again to Weymouth she was like a welcome guest there too.

All three households were well-to-do, and two of them were bookish. Her clergyman father was a reader and lender of books. In his library she browsed through many a volume. Parson Smith's salary was not large in cash, but he got the parsonage rent free with it, and was besides an able farmer. By the time Abigail was nineteen her father had made, saved, or inherited enough to buy an additional farm at Medford.

Parson Smith was not fluent with his pen; he did not run to words, but scratched a hasty line, day by day, of the day's main event in the blank pages of his interleaved almanacs. But these entries in his skeleton diary, scant and curt as they are, reflect the healthy, thrifty rhythm of the home; the easy swing of the parson's mind from the sheep of his congregation to the sheep of his fields. One day (May 16, 1751) "We kept a fast to bewail the burning of our Meeting-House." And another (December 1761), "My winter stock of sheep is 26." A September Sabbath notes "A proclamation for a day of general prayer thro' the province on account of a severe drought. [September 3, 1761.] I prayed from 5 James V. 7." Monday (September 4, 1761) laconically records "A remarkable rain." One day he will kill two hogs, and another he will baptize a baby. The scales swing equal. Life has more than one side. He will pay for his firewood with his hay, but he will hand out cash for a volume of Virgil. He will risk in the lottery (January 5, 1759) — result, "perdu" — but he will sell a horse

(April 11, 1749) for a good price, and will lend half of it to brother Isaac Smith (December 31, 1755). It is a vigorous, prosperous, practical, not narrow, not ungenerous character that emerges as Abigail's father.

It was a great change from country living to be in the Smiths' Boston house. She could feel the exciting stir of the town about her, a town which was the largest city * in the colonies, and the most thriving port. She could go down to the wharf, carefully accompanied, and see the forest of masts, the clean-cut angles of rigging and spars against the blue New England sky, and the bright figureheads and scrollwork of the sea-clean ships. Bran † sometimes flew in the air, from the opening of a bale of perishable goods packed in it, and she could catch a glimpse as she passed of "bran-new" porcelain from Sèvres, or glass from Venice, twinkling in the sun. She could go with dazzled eyes into the pleasant dimness of her uncle's warehouse, which smelt of coffee and wine and spice and sugar from the West Indies and Madeira; tea from the Far East via England; and salted herring and mackerel from the native fisheries. For a special treat she would sometimes be taken by dinghy to one of her uncle's ships and would see the cabin, with its plush and leather, look out through the dark porthole into the bright water, and feel how the great hollow shell rocked gently in its berth on the tide. The tide of Boston Harbor would soon rock the British Empire itself. But now all the ships flew the Union Jack, all owed allegiance to Great Britain, were manned by colonial-born men who called themselves English, and were protected by British men-o'-war.

But it was when Abigail visited Grandmother Quincy that she truly breathed what was to become her native air. There in the township of Braintree ‡ by the sea she was to pass the major part of her life. Whatever part of the world she was in, she was to look

---

* Philadelphia was the largest less than forty years later.
† Sawdust was then called bran, and was the chief article used for packing perishables of all kinds.
‡ The New England word was "town" for the aggregation of community called in other places "township." There was no town then at Braintree in the modern sense.

back, not to Weymouth, not to Boston, but to Braintree as her heart's home. Though not to her grandfather's house, but to another, outwardly more modest.

Her grandfather's homestead was on a spacious scale for those parts, not to be compared with the large mansions of the South, run by slave labor and built for lavish hospitality, but distinctly the great house of the neighborhood, with grounds that ran down to the sea's edge. It was a good playground for a delicate little girl. Inside the house there was a dignity and order not possible in the bustling Weymouth parsonage. The type of life was the same — the farm life, and abundance from the farm — but there was more time, more leisure to read, discuss, think, and enjoy — because there was more money. The Honorable John Quincy had regarded wealth as an instrument for the public service. For twenty-one years he was annually elected to the Massachusetts House of Representatives from Braintree, and for fourteen of those years he was Speaker of the House. For even longer he had been elected each year Moderator of the Braintree Town Meeting, succeeding in that office his Uncle Edmund, Judge of the Supreme Court of Massachusetts. John Quincy was also chairman of the Massachusetts committee on currency and chairman of the legislative committee with the duty of sending instructions to the agent of the Province at the Court of Great Britain. At home he did not scorn to accept appointment, at their own request, as guardian of the remnant of Massachusetts Indians, the Ponkapoag Indians, who tramped the twelve miles to his home from their reserve, consumed his beer and cider, told him their troubles and got redress, camped on his land and fished his ocean beaches, broke his fences and burnt his wood; which he bore with patience equal to any Quaker's. As her father's home, then, was pervaded by the air of church and parish matters, so Abigail found her grandfather's home pervaded by the air of the state,* politics, and the law. Sitting quietly on her stool in a shady corner, her chin in her hand, she listened to many a hot conversation among the gentlemen, debates on freedom, the constitution of England, Magna Carta and

* I.e., the American colonies.

rights of Englishmen. She heard heated arguments on the right of
the government to search citizens' property for contraband, to
break open chests, burst locks; yes, in a man's own store, sir, or
worse, his house! And there was sharp comment on the British-
appointed Governor of Massachusetts Bay, Sir Thomas Bernard,
and his part in the increasing tenseness between the colonies and
Parliament.

So Abigail as a girl breathed in the air of liberty and was conscious of the fast-moving current of her times. She also read
Shakespeare, Molière, and "the poets," Locke, and the *Spectator*,
learned to cook and sew — both plain and fancy — and was taught
the importance of grace and softness to a woman's manner.
Grandmother Quincy was as keen as any Southern lady to cultivate the gentle exterior, the controlled movement, the voice without edge.

By the time John Adams noticed Abigail Smith she was so
worthy of his notice that his hesitation, his caution, could be
caused only by the fear that she was too good to be true.

John Adams found Abigail the best-educated woman he had
ever met. Adams's very first letter to her — or rather aimed at her,
for it was addressed to her sister and enclosed in one of Dick
Cranch's — referred to some lively political opinions she had been
expressing. "Please give my — I don't know what! — to Mistress
Nabby. Tell her I hear she's about commencing a most loyal subject to young George; and although my allegiance has been
hitherto inviolate, I shall endeavor all in my power to foment
rebellion." [6]

That was 1761, the year that George III was crowned in a
blaze of youth and popularity; but it also was the year of the
Writs of Assistance in Massachusetts to help enforce the British
Acts of Trade. Only a few weeks after writing that ambiguous
message to Mistress Nabby, John Adams gave a remarkable account, in the Mount Wollaston circle, of his first full-dress day in
court, when the test case concerning the Writs of Assistance came
up for trial. John Adams's patron and sponsor, Benjamin Gridley,
had been counsel for the Crown, and James Otis against him.
Young Adams had been deeply, passionately stirred.

"In the noble Council Chamber," he said, "round a great fire were seated five judges, with Lieutenant-Governor Hutchinson at their head as Chief Justice, all arrayed in their new, fresh robes of scarlet English broad-cloth, with their large cambric bands and immense judicial wigs. Sam Quincy and I sat there in our new black gowns and bands and wigs, according to Chief Justice Hutchinson's new rules of costume on the model of the English lawcourts. I was the youngest present, looking, I dare say, like a short, thick Archbishop of Canterbury in that outfit! But I tell you, sir, I sat there at the table, pen in hand, lost in admiration. Mr. Otis, as you know, was once Mr. Gridley's pupil. Well, Mr. Gridley made a learned, well-reasoned speech supporting the right of government to search for contraband. Then Mr. Otis demolished it; more than demolished it, blew it all to pieces; not troubling to take it up point by point, but setting principle against principle. And yet, while he refuted all Gridley's arguments and swept on to overwhelming victory, he treated his old master with all the deference of a son to a father!"

"I hope you took notes?" said the Honorable John Quincy.

"Having my pen, I did take some. But my feeling was too great for me to take many. My eyes were constantly on the drama before me. Mr. Otis was transformed by speaking. One forgot he was plump, round-faced, short-necked; one saw only that he had the eye of an eagle, a voice and style worthy of antiquity. I can imagine Cicero spoke like him! His view of the attitude of England toward the colonies seemed to me, as he unfolded it, incontrovertibly true. And a contest appeared to me to be opened to which I could foresee no end, and which would render my life a burden, and everything — property, industry, everything! — insecure!" [7]

Abigail, listening to young John Adams, forgot that he also was plump and short-necked; she noticed only that he too had the eye of an eagle.

"As to your life being a burden," said Quincy, "that might depend on which side you take. Mr. Hutchinson has shown us the shortcut to prosperity!" He glanced keenly at the young man.

"There is no alternative left but to take the side which appears to be just," said Adams, with a downcast look of somber meditation, "and to trust in Providence for the protection of truth and right." [8]

Preoccupied as John Adams was with thoughts like these, thoughts at war with his private ambition, he found refreshment whenever he came to the Weymouth Parsonage with Dick Cranch. He loved to hear that saucy Mistress Nabby talk. His manner to her might at times be forbidding or overbearing, but it was never tainted with patronage. And when he found out at last what he had to give her, there was nothing cold about that.

"Accidents are often more friendly to us than our own prudence," [9] he wrote her in February. "I intended to have been at Weymouth yesterday, but a storm prevented — cruel yet perhaps blessed storm! Cruel for detaining me . . . perhaps blessed to you or me or both for keeping me at *my distance*. For every experimental philosopher knows that the steel and magnet or the glass and the platter will not fly together with more celerity than Somebody and Somebody when brought within the striking distance." And in August — "Could my horse have helped me to Weymouth, Braintree would not have held me last night. I lay in the well-known chamber and dreamed I saw a Lady tripping it over the hills on the Weymouth Shore and spreading light and beauty and glory all around her."

John Adams had no reason to complain that his ardor was not reciprocated, or that his lady's lively brain had cooled her heart.

"My Friend," she wrote, "if I was sure your absence to-day was occasioned by what it generally is, either to wait upon company or promote some good work, I frankly confess my mind would be much more at ease than at present it is." There are bonds of humanity, friendship, and "a type more binding than either. Unite these and there is a three-fold cord — by this I am not ashamed to own myself bound, nor do I perceive that you are wholly free from it." She pressed a flower in there. "Accept this faulty scrawl warm from the heart of Your sincere Diana." [10]

Since they lived only four miles apart, there was not much

occasion for love letters. But the last ordeal of the long period of courtship was a six weeks' separation while John Adams underwent inoculation for smallpox. This practice (introduced into England by Lady Mary Wortley Montagu, who had discovered it among the Turks, and into Philadelphia by Dr. Benjamin Rush) had been introduced into Boston by John Adams's uncle, Dr. Boylston. It was nothing less than having smallpox on purpose. The theory, supported by a good deal of evidence, was that smallpox induced in a healthy person, well-prepared by diet and drugs, and under the constant supervision of a physician, would insure him against a painful, disfiguring, and perhaps fatal attack of smallpox accidentally acquired. The chances of the latter were so high that inoculation was preferable.* Yet there were risks. Jonathan Edwards's son-in-law, President Burr of Princeton, father of Aaron, died of it.

John Adams, in April 1764, wrote to his lady — "(Just off to enjoy the Small Pox) Saturday eve. Eight o'clock. My dear Diana — For many years past I have not felt more serenely than I do this evening. My head is clear and my heart is at ease. . . . My room is prepared for a seven days retirement and my plan is digested for 4 or 5 weeks. My brother retreats with me to our preparatory hospital and is determined to keep me company through the Small Pox." He comforts her "tears and anxiety," his hearty confidence sets to work to soothe her fears. "For my part I believe no man ever undertook to prepare himself for the Small Pox with fewer than I have at present. I have considered very thoroughly the diet and medicine prescribed me and am fully satisfied that no durable evil can result from either, and any other fear from the Small Pox or its appurtenances in the modern way of Inoculation I never had in my life. Present my duty and gratitude to Papa. Next Fryday we take our departure for Boston. To Capt. Cunningham's we go. And I have not the least doubt of a pleasant three weeks not withstanding the distemper. Good-night, my Dear, I'm agoing to Bed!" [11]

A note from Abigail, brought by her brother, cheered his

---

* The young Jefferson went to Philadelphia to have his under the famous supervision of Dr. Rush.

pillow. "Sir — I feel much easier than I did an hour ago, my
Uncle having given me a more particular and favorable account of
the Small Pox or rather the operation of the preparation, than I
have had before. He speaks greatly in favor of Dr. Perkins,* who
has not lost one patient . . . and knows better what to do in case
of any difficulty. He allows his patients greater liberty with regard to their diet than several other physicians. Some of them,
such as Lord, forbid their patients a mouthful of bread. My
uncle" (she means her uncle Dr. Tufts, himself a physician) "says
they are all agreed that 'tis best to abstain from Butter and Salt —
and most of them from meat. Keep your spirits up. Shall I come
to see you before you go? No, I won't, for I want not again to
experience what I this morning felt when you left — Your A.
mith." [12]

The Reverend William Smith, already Papa to his intended
son-in-law, sent by request all his volumes of Swift, and by personal concern his manservant Tom, to wait on the Adams brothers
for the few days until they went into Boston.

The probation week over, John Adams next reported from
Captain Cunningham's home in Boston, one of the houses which
had been set aside for the smallpox party. Often a group of relations and friends arranged to be "done" together, but John
Adams's companions in the adventure were not all under the same
doctor. Dr. Perkins's patients were well treated. "We have new
milk in abundance and as much pudding and rice and indeed anything of a farinacious kind we please, and the medicine we take is
not at all nauseous or painful. Five persons in the same room under the care of Dr. Lord are starved and medicamented with the
greatest severity. No bread, no pudding, no milk (except half
milk, half water) and powders that keep them sick and weak."
Inoculated patients felt pretty uncomfortable "just before the
pock came out . . . some general languor, some fever and
others," then their aches and pains departed — "Their spirits rise,
tongues run and they eat, drink and laugh like prisoners released."
Abigail's brother and uncle, who had been done in another house,

The doctor of Adams's choice.

"have been here to see us this morning. They are charmingly well and cheerful, tho' they are lean and weak." The Quincy brothers, Sam and Josiah, were fellow patients of Perkins near by. "I asked Dr. Perkins how they had it. He answered — 'Oh Lord, Sir, infinitely light.' It is extremely pleasing, says he, wherever we go we see everybody passing through this tremendous distemper in the lightest, easiest manner conceivable. The Doctor meant those that have the distemper by inoculation in the new method, for those who have it in the natural way are objects of as much Horror as ever." John Adams was exasperated that with this contrast "before the eyes of the whole Town," as plain as the nose on your face, there were still at least five hundred persons who refused to be inoculated. Clergy and selectmen expostulated in vain. "Is man a rational creature, think you?" he demanded. "Conscience, forsooth, and scruples are the cause. I should think myself a deliberate self-murderer!" [13]

But these charges hit closer home than he remembered. Abigail herself had not been inoculated, and her father could not bring himself to risk her beauty in that way. John converted and thoroughly scared her, and she bewailed her dangerous situation to him. He replied fervently — "I join with you sincerely in your lamentation that you were not inoculated. I wish to God the Dr. wd sett up an Hospital at Germantown * and inoculate you. I will come and nurse you, nay, I will go with you to the Castle or to Point Shirley or anywhere & attend you. You say rightly safety there is not, and I say safety there never will be!" [14]

He knew that even his letters might carry contagion. And so did Abigail's mother. At the height of his illness John hesitated to obey Abigail's demand for letters — "I am infected myself, & every room in the house has infected people in it, so that there is real danger in writing." [15] But his scruples were earnestly set at rest. The letters were fumigated. "Your friendly epistle came like an infernal messenger through fire & brimstone," [16] Abigail assured him. And she described how her impatience pestered the manservant at his task.

* A part of Braintree.

"Mamma is so fearful I should catch the distemper that she hardly ever thinks the letters are sufficiently purified. Did you never rob a bird's nest? Do you remember how the poor bird would fly round and round fearful to come nigh, yet not know how to leave the place? Just so they say I hover round Tom while he is smoking your letters."

She makes sport with his baby goddaughter, Betsy, one-year-old daughter of Richard and Mary Cranch. "Betsy sends her love to you, says she designed to have kissed you before you went away, but you made no advances & she! . . . know you of any figure in the Mathematics whereby you can convey one to her? Inclining lines that meet in the same center, will not that figure come as nigh as any?" [17] And she can be as outspoken as himself at times. "Unsociable being" is a charge that has been laid against him. She quotes one of his fellow sufferers as saying — "I did expect this purgation of Lysander to have set us on a level & have rendered him a sociable creature, but ill-luck, he stands it like an oak and is as haughty as ever!" "I expect you to clear up these matters without being in the least saucy!" she warns him. But before she can offend and wound, she hastens to take his part. "As to the charge of haughtiness, I am certain that is a mistake, for if I know Lysander he has as little of that in his disposition as he has of ill-nature. But for saucyness no mortal can match him, no, not even his Diana." [18]

Never does she forget her masculine lover's dictum, commenting on other ladies, that no vivacity or fire or intrepidity or whatever will take the place for him of "the kindness, the softness, the tenderness that constitute the characteristic excellence of your sex, & for the want of which no abilities can atone." [19]

She freely expresses her longing to see him, as the quarantine wears to a close, yet, since "not sight alone would please," it would be advisable to keep at an unseeable distance "till any approach would not endanger." She laughs at cool and prim lovers. The other day she saw a couple meet — "no danger and no fear — a how do-ye-do and how-do-ye-do was exchanged between them, a smile and a good-natured look — upon my word I believe they were glad to see each other. Yet I thought whether Lysander under like circumstances cd thus coldly meet his Diana, and whether Diana cd with no more emotion receive L. What think you? I dare answer for a different meeting on her part were she under no restraint." [20]

But that word "restraint" falls into place like a boulder blocking a torrent. And she is not only thinking of quarantine. How comes it, she inquires, that he can read *Sir Charles Grandison* yet be the very reverse in practice? "Sir Charles called forth every one's excellencies, but never was a thought born in Lysander's presence." This is a heavy charge. She amplifies it in many places. "Sometimes, you know, I think you are too severe, and that you do not make quite so many allowances as human nature requires, but," she is quick to add, "perhaps this may be owing to my unacquaintance with the world. Your Business naturaly leads you to a nearer inspection of Mankind, and to see the corruptions of the heart."

She can bear with it the more easily because he assures her "my affection for a certain Lady (you know who, my Dear) quickens my affection for every Body else that does not deserve my hatred." And because he is impatient for their marriage and says, "I am, and till then and ever after will be, your Admirer and Friend and Lover, — John Adams." Because he says, after his six weeks' quarantine are over, and they are reunited, and then she goes to Boston on a visit, "My soul and body have both been thrown into disorder by your absence, and a month or two more would make me the most insufferable Cynic in the world. I see nothing but Faults, Follies, Frailties and Defects in anybody lately. People have lost all their good properties. But you who have always softened and warmed my heart shall restore my Benevolence as well as my Health and Tranquillity of mind. You shall polish and refine my Sentiments of Life and Manners, banish all the unsocial and ill-natured Particles in my Composition and restore me to the happy Temper that can nourish a quick Discernment with a perfect Candour."

Yet again he comes to see her and creates "an intolerable forbidding expecting silence which lays such a restraint upon but moderate Modesty that 'tis impossible for a Stranger to be tranquil in your presence. What say you to that charge? Deny it not, for by experience I know it to be true." . . . And she confesses that she has often examined his countenance to see whether there was anything austere in it. "Indeed . . . when I have been most pained I have thoroughly studied it, but never could discern one trace of the Severe. Must it not then be something in Behaviour, else why shd I not feel as great restraint when I write?" [21]

Sometimes she is half afraid of the ease with which she pours herself forth in written words, but she lets herself go none the less. "This is a right girl's letter." She suggests that it will serve to light his pipe with!

And yet deep down, can she not judge of his heart by her own? "When I have often been tempted to believe that they were both cast in the same mould, only with this difference, that yours was made with a harder mettle, and therefore is less liable to an impression. Whether they have both an equal quantity of steel I have not yet been able to discover, but do not imagine they are either of them deficient." [22]

Perhaps the fact that he could daunt her was, to a woman of her strength, a vital part of his charm.

Three years of courting and waiting were too long, and both were irked by it. At last, delays were over, his house was ready for her, the Adams cart came to Weymouth in bright October weather to carry away such furniture and goods as the bride would bring to the new home, and she could write — "And — then Sir if you please you may take me."

The fall was a good time for country weddings, the harvest gathered in and carts and horses and their owners free for other doings. Two years after Mary's wedding, Richard Cranch brought his wife and baby Betsy to John and Abigail's wedding, October 25, 1764. Rumor has it that Abigail's mother was reluctant to the last. Some have written that it was because John Adams was a lawyer; but that will not hold water. Dick Cranch too was a lawyer, and Uncle Edmund Quincy, and nephews Sam and Josiah.

More likely she felt the difficulty of Jack Adams's temper, without feeling the ameliorations that made up for it. At all events, the Reverend William Smith, with his usual sardonic humor, preached the wedding sermon from the text "John came eating bread and drinking wine and ye say He hath a devil."

Braintree

THE town of Braintree, classified for muster-roll purposes into the North Precinct, Middle Precinct, and South Precinct, numbered around two thousand souls, averaging seven to a family. It was a farming community, and people lived scattered on their farms, with wide fields about them, though all set their houses on the highway.

The small and modest house in Braintree to which John Adams took his bride was just across the garden from his old home. It was his own property, having been left him by his father, along with nine and a half acres of farm and garden land. The homestead and the main farm of one hundred and forty acres had been left to his next brother, Peter Boylston Adams, who had not been given a Harvard education. The youngest brother, Elihu, had been left a little farm in another part of Braintree. Deacon John Adams — or Ensign Adams, according to whether you regarded his rank in the church or in the militia — died three years before John's marriage.

John's house was rented by a Dr. and Mrs. Savil until the heir should want its use. But all summer the house had stood empty while John employed what time he could spare from "attending courts and pursuing my studies" in getting house and garden in readiness for his bride. Like the parent homestead its walls were of brick and clay sheathed in wood, built above a deep stone cellar, round a massive central brick chimney, with enormous fireplaces and deep brick ovens. It had been built to last. The outside walls had no paint or whitewash, and when John brought home his bride, the sturdy wood — more than fifty years old — had weathered to a neutral brownish gray. Before John's father's time, a leanter * had been added at the back of each of the Adams houses. This was a long, sloping roof above a roomy kitchen, with another chimney and additional room, and a tiny crooked stair climbing to the upper floor.

The two houses, similar in appearance and in size, stood near together, but not side by side upon the highway, nor back to back, nor staring into each other's faces. The father house looked rather toward the son house, as if in not too intent but rather casual oversight, and the son house turned away its shoulder in an independent but not brusque manner. They looked companionable set there in the quiet fields. In front of them, across the Old Shore Road to Boston, rose the steep green slope of Penns Hill, from the top of which one could get a good view of the near-by sea. And behind the farm stretched the long ridge of the Blue Hills. There was something about the region which had made its first settler, Morton of Merry-Mount,† who had established himself on what was now Abigail's Grandfather Quincy's farm, Mount Wollaston — break into a kind of rough blank verse: "So many goodly groves of trees; dainty, fine, round, rising hillocks; delicate fair large plains, sweet crystal fountains and clear running streams that twine in fine meanders through the meads, making so sweet a murmuring noise to hear." The landscape, now somewhat tamed by the hand of man, was still unspoiled. The weathered houses took their quiet places in the scene, and the lines of farm fields and crops looked calm against the background of wild woods. The main road, a rough track running north to Weymouth and Boston, and south to Hingham and beyond, still passed through some virgin forest. Braintree's one industrial enterprise was the glassworks, a large round building which had been erected upon a peninsula between the river and the sea by newcomers from England, Joseph Palmer and Richard Cranch. Because Palmer had imported German glassworkers, it was called Germantown. Here Mary Cranch, recently Polly Smith, was settled, in close neighborhood to her sister.

* Or lean-to. The New Englanders pronounced and spelled it as above.
† A renegade Puritan who frivolously set up a maypole, and had it cut down by Endicott.

When John Adams ushered Abigail into her new home, it is doubtful whether the two of them could stand together in the tiny entry. In front of them rose the precipitous, irregular stairs, roughly curved around the main chimney. On the right of the entry was the parlor, distinctly the room of state; on the left was John's office-study. Behind the office, and opening from it, was the dining room, in the leanter, with the kitchen next it. The parlor also opened back into the kitchen, so that one could pass freely about the house. The office had an outside door for the use of clients. Upstairs there were two good bedrooms, and a tiny one, for a nurse or a child, opening off the chief room. There was attic space above the leanter on this floor, and the whole of the third floor under the rafters could be used for overflow guests or servants or children. It was simple, solid, and adequate. Abigail was charmed with it.

One of John Adams's last chores before his marriage had been the finding of a suitable maidservant. He discussed with Abigail the merits and demerits of several applicants by letter, and they compromised on John's mother's slave girl, Negress Judah, whom they could have for the autumn and winter but must return in the spring. Abigail did not take to this idea or to Judah, but she submitted because it was an economical arrangement. They needed to count their shillings carefully at first.

Now the bright October day faded, and she was shut up in the house with him — him of the sometimes corrosive tongue, critical glance, forbidding silence — with his widowed mother and his two brothers across the yard, and his mother's old servant was at her elbow. Does it promise fair?

Elizabeth Quincy Smith, and many others, said to themselves No!

When night closed down, Judah went up the tiny back stairs to her attic. John and Abigail took their candle and went up into that simple bedroom, with its windows facing east and south, its scanty, well-made furniture, and its high canopied bed. There they began their life together, each with a humble heart but with an ardent hope.

In her first letter after marriage, Abigail compared her husband's presence to the sunshine, while John Adams wrote in his diary that his marriage was the source of all his felicity. Yet the strains and tests which lay ahead were beyond anything foreseen.

The first weeks were a kind of true honeymoon, and there is no honeymoon more delightful to a young bride than settling into her own house, feeling herself mistress of all she surveys.

John Adams could be good company, the best in the world;* and that Abigail was good company, with the "saucy spirit" that her friends had admired, no one would deny. They entertained each other well. Then, too, John Adams was not only a man of books, pen, and words; he was also an outdoor man, skilled in the farm. He could mend the fence and clear the spring, cut the firewood, keep an eye on horse and cow, and direct sowing and harvest. It was recreation for him. He loved the land. His hands were as much his servants as what he called "that great gland, the brain." He would come in after a day or an hour of outdoor work, invigorated and glowing, with an appetite as hearty as his laugh. And his young wife could work with her hands. She could cook and bake with the best. And with Judah to do the heavy work, she could sit down to the well-filled table fresh and neat, hair well-arranged, eyes bright, bent on sharing her husband's interests, whatever they might be.

The only drawback to her marriage that Abigail noticed was that her husband's law business took him away so much, not only riding circuit but taking cases far afield — even as far as Martha's Vineyard.†

Part of their pleasure the first winter lay in the feeling of growing prosperity. Upward climbing, forward-looking feeling, that is the essence of energy and hope. And from the first, the husband, coming home with a wallet full of fees, would empty his leather pouch in his young wife's lap for her to administer the domestic economy. Discontent or argument over money was never known between them. Each was generous and open with the other, and each knew how to "make do" with what they had. They were partners in the building of a life together on a pattern that was

---

* According to Jonathan Sewall and Thomas Jefferson.
† An island off the coast of Cape Cod.

agreeable now and promised affluence and larger influence in time to come. John Adams already belonged to a Boston club, and looked forward to a Boston practice. But private ambition and thrift did not begin to quench their public spirit. John Adams gave his time freely where he could to the service of his township, acting as surveyor of highways and selectman, attending town meeting and serving on committees. And Abigail took it for granted that he should. It was in her family tradition.

Abigail had little time to realize that she was a wife before she had also to realize that she was a mother. Nine months after the wedding a daughter was born, whom the proud father named by the best name he knew, and that only — Abigail. Elizabeth Quincy Smith was at the bedside through the long hot hours, to aid her daughter in every way that love and experience could devise, to supplement midwife and doctor with comfort and cheer, to welcome the little grandchild with true affection. Parson Smith's diary reads, "July 14th, 1765. Mrs. Adams deliv^d. I Bap^d the Child Abigail — pd from 2 Luke."

But at this crucial time a sharp crisis arose unexpectedly and forced John to make a sudden decision between private and public interest. The Writs of Assistance in Massachusetts had been repealed, the Acts of Trade modified. But the Stamp Act, put on by the British Parliament as an easy way of collecting a uniform tax throughout the colonies to pay for their own defense in time of war, affected all the colonies. The French-Indian, or Seven Years' War, just past, had provided an object lesson in the injustice which arose when each colony had to manage its own war financing, for the ones in the front line were forced by circumstances to pay more than their share in both money and men.* This tax, imposed in the form of payment for stamps to be placed upon writs, wills, bills of sale, and other legal documents, had seemed reasonable to most of the English Parliament. But it proved to be dynamite, and one of those who lit the fuse was John Adams.

The Stamp Act had been discussed for several months before it passed. Cousin Sam Adams had drawn up a statement against it for

---

* Braddock and an army had been also sent over at Britain's expense to defend her colonies.

the Boston Town Meeting in the spring of '64. "There is no room for delay!" he said. "Those unexpected proceedings may be preparatory to more taxation. This annihilates our charter right to govern & tax ourselves. We claim British rights, not by charter only; we are born to them!" And he urged the men of Massachusetts — "Use your endeavors that the weight of the other North American colonies may be added to that of this province, that by united application all may happily obtain redress." [1]

These matters were part of the table conversation in the farmhouse below Penns Hill. In the close association of domestic life Abigail was learning to understand her husband's temperament. It was like her own, warm and quick, but never nursing a grudge. It was unlike her own in being instantly expressive, whereas Abigail was more fluent with pen than tongue. John was affectionate, loyal, easily wounded, quick in remorse at wounding others; and in private or public, always consistent, honest to the core. He had a large heart and a large mind. He fed eagerly on the admiration of other men. But sharp with himself, he could be sharp with others, and too much of the schoolmaster sometimes lingered in his strictures, rousing resentment in the wounded vanity of others who considered themselves his equals or superiors.

With qualities like these, John Adams could easily have become a domestic autocrat, and perhaps that is what Mrs. Smith had feared. A meek woman would have been crushed by him, a woman of average intelligence would have been reduced to silence, an assertive woman, like Mercy Otis Warren,* would have found life a misery of continual battle. But Abigail's lively and natural self-confidence, her deep and wide intelligence, and her feminine softness made the ideal combination. Add to these her loving, heartfelt admiration of her husband, and one perceived that John Adams, alone among the leaders of his time, had achieved a perfect mating. Familiarity, sickness, all the ups and downs and intimacies of married life in a cottage, never dulled his perception of that fact. And as the months passed, Abigail became more queenly, more

* Brilliant daughter of James Otis. She was a poet and playwright much admired by John Adams. Her works were admired by George Washington. She wrote a history of the Revolution.

assured, more his true companion in the heart-warming consciousness not only of his ardor but of his increasing respect. He did not
scorn to share with her a man's world.

In May 1765 news arrived of the passing of the Stamp Act, to
take effect in November. In June, James Otis made his great speech
in the Boston Assembly proposing the calling of a convention in
October of representatives from all the colonies to discuss the
Stamp (and Sugar) Acts and arrive at a united policy. The circular
letter of invitation had just gone out to the colonies when news
arrived in Boston of Patrick Henry's fiery resolutions in the Virginia House of Burgesses. The combination was combustible. A
band calling themselves Sons of Liberty immediately formed in
Boston, found out that Peter Oliver had been appointed to be
stamp distributor for the town, marched his effigy in a roaring
mob right through the lower part of the Town Hall while Governor Bernard and Lieutenant Governor Hutchinson and Council
were sitting in conclave in the council room above, hanged Oliver
in effigy on a large tree in the main street, and wrecked Oliver's
house. The insult was not lessened by the fact that Oliver was
Hutchinson's brother-in-law. This demonstration had just shocked
the town when John Adams, having seen his wife and child safely
through the first month after the birth, left home on a long visit to
Martha's Vineyard on legal business.

Abigail's mind, filled with the deep contentment and extraordinary tenderness of new motherhood, had no thought for politics.
The Stamp Act would go the way of the Writs no doubt, in time.
It was late in August and John had been gone about a fortnight
when she drove over to take tea with her Quincy cousins, eager
to discuss infant care with her aunt. She had been reading some of
the back numbers of *"Ames Almanack"* on the subject.

"I'm not swaddling my baby," she explained. "When the bodies
of tender infants are done up tight in swathing, neither their
breast nor belly can rise so freely as they ought to when the child
draws its breath, Dr. Hales says."

"Well, my dear, say what you like, it's a great preventive of
colic!" said Grandmother Quincy. "I always swathed mine. . . .
Why, look who's tying his horse outside! Grandson Josiah!"

In came young Josiah Quincy, now twenty-one, and beginning law in Boston. He was full of agitation and a tale. His father, Colonel Josiah, met him at the door. His voice was sharp. "Hutchinson! What, Hutchinson mobbed?"

"It was the night before last," said Josiah. "Mr. Hutchinson came into court the next morning. I was there. You never saw anything like it! In his shirt and small-clothes! The stripped Chief Justice — such a man! — tears starting from his eyes — destitute of everything — no other shirt even! He was sitting at supper with his children when somebody ran in and said the mob were coming. The evening being warm he had taken off his coat, and put on a thin camlet surtout over his waistcoat. But he had to flee just as he was — got out by the back way and through into another house. His own house was completely broke up with axes and crowbars. Even the trees and garden-house were laid in ruin. The mob looted plate and family pictures, apparel, books, papers — thirty years collection, he said — and nine hundred pounds in money. The poor gentleman was distraught, and denied he had encouraged the Stamp Act." [2]

"Well, I'm sorry he was treated so," said Abigail, "but I have heard that many a member of both houses * labored to obtain a resolution to send home a petition to the King and the Parliament against this Act, and that the Lieutenant Governor prevented it. And I know, and we all know, that he is greedy of power, holding as he does four of the chief offices of the province. No one man should be Chief Justice *and* Treasurer *and* Lieutenant Governor all at once, and then appoint his brother-in-law Stamp Collector, if he wishes to be thought disinterested."

"Whatever the provocation, there's no excuse for mob violence!" said the Colonel.

"The weather's partly to blame," said Josiah. "The town's a furnace. People get hot, and then they get thirsty, and then they take too much cider and rum, and their grievances run away with 'em. Good thing the Act isn't to operate until November. Everybody will feel cooler then."

A few days later John Adams came home, and though his young

* The Assembly and Council of Massachusetts.

wife had much to tell him about the baby's charms, she had other things to talk of too. How much this Stamp Act and the resistance to it was to affect their personal lives, in ever widening ripples, they could not guess.

* * * * *

No map of the American colonies, pored over by a tax-imposing Parliament, was likely to carry the name of Braintree. King George had never heard of its town meeting, or its nine selectmen. And since the King was a man of regular and simple habits, and the clocks of London were five hours ahead of the clocks of Braintree, no doubt George III was sound asleep on that mild fall evening when Abigail kissed John good-by as he set off to town meeting, and herself stepped across the garden to sit with Mother Adams.

"I doubt Jack is fussing himself too much about this new stamp duty they talk of," grumbled Mrs. Adams, as they settled to their knitting. "Peter tells me it's Jack that has stirred up the folk to call this here town meeting. What does Jack care? It's the lawyers that stand to *benefit* by the stamps, as far as I can see. He's got a wife to support, and now a child. He'd better keep his nose close to his business!"

"John minds his business," said Abigail mildly. And Mrs. Adams was silent, uncomfortably remembering a time when she had unwisely and, "with cruel reproaches," [3] urged her son to undertake business for which his inexperience was not ready. That was when John had come home to start his law practice, and she had thought it was time he earned his keep. He was then only twenty-three. But now at twenty-nine he was earning well and had married into the best family in the neighborhood. His decisions had for a long time been his own.

"John and Grandfather and my Uncle Josiah are all of one mind about this Stamp Act," went on Abigail presently. "They are quite certain that if it is enforced, when it comes due in November, it will mean our ruin. I mean the ruin of the Colonies! We all know what the Acts of Trade and the Writs of Assistance were like. This is worse. John has drawn up a paper in which he

has clearly stated that the Stamp Tax is 'a burthensome tax because
the duties are so numerous and so high, and the embarrassments to
business in this infant, sparsely-settled country so great that it
would be totally impossible for the people to subsist under it
even if we had no controversy at all about the right and authority
of imposing it.' " ⁴

"Why, that last sentence," said the older woman, "is as good as
treason. Colonies or none, Jack will ruin himself! Did he take that
paper to the meeting?"

"Why, certainly! He's going to try to get it passed as a resolution to instruct the Braintree delegates to the House of Representatives what to do when the Stamp Act becomes law a few
months from now."

"Child, he'll be a marked man! And for nothing. What does it
matter what we do in a little place like this? Why does Jack
have to make himself conspicuous, talking like that in public,
when all it will result in will be getting Hutchinson against him?
'Twon't affect the Stamp Act one way or 'tother. But a black
mark from the Chief Justice can keep a man down!"

Abigail listened to her mother-in-law's words, and she could
not deny them. But her mind flew to the town meeting, now in
progress. She saw the gathering of the men of Braintree in the
meetinghouse of the North Precinct, saw the two or three hundred men sitting in the backless benches on the men's side. Most
of them she knew, at least by sight. Her mother's cousin, Edmund
Quincy, was presiding as Moderator. Dignified in wig and ruffles,
he sat in the Deacons' bench below the empty pulpit, his fine
figure casting a great shadow on the whitewashed wall, the candles in front of him accentuating the lines deep-graven in his
thoughtful face. Jo Cleverly and Major Miller, William Veasey
and Jonathan Bass, and Captain Thayer would be sure to be there.
And there for sure was Peter Boylston Adams, John's brother,
who had accompanied him to the meeting, his loyal supporter and
lieutenant in every plan. Now Abigail imagined her husband had
the floor. He was addressing the meeting with that fire and vigor,
that complete conviction, which she knew so well and which compelled attention, even from opponents. She could feel the meeting

tighten up, she could see them all lean toward him, deeply stirred.

"Oh, Mother," she replied at last to Mrs. Adams, "John thinks, and I think too, that this is no time for private interests to come first. He is saying tonight, 'We further recommend the most clear and explicit assertion and vindication of our rights and liberties to be entered on the public records, that the world may know, in the present and all future generations, that we have a clear knowledge and a just sense of them, and, with submission to Divine Providence, that we never can be slaves.' " [5]

There was a long silence. Slow tears gathered and fell, in the candle shine, on the little woolen hood Mrs. Adams was knitting for her first grandchild.

"Ay," said John that night, holding Abigail to his heart, "carried unanimously! including the key sentence." [6]

A day or two after the town meeting John Adams rode into Boston to deliver a copy of his Resolutions to Draper the printer, who had asked permission to publish them in his weekly newssheet, and on the way called on his father's cousin, Samuel Adams. The name of Sam Adams was beginning to be heard in Boston in the way of politics, for by means of the powerful private caucus created by his father, Sam Adams had been elected this year to the Massachusetts House of Representatives.

He was a graduate of Harvard, but up to this time he had not found his métier. He had dabbled a little in law, a little in trade, and failed at both. But his powerful mind and brilliant conversation had always commanded his younger cousin's admiration. John found him now in his stuffy dark little office, driving his quill across the paper in clouds of tobacco smoke. Now forty-two, he looked much older. He had a blunt, strong face, but his hair was already gray, and he had fallen prey to an infirmity, which kept his head and hands shaking like those of a paralytic. He welcomed John Adams eagerly.

"Now, John, you're just the man I want. I've been appointed by the town of Boston to draw up a set of instructions for their representatives in the House with relation to the coming Stamps. And I feel an ambition which is apt to mislead a man — that of doing something extraordinary.[7] Here, cousin, read over what

I've put here, and give me your comments. Frank and honest I know they will be. And to the point, I dare swear."

"I read his instructions," said John to Abigail afterwards, "and showed him a copy of mine. I told him I thought his very well as far as they went, but he had not gone far enough."

"And what did he say to that?" said Abigail.

"Well, upon reading mine, he said he was of my opinion, and accordingly took into his some paragraphs from mine." [8]

"But then he will get the credit for them!" said Abigail, jealous for her John.

He laughed out, as surprised as he was amused. He had not yet got used to the odd combination of her clear mind and her woman's point of view.

"My dear," he said, "we are out for bigger things than any man's credit."

John Adams's Resolutions for the town of Braintree, circulated in the press, went through the province like wildfire, and were adopted verbatim by forty towns in their town meetings. They even found their way down to Virginia and rang familiar echoes in the heart of Patrick Henry.

* * * * *

Abigail got early notice from her cousins when the ship bearing the stamps arrived in Boston. But since to unpack and distribute the stamps was obviously to provoke riot, the bundles were dumped in the Castle, three miles out of town. Every province was in the same predicament; no one would unpack and distribute the stamps. Appointed distributors everywhere went in terror. But Lieutenant Governor Hutchinson of Massachusetts was an astute and obstinate man. He advised Governor Bernard to exercise pressure by closing all law courts and public offices in Massachusetts, on the grounds that all legal documents not bearing the new stamps would be ineffective, and all writers of same would be liable, under the Act, to a fine of ten pounds for each offense. With this encouragement, Peter Oliver quietly took over again the potentially lucrative office of collector of the Stamp Duty.

All the Massachusetts counties except Suffolk County, in which were Weymouth and Braintree and the city of Boston, found ways of getting around the court closure by opening the inferior and probate courts under local judges who defied the stamps and refused to issue fines. But Abigail's husband practised in Suffolk County, where Hutchinson was in complete control of the machinery, and so found himself, with all his fellows at the Boston Bar, suddenly deprived of livelihood. It looked like ruin.

"The bar seem to me to behave like a flock of shot pigeons," he complained bitterly to Abigail.

John was sitting in the quiet house at Braintree, posting his books, regulating his accounts, making himself out a course of reading for the winter, and trying to calm his fretted spirit with Abigail's cheering company, when a deputation suddenly rode up through the December mud to summon him to public action. The Boston Town Meeting had unanimously voted to appoint him, along with Mr. Gridley and James Otis, as counsel to appear before the Governor "in support of their memorial that the courts of law in this province be opened."

John Adams called his wife aside, showed her the letter. "What shall I do? What do you say?"

Abigail's heart throbbed.

"Ah — what an opportunity! How did it happen?"

"Opportunity; not risk." He laughed short, and embraced her.

"The reasons which induced Boston to choose me, at a distance and unknown as I am," he remarked to his Braintree friends, "I am wholly at a loss to conjecture." [9] But it is perhaps not irrelevant that Cousin Sam Adams was chairman of the town committee.

The next day Abigail and baby Nabby waved farewell as John rode off to Boston to discuss with Gridley and Otis and Cousin Sam the line of argument to be taken.

At candlelight the appointed three were summoned before the Governor to present the memorial and to speak for it.

They stood there in the stately council chamber, three men, the wedge of opposition to royal authority, before the King's representative of that authority. But which of them was to be the point of the wedge? Not till that moment did it occur to them that in their consideration of impersonal ideals and high principles they had omitted to arrange the detail of which of them should speak first. Gridley claimed to speak last; Otis claimed to speak second; they laid the difficult opening on their junior, John Adams.

"Then it fell upon me," said John Adams to his wife, when he got home on Sunday, "without one moment's opportunity to consult any authorities, to open an argument upon a question that was never made before, and I wish I could hope it never would be made again! That is, whether the courts of law should be open or not!" [10]

He was not proud of his first appearance upon the stage of history. He gave all credit to Gridley and Otis.[11] And the whole course of the unsuccessful struggle with the Governor stimulated his admiration for his cousin Sam Adams, who with integrity, "an artful pen," genuine piety, and charm of manner, had "the most thorough understanding of liberty." [12]

Sunday he spent at home, "thinking." But what different lively thoughts. And on Monday, back to Boston, to the arena of events, in which he now had a leading part. No more was the winter lean and dull. The lightness of his purse no longer worried him. His mind was keenly bent on studying out the most difficult legal case of his career, making precedents as he went. He worked not in loneliness and solitude but in daily association with the cream of the city of Boston. His companions drew his admiration and pleased him greatly, for it is a delight to a brilliant talker to meet with his peers. Each day he felt more vigorously at the hub of affairs, but deep in his heart, base of his confidence and good humor, was the thought of Abigail, happy at home at Braintree with her baby, sending her thoughts constantly to him, fully understanding the nature of his task. Good humor is the source of moderation. Your happily married man may be a fighter in a good cause, but he is never a sour one. And Sam Adams, chairman of the committee, appreciated this quality in his cousin.

Abigail had no time to be lonely. Friends and relatives were

always dropping in to tea. Her precious Grandmother Quincy
was an easy walk away; Weymouth was comfortably close; and
Boston was not too far for John to come home often. Christmas
came on a Wednesday and John rode home on Christmas Eve to
spend the holiday with his family. It was a perfect day. They did
not even go to meeting. John took the time "thinking, reading,
searching, concerning taxation without consent." They had a cosy
dinner at home; and then they walked through the brisk frosty
air to drink tea at Grandfather Quincy's. Old Colonel John had
always regarded John Adams as a young man with a future.
Grandmother had long since lost her prejudice against him, seeing
that he made her beloved granddaughter so happy. Welcome and
love and elegance and grace awaited them there. The low winter
sun shone on fine china and silver, on polished walnut and maple.
The tea table was drawn to the fire, and the white-haired hostess,
erect and dainty in her beautiful striped satin dress and white lace
cap, had eyes as bright and dark as Abigail's own. There was good
talk, as good as Boston's; "the old gentleman inquisitive about
the hearing before the Governor and Council; about the Governor's and Secretary's looks and behavior, and about the final
determination of the board. The old lady as merry and chatty
as ever, with her stories out of the newspapers."

But when the candles were brought, John and Abigail took
their leave, before the country lanes got too dark, and went
back to relax by their own fireside and savor their supreme content. "Spent the evening at home with my partner and no other
company." [13]

It was good that they took that chance while they had it.
It was the last Christmas of their lives of which that might be
said.

*   *   *   *   *

In many ways that winter of the Stamp Act was an extraor-
dinarily happy time for Abigail. Her husband was frequently at
home all day. "Mr. Hayward dined; Town politics the subject.
Doctor Tufts here in the afternoon; American politics the subject." And Abigail, presiding at the table or part of the group

on the settle beside the hearth, was a partner in the talk. Modest and discreet, more a listener than a talker, she was learning the arts of politics and feeling under her finger the throbbing pulse of the time. The little cottage at the foot of Penns Hill had become one of the arteries of American opinion.

Severe cold and deep snow shut the house in that winter. The three main fires, kept up day and night, maintained a central triangle of warmth. One bundled up in clothes. Men wore their overcoats to sit down at the table, a few feet from the genial circle of heat, and Abigail had layers of petticoats that made her look like a large rose and feel like a feather bed. It gave her girlish figure a matronly dignity. She had also a dignity of mind, along with her youthful zest, which struck her husband's visitors forcibly. Not many strangers, however, were likely to find their way to Braintree at that season. The outer world entered by way of the newspaper and the mail. Uncle Tufts and brother Peter Boylston Adams, neighbor Field and Parson Wibird and Mr. Cleverly and Cousin Josiah Quincy and Dick Cranch were the ones who came, slamming the door to quickly, stamping off the snow in the little entry.

As they stared into the glowing logs at that simple fireside their eyes ranged over the colonies.

Led by John Adams's bold mind, his wife and brothers and friends lost that strong parochial feeling engendered by close living in one place. Abigail lifted her attention from the cradle, from the flickering shadows of the room, from the small snug house, from the village; nay, from Boston itself and from the province of Massachusetts. Was she a villager — or a Bostonian — or a colonial? Something much more than, and different from, all these. John had the word.

"Wretched blunders do they make, these British," said her husband, "they know not *the character of Americans!*" [14]

As Abigail's political education proceeded, there was no inner conflict set up in her by difference of opinion among those whom she held dear. Wherever she went, there was the same spirit.

John harnessed the sleigh and drove with Abigail over the smooth surface of the packed, hard snow to Weymouth, a de-

lightful drive in the sharp, glittering air. And there at dinner with
Abigail's father and mother and young sister Elizabeth they
heard that Parson Smith had recently preached a fiery sermon
from the text — "Render unto Caesar the things that are Caesar's
and unto God the things that are God's." The tenor of the sermon
was to recommend obedience to good rulers and a spirited opposition to bad ones, and its lesson was brought right up to date, in
Parson Smith's best manner.[15] The congregation wanted to
print it.

Abigail could not even conceive of a contrary opinion. The
principal local Tory (as government supporters soon came to be
called), Mr. Cleverly, was to her "that unaccountable man, who
goes about sowing his seeds of Mischief." Other Tory neighbors
were also "poisonous talkers," though not so bad as Cleverly.
The "Tories" were trying to divide and disunite the people. That
the resisters to the Stamp Act might be regarded as striving to
divide people who had all been loyal subjects of the King never
entered her head for a moment.

There was a Sunday when Parson Wibird at Braintree warmed
her up in the freezing cold unheated meetinghouse — where the
congregation would sit on the uncushioned benches, men to the
right, women to the left, boys in the gallery, from ten-thirty
to twelve-thirty and from two to four, weekly, regardless of
weather — by preaching from the text, "I have nourished and
brought up children and they have rebelled against me." Mr.
Wibird certainly got attention that day, nobody went to sleep
on him; all had their ears pricked indignantly for the expected
Tory lesson to be drawn. But none was forthcoming. Mr. Wibird
skillfully skirted round the subject, and let his text speak for
itself.

Every week John Adams spent several days in Boston and
always came back full of tales of elegant dinners and political
talk.

He described the rich furnishings of his kinsman Nick Boylston's house: "Turkey carpets, painted hangings, marble tables,
rich beds with crimson damask curtains and counterpanes, the
beautiful chimney clock — the spacious garden." He was struck

with unwilling admiration. "It was altogether magnificent. Fit
for a nobleman, a prince." [16]

Abigail was intensely curious and felt she would like to see it
sometime. It was the nearest she was ever likely to get to any
nobleman or prince.

"But tell about the Sons of Liberty. Were they a very wild
crew?"

"Not at all. You'd be surprised — as I was! No doubt their
methods attract the rowdy element, and give the riff-raff of the
town a chance to riot and loot, as we saw in the sad case of
Mr. Hutchinson. Mob law is no law. But the Sons of Liberty
are a very respectable organisation. They meet in a counting-
room in Chase and Speakman's distillery, in Hanover Square,
near the liberty tree. A very small room it is. John Avery was
chairman — a distiller and merchant, a man of a liberal education,
and he invited me. There were present Smith, the brazier, Crafts,
the painter, Edes, the printer, Chase, the distiller, Field, the
master of a vessel, Trott, the jeweller, and a few other reputable
tradesmen. I was very civilly and respectfully treated by all
present. We had punch, wine, pipes and tobacco, biscuit and
cheese, etc. I heard nothing but what passes at all clubs, among
gentlemen, about the times. No plots, no machinations. They
were so certain of repeal that they were appointing a committee
to be in charge of grand rejoicings when it should occur — such
fireworks, bonfires, illuminations and the rest as were never before
seen in America! I wish they may not be disappointed." [17]

"Be sure you take me in to see it!" said Abigail.

"Indeed, then, madam, you had better start to make payment
in advance for it."

"And how, sir?"

"Why, by paying me back some of those kisses you owe me.
I am sure you are in my debt three million at least!" [18]

Abigail perceived that her husband had quite suddenly become
an important man, whose influence was sought by many groups,
and her pride in it was the greater that it had happened through
no one's patronage, but by his own inherent qualities backed by
steady self-preparation.

The same outspoken honesty that had made him enemies was now making him friends in every quarter of the town.

Although the Superior Court remained closed, the Gridley, Otis, and Adams committee, backed by the House of Representatives, succeeded in forcing the reopening of the inferior Court of Common Pleas in Boston, and through the late winter and spring, John Adams had resumed that part of his law business. Late in March, Abigail's uncle, Dr. Tufts, came for the night, bearing the newspaper account of Pitt's warm speech for repeal in the House of Commons. And two months later, in the middle of May, 1766, the news of the repeal of the Stamp Act reached Boston.

That was the great day for the fireworks, the bells, the bonfires, the cannon and all the rest, and the well-prepared Sons of Liberty did their part. Boston went mad. The glow of torches and the flare of rockets in the sky could be seen from the top of Penns Hill. But Abigail did not even get that satisfaction, confined to the house, she and her baby both, with whooping cough. In all this passion of national joy it was not much to light up the house with candles to surprise their quiet cow and dazzle passing owls. For once both she and her husband felt that their country seclusion was almost too complete. "A duller day than last Monday, when the Province was in a rapture for the repeal of the Stamp Act, I do not remember to have passed . . . unable to go to Boston, and the town of Braintree insensible to the common joy." [19]

But the Superior Law Courts were immediately opened everywhere, business was pressing, whooping cough passed away in the summer sunshine, and Abigail and her child recovered their color and liveliness. On Sunday the twenty-fourth of July, appointed as a day of religious Thanksgiving for the repeal, they all three drove in the chaise to Weymouth to hear Father Smith preach. His happy knack with texts was once more exemplified. "The Lord reigneth, let the earth rejoice, and the multitude of the isles be glad thereof." [20] The application was all that his congregation — and those that came over from Hingham — had hoped for.

At home in Braintree, Parson Wibird, whose political opinions had been suspect but elusive, diddled them again. He chose a text from Genesis — "But as for you, ye thought evil against me; but God meant it unto good, to bring it to pass, as it is this day, to save much people alive."

John Adams, hearing of it, chuckled to Abigail — "Wibird shone, they say!" [21]

There were some rewards to be gleaned in those days for the excessive length of the church services.

A storm had blown over; the colonies had waked out of a nightmare. "The repeal of the Stamp Act had hushed into silence almost every popular clamor, and composed every wave of popular disorder into a smooth and peaceful calm," wrote John Adams in his diary.[22] Every letter and newspaper that came from England breathed benevolence and peace. It was a new era of better understanding and advancing prosperity.

In August, Abigail, dressed in her best summer things and radiant with smiles, drove over with John to visit her sister and husband, who had recently moved to Salem. They dined at Boston, drank tea at Dr. Tufts's at Medford, lodged for the night, set off next day, oated at Martin's, and reached brother Cranch's at twelve o'clock; dined and drank tea, and then went eagerly about through the flat, level town to see the sights. Next day the two sisters, Mary and Abigail, got into a chaise and drove to Marblehead and back, John Adams escorting them on horseback.[23] It was a delightful holiday.

In November, when John Adams had to attend court in Salem, they repeated the visit. "Arrived at my dear brother Cranch's about eight, and drank tea and are all very happy." The sisters had a marvelous gossip, about children, neighbors, all kinds of woman things. It did John good to hear them. "Sat and heard the ladies talk about ribbon, catgut and Paris net, ridinghoods, cloth, silk and lace. Brother Cranch came home, and a very happy evening we had." [24] Four people more congenial with each other could hardly have been found.

"My love to Mr. Cranch and his lady," said John Adams when he saw his wife writing her bread-and-butter letter, "tell them

I love them, I love them better than any mortals who have no other title to my love than friendship gives." [25]

The year that had opened with such serious public thoughts, with events that lifted their eyes to wide and bleak horizons, closed by bringing them back to the snug private circle of their little house at Penns Hill and their nine and a half acres. The unease of change had touched that circle too. Faithful old Tom at Weymouth — he who had smoked the letters — had died, sincerely mourned; Mrs. Adams senior was being courted by a Mr. Hall, and expected to marry again in December; Abigail herself had entered on what her husband called "all the Qualms that necessarily [are] at end or beginning pregnancy, in all other respects very happy." But in all these changes, the land remained, solid and familiar under their feet. In deep serenity, under the blue November sky, Abigail strolled up the woods pasture with John, learning woodcraft from him as she had learned politics. The brilliant sunshine above the arches of red and golden leaves made a rich-colored gloom in the thick woods. The little stream could be heard struggling with choking rocks and dead leaves.

"We must prune these oaks and buttonwoods and maples," said John Adams, "and fell without mercy all these irregular misshapen pines. Ay, I'll have them all out. I am desirous of clearing out the rocky gutter — maybe clear out the rocks and make a ditch for the water. But first and foremost we must let in the sun and air to sweeten the grass." [26]

I I I

Boston

A BIGAIL'S second child was born on July 11th, 1767. Elizabeth Quincy Smith presided over the agony attendant on the coming of life, all the while holding in her heart the picture of another candlelit room just left, in her father's house by the sea, where life was ebbing out. Parson Smith's diary laconically notes that the Hon. John Quincy died July 13th, in the seventy-eighth year of his age. On the day of his death, his great-grandson was duly christened John Quincy.

Abigail, lying in the big feather bed, exhausted, happy, and sad, had no suspicion that the two men who, each in his own way — one so earnestly masculine, one so nuddling and small — comforted her sorrow, were both incipient Presidents of a republic yet unborn.

But Fate was busy at the loom. The King was exasperated with his Parliament for repealing the Stamp Act. He regarded the colonies as naughty schoolboys who needed the rod, and resented their triumph. To give in to them was a dangerous precedent. By January 1767, the King and Townshend in England had concocted another act, behind the back of the dying Pitt, setting new duties to raise colonial revenue. William Pitt, Lord Chatham, was not only old and sick; his attention was distracted from colonial affairs. A new object dazzled him. He confessed to Townshend, "I need not tell you how entirely this transcendant object, India, possesses my heart and fixes my thoughts." [1] The House of Commons passed the Townshend Bill to raise revenues in the American colonies by customs duties on glass, paper, painters' colors and tea, none of which were produced in America, the duties to be spent in maintaining a standing army for defense of the colonies and providing permanent salaries for colonial governors and judges.

Benjamin Franklin, agent for several colonies in London, had seen nothing wrong with this measure. "The Americans," he said, "think you have no right to levy excise within their country on native products. But the sea is yours; you maintain by your fleets the safety of navigation on it, and keep it clear of pirates. You may have, therefore, a natural and equitable right to some toll or duty on merchandise carried through that part of your dominions, towards defraying the expense you are at in ships to maintain the safety of that carriage." [2]

But the money was not to go for ships. And Franklin missed the main issue — the same as in the Stamp Act. The issue of the right of Parliament to tax the colonies, fairly or unfairly, directly or indirectly.

Paxton, Marshal of the Boston Court of Admiralty, was in London, advising his friend Townshend that "ships of war and a regiment" would be needed "to ensure tranquillity," and then all would go well.

The Sons of Liberty in Boston replied with a campaign to refuse use or purchase of any of the taxed imports. And so did Dickinson in Pennsylvania and Patrick Henry and George Washington in Virginia; the movement was taking hold throughout the colonies. The French naturally had secret agents in America noting and fomenting discontent. Governor Bernard, backed by Hutchinson, was sending home to England for troops to break up resistance and enforce the Townshend Act, when it should go into effect.

At present Abigail Adams's mind was wholly in her home, but what security and warmth she gave her husband! He always kept with him one of her letters from the fall of '67, telling him that the baby was "better" and that little Nabby, three years old, "rocks him to sleep with the song of 'Come, papa, come, home to brother Johnny.'" And then Abigail adds — though writing on a visit to the Parsonage, her old home — "Sunday seems a more lonely day to me than any other when you are absent; for though I may be compared to those climates which are deprived of the sun half the year, yet upon a Sunday you commonly afford us your benign influence! I am now at Weymouth, my father brought me here last night. Tomorrow I return home, where I hope soon to receive the dearest of friends and the tenderest of husbands." [3]

The physical setting of that spiritual entity called "home," however, was soon to change. In the spring of 1768, the demands of a growing law practice induced them to move to Boston, where they rented the White House, Brattle Square.

John had talked things over with Abigail and resolved to avoid further entanglement in public affairs which brought no grist to the mill. He now had two children, and his family responsibilities must come first. He refused re-election as selectman at Braintree. He would not even attend town meeting at Boston. Indeed his avoidance of entanglement was so marked and his determination to get on with his job so openly declared that Otis accused him of caring for nothing but making money, and Hutchinson, who had successfully limed Sewall by creating for him and placing him in the office of Attorney General of the Province, thought the time was ripe for catching John Adams also.

One afternoon, near the three o'clock dinner hour, the maid, answering the knocker's clamor, ushered in Jonathan Sewall, dressed ceremoniously in best scarlet coat and fresh ruffles. With an ingratiating bow to Abigail he claimed the privilege of old friendship to invite himself to dinner. Abigail was charmed. She liked company, and Sewall, who had married her cousin Esther Quincy, was a clever and likable man. John Adams too, coming in from his office, gave hearty welcome. Differences in politics should not dissolve friendship. They sat down together to the family table, happy and easy in talk of people and scenes near and dear to them all. Little Nabby, aged four, comported herself daintily.

Sewall's eye quickly discerned in his hostess's figure the signs of coming motherhood. And here was one child at table, and another upstairs with its nurse. A man who is giving these hostages to Fortune is in a conservative — as Hutchinson would say, a reasonable — frame of mind. John Adams had sown his political wild oats and should be ready to settle down, especially if it were made worth his while. His value to the Tory cause could hardly be overestimated. After dinner Sewall made it courteously clear that he had business to discuss — should they perhaps adjourn to the office? But Abigail rose pleasantly and taking her little girl by the hand said that she was going upstairs to her chamber and would bid the gentlemen good evening.

The gentlemen lighted their pipes and drew their chairs to the window which opened at the back over the green, shady garden, and without further preliminary, and with good hope of success, Sewall broached his errand.

An hour later John Adams came upstairs to his wife.

"Put on your bonnet, my dear. I have ordered the chaise to be at the door in ten minutes. I'm going to take you for a drive in this fine evening air!"

Abigail saw that he was excited and stirred, but she had learned that he would tell her the quicker if she restrained hasty questions. So she put on her light summer bonnet before the glass and pushed her dark curls becomingly into place, while her husband took a turn about the room.

"What do you suppose Sewall came for?" he burst out. "You'd never guess. . . . Why, to ask me, on Governor Bernard's behalf, to take the office of Advocate-General in the Court of Admiralty. To bribe me, in fact, with immediate fortune and a sure career of advancement. . . . Sewall could not bring himself to take my refusal seriously. He said I could not refuse off-hand like that — I must take time to think it over! I reminded him of my political opinions, which were not likely to change overnight. He replied that he was instructed by the Governor to say that I should be at full liberty to hold my opinions — which were well known — and that the Governor *did not wish to influence me* by this office. He had offered it to me merely because he believed I was the best qualified for it and because he relied on my integrity! . . . Well, my dear, what ought I to have said?"

Abigail came to him and put her hands softly on his shoulders.

"Just exactly what I know you did say!" she murmured, as one putting a secret in his ear.

His strong arms came round her waist.

"What? What?"

"Why, that it would put you under obligations and restraints that you could not in honesty accept!"

"Right, right, my lass, my dear girl, my Portia!" He kissed her lips in his eager ardent way. "And yet Jon Sewall was astounded and vexed! Kept saying 'Why are you so quick and sudden? You'd better consider it and give me an answer another day!' I told him my answer was ready because my mind was clear. But he went away sulky, swearing he would be back in three weeks and would hope I'd changed my mind." [4]

"He can't bear to see another man firm and clear where he himself fell into the toils!" said Abigail.

John was silent and took her down to the waiting chaise. They drove away in a companionable thoughtfulness through the sunny streets. Long evening shadows stretched across the way. There were many trees to spread the refreshment of greenness and shade. Gulls wheeled and floated above their heads against the blue, and an evening breeze, smelling of seaweed and fish, came up from the sea. Abigail remembered a time when her husband had said that he couldn't think in Boston, what with the distractions of the passing traffic, the "rattle-gabble" of the streets. But now the varied sights and sounds fell into place as an undercurrent to their thoughts. Love of the hilly, salty city had taken hold of them. This was the kind of life they wanted: Boston and Braintree, city and country, in a steady re-creating rhythm; a life mainly private, centered in the home, with their children growing up around them and their friends freely passing in and out; and later on, when the basis of secure prosperity was well laid, acceptance of public responsibilities without compromise of principle. The times were restless now but they would settle. Refusal to buy British imports was essential. Townshend himself was dead,* and repeal was only a matter of time, patience, and law-abiding pressure. John Adams, giving his wife her airing, reflected that a man's first duty was to his wife and family. Not riches they wanted, merely security; to have necessaries and com-

* Died September 4, 1768.

forts and books, to send their sons to college, start them in a respectable profession or business, and keep out of debt.

Men like James Otis, with security established and family grown, or like John Hancock, not yet married and rolling in riches, they were the ones to give their time to the nonremunerative tasks of public reform. While John was expressing this to Abigail they caught sight of Samuel Adams marching along the pavement, a conspicuous figure with his shaking head and occasional involuntary gesture. Now there was a case in point! . . . They drew up beside the curb.

"Come, Cousin, drive with us! Come home to supper!"

Sam Adams got in, with his shabby, ill-brushed coat and well-concealed linen contrasting with John's trim suit and ironed ruffles, and at once said:

"John, I want thee to harangue the public meeting I have persuaded the Sons of Liberty to summon next week on the legality of the Townshend Revenue Act. I was walking now to thy house."

"I shall be away on circuit," said John, "and I have told you and my friend Dr. Warren I will harangue no meetings. That way madness lies.[5] Even the great Otis is driving himself crazy with constant eloquence to work up public feeling! Tell me, Cousin Sam, did you never, when you were my age, with a young growing family, feel the necessity of laying by and planning for the future?"

"No, I have to confess," said Sam Adams thoughtfully, "I have never in my life looked forward; never made any plan or scheme of laying up anything for myself or others after me."[6]

His discourse that evening on political matters so enthralled John that he almost regretted that he would be absent from the planned town meeting. Dr. Warren was most urgent that John Adams should address it, most disappointed that he would not. But before Sam Adams left, he drew John aside and quite naturally and simply asked him for a loan. And John Adams, unlocking his desk drawer and taking out the cash with generous readiness, was privately confirmed in his decision to give attention to the necessary task of paying his own way.

So he was away on circuit when the town meeting met, and had nothing to do with the letter it sent out to invite all select-men of the other towns in Massachusetts to a convention in Boston. The convention was in its closing session when fifteen British men-o'-war sailed into Boston Harbor, carrying on board two regiments of soldiers.

Abigail's condition prevented her from being among those who put off in boats to see the ships near to — and who came back with their sight-seeing ardor damped by observation of cannon in readiness upon the decks. But even from Brattle Square she could see in the deep night sky the falling stars of rockets which the soldiers and sailors, in a surprising burst of gaiety, sent up from the ships. And together with everyone else who could look from a window or walk to the end of a street, she saw the amazing march of the troops into the town a few days later.* They marched through the quiet crowds with their muskets charged and bayonets fixed, drums beating and fifes playing, with a train of artillery and a couple of cannon.[7] But there was a sad fizzle out at the end of the march when there was nowhere to go but the Common. The citizens of Boston sardonically refused billet. The soldiers, some seven hundred of them,[8] deployed on the Common and pitched tents, and, unable to get firewood except by paying for it, ate cold rations around their cold artillery.

Abigail was startled and indignant at all this martial display. Wherever she went, at Uncle Isaac's or at the Otises', where young Sam Otis was courting her cousin Mary, Isaac Smith's daughter, or at the houses of any of the Quincy connection save one (the Sewalls), the talk was the same. Why all these guns and fixed bayonets? Are we an enemy town?

It was not more soothing to Abigail that she was wakened every morning early by "the spirit-stirring drum and the ear-piercing fife" when Major Small marched his regiment up to drill in Brattle Square right in front of her house. There they were, the ridiculous lobsters — and the street boys showed their usual uncanny aptitude of phrase in calling them so. In scarlet coats and

* On October 1, 1768. The Townshend duties were to go into operation on November 20.

high pointed caps, with bayonets for antennae, they turned and wheeled and clanked about, both picturesque and silly in the autumn sunshine. John Adams came back and heard and saw everything, and his comments were caustic. He told her a bitter joke that was running the town: " 'Our grievances are reddressed!' But patience. We must help the town to hold itself steady. Our method of resistance is the lawful, pacific one of passive resistance. Violence in word or act will only weaken our cause. The embargo on all British imports, steadily, unitedly applied, must win. It will hurt us and our trade, but it will hurt the English more. They can't afford to bear it."

"Well, at any rate," said Abigail, "they can't use their bayonets to force me or any other housewife to buy what we don't want to!"

John Hancock's sloop the *Liberty* had been searched for contraband wines by suspicious customs commissioners, who found the cargo had been unloaded at night on Hancock's Wharf to avoid paying the duty. Hancock was prosecuted to the tune of £100,000 sterling. He engaged John Adams as his counsel, and the case greatly inflamed public opinion.

Parson Smith did not step aside from his duties to enter politics, though his opinions were well-known, and his laconic diary contains, except by implication, no comment on the times. As the year 1768 rolled to its quiet but storm-laden close Mr. Smith impartially notes — "Dec. 1st. Thanksgiving Day. 14th brot my sheep from Hingham. 23rd Mrs. Adams deliver^d of a daughter." This third child was christened Susanna.

So this year Parson and Mrs. Smith spent the Christmas season with their daughter Abigail in the White House, Brattle Square. And they too could join little Nabby and Johnny at the window to watch the redcoats drilling in the falling snow.

*   *   *   *

It was hard on a baby to be born in a Boston winter. Little Susanna was a frail child, and her weak cries of discomfort and protest absorbed her mother's attention almost to the exclusion of the sound of drum and fife outside the door. Yet when Abigail

passed about the streets on marketing or social affairs, the town
seemed full of soldiers. Their conspicuous red coats met one at
every turn. Four regiments were now in Boston, two from Halifax and two from Ireland, totaling upwards of two thousand men.
And that number is not easily absorbed by a population of sixteen thousand.[9] The soldiers were under strict orders from General Gage and their officers to behave with circumspection
and provoke no incident. But the offenses of soldiers everywhere — drunkenness, sex, hectoring — were of constant occur-
rence.

Their presence in fact was a continual provocation and a
nuisance rather than a punishment. The Governor found himself
unable to administer the Quartering Act requiring free lodging
and firewood against the steady passive resistance of intelligent
Boston. The soldiers paid. The canny Yankees set to work to
make money out of them in other ways too — firewood, candles,
food. It was exasperating to the high-tempered Governor to see
his protecting troops, meant as terrorists, treated as customers.

No one, in fact, was afraid of the soldiers, after the first shock.
Street boys booed them — at a safe distance. John Adams had no
qualms about leaving his little family unprotected when it was
time to go away again on circuit.

Yet the White House on Brattle Square was not unmarked.
Leaving her ailing baby with the nurse, Abigail would come
downstairs to pour coffee or chocolate (tea being now tabooed)
for Cousin Sam Adams, for handsome John Hancock, for Mr.
Gridley, Mr. Cushing, and many other habitual visitors of note;
and would take part in talk which would find its outcome in
action. She would listen to constant plans to keep the peace between the population and soldiers. She would see her husband
consulted at every turn. John Adams's draft instructions, throughout '68 and '69, though he never attended town meeting, were
adopted without alteration by the town,[10] and no instructions
were drawn up unless he had prepared the draft. She felt and
approved of the steady moderation and conservatism with which
he curbed his fiery, positive energy. And in all the discussions to
which she was a part, these keen, farseeing men carefully refused

to look farther into the future than to the withdrawal of the troops, the repeal of the Townshend Act.

Often of an evening, especially as the weather grew milder, the sweet plaintive strains of violins and flutes, accompanied by songs, rose under the windows. Nabby and Johnny, preparing for bed, would scramble to the window and look out between the curtains.

"Who are those men, Mama?" asked Nabby the first time.

"They are the Sons of Liberty, your father's friends. At least," said Abigail, looking down too, with a quickening breath, "they think your father is one of *their* friends. . . . Come, Johnny, now the song is done, come say your prayers!"

John Adams, entering the bedroom, hushed the comment he was about to make concerning the serenade. His baby son was kneeling with fat hands pressed together against his mother's knee. The white homespun linen nightshirts made both children look like cherubs. Curly-haired Nabby was earnestly listening to Johnny's performance, her lips silently moving with his.

"Now Ilayme darnter seep . . . "

The drowsy baby lisp of not understood but holy words made something better to listen to than violins.

Abigail presently laid her husband's hand against her cheek.

"You won't let the Sons of Liberty draw you out into their doings?" she murmured.

"No," said the firm decided voice she trusted. "I'll take no part in public. I've no time, in any case. You and the children come first and I'm even half sorry I undertook John Hancock's case in regard to the customs' seizure of his sloop *The Liberty*. It drags on and on, and is a lot of work for little return. I've far more business than I can handle, even with an office down town and two clerks."

Abigail remembered what cousin Esther had said yesterday, when she was making a visit at the Sewall house.

"Although you know my Jonathan doesn't hold with your Mr. Adams's politics," said Esther, "he said to a group here 'tother day that 'John Adams is as honest a lawyer as ever broke bread.' And then another gentleman present spoke up and said now that

James Otis was failing in his mind, it was pretty generally recognized that John Adams was the first lawyer in the province!"

Abigail repeated this now to her husband, and saw the quick gleam in his eye which showed his pleasure at the tribute. But he picked up his little daughter, ruffled her curls, and pressed several warm kisses on her satin cheek as she flung her arms round his neck.

"I will hear Nabby's prayers!" he said.

Though this new struggle over tariffs seemed to Abigail to be taking rather longer than the one over the Stamp Act, there were signs of victory in the air. A circular had come from the English Parliament saying that no more duties should be imposed against the will of the colonists and that the ones on paper, colors, and glass should be removed. That only left the tax on tea. Then Governor Bernard, who had been trying to work the home government in London up to violent measures of repression, was recalled, to his own surprise and chagrin; and less than a year after the troops had sailed into Boston, the Governor sailed out. The city rejoiced. As he drove away he saw flags flaunting on the Liberty Tree, and the last sound he heard over the quiet harbor was the impudent roar of the province-owned cannon fired in good-riddance salute from Hancock's Wharf.

"Well, we are getting on!" said Abigail, delighted as bonfires flared in the July night.

"Ay," said her husband and his friends, sipping their cold beer, "but not fast enough. Hutchinson is as bad as Bernard; maybe worse. And a tax on tea is still a tax."

"Will the non-importation continue, then?" said Abigail.

"Non-importation will continue and will be enforced!" said Sam Adams.

"And Hutchinson's sons are in the tea business!" grunted John Hancock with a wry grin.

"I said 'enforced,' " said Sam Adams, his palsy intensifying with his emotion. "Them Hutchinsons will find themselves a boiling in their tea if they don't look out!"

Abigail, alert lest John should take fire and commit himself to something, hastened to give the talk a lighter turn.

"My little son is by way of being a Tory!" said she. "He glues his nose to the window when drill is on, and admires the redcoats!"

"So?" said Sam Adams. He did not join the laugh. Next day Abigail was greatly amused to see her son waddling along beside Cousin Sam in the cool of the summer morning. Held fast by Adams's shaky grip, he was being conducted all around the square to watch the drill. She saw the baby's hand eagerly pointing, heard his shrill voice say, "Pitty wedcoats! Pitty sojers!" — heard the stern, gruff denial of his companion. As they went out of earshot she could discern by Sam Adams's denunciatory gestures that he was telling the boy — "Naughty redcoats! Wicked redcoats! They must GO AWAY." So Sam Adams gave his tiny distant cousin a lesson in political theory; and the intelligent little boy heard and understood, and was convinced. Sam Adams did not waste his time that morning. To the end of his life John Quincy Adams remembered and told of it.

But as the heat of summer wore on the city, tempers grew short. Ugly possibilities raised their heads.

Abigail, having returned with her children from an August spent at Penns Hill and Mount Wollaston, where her Uncle Norton Quincy had inherited the big house on the seashore, had a caller early in September. Her friend Mrs. James Warren was grief-stricken and indignant. Her father, James Otis, had been assaulted in the street by a customs officer and badly hurt.

"He's not responsible for what he says, you know!" she said, through her tears. "He's been liable to attacks of wild temper — well, really madness — for some time. Everybody knows it! I suppose this brute said something to vex him, and he roared out, and the next thing the wretch hit him over the head — knocked him down and struck him repeatedly. He was all bloody before others could run and help him — "

She broke down in Abigail's comforting arms. But a cold chill seized Abigail, none the less. This — in Boston — to a man like James Otis? A leading citizen — recently speaker of the Assembly? The chill returned in even worse form in October. John was away, Nabby and Johnny were in bed and asleep. Abigail and the nurse were in the chief bedroom, tending little Susanna. Several candles made the room bright, and a glow of firelight spread rosily over the walls as the nurse moved to and fro about the hearth stirring a poultice in a little saucepan. Abigail was walking about, rocking the colicky child against her shoulder, patting its back gently, trying to ease its obvious pain, while its little mouth wailed in her ear. But suddenly another sound roused her attention with an uncomfortable start. It was a distant sullen roar, like a herd of beasts, or like storm on the sea, but Abigail knew it at once for what it was, the sound of a mob. It drew slowly nearer, and now there were running feet on the pavement. Men's voices shouted —

"Light up, citizens! Light up! We need the lights of the windows to show up traitors!"

Knockers banged all along the row. Abigail looked out and saw some young men running. One of them glanced up at the lighted window and recognized her. He doffed his cap in a moment.

"Yer servant, Mistress Adams!"

He was gone into the soft fall darkness. His face was excited, wild. His automatic courtesy to her seemed grotesque, as if a bear should show manners. She believed he was a journeyman ropewalker, a Son of Liberty named Gray, whose rough bass sometimes joined the serenaders.

And now the roaring of the mob came close, reached the end of the square, came on rolling slowly, past the house. Abigail, hugging her baby, looked and shuddered. In the center, lit by a few torches, were two creatures riding a rail. One was shapeless, white and fluffy, more like a gigantic owl than anything human; the other was a well-dressed man in a dark coat, his face twisted with agony, whom Abigail recognized as a printer who had recently libeled many of the people's leaders in a scurrilous newssheet violently attacking non-importation. They passed with their tormentors, all too slowly. Abigail put her baby gently into the cradle, then dropped down on the bed, sick and faint.

"Oh, ma'am!" cried the nurse, turning from the window where she had been leaning out to miss no last vestige of the spectacle, "you shouldn't have looked on that in your condition! God help us that it don't mark that which is within your womb!"

She brought vinegar to bathe her mistress's brows, singed a feather and waved it under her nose.

"What was it? What was it?" gasped Abigail.

"A sailor, ma'am — an informer. They'd tarred and feathered him, and serve him right. Forget it, ma'am, don't think of it. . . ."

But when John Adams returned a few days later Abigail was glad to find that in his harder man's way he disliked it as much as she did.

"Mob justice is injustice, even if the man was guilty. Such things mar our cause."

Sam Adams, however, felt differently.

"Action is felt and noticed when words are disregarded. It will be a useful lesson," said he.

He had not been in the mob, but it was rumored he was among those who high-handedly released eight members of the mob whom Hutchinson had arrested and jailed. The jailer could not resist the town pressure. He let them out willingly.

"The troops were in the streets that night, bayonets and all," said Abigail, "I saw several of them, coming along at the rear. Why couldn't they interfere and stop it?"

"The city is not under martial law, my dear!" said John Adams. "Until it is, or unless a civil magistrate gives the order to disperse a riot, the troops are helpless. And well Hutchinson knows it. However, if he don't soon move them out to the Castle, there'll be an incident. There's bound to be. And we shall all be sorry."

"Except me, cousin!" said Sam Adams.

*　　*　　*　　*　　*

Little Susanna died in February 1770, having managed to pass her first birthday but not to win the struggle against a second Boston winter. Frail as her hold on life had been, her loss brought a peculiar sorrow to her mother's heart through the tenderness aroused by caring for the sickly little creature. But her second mother, Aunt Elizabeth, wise in living, urged philosophy and religious resignation. Children were delicate vessels, her friends said, one could not expect to raise them all. Hardly a mother of their acquaintance had attained middle age without losing one or more children, and was not Abigail expecting another child in May?

John Adams, leaving his wife to Aunt Elizabeth's ministrations, rode himself to Weymouth carrying the tiny coffin on the back of his saddle for burial by Parson Smith. After the service in the church and a night at the Weymouth Parsonage, it was cheering to ride the familiar road to Braintree, to call on his mother and see her well settled, to call on his brother and see his married state with his prim Puritan wife, and to look over his own house and find it weather-proof and in good condition. So, after visiting the blacksmith to have his horse shod, he rode on back to Boston.

He reached Boston, late that February afternoon, at a critical moment. As he told Abigail over their hot supper, drawn up before the roaring fire:

"When I came into town I saw a vast collection of people near Liberty Tree and found it was the funeral of that boy that was shot in the streets a few days ago.* Sam Adams and others begged my company. So after I had warmed me at the house of a friend, and put up my horse, I walked with them in the procession. We went from Liberty Tree to the Town House and thence to the burial ground. It was a solemn and quiet occasion. I hope it will be marked as a lesson to the practicers of violence on both sides."

"It is the first blood," said Abigail somberly, "the first death.

* The first incident — that is, the first involving death, as distinguished from the innumerable little clashes involving manhandling and blows — was not a clash between soldiers and citizens but between citizens determined to enforce the embargo and citizens determined to exercise their individual rights and resist it. Stores that ignored the embargo and took the opportunity to sell English imported goods at a high profit — including tea and molasses — to such citizens as would patronize the "Black Market," had their shops picketed by the Sons of Liberty. The neighbor of such a picketed shop, himself a minor customs official, came out and protested the picket. A mob joined the pickets in no time, the man Richardson was forced to seek refuge in his house, and since even there he thought the enraged mob would storm the door, his terror caused him to bring out a pistol and fire into the crowd. He killed a boy.

But I fear me it won't be the last. . . . It is too sad it had to be a child."

"Ay. But that it was a child," said John Adams, "made it appeal to young and old. A vast number of boys walked before the coffin; a vast number of men and women after it, and many carriages. My eyes never beheld such a funeral. The procession stretched away into the distance. . . . It shows the ardor of the people!" [11]

Yes, but where is that procession marching to? What is its real destination? Time alone, sighed Abigail, can show. Fresh from the funeral of his own child, it was no wonder that John had impulsively joined in the funeral of another. But she prayed he would remember his living children, and the ones that were yet unborn. She felt unwell, dispirited and sad. She would gladly have drawn him back from that procession. Too late. He had taken that fatal step, and what would the next be?

"I'm sorry for James Otis!" said John, his active mind running on, unsuspecting. "He has often told me that his wife was a high Tory and read him the most unmerciful curtain lectures.[12] It's my guess that friction at home as much as anything has been the cause of the irritability that has broken up his fine mind and got him into trouble. Now that's a thing I could not stand. I thank God for *my* wife!" His vivid affectionate glance flashed on her and drew its usual response, but she was pale. "Nay, my dear, don't be in the dumps!" He strove to cheer her with all the home gossip that he had collected. But — though she made him think he had succeeded — real cheer was more than she could summon, and she went to bed homesick for Weymouth and Braintree and the old quiet days. Boston was a vortex. Boston was dangerous.

That was the twenty-sixth of February. Six days later Abigail heard of a rumpus between the journeyman ropewalker Gray and his friends and some men of the 29th Regiment. The soldiers, either outnumbered or afraid to disobey orders, had got the worst of it, and one of them was said to be dangerously wounded. No one had been arrested. Apparently no one could be found to identify the guilty party.

Abigail, well bundled up against the snapping cold, went stepping cautiously about her business in the slippery streets, where cinders and oyster shells had been scattered to make walking safer. She saw the soldiers gathered in sulky groups, their scarlet coats conspicuous against the white snow. And now a snowball whizzed through the air, edgy with cinders, and caught one hard on the ear. No use to turn sharp to see who. All the boys in sight were looking the other way, hands in pockets, or intent on playing an absorbing game with each other. As for pouncing and catching one, as easy catch a fish in the hand. They slid away on the icy gutters, dodged, twisted, disappeared in doorways, up alleys. Chase by the military was undignified and futile. The soldiers resumed their sullen talk, and now a volley of snowballs hit them in the back like stones, melted down their collars, knocked their tall hats sideways. Abigail thought that Providence had been inconsiderate of the soldiers in filling the streets of Boston with piles of snow, the street boys' ammunition. But she was surprised at the youngsters' bold, repeated rudeness.

"They've been intentionally wrought up by designing men!" [18] said her husband when she told her anecdotes at the dinner table. "There have been some for many months trying to stir up quarrels between the lower sort of people and the soldiers. The night brawls are the worst. I wish Sam Adams would exert himself against it. Some think they have his encouragement. But I can't believe it of him."

The next day was March 5th. A lonely sentry, on guard at the customhouse in the frosty evening, found himself a target for hard snowballs and lumps of ice, thrown with savage intention and deadly aim by a gang of toughs. These were not boys but men. Their leader was Gray the ropewalker; and his most eager and skillful adjutant showed, in the intermittent light from the customhouse window, the dark face and brilliant teeth of a Negro.* The sentry was not only angry and bruised, he was frightened, and shouted for the guard. Half a dozen of his comrades came at the double, headed by a sergeant, and almost at once Captain Preston joined them. He was in command of the guard that night and anxious to prevent any shooting. How did it happen then that there was shooting? Who gave the command to

* Crispus Attucks.

fire? Did anybody? Certainly not Preston. The mob, terrifying
and elusive in the half-dark, taunted the soldiers to fire, being
certain, from months of experience, that they would not. But
suddenly the crack of muskets roused echoes along the Boston
streets, and life was snapped in two like a brittle stick. Gray and
his Negro follower fell dead, and another young man staggered
and died beside them; sixteen others were wounded, two of them
mortally. Their blood ran out on the snow, as scarlet as the sleeve
of the drummer boy who held up a lantern for the captain to
see by. And the soldiers were appalled and still.

Abigail was sitting alone by the fire, musing and reading. John
had gone off to his club, at Mr. Henderson Inches's house at the
south end of Boston. Of a sudden, about nine o'clock, the bells
began to ring. Startled, Abigail went to the window, drawing her
shawl about her, thinking it a fire alarm, and looking for the glow
of flames in the sky. John, at the other end of town, thought the
same, and so did his companions. They snatched up their hats and
cloaks and rushed out into the streets. They found a crowd of
people all flowing down the street one way; and the word was
passed from mouth to mouth that the British had fired on the
people, "killed some and wounded others, near the town-house."
Abigail's boy ran out of her front door and brought back to his
mistress the same news. Now, while Abigail's heart beat wildly,
Brattle Square began filling up with soldiers, summoned by the
sharp beat of the drums. There, silent except for shouted com-
mands, they formed their ranks, muskets shouldered, bayonets
fixed. So they stood ready when John Adams came into the square,
hurrying home at a smart pace to take care of his wife. There was
just room for him to walk along the whole front of the company
in a narrow space they had left for foot passengers. He pursued
his way "without taking the least notice of them," as he told
Abigail presently, "or they of me, any more than if they had been
marble statues." *

His strong arm around her, his reassuring companionship, his

* John and Abigail Adams were at this time living in "Mr. Fayerweather's
house" in Cold Lane, just off Brattle Square, to which they had removed
in the previous spring. Soon after these events they moved back to "another
house in Brattle Square."

firsthand news that all the town was quiet, "in a sombre, tragic, but not violent mood," steadied her racing nerves. She drank a little mulled wine and her color came back. She was preparing for bed before she heard the soldiers march to their barracks. The commanders had agreed that the first necessity was to get the soldiers off the streets and out of sight.

"We had nothing," said John Adams, "but our reflections to interrupt our repose." But those were disquieting enough.

IV

The Die Is Cast

THE day after the massacre was almost like a Sabbath. No drum and fife broke the morning stillness, no soldiers came to drill in Brattle Square. The forest birds flew undisturbed about the trees, catbird, redwing and scarlet tanager, brown thrush, robin and bluejay, and sea birds sailed above.

The front door opened and shut, and John Adams's breezy presence filled the house.

He entered the room with a quick, hearty greeting to his aunt-in-law, and came directly up to his wife. She, who knew him so well, knew instantly something important had happened. His bright, eager eyes were searching hers, with a serious, intent gaze that yet held a gleam of humor. His firm arm was round her waist.

"What think you, Nabby," said he, "I am about to lay myself open to a charge of Tory!"

Her face lit up, confident even in her question.

"And how do you manage that miracle, sir?"

"Nabby, let me first ask you some questions. Were those soldiers last night monsters of iniquity, or were they stupid men in a tight place who made an error? Which is your opinion?"

"The second is my opinion!" she said thoughtfully.

"And it's mine too. So when a redcoat — an officer, Mr. Forrest, whom they call the Irish Infant — came to my office this morning, and with his eyes streaming with tears implored me, in a broken voice, as if he thought I held his friend's life in my hand, to help his friend get justice, what ought I to have said? He came from Captain Preston; and Captain Preston is in the town jail, having given himself up — he and his eight men — to stand their civil trial according to English law. Are we in Boston to deny them law?

Shall we, who are claiming one part of the British Constitution, deny another part? Shall we?"

"Oh, no!" said Abigail fervently.

"So I accepted the charge of the defense of Preston and those eight accused men, and took his guinea. And your cousin Josiah Quincy is my partner in it. I could not wish a better! They went to him first, on their way to me, and he said he would engage if I would. . . . And meanwhile, my dear, while I sat there listening to Forrest, I saw out of the window my friends John Hancock and Sam Adams pass by more than once, going up and down the Court House steps carrying word from the Town Meeting to the Lieutenant Governor and his council. From time to time a messenger would slip in to me to tell me how things were going — how the Town Meeting was standing out for the withdrawal of the regiments to the Castle, and how they were strong for the immediate and condign punishment of Preston and the guard, and were calling in and examining many witnesses of last night's affray. I saw the temper of the town was hot and growing hotter. And but for you and the children, *I* should have been in there with Hancock and Adams, helping to force the town's demands down Hutchinson's throat. Why then should I find myself compelled to go against the tide? . . . Just because, as I said to Forrest, the law is neutral, and counsel ought to be the very last thing that an accused person should lack in a free country. But I told Forrest plain I would use no tricks, no arts. If I undertook it, my argument would depend only upon facts, evidence and law. Forrest eagerly assured me that Captain Preston desired no more. 'As God Almighty is my judge,' he said, through his tears, 'I believe Preston to be an innocent man.' 'Well, that the trial should show,' said I, 'and if he thinks he can't have a fair trial without my assistance, then without hesitation he shall have it!' " [1]

"You did right!" said Abigail with all her heart. "We will show the world that we are a just and law-abiding people."

Aunt Elizabeth was amazed at her. Not a word of caution or regret — nothing about John's health, or taking on too much, or the risk of losing his popularity, his carefully built-up career, on this quixotic case. Were there no Tory lawyers to undertake it?

What about Sewall, for instance? She ventured to say something of this as they all went into the dining room.

"There are Tory lawyers, yes," said John Adams, "many and good ones. Why did not Preston choose one of them? I can only answer — he did not. He came to me. And a man on trial for his life is entitled to the counsel of his choice."

The trial would not come on until the autumn assize.

Abigail's fourth child, a son, was born on May 29th, 1770. He was christened by his faithful grandfather, Charles. He was from the beginning happy and cheerful and Nabby and Johnny soon found how delightful a plaything a baby brother can be.

For three months life had been almost normal. Abigail and many others began to believe the worst was over. If a new and more liberal governor were sent across from England to replace Bernard, instead of the crass, though American-born, Hutchinson, there was room for hope. And in the meantime, the very fact that John had engaged to defend the soldiers had roused such a clamor in the town that it seemed to Abigail an added safeguard against his being drawn into the vortex of the patriot cause. There were plenty of people now, she was well aware, who were calling John Adams traitor and timeserver; and the House of Representatives itself had issued a printéd statement of the massacre [2] which prejudged the case before trial, and condemned the accused out of hand.

So the shock was the greater when John came up to her room on the evening of June 5 with that look of kindled fires within him and of grim resolution which warned her of danger. He told her the worst at once.

"Abigail, what will you say to me? I have accepted election to the House of Representatives!"

"But — John — how is it possible? You were not at Town Meeting?"

"No. I've never attended Town Meeting in Boston, as no one knows better than you. I was not there this morning when my election took place. I had no idea of it until a messenger brought the news to my office. Then I went over to Faneuil Hall, where a very large Town Meeting was assembled, and expressed my sense of the honor of their choice of me, and my own unworthiness and unreadiness, in a very few words."[3] He sat down beside the bed, and took his head between his hands. "A few words in which to throw away the hopes of a life-time."

"But John — when your prospects were so good —" she faltered. "Your future — your children — "

"Ay. I've thrown away to-day as bright prospects as any man ever had before him." He got up and paced restlessly to the window and back. "In my heart, which I ever show you, I'll confess to you I consider that this step likely condemns my little ones and you to ruin. And myself to worse still!"

"John — *death?*"

"Ay. Hutchinson has already threatened to invoke high treason against patriot leaders. The King may do so in any case, at any time. *May?* Nay, is *certain* to if things go on."

Now the full realization had sunk deep into Abigail's heart, and her numbed feelings woke into agony. She burst into tears.[4]

"Ah, John, John — why must you?"

"For the same foolish reason that I must defend the soldiers, my dear — nothing except a sense of duty. And I can't escape it."

Her tears moved him unbearably. She — "that excellent lady who had always encouraged me" — so broken as this.

"Was I a fool, dear wife? Did I act wrong? . . . When my fellow townsmen turned to me in their need, overlooked more obvious claimants, paid me the high compliment of selecting me, not only without my candidacy but in my absence — should I have said No?"

She sobbed and wept, speechless, but she shook her head. She struggled for control, while he stroked her hair. At last she could trust her voice to speak as firmly as she wished.

"She said she was very sensible of the danger to her and to our children as well as to me," wrote her husband in his diary, "but she thought I had done as I ought; she was very willing to share in all that was to come and to place her trust in Providence."[5]

One of the minor results of this unexpected turn of affairs was to deprive Abigail of her husband's company. The General Court — the full unit of government composed of the acting Governor, the Council, and the House of Representatives — was in session at Cambridge, where Hutchinson was insisting on its meeting as a punishment to the cantankerous town of Boston. To Cambridge therefore John Adams had to go, and immediately went, next day. Since the village was separated from Boston by the Charles River, and there were no bridges across the Charles, the delegates had to find lodgings in the village. Overcrowding made them uncomfortable. Sessions were held in the halls of Harvard College.

Abigail soon learned, both from her husband's brief letters and from the comments of her friends, that John Adams, on entering the sessions, was at once not only involved in all the arguments, but actually made the leader of them. The anti-government party, now definitely calling itself the "patriot party," had been in sore need of a first-rate lawyer, one whom they would not be afraid to pit against the highly trained legalism of Hutchinson himself.* John Adams was their man.

As he told his wife — "This was to me a very fatiguing session for they put upon me all the drudgery of managing all the disputes." [6]

When the July recess came he had to be away riding circuit, and catching up a little on his law business. Wherever he went, as he told Abigail on return, he observed how "the spirit of liberty circulated through every minute artery of the province." [7] No one would buy British goods, no one (he boasted ruefully) would offer you a cup of tea; and farmers, innkeepers, country lawyers all over the place proved to be patriotic Sons of Liberty.

In October he had to absent himself from the General Court. The trials of Captain Preston and the soldiers came on. So certain was everyone of a verdict of "Guilty" and a sentence of death that a sermon was preached in Boston anticipating not only the sentence but a reprieve by the Acting Governor, and arguing against reprieve.

Abigail, present among the spectators in the packed courtroom, was aware of all the prejudice built up around the trial, of the desire for punishment, and the positiveness of guilt. She knew too

* Hutchinson was Chief Justice as well as Lieutenant Governor and a very able and tricky lawyer.

about the illegal circulation of evidence taken down from witnesses who had not been subjected to any responsibility for proof. On the first day of the trial, the prosecution seemed to have an overwhelming case. And with the rest of the hushed audience she felt the thrill that ran through the room when, on the second day, after the opening by Quincy, John Adams rose for the defense and his first words, passionate, unequivocal, human and sincere, reminded the court at once that they were dealing with no mere affair of party politics, or prejudiced opinion, but nothing less than life and death, justice and law.

John Adams's insistent return to fundamental principles, his stirring oratory, and his destructive cross-questioning of witnesses succeeded in getting a verdict of acquittal for Preston and for all of the soldiers but two, the only two who could be positively identified as having fired. Those two were found guilty of manslaughter and were condemned to be burned in the hand, a light sentence as things were considered.

Abigail felt all the thrill of a girl at her first conquest to have this great man, this public figure, escort her home, and to hear him say with vehement conviction:

"The jury did exactly right — exactly right — and come what may, this was the best action of my life." *

As winter came on, John Adams's health began to break. Complicated legal cases, political engagements, a slender diet — the doctor's remedy for nervous indigestion — and especially "constant speaking in public almost every day for many hours," [8] finally brought on serious illness. At the height of the winter a "complaint in his lungs" threatened his life. To Abigail, this seemed a heaven-sent reprieve from duty. Not the King's threat against treason, but Nature itself compelled a halt. The doctor backed her up — good Dr. Warren, himself a patriot. It "compelled me," said John Adams, "to throw off a great part of the load of business both public and private, and return to my farm in the country."

Joyful illness that demanded such a convalescence! Little Nabby

---

* It was also the least rewarding financially. John Adams's total fee, including retainer, for his nine clients was fourteen guineas.

and Johnny, in their wild delight at going back to the farm, felt nothing like the deep excitement of their mother. "Last Wed. my furniture was all removed to Braintree. Sat. I carried up my wife and youngest child," records John's diary. "The air of my native spot and the fine breezes from the sea on one side and the rocky mountains of pine and savin on the other . . . daily rides on horseback and the amusements of agriculture, always delightful to me, soon restored my health." [9] April was sweet upon the hills.

Abigail heard, by report at week ends, all the talk of the town. And though, as John said, "England and America are staring at each other and will continue to stare for a long time to come," America was also staring the other way. There was west on the compass as well as east. Stories were being told of one Daniel Boone.

"Yes, America is a continent, and let us never forget it," said Abigail to her little son Johnny. "It is not just Boston and New York and Philadelphia, nor even just the Northern Colonies and the Southern Colonies. It spreads away so far — "

"How far?" said Johnny. He was so keen and quick and sensible that his mother sometimes forgot how young he was. Now six, he seemed often more mature than Nabby.

"As far — as the sunset!" said Abigail.

Johnny had already learned to read. She was teaching him a lot of her favorite poetry by heart. And John Adams was eager to apply his educational theories to his young son. Copying out, copying out was the thing — "make my sons copy out the Preceptor's *Elements of Logic* entirely with their own hands in fair characters as soon as they can write in order to imprint it on their memories!" [10]

"And what about your daughter?" said Abigail, lifting her chin.

"Well — 'twouldn't hurt my daughter to do the same!" [11]

They all drove over to Weymouth on a summer Sunday, a happy family party, the sweet scent of new-mown hay blowing across the fields. Young Isaac Smith was there with a letter in his pocket from England giving the news. It was from an American, John Adams's relative John Boylston, who wrote — "Lord T——'s avowed and publicly declared reason for keeping a Military and Naval force at Boston is to corrupt the morals of the inhabitants in order totally to enslave them, and I sincerely hope and wish the principles of the Revolution will have no period but with the Existence of the planet we breathe on." [12]

That word "revolution" seemed to explode and thunder in the room. But John Adams, though he paced up and down restlessly in the ensuing hush, finally stared out of the window and avoided comment.

On September 15th, 1772, Abigail's mother and father were at the Penns Hill farm to support their daughter in the agonizing hours of childbirth; and a son was born and promptly christened Thomas Boylston. This was Abigail's fifth child, there were difficulties and complications, and her recovery from the birth was slow.

They had now been back at Braintree two springs, two summers, two autumns, and one winter. They had tried all the possible ways but the arrangement hadn't worked. John and Abigail Adams were not happy apart. John might think at first how nice to have long undisturbed evenings in his office "which I never cd do in my family," but presently his spirits sank — "walking about the streets of Boston as hipped as old Father Flynt at ninety," James Otis told him angrily. Abigail alone could make him see the world in pleasant colors. He hungered for sight and sound of her, and he needed her as companion, comforter, and sounding board for his thoughts.

Abigail too needed the pungent, vitalizing quality of John's presence, the smell of his tobacco, the firm step, the almost rough caress, above all the support of his strong, decided nature. Country life of course was good for the children but, in Abigail's opinion, their father's company was better for them still.

So when John presently had the offer of a house in Boston that was within his means and situated where he wanted it, he purchased it, "having found it very troublesome to hire houses, and be often obliged to remove." In September 1772 he moved his office into it and began to get it ready for his family.

When little Tommy was a month old, and Abigail, pale and

languid but on the mend, was able to be taken out onto a couch under the trees, they celebrated John Adams's birthday, October 19th. A party gathered — Grandmother Elizabeth Quincy and Uncle Norton, Parson Smith and his wife and young Betsey,* brother Peter Boylston Adams and the prim Mrs. Peter — whom John could not help pitying Peter for marrying! — Mr. Hall and his wife, John Adams's mother — Edmund Quincy and his lovely youngest daughter Dorothy, the flower of the flock (now being courted by John Hancock) — and Parson Wibird, the cultured but elusive bachelor, John Adams's old crony. These and others of the neighborhood gathered to drink John Adams's health and wish him well — and to toast the new baby. And John Adams told them that this was both hail and farewell — that his mother and father-in-law (current for stepfather) were going to occupy his farm, and he and his family were going to return to Boston before winter.

When the guests had taken leave, and the children were in bed and John and Abigail were left alone to watch the sun's last after-glow along the west, reflected in the autumn gold of the maple leaves above them, John fell into a mood of melancholy.

"D'you realise, Nabby, what this day marks? Thirty-seven years of my life are run out, more than half the life of man! The re-mainder of my days I shall rather decline, in sense — in spirit — and in activity! And yet I still have my own and my children's for-tunes to make!" [13]

"Tush!" said she. "Why, your boyish habits and airs aren't yet worn off!"

On Tuesday, November 25th, Abigail and the children moved into Boston to take up residence in the house in Queen Street.† Although John Adams spoke of it disparagingly — "inconvenient and contracted as it was" — Abigail was pleased with it because it offered better opportunities of constant companionship than any other they had had. It was just opposite the Courthouse. But as the house took order under her hands and cheerful children's voices rang in the halls, he insensibly cheered up. A feeling of

* Abigail's youngest sister.
† Now Court Street.

content and hope began to take possession of him. He did not feel quite so old.

"My father-in-law * Mr. Hall and my mother are well settled in my farm at Braintree," he wrote in his diary. "The produce of my farm is all collected in; my wood and stores are laid in for the winter. I am disengaged from public affairs — with a fixed resolution to meddle not with them — and I now have nothing to do but mind my office, my clerks and my children." [14]

As Abigail and Dr. Warren both pointed out warningly, though the excursion into the country had partly recovered his health, he was an infirm man yet. The strenuous Boston hours had not agreed with him. They hoped that by this time — and with his wife there to take care of him — he had learned how to live in Boston. If not — if his health should again decline — he must return to Braintree and give up the town entirely. Above all, the doctor reiterated, Mr. Adams must remember — no clubs, no meetings, no politics! His recipe for living must be temperance, exercise, and peace of mind! He must ride frequently to Braintree to inspect his farm, and spend evenings in his office or with his family, with as little company as possible. [15]

The lion seemed to purr drowsily in complete agreement, blinked mildly at the fire, and appeared quite domesticated.

His wife, peeking into his diary to see what he was putting there, was well satisfied. He had taken the lesson to heart, and repeated it verbatim.

Abigail found the resumption of social life in Boston very pleasant. But the British Admiral's wife, Mrs. Montague, was giving offense by disdaining the colonial ladies. "Pray, can Mrs. So-and-so *afford* the dress and jewels she wears?" And — "Oh, that my son should ever come to dance with a mantua-maker!" The Admiral was more restrained, and therefore, in the presence of ladies, comparatively tolerable. But John Adams's fashionable young clerk, Will Tudor, could cap these stories with anecdotes of the Admiral as a foul-mouthed fellow, with "hoggish, brutal manners," a disgrace to the King's navy. [16]

Such minor annoyances gave outlet to Boston's deep-seated irri-

* I.e., stepfather.

tation at having the Navy and Army still present; the uniforms of officers might add picturesqueness to a ball, but they were a reminder of the incubus that had only been moved three miles away.

Abigail, anxious to keep the family temperature down, took a good-humored and tolerant view. She thanked her stars that after safely skirting the reefs and shoals of two evenings running with Sam Adams, they were going to see the old year out in the peaceful security of the Cranches' house. A quiet family circle. Just what the doctor ordered.

John was in excellent spirits that evening. "I never was happier in my whole life than I have been since I returned to Boston," he said when Richard and Mary inquired how the move was working out. "The year to come will be a pleasant, cheerful, happy and prosperous year to me. At least, such are the forebodings of my mind at present." [17]

"John doesn't feel the weight of middle age half so badly as he did a few months ago!" said Abigail.

But it is in Eden that one must look for the serpent. And here it was indeed, in the person of a harmless-looking Englishman, a friendly and courteous fellow — one who was struck, moreover, with admiration for Mrs. Adams. A cosmopolitan and a stranger, he was perhaps the first person who ever recognized her quality. He thought her the most accomplished lady he had seen since he came out of England.

All was calm, warmth, and mutual friendship. But someone mentioned the *Gaspee* and court of commission. And Mr. Collins, not unnaturally sticking up for his country, ventured to say something mild about the high reputation, after all, of British justice. The resulting explosion astonished everybody — perhaps even Abigail. It certainly astonished in retrospect the remorseful John.

"I found the old warmth, heat, violence, acrimony, bitterness of my temper and expression was not departed. I said there was no more justice in Britain than there was in Hell — and that I wished for war." [18]

So the dream of maintaining a private life went up in smoke.

After such an uprising from the subconscious John felt he must consent when asked to serve the patriot cause again. This time it was to involve a direct challenge to the Crown, and both John and Abigail perceived its full consequences and weighed them well before taking the irrevocable step.

In January '73 Hutchinson opened the General Court with a subtle and carefully prepared speech to the effect "that Parliament was our sovereign legislature and had a right to make laws, lay on taxes, etc., for the colonies." [19] The two Houses appointed a committee to take into consideration the Governor's speech. Their need, they soon saw, was a lawyer, and experience had taught them who. No matter that John Adams was not now a member of the House, they urged and entreated him to meet with them and give them the benefit of his advice, and so he did every evening until the report was finished. The committee had the draft of an answer prepared when he arrived first — the joint production of Sam Adams and Dr. Warren — but it was full of high-sounding phrases about liberty and rights without meeting the legal arguments in the Governor's speech.

John Adams detected the legal flaws in these arguments, saw that the Governor could be hoist with his own petard. But John Adams perceived that he would have to rewrite the answer himself, since he alone had the requisite knowledge and skill. But *if* he rewrote it, he would be personally responsible for it. And his head might be the forfeit.

"I have a wife — and what a wife! I have children — and what children!" he groaned to Abigail.

But this time she was in full health and had two years more experience behind her, in which she had watched both her husband and the progress of the struggle. No tears now.

"You must not think of us first," she said, "in times like these. The challenge has been made, and I'm proud that you are needed to meet it! You can't be, I know, nor do I wish to see you, an inactive spectator! I will try to be a good Portia to your Brutus!" [20]

He looked at her glowing beauty, illuminated by the leaping fire, and thought of the security that he longed to give her, the bleak dangers and uncertainties that threatened if he took the part his nature — and hers — urged him to.

"I should think myself the happiest man in the world," he said

involuntarily, "if I could retire now to my little hut and forty *
acres which my father left me in Braintree and live on potatoes
and sea-weed for the rest of my life [21] — sooner than expose you
and my little ones to what may come! For that which I am to
answer the Governor — if I do answer — means revolution, nothing less."

"Dear heart," she said, "you have often read to me that all the
misfortunes of Sparta were brought on by their being too anxious
for present tranquillity — is it not so? Loving peace so much,
clinging to peace, they neglected the means of making it sure and
lasting. Ah, peace can only be founded in justice and honor; it
can't be purchased at the price of liberty!" [22]

No word now about his health or her children. He was not
forcing her, not even persuading her. She was in equal step at his
side.

"Then," said he, "I will set friends and enemies at defiance and
follow my own best judgment whatever may fall thereon!" [23]

"Don't fear for me!" said she. "I long impatiently to have you
upon the stage of action!" [24]

So John Adams arrived at that main crossroad at which everyone arrives sometime in life, and chose his path. And his wife
chose it with him.

It would not be true to say that they never again looked backward, because they often longed to be able to steer out of the
turmoil into the quiet backwater. But since the path of duty led
them ever deeper into the thick of affairs, they never after did
more than cast a wistful look behind, a mere sigh of relinquish-
ment of a loved pattern of living.

And that this sigh sometimes escaped them only shows the more
that John and Abigail Adams were not — as were Patrick Henry
and Samuel Adams — the type of people naturally thought of as
revolutionary. They belonged to the type of people who valued
comfort and culture, who were easy in the established order, successful and at home in it, and normally to be found among its
firmest supporters.

* He had added to his original nine and one half by purchase from time
to time.

Two mortal blows were dealt that winter to Hutchinson's schemes, and both were dealt by John Adams. One was the reply to Hutchinson's address, and the other was the impeachment of the Chief Justice, Peter Oliver of effigy fame, for accepting salary from the Crown when he was an official of the colony.

But the slow transit of mails, in the bottoms of leisurely sailing ships, diverted by winds, delayed by calms, gave plenty of opportunity for the Devil and his servant mischievous Chance to tangle up the skein. Perhaps, too, it was less Chance and the Devil than the familiar human motives of greed and obstinacy that sped catastrophe.

There were quantities of tea stored up, because of the boycott, in English warehouses. Parliament gave attention to the affairs of the East India Company, in which private and national revenue was tied up, and resolved to send some of this tea to America willy-nilly "to habituate the colonies to parliamentary taxes." [25]

Protesting voices were heard in London, from many Englishmen as well as from Americans. But the Prime Minister, Lord North, said publicly — "It is to no purpose making objections, for the King will have it so. The King means to try the question with America." [26]

When news of this reached America the reaction was immediate and violent. The committees of correspondence between the colonies passed around word to form plans for a determined and united stand — as with the stamps ten years before. Philadelphia passed a resolution first this time, not to allow the tea to be put on shore; Boston second. New York followed suit.

Three ships, it was learned, were on the way to Boston, two to New York, one to Philadelphia, one to Charleston, South Carolina. In Boston the consignees to whom the tea was to be delivered included Hutchinson's son. An orderly gathering of the people at the Tree of Liberty, under the British flag, headed by Samuel Adams and John Hancock, Dr. Warren, and the Town Clerk, William Cooper, summoned the consignees to appear and to agree to send back the tea. The consignees not unnaturally refused to appear or to repudiate the tea.

Town Meeting met at Faneuil Hall and passed a vote of censure on them.

The three tea ships were expected every hour. Boston grew feverish.

One of the consignees (Clarke) had his windows broken by a mob, and replied by firing out of the window over their heads. It dispersed the crowd, but only added to the anger of the town.

The consignees appealed to the Governor, their silent invested partner, to protect them and their tea.

On the last Sunday of November one of the tea ships arrived and anchored below the Castle. Abigail heard the news given out from the pulpit in meeting, where she sat beside her husband and elder children. Deep and passionate were the prayers. Being Sabbath, there could be no movement on either side.

On Monday morning, when Abigail went out to her early marketing, she saw notices posted on tree trunks and walls, surrounded by rapidly shifting groups of readers. She paused to read one:

Friends! Brethren! Countrymen! That worst of plagues, the detested tea is now arrived in this harbor.

Every friend to his country is now called upon to meet at Faneuil Hall at nine o'clock this day at which time the bells will ring, to make an united and successful resistance to this last, worst and most destructive measure of administration.

Abigail hurried home before the bells should ring. The streets were already filling up with horsemen, chaises, chairs, wagons, people on foot. A crowd predominantly male was flocking into Boston from all villages and towns within a dozen miles. Hancock's partner, John Andrews, wrote to London next day —* " 'Twould puzzle any person to purchase a pair of pistols in town, as they are all bought up, with a full determination to repell force to force." [27]

The Governor and council sat in the council chamber opposite Abigail's door, while the Body Meeting † sat in Faneuil Hall not far off. Watching from the window she could see John Hancock

* December 1st, 1773. See *John Hancock's Book*, p. 179.
† Body meeting comprising several towns, as distinct from town meeting, representing only one.

and another go up the steps, an evident deputation to wait upon the Governor; she saw them return, hats pulled low.

"What will happen?" said Abigail to her husband.

His face was grave and steady.

"We shall continue to the last to try for one of two things: to persuade the consignees to repudiate, as the consignees have done in New York before their ship even reached port; or to obtain a clearance from the Governor to allow this ship to return to England without unloading."

"And if not?"

"You may be sure, my dear, the tea will not be landed in Boston."

Abigail was silent. But at last she found her voice, although it trembled.

"And what consequences will follow such unmitigated resistance?"

"The worst might follow," said John Adams. "The very worst — except one. It might be civil war, no less."

"What can be worse?" said Abigail with trembling lips.

"Why, slavery!" he said vehemently. "If freedom can only be bought at the price of civil war, then I say it is worth the price!"

The days passed without any show of violence. The town resumed its normal life, but under tension, vigilant for signal. The appointed Committee of Vigilance and Safety met every day. And the tea ship was under armed surveillance, by volunteer shift, day and night.

On December 5th, Abigail Adams wrote to her dear friend Mercy Warren at Plymouth — "The tea, that baneful weed, is arrived. Great and I hope effectual opposition has been made to the landing of it. . . . The flame is kindled and like lightning it catches from soul to soul. Although the mind is shocked at the thought of shedding human blood, more especially the blood of our countrymen, and a civil war is of all wars the most dreadful, such is the present spirit that prevails that if once they are made desperate, many, very many, of our heroes will spend their lives in the cause. I tremble when I think what may be the direful consequences, and in this town must the scene of the action lie. My heart beats at every whistle I hear, and I dare not express half my fears." [28]

The committees of correspondence of all the towns within a radius of twelve miles of Boston sat daily in united session in Faneuil Hall. The Boston Committee of Safety, with Sam Adams and John Hancock leading, had the town in complete control. Two more tea ships arrived, and were ordered by the Committee, along with the first, to move in to Griffin's Wharf, in the heart of maritime Boston. The twenty days of grace ran out, one by one, like a string of broken beads. At their expiration demand for duty must be made by the customs, and if it was not paid, ship and goods must be seized by the fleet. Mr. Rotch took an encouraging step when he agreed to order his ship away without unloading.

So quiet was the town, so competent the Committee, that John Adams went on circuit as usual. He had been away a week, and was expected back next day, when Thursday, December 16th, 1773, the last day of grace, dawned on Boston. It dawned with the news flying from mouth to mouth that Rotch had withdrawn his promise.

"And why has he so?" said Abigail to her young cousin Will Smith, Isaac's younger brother, who brought the word to her breakfast table.

"Because he finds that to send back the *Dartmouth* without a clearance from the custom house would lose him his ship! The Admiral keeps a ship o' the line in readiness to seize it should it sail under those circumstances. The Governor won't give the ship a clearance to sail away without a clearance from the Customs. The Customs won't give a clearance without landing tea and paying duty. You see? It goes round and round. A perfect deadlock. Farewell! I am off to Town Meeting with my father — or it's more than that! Look at the crowds out of window! It's a muster! Faneuil Hall's too small, we are gathering in the Old South. There go the bells!"

Abigail's heart beat with them. Lessons that morning for Nabby and Johnny were divided between the window and the book, while the cadences of patriotic verse fell on their impressionable ears. What the town does now will be history, and we are in and with the town! An ominous quiet fell on the silent and deserted streets. Abigail, like the other women of Boston, went about her daily domestic tasks with an ear cocked to the outer world for sounds of — what? — while she waited for the returning men to bring some news.

Her loved young cousin Will, her favorite, looked in again.

"They've passed a unanimous vote that the tea shall go out of the harbor this afternoon. A committee was sent with Mr. Rotch to the customs to demand a clearance, and when 'twas refused unless they would pay the duty on the tea, the committee and Mr. Rotch set off for the Governor's house at Milton village to beg his clearance for the ship to sail without unloading. There are ten thousand men in the Old South awaiting the Governor's reply!"

Abigail's house boy came in with lighted candles, and replenished the fire; one of the maids followed promptly with the tea tray. Behind all the lighted windows of Boston the womenfolk and their callers sat down — without their menfolk — to their tea. Will sat down for a cup. But suddenly there fell a sound of distant shouting from a thousand throats. Will ran out and back to the Old South, while Abigail, wrapped in a cloak, stood at her door, straining eyes and ears through the winter dusk.

She heard, indeed, pandemonium.

As she was told afterwards by many witnesses Rotch came back with the not unexpected message that the Governor could not give a pass for the ships without a clearance from the customs. Thus the vicious circle closed complete. The candles had been lit in the church, and threw into chiaroscuro the sea of faces on floor and galleries, and a great black shadow wavered up behind Rotch above the pulpit. As soon as he had spoken "such prodigious shouts were made" that people not in the meeting came running to learn the cause of it. Samuel Adams, moderator, immediately declared the meeting dissolved, which caused another general shout and three cheers, hip-hip-hooray! [29] Then as the thousands poured out and joined the crowds in the streets, the noise was as if the infernal regions had broken loose.

Those who knew their parts were fully prepared, and lost no

time. They mustered on Fort Hill, a convenient spot not far from Griffin's Wharf, roughly disguised in soot, paint, and blankets as "Indians from Narragansett." Armed with hatchets and pistols, they marched two by two, in perfect order, to the wharf where the *Dartmouth, Eleanor,* and *Beaver* lay, vigilantly guarded by the Committee of Safety, each with 114 chests of tea on board. The first two ships' sole remaining cargo was tea, but "ye latter had arrived at ye wharf only the day before, and was freighted with a large quantity of other goods which the Mohawks took the greatest care not to injure in the least, and before nine o'clock in ye evening, every chest from on board the three vessels was knocked to pieces and flung over ye sides" [30] into the salt water. Almost the entire population of Boston watched along the shore, in the flare of lanterns and torches. Yet in spite of all the witnesses not one of the names of the Mohawks was ever given. Hutchinson, who had taken refuge with his sons in the Castle, said there were fifty Mohawks.[31] Hancock's partner, John Andrews, an eyewitness, said there were two hundred. "Not the least insult was offered to any person," added Andrews, "but a horse-dealer who was discovered to have ript up the lining of his coat and to be stuffing it full of tea was handled pretty roughly. They not only stript him of his clothes but gave him a coat of mud with a severe bruising into the bargain; and nothing but their utter aversion to make any disturbance prevented his being tar'd and feathered." [32]

This modest aversion to making a disturbance would have sounded strange in the Governor's ears, but John and Abigail Adams accepted it at the foot of the letter. John had arrived home from Plymouth early the morning after [33] and was at once informed of everything. He and Abigail watched the Governor drive by their house with the Secretary. "Notwithstanding the forlorn state he was in," wrote the ruined Governor of himself, "he thought it necessary to keep up some show of authority." [34]

"I suppose they're framing a proclamation with reward for names of the ringleaders!" said John Adams. "Take care to mention none in my hearing! I'll likely be called on by some of them to take charge of their defence!" [35]

"What's your opinion of the action, cousin?" said Sam Adams, alert as usual to get John Adams to commit himself. John did not hesitate.

"It was magnificent!" said he. "Sublime!"

It was astonishing how gay everyone seemed. Suspense and tension had been broken by a simple satisfying action. An inextricable tangle, a complete Gordian knot, had been neatly cut. It was an action too that had an element of laughter in it, a saucy and audacious good humor. It was no child's play, it was the stern action of a man, but of a young man.

"Such is the present calm composure of the people," wrote Andrews to Hancock's business friends in London, "that a stranger would hardly think that ten thousand pounds sterling of the East India Company's tea was destroy'd the evening before last." [36]

But other letters reached the King from his Tory friends in Boston dictated by panic and fury. They said that Boston was full of wild rioters, that there was a terrorist committee to tar and feather people, and that the Governor himself was liable to be its next victim.

Abigail was sent to Weymouth to rest from the prolonged strain, and have a brief holiday from domestic duties and child care. There the eventful year closed for her.

"Alas!" she wrote to John, "how many snow banks divide thee and me and my warmest wishes to see thee will not melt one of them. . . ."

As winter wore into spring John worried increasingly about Abigail. She was far from well. The return to Boston had brought back distressing symptoms. "I cannot get the thought of her state of health out of my mind," [37] he wrote. Nevertheless they were pleasantly occupied making plans for Braintree. John had purchased from his brother his father's homestead and farm. "How shall I improve it?" he wondered. "Shall I try to introduce fowl-meadow and herds-grass into the meadows? or still better, clover and herds-grass? I must ramble over it and take a view." [38]

V

War Comes to Braintree

IN the month of May, 1774, the height of the dazzling brief New
England spring, the season of singing birds and of a thousand
flowers, General Gage arrived in Boston as the new governor,
straight from England, with the Parliamentary Edict in his pocket.
Abigail was not there to see his entry in state, Union Jacks flying,
Colonel Hancock and his cadet corps, under British commission,
forming an escorting guard of honor, and the citizens of Boston
and near-by towns lining the streets in a grave and noncommittal
mood. John's anxiety for her health — she suffered from a terrible
recurrent migraine — had sent her to Weymouth, where she was
basking in country peace under the tender care of her mother
and lively young sister Betsey. So she did not watch the inauguration of the last royal governor of Massachusetts. After the pageant
before the Courthouse, General Gage expressed formal regret at
his immediate duty, cleared his throat, and read the Parliamentary
Edict rescinding the charter of Massachusetts and — as John
Adams expressed it to his wife succinctly — "blocking up the
Harbor of Boston and annihilating the trade of this town." The
audience dispersed in silence. It was, in fact, dangerously quiet.

Abigail, lying very unwell under her father's trees, suffering
agonies of headache and a kind of influenza prostration, received
John's letters by the manservant next day —

> The Town of Boston, for aught I can see might suffer mar-
> tyrdom. Our principal consolation is that it dies in a noble
> cause. . . . Let me know what is best for us to do.

But while he paid her the compliment of not painting the picture less dark than it really was, he did not expect to depress her
or himself.

Don't imagine from all this that I am in the dumps. Far
otherwise. I look upon this as the last effort of Lord North's
despair.

I am, with great anxiety for your health,

Your

John Adams.[1]

When Abigail returned to Boston, she found it apparently so
normal that only in conversation did impending crisis appear. But
on the first of June, as the clock in the belfry of the Old South
chimed the last heavy stroke of noon, the waiting warships moved
in and closed the port. And as the days went by, the cruel consequences of the blockade became apparent. Abigail wanted to
move her household goods to Braintree by water, on the slow, safe,
easy barges; but not a boat could move at Boston, no, not to bring
in produce from the harbor islands, nor so much as to make traffic
from one wharf to another. All fresh milk, food, and goods coming into the city must travel by wagon along the hot road into the
Neck. And there one could see the congested traffic lined up,
while milk and butter soured and vegetables wilted.

Taking a drive about the city with Dorothy Quincy that first
week, Abigail found it already like a place quarantined for sickness. Ships lay idle at the wharf; warehouses, having sold all their
store, lay open to the casual entry of wandering cats and birds.
Men thrown out of employment loitered at street corners. The
populous traffic of the streets had shrunk to a thin trickle. The
poor were in terror of the winter.

Abigail was trying to get ready to move to Braintree but now
more than ever John Adams's office was full, if not with private
clients, then with public ones. Said Gridley, "Brother Adams, you
keep late hours at your house! As I passed it last night long
after midnight I saw your street door vomit forth a crowd of
senators!"[2] At last the main part of the furniture was got
off. The family only waited conveyance and John Adams's
escort.

On June 14th the 4th Regiment landed, marched into Boston
and encamped on the Common, followed next day by the 43rd.
Two companies of artillery and eight pieces of ordnance were un-

loaded at the Castle. More battalions of infantry were hourly expected.

On the seventeenth the bells rang to call Town Meeting in Faneuil Hall, and the male citizens of Boston jammed it to overflowing. John Hancock and Sam Adams were away at Salem, where the Governor had called the General Court. So John Adams, new to Boston Town Meeting, was elected Moderator. He at once put the question to the meeting: any in favor of buying off the blockade by paying for the tea now rise and freely argue their case. But the sight of the soldiers again in Boston had put so much iron into Boston blood that not a man stood up.

Abigail, sitting by the window in the dusky, dismantled room, looked anxiously out into the street. The lanterns, hung to walls at intervals — John Hancock's new system of lighting the town — caught the gleam of scarlet and the flash of steel from passing soldiery out to explore their new location. Well she knew that the temper of the city was so much tinder, and the soldiers were the spark. Some hour, hidden in the not far distant future, would inevitably bring the explosion. "Did ever any kingdom or state regain its liberty, when once it was invaded, without bloodshed?" [3] She had said, "Yet, if the sword be drawn, I bid adieu to all domestic happiness." [4]

Boston had been forbidden "by the King's command" to summon a Town Meeting, but John had shown a way out of that. The Town Meeting was not, he said, fresh summoned; it was considered adjourned from the last one.

At last Abigail heard the familiar noise of the crowd issuing into the streets from Faneuil Hall; and presently she discerned her husband's figure coming at a brisk pace. The nearest lantern caught Richard Cranch's long, thin face. His hand was pressing John's shoulder in affection and congratulation as he bade farewell. There was a flourish of hats, a murmur of men's resonant voices, and then John Adams came in alone.

She met him at the door of the room, her pulses throbbing with portent. He gathered her to him in the dusk, and held her to his own hard-beating heart. She felt its strong pulsation more than she felt her own.

"John?"

"Ay, Nabby. Ay, my Portia. . . . A messenger rode hard from Salem to our meeting. . . . There's a new and grand scene opening before me! A Congress! [5] Ay, a Continental Congress is to meet on the first day of September at Philadelphia. So well have our Committees of Correspondence functioned, so quick has the word been got from one to 'tother. Cushing, Bob Paine, Cousin Sam Adams and myself are appointed Delegates from this province. . . . Ah, this will be an assembly of the wisest men upon the continent. I feel myself unequal to this business!" [6]

Next day John Adams with coach and chaise and wagon removed his family to Braintree "to prepare myself as well as I could for the storm that was coming on. They could not indeed have remained in safety in Boston." After a few days to settle them there, he returned to Boston, left three of his clerks in charge of his office in Queen Street, sent two to Braintree to protect his wife, and rode away with Josiah Quincy for the tenth and last time on the eastern circuit.

"My refreshment," Abigail read in one of his treasured letters, "is a flight to Braintree, to my Cornfields and Grass Plotts, my Gardens and Meadows — my Fancy runs about you perpetually, frequently takes a walk with you and your little prattlings. We walk all together up Penns Hill, over the Bridge to the Plain, down to the Garden. . . ." [7]

She loved this simplicity in him. And she loved his earnest attention to the children's training which urged her — "above all Cares of this Life let our ardent Anxiety be to mould the Minds and Manners of our Children, not only to do virtuously but to excel." And, by way of concrete suggestion — tribute also to her culture — "It is time, my dear, for you to begin to teach them French." [8]

But she could not fail most to value in his letters their constant elevation of herself to true equality with him. "My dear Partner" was no empty phrase. "I must intreat you," he said, "to take a part with me in the struggle. [9] . . . I have a Zeal at my heart for my Country and her friends which I cannot smother or conceal. This Zeal will prove fatal to the Fortune and Felicity of my

Family." [10] Yet she was willing to take part with him; she encouraged his zeal; she shared it.

Refreshed by the country life, Abigail and the children — Nabby, now nine, and Tommy, the youngest, two — welcomed him home in July for a brief time of rest and preparation for what lay before him. And before the middle of August she drove into Boston with him where he joined his fellow delegates. There was a good send-off at Mr. Cushing's house, with a dinner and speeches, and the four delegates set out on their journey together in one coach. [11]

It was well-organized, open and dignified, yet Abigail realized, in a sickening stab of panic, that bloody rebellion, wounds and death, might be the end. But what weighed upon her husband, as he had told her in the intimate night watches, was a sense of his own inadequacy. Only she knew his humility, his honest self-criticism, and his often too harsh self-depreciation. He expected to find the representatives from other provinces a dazzling group of superior beings among whom he would be constantly at a disadvantage. He regretted that riding circuit had prevented him from brushing up on his law and history that "I might appear with less indecency before a variety of gentlemen whose education and experience, family, fortune and everything will give them a vast superiority to me." [12]

A gigantic responsibility rested on this congress, he felt, of which he was only too unworthy. "Should this country submit, what infamy and ruin! Death in any form is less terrible!" But who among his acquaintance were fit for the untried task? That was when his heart sank, for he could see no one.

"We have not men fit for the times!" [13]

Abigail's own duty was clear before her: to administer her household with the utmost thrift, keep a lively oversight of the farm, cherish and educate her children, and keep her husband in touch with home by long and frequent letters. The sad part was she got no letters in return. Hers seemed to be carried off into a void, buried perhaps in the pockets of the friends who, being about to travel, had taken them along. Five weeks dragged slowly by, and she had not had a line.

What, then, about the postal system? It had two drawbacks. It was not considered so safe as private conveyance, and it was ruinously expensive. Said John Adams, in one of the letters she had not yet received — "I have not found a single opportunity to write since I left Boston excepting by the post, and I don't choose to write by that conveyance for fear of foul play. . . . I hope to find some private hand by which I can convey this." [14] And Abigail at last, guessing the cause was lack of "safe conveyance," wrote desperately — "I would rather give a dollar for a letter by the post, though the consequence should be that I ate but one meal a day these three weeks to come." [15]

She laid down her pen and got ready to walk over to Mount Wollaston to spend the day with her Uncle Norton Quincy. Little Nabby and Abigail's younger sister Betsey accompanied her. It proved a lively visit. Josiah Quincy and his wife came in, and presently Sam Quincy's wife and a Mr. Sumner followed. "A little clashing of parties you may be sure!" [16] said Abigail, "especially as the conversation turned upon the recent speech in the House of Lords by the Bishop of St. Asaph, defending the colonies' cause." But there was no ill-will between Quincy and Quincy, differ and argue as they might. All were agreed at last in praise of the Bishop. They strolled home refreshed in the grape-scented September dusk, with tall goldenrod and purple asters by the wayside catching the light of their lantern, and the half-moon shaping a sickle in the sky. The murmur of the sea grew fainter behind them as they turned inland toward Penns Hill. And then, just when expectation was dormant, "Mr. Thaxter met me at the door with your letter. . . . It gave me such a flow of spirits that I was not composed enough to sleep until one o'clock." [17]

John Adams had gone to the heart of the political world, for such this modest-looking gathering of fifty-six gentlemen had become. All that then seethed in conscious importance in Moscow, Berlin, London, and even Paris was to weigh lighter, was to mark the future less, than the unpractised deliberations then going on in Philadelphia.

But Abigail had not been left in a backwater. When the family gathered at table there were two young men to contribute news and intelligent discussion, the two law clerks brought out from Boston for protection. They were Nathan Rice, just graduated from Harvard, and John Thaxter, who was Abigail's own cousin,* a grandson of John Quincy. "Never were two persons who gave a family less trouble than they do," [18] said Abigail. All their time seemed spent in the office, except that Mr. Rice was now teaching the Braintree school and John Thaxter was tutoring young Johnny. Those two liked each other so well and Johnny was getting on so fast that his mother decided to continue the plan and not send him to school. But though Johnny had thus graduated to a tutor, shared also for some lessons by Nabby, he would sit by his mother in the evening and read aloud, stumbling through a page or two of Rollin's *Ancient History*, in which she was passionately interested. Then Abigail would lay down her sewing and finish the chapter. Nabby would get her sewing and listen too while Abigail made the old, far-distant story vivid to her children by relating it to the present time.

Johnny liked to pass by the muster field beside the meetinghouse at sunset, for there he could watch the young men, fresh from the fields, getting to work at their drill, and hear the rattle of old muskets at the loading. "Indeed, yes," said Abigail, "this town appears as high as you can well imagine, and if necessary would soon be in arms." [19]

But in the meetinghouse on Sunday the thought of arms was laid aside. Nor was the powder stored, as it was at Weymouth, in the church tower. The Reverend Mr. Wibird preached cautious, neutral sermons, expounding obscure texts which had no political undercurrents. But it was a great social occasion and word passed rapidly, with minimum machinery, from man to man, as need arose, at or after meeting, let the pastor be as neutral — or as Tory! — as he liked.

At sunset on a Sabbath the first breath of coming storm came to Braintree. It was right in the middle of the reading of Rollin's *History* that the unmistakable rhythmic beat of marching men broke on their ears in the cool parlor at Penns Hill. Johnny

* Her mother's younger sister, Anna Quincy, married John Thaxter of Hingham.

Mount Wollaston in Abigail's grandfather's time

FROM A SKETCH BY ELIZA QUINCY

dropped the printed pages and ran to the window. A thousand years vanished in a flash; not Roman legions but American farmers were filing past. "About two hundred men, preceded by a horsecart; they passed without any noise, not a word among them." [20]

"Where are they going, Mother?"

"I don't know!"

"They're fetching the powder from the powder-house," said John Thaxter, buckling on his belt. "A soldier — they suppose a spy — was seen lurking about here this morning. So we expect a redcoat raid to steal the township's store of munitions, such as was made at Charlestown 'tother day when the province's store of munitions there was captured by soldiers and carried off in a boat. Now Gage means business; he's mounted a cannon on Beacon Hill; he's fortifying the Neck; what does he mean, anyhow? And if he takes all our munitions, what protection shall we have? . . ." He went out, and joined the rear of the procession. When they came back, with the loaded cart and a captured Tory walking between them — caught with writs to summon juries in his possession — they saw Mrs. John Adams and her children at the open casement level with the road.

"Hey, ma'am!" cried one of them jovially. "Are you wanting some powder?"

She laughed, and shook her head. Her dark curls ruffled in the evening breeze, her eyes and cheeks were bright with excitement like their own.

"No, no!" she said. "Not now it's in such good hands!"

And the men laughed softly, passing on.

Soon they halted and asked their Tory to hand over his writs, which he did, and they made a circle round, and burned them. Then they wanted to huzza, but someone objected that it was Sunday; "Those in favor say Ay! — Contrary, contrary sign!" The Nays had it. So after making the Tory swear not to administer the new acts, they let him go unhurt, took the powder to a safe hiding place in the next parish, and dispersed. [21]

This sudden appearance and disappearance of large bodies of men under discipline — summoned how? by whom? — made the country Tories blench, and made Governor Gage prickle nervously in Boston.

Suffolk County, in fact, had a little Congress of its own, organized * and dominated by no less a person than Dr. Joseph Warren. It kept up law and order by its own methods now that law courts were "out." In fact, wrote Abigail to her absent husband, the people's committees had now taken matters into their own hands in all the places round, and would not permit any of the courts to sit. Last week in Taunton, she had heard in a letter from Robert Treat Paine's sister Eunice, that two thousand disciplined men assembled round the courthouse and prevented entry. They waited for two hours to gain their point, keeping ordered rank in the hot sun. The same happened at Springfield, with drums and trumpets and this time a flag — plain black. A flag not yet completely rival to the British flag; not yet affirming another allegiance; a flag that simply said No. . . .

With the first leaf fall of late September Abigail left home to visit her brother, William Smith, near the town of Salem. William was now married to an attractive and suitable wife, had some children of his own and a commission in the militia, but had fallen into the private difficulties that were to pursue him to his end. Salt meat and salt fish led to cider and to rum. The sin of New England was intemperance. Before other issues claimed him, John Adams had inveighed hotly in speeches and in the press against the too numerous taverns and their lack of conscience in pursuing trade. William and his painful affairs were covered by his sister with the charity which is a cloak for all sins and the silence which was the best policy for all parties. The subject of Boston was more interesting to her husband and more urgent. "I called here on my return to see this much injured town." [22] It was the corpse of a city, "the body of a departed friend." The soldiers were now in constant evidence, passing and repassing, the only people who were busy. Many of the principal merchants had moved out of town. Uncle Isaac and Aunt Elizabeth Smith had moved to Salem.

* In consultation, before he left, with Samuel Adams. See Bancroft, IV, p. 379.

Abigail looked in at her husband's office in Queen Street, and saw that the three young men left in charge there were making the best possible use of their time, and needed the books and papers to study with. By their articles, John Adams was responsible for them, and they wished to avail themselves of the shelter and resources of the office. So she decided against removing the books to Braintree. She went to Judge Quincy's house across the way for rest, a meal, and a family visit. Lovely Dorothy Quincy had a story to tell of an evil undercurrent in the town — a conspiracy of the Negro slaves. It was no idle rumor. The leaders had got an Irishman to draw up a petition for them to Governor Gage, offering their services against the colonists if he would arm them and promise them their liberty. A Negro who was a patriot (like Crispus Attucks) had tried to persuade his brethren against this course, and when he found himself in danger of his life had come secretly to Judge Edmund Quincy for protection and had revealed the plot. "There is but little said," her relatives warned Abigail. "The less this gets about, the better!"

"Well," said Abigail, "I wish most sincerely there was not a slave in the province! It always seemed a most iniquitous scheme to me to fight ourselves for what we are robbing the Negroes of, who have as good a right to freedom as we have! You know my mind upon this subject." [23]

"Yet, cousin, I once heard that your kinsman Thomas Smith, who is so excellent a patriot in the south, had given your Uncle Isaac a figure upon slave cargoes — something about five per cent?" [24] said Dorothy slyly.

"That was at any rate before importing slaves became contraband, like tea!" said Abigail good-humoredly. "The last I heard from Charleston was of a cargo of three hundred slaves being sent back to base by its own consignees, not being allowed to land! [25] But all this talk of five per cent from *you*, lady? It's my guess you've been listening attentively to one John Hancock!"

"There are others!" said Dorothy.

In October John Adams came home to his wife and family after ten weeks' absence. The warmth and *élan* of his presence had not been exaggerated in their hopes and dreams. Wife and children alike felt as if the sun had come out on them. Johnny was praised for reading to his mother so manfully — such a hard book! — and for writing to his father. Nabby was eagerly thanked for her letters — "My dear, they gave me great spirit!" [26] Charley and Tommy were tossed up and hugged. Each child felt its own place secure in its father's heart, without pretense or patronage.

But presently he turned to their mother and spoke of matters they could not understand. "You ask me am I satisfied with the Congress? Tolerably well, tolerably. We should have done more. We were slow! Slow as snails. I have not been used to such ways! [27] . . . And yet . . . we have had as great questions to discuss as ever engaged the attention of men. There is a great spirit in the Congress! Above all, there is in the Congress a collection of the greatest men upon this continent. Here are fortunes, abilities, learning, eloquence, acuteness, equal to any I ever met with in my life. There is a magnanimity and public spirit equal to any in ancient history. . . . When we got the false news of the bombardment of Boston every gentleman seemed to consider it as the bombardment of the capital of his own province! I was particularly struck with the Southern gentlemen from Virginia — Mr. Peyton Randolph, whom we made our President, and Mr. Patrick Henry, and Colonel Washington and Mr. Richard Henry Lee. The Virginians have called Lee their Cicero, Henry their Demosthenes."

"Did you accomplish anything definite?" she said.

"Not what I hoped, I confess. I feel — and I urged — that there is a necessity that an American Legislature should be set up without delay.[28] But others thought that that would bar the way finally for reconciliation with the British. Finally, a committee was appointed to draw up an address to the King — Lee, Henry, myself and two others. The address we prepared was not considered conciliatory enough, by Mr. Dickinson especially. And Mr. Dickinson — the Philadelphia Quaker whose writings you know well [29] — was added to our committee to help re-draft it, which he did — adding softening touches to the document already prepared but not changing its main arguments. This has gone to London, and we must hope for result. It was at least a clear statement and a loyal one. Well, my love, your informative letters have not only cheered me but done us vast service! Tell me about yourself! How have you managed?"

"I've lived a very recluse life since your absence, my dearest!" said Abigail. "Seldom gone anywhere except to my father's! My mother has been exceedingly low, but is a little better. Uncle Quincy often visits me to have an hour of sweet communion upon politicks with me! And Dr. Tufts comes in, and Colonel James and Mrs. Mercy Warren were here on Monday, and Mrs. Warren will spend a day or two on her return with me. I've spent one Sabbath in town since you left — well, I wrote to you from Boston. What struck me was that the city people don't know yet that luxury and fashion are out of date — they haven't the resolution to encourage our own manufactories * which people in the country have! We must return a little more to the simplicity of our fathers! But, dearest — how do you think I look? My health is much better than it was last fall! Some folkes say I grow very fat!" [30]

He had listened to all she said with kindling interest, and now he laughed out. She was always taking him by surprise.

"Down, vanity!" he said. But he showed her what he thought of her looks. Then he set straight the lace on her hair and taking her arm in his drew her out into the yard. Ankle-deep in the golden leaves he looked out eagerly over his farm, his walled byre and pasture, his browsing cattle, the well-cut stubble of the sickled corn. Between the fields ran the road, deep in dust.

"And here you saw them pass to get the powder, in armed array!" he said, musing. "Ay, but our people must be peaceable! Let them exercise every day in the week, if they will — the more the better! Let them furnish themselves with artillery and arms and ammunition. Let 'em follow the maxim which you say they have adopted — 'In times of peace prepare for war.' — But let them avoid war *if possible, if possible* I say." [31]

On November 23rd, with John Adams's assistance, the Provincial Congress of Massachusetts (formed from the dissolved

* This alludes to the hand spinning and weaving etc. being encouraged to substitute for the finer imported goods. In those days the word "manufactory" clung to its Latin meaning and meant "made by hand."

Assembly during his absence) voted to enroll twelve thousand minutemen, who — as in the times of the Indian wars — would go about their labor with weapons at hand, ready at a minute's notice to follow the call to arms.

A game of seizing the arms of the province was on. First the British made a successful coup, then the provincials, in a tremendous hide-and-seek in which the advantages were all on the side of the provincials. They knew the terrain, they knew good hiding places, and they were almost always informed in time of British intentions. Since minutemen and militia were openly drilling everywhere, three times a week and oftener, it was natural that Gage, who could think of nothing else to do, should try to seize the small local stores of munitions and arms.

Abigail Adams would stroll down to the North Precinct muster field with her husband and son and hear John groan with envy of his youngest brother Elihu, the captain of the local troop. "Oh that I were a soldier! I will be. I'm reading military books!" [32] And he gave thought — and poured it forth to her — on the problems of the organization of an army. Little enough had been done yet but at least some general officers had been appointed: General Ward, a veteran of the French and Indian War, and two major generals, of whom Dr. Joseph Warren was one. Powder and guns were being assembled in a central spot.

It was five months later that the skirmishes of Lexington and Concord were fought. As soon as the news reached Braintree, Captain Elihu Adams and his band of minutemen lit out to join the others. All night minutemen and militia poured into Cambridge. The Penns Hill farm, right on the Old Shore Road, became a scene of bustle and confusion as passing minutemen paused for a drink and a rest. More came and more and were offered supper — breakfast — a night's lodging. Johnny ran to and fro with big mugs of water from the well. His father brought cider from the cellar. His mother was cutting slices of salt meat and bread on the living-room table, and ordering a large kettle of meat and vegetables to be put on to boil in the kitchen. The good smell of baking bread floated out of the door to the tired and dusty traveler. The barn became full of men bivouacking there for the night and every corner of the house was full.

John Adams came into the barn, a cordial host to his guests.

"Ye've got a fine little soldier coming along *there*, sir!" said one, pointing to Johnny.

"Ay, and he knows his drill, I'll warrant!" said John Adams. "He's always down at the muster-field, or playing at drills with his brothers."

The militiaman arose, and gravely handed the little boy his musket.

"Now then, sir — shoulder *arms!* — right *turn* — slope arms — ground arms — "

The lantern hanging in the barn door shone out across a strip of emerald grass and illuminated the slender boy's figure, gallantly handling the heavy weapon, exactly and smartly performing the manual exercise of the musket at the word of command; while in the shadowy barn, a ruddy cheek, a bright eye, a boot, the gleam of a silver button, a hand playing with the straw, indicated the crowd of intent, resting men.

Abigail had come out to watch, and her hand tightened on her husband's arm. Eight years ago Johnny was born and the time was short to look back on. Eight years from now he would be as old as some who were present there now in the barn. And what would he be then? A soldier? There were people — Sam Quincy, for instance, Jonathan Sewall — who said that if the war began it would last for twenty years.

Next day, John Adams took horse and rode over the route of the battle, collecting information from witnesses of all kinds; visited the camp at Cambridge, and listened to his friends, General Ward, General Heath, and above all General Joseph Warren.[33]

So Abigail presently learned from him the full story.

"This battle of Concord has cost the British more than it cost them to take Quebec!" said John Adams. "And what have they got to show for it?"

"But what have we got to show for it?" stammered the Reverend Isaac, who had ridden back with John from Cambridge. "Their revenge will be terrible."

"Indeed, what I saw and heard yesterday convinced me," said

John Adams, "that if we do not defend ourselves, they will kill us!"

"B-but how can we defend ourselves?" said Isaac, despairing.

"What can we do to help?" said Abigail. "Us, I mean — here? How were things at the camp?"

"Confusion and much distress!" said John. "No artillery — little in the way of arms, short of clothing and blankets — short of provisions. But I'll tell you what they're not short of — resolution and spirit!" [34]

He looked fiercely at Isaac, and the gentle young man quailed and glanced appealingly at his beloved cousin Abigail.

"I must say farewell, my dear, dear cousin!" said he. "I am for England until this trouble is past! I am a man of peace, and out of place here in this distracted province. My mind is full of perplexity and concern! . . . My mother and father agree to my going. . . . I can't be useful here! . . ." His eyes filled with tears. He hated to be the only one of his family of another opinion. He was homesick for return almost before he started. But go he must.

Abigail took his hand.

"You are always," she said, "my dear cousin and friend! You will pray to God for Boston — and for our country!"

Now the Second Continental Congress came on, and John Adams, again a delegate, left his wife and children with reluctance, though he left them in a place as safe as any. He did not anticipate immediate trouble.

Had Abigail been inside Boston, her situation would have been intolerable. But her farsighted husband had got her out in time — well ahead of time. She tried to feel worthy now of his bracing letters. He was more afraid, it seemed, that she should feel nervous than that she would be unsafe — "surrounded as you are by people who are too timorous. Many fears and imaginary dangers will be suggested to you but I hope you will not be impressed by them! In case of real danger," he added, a bit offhand, "fly to the woods with our children."

Abigail did not feel heroic. The idea of the woods was not appealing. She had now no men in the house. Her work people and her neighbors were indeed "timorous." "I feel somewhat lonely. Mr. Thaxter is gone home. Mr. Rice is going into the army as captain of a company. We have no school. I know not what to do with John." The young men "seem to be discouraged in the study of law and think there will never be any business for them." But she felt they were prematurely discouraged. A pity they didn't talk it over with John Adams before they left.

"As government is assumed," she said with perfect simplicity, "I suppose courts of justice will be established and in that case there may be [law] business to do." [35]

Not "resumed" — "assumed." This telltale word reveals that by May 4th, 1775, Abigail Adams and her husband — for from him she derived the idea — looked forward to nothing else but complete independence.* And John Adams had driven up to the Congress in his sulky, his manservant on horseback behind him, with a scheme for independence completely formulated in his mind.

*   *   *   *   *

Before May was out, Braintree discovered that it was not, as John Adams had cheerfully supposed, out of the war zone. In the dark of a Sunday morning the warning drum began to beat, and Abigail wakened to its distant sound. As she came downstairs, a farm hand ran into the kitchen with word that the bell on the meetinghouse in Braintree South Precinct was ringing like mad, and beyond to the southwest the bell of Abigail's father's church in Weymouth was heard faintly on the breeze by villagers down that way. The man Isaac came back breathless before they had finished their hasty meal — mistress, maids, and children all sitting down together in the twilit kitchen.

"Three sloops and a cutter have anchored just below Great Hill. Some think they're for Germantown — some say Weymouth. The road's full of folk from Germantown, loaded with their goods, flocking inland this way! And the folk from Weymouth

---

* See among many incorrect statements re John Adams and Samuel Adams in *American Statesmen* series this error in particular, that Samuel Adams alone stood for independence at the start of the Second Congress — "Even John Adams and Jefferson were as yet far from being ready for such a step." (P. 333.) The exact contrary is the case.

are all going back from the coast into the country — Parson Smith and his family have taken their chaise and gone, and the Parson loaded his waggon with women and children of his parish and took 'em along. Your Aunt Tufts had a bed thrown into a waggon and ordered the boy to drive her to Bridgwater, and your Uncle the Doctor is distracted, whether to go or not. They say three hundred men have landed somewhere, and our minute-men are mustering. . . . Well, mistress, there'll be no church this Sabbath!"

Peter Adams hurried in, his honest face anxious.

"Sister, won't you let me move you and the children and any of your valuables back into the country, to my house? You're in an exposed place here on the highway — if — !"

"I do thank you, Brother Peter! Indeed I will go thankfully if we're really in danger! But John is always warning me against false fears. Let me wait awhile and see. I can be useful here, 'I hope."

Thinking of the panic-stricken women all around, Peter gazed at her with admiration as she bundled the children out of the kitchen and directed her work people to push aside the table, get out the wooden mugs and bowls and all the spoons — two more buckets of ice-cold well water —

Elihu Adams appeared at the kitchen door, dressed in his hunting shirt with his musket slung on his back.

"Good morning, sister! There's a dozen men out here from Weymouth who have packed off their womenfolk and hurried to help us without breakfast. . . ."

"We have some pease-porridge and coffee ready!" said Abigail. "Will they come in?"

A moment or two later Elihu, stepping to the big kettle to ladle out some porridge, exclaimed at the spoon in his hand.

"What, sister, *pewter?* The men in my company have so few bullets that some of them, if they fire once, can't re-load. They'd give their ears for pewter this day!"

"Take it, take it!" said Abigail. "Take all my pewter spoons! I've at least two dozen, that we use here in the kitchen." She caught them down from hooks, pulled them out of the dresser.

"Look, have you your bullet-moulds? Use that heavy iron kettle!"

Johnny, coming into the kitchen, saw the spoons going into the kettle. The long handles of the bigger ladles stuck up. He squeezed through the people to see closer.

"Why, Uncle, what are you doing? What funny soup!"

"Bullet soup!" said his uncle. "You've seen your father run shot. We're going to run bullets!"

Johnny understood, and his heart jumped. Danger was close. Why didn't they go all away in the cart to Uncle Peter's? But just as he began to feel that sickening stab of fear, he turned round to look for his mother. When he saw her standing so calmly in the doorway between kitchen and living room, directing things in her quiet voice as if everything were going on just as she expected, his heart, if it did not return to normal, exchanged fear for excitement. He and his mother were sharing in a great day. Her eyes suddenly met his in warm, proud sympathy. She was glad to see him there. "Do you wonder," said John Quincy Adams, sixty-eight years later, "that a boy of seven who witnessed this scene should be a patriot?" *

The road outside was now cloudy with the dust of passing feet. The minutemen came flocking down, even from towns twenty, thirty, and forty miles from Weymouth, till two thousand were collected.[36]

The lookout men soon reported that the enemy's objective was now apparent. It was a redcoat raid on Grape Island to gather hay. They couldn't be reached there for want of boats; but the formidable array of minutemen on the shore, and the firing of muskets which splashed ball into the sea around them, flustered the redcoats and "prevented their getting more than three tons of hay though they had carted much more down to the water. At last a lighter was mustered and a sloop from Hingham which had six port-holes. Our men eagerly jumped on board and put off for the island. Your brother Elihu was one of the first on board,"[37] wrote Abigail to her husband. The British, who had probably intended to get the hay while all the inhabitants were in church,

* Speech delivered in 1843.

were unprepared for such resistance and hurriedly decamped.
"Our people landed upon the island and in an instant set fire to
the hay. Both your brothers were there; your younger brother
with his company gained honor by their good order that day."
Dr. Tufts, too; "danger, you know, sometimes makes timid men
bold. He stood that day very well, and generously attended,
with drink, biscuits, flints etc. five hundred men without taking
any pay. He has since been chosen one of the committee of correspondence for Weymouth, establishing a regular method of
alarm from town to town."

The Monday morning sun saw peace restored to Weymouth
and Braintree, evacuated families back in their homes, minutemen
laying aside the musket for the hoe, and only the lookout men
on duty. Nabby and Johnny settled to lessons with their mother,
doing some of that "copying out" their father favored, in the
delicate, clear handwriting taught them by Mr. Thaxter. Charley
began to read the primer, and three-year-old Tommy learned his
letters from the hornbook. Their little lives were steadied and
reassured.

Yet as the days passed it became apparent that not only occasions of critical alarm, and not only soldiers, were now taxing
the resources of the Penns Hill farm. "Sometimes refugees from
Boston, tired and fatigued, seek an asylum for a day, a night, a
week. You can hardly imagine how we live," wrote Abigail to
her husband. "Yet —

> "To the houseless child of want
>   Our doors are open still;
> And though our portions are but scant
>   We give them with good will." [38]

John Adams's passionate love for his wife did not in the least
diminish his hardihood. He wrote back cheerily — "Was you
frightened when the sheep-stealers got a drubbing at Grape
Island? Father Smith prayed for our scow crew I doubt not!"
And with a tonic stoicism he acknowledges necessity — "My
health and life ought to be hazarded in the cause of my country
as well as yours and all my friends. . . . I hope you will maintain

your philosophical composure. I think you are in no danger." [39]

But Abigail knew better. Before those letters reached her she had written again, not minimizing for his sake the increasing tenseness of the situation at Braintree. "We now expect our sea coast ravaged. Perhaps the very next letter I write will inform you that I am driven away from our yet quiet cottage. Necessity will oblige Gage to take some desperate steps. We are told for truth that he is now eight thousand strong. We live in continual expectation of alarms. Courage I know we have in abundance; conduct I hope we shall not want; but powder — where shall we get a sufficient supply?" [40] She added — "I never trust myself long with the terrors which sometimes intrude themselves upon me."

V I

The Battle of Bunker Hill

THE bell of the North Precinct Meetinghouse and the marching drum were silent. But something unusual wakened Abigail
at three o'clock that Saturday morning the seventeenth of June.
It was thunder. At first, people waking in the dim blue-gray
dawn in the peaceful bedrooms of Weymouth and Braintree mut-
tered to themselves, "A storm." But when they leaned out of
window, anxious for standing crops, the air was fresh, a few stars
hung silver in the pale sky, a light breeze ruffled the leaves; all
the farmer's signs pointed toward a fine day. But again that clap
of thunder rolled across the sea. . . .

Guns at Boston. It had begun.

The whole house roused; all dressed in haste. As soon as Abigail was ready she set off impatiently to climb Penns Hill, spyglass
in hand. Her eldest son ran after her, and she welcomed his company.

Up through the orchard, and over the coarse turf at the top
of the hill where the bare rock made a rough seat facing Boston.
Yes, the intermittent flash of cannon and puffs of smoke could
be seen clearly even without the glass. Evidently the ships of
war lying in the channel between Boston and Charlestown were
firing at Charlestown; she could learn no more than that.

"You see, Johnny?"

He saw.

"Is this a battle, Mother?"

"This is a battle. The day is come . . . perhaps the very day
on which the fate of America depends!"

The little boy's heart beat hard. He shared her emotion more
fully than she would have believed possible. To eight-year-old
John Quincy this was like the great battles in the Bible — "the

sword of the Lord and of Gideon." Right was marshaled on one side, wrong on the other, and he saw the flash and heard the thunder of their conflict. It was almost more than he could bear. Exalted at being within sight and hearing of such an event, he clasped his mother's hand fervently, and they went down the hill together.

"Is it dangerous, ma'am? What shall we do," cried the servant Patty. "That roar — it makes me jump so, I don't know what I'm about!"

Baby Tommy was wailing, and Nabby, pale and anxious, was trying to comfort him. Charlie, with a quivering lip, was trying to show off to Tommy that he was *too big* to be scared by that horrid noise. But when their mother appeared they all flung themselves upon her. She did not need to say much to reassure them. Her paleness and overbright eyes escaped their notice. Here she was, and they were with her. Everything was all right with them.

"Breakfast!" she said. "We must eat all we can. Perhaps we shall go to visit Uncle Peter! No, Patty, it's not dangerous to *us* — yet. But after breakfast we will pack some things in case we think it best to leave the house."

Her brothers-in-law called to see if she was all right, and Peter again offered refuge at his house.

The hot, bright summer day wore on and, duties attended to, she could not restrain her desire to see the distant battle, as she could not fail moment by moment to hear it. And, like a mother of ancient Rome, she believed it was a good thing for her son to see that spectacle, to observe history being hammered out on the anvil before his eyes. So again she took Johnny with her up the hill, and as they climbed the hot slope under the thin speckled shade of the apple trees she told him what she thought: in time to come boys in school would learn from their history books the date of this day, June 17th, 1775, and when he was an old man, he would be able to tell his grandchildren and his great-grand-children, "Yes, I *saw* it!" *

* In 1843, when John Quincy Adams was an old man, a granite monument was set up on the site of the battle, and a great day of celebration was ap-

They came out onto the hilltop. The sun beat fiercely down. The rocks were too hot to touch. But what was that which, in midafternoon, sent great black clouds of smoke volleying into the blue sky over there beyond Boston and the glittering Charles?

"Good God," said Abigail, "they are burning Charlestown!"

All night and all day Sunday "the constant roar of the cannon is so distressing that we cannot eat, drink or sleep." On Sunday afternoon, Peter Adams came back with heavy news. Abigail, stricken, turned in spirit to her distant husband. "My bursting heart must find vent at my pen. I have just heard that our dear friend Dr. Warren is no more, but fell gloriously fighting for his country. . . . Great is our loss . . . his courage and fortitude animating the soldiers. . . . Charlestown lies in ashes. . . . It is expected they will come out over the Neck tonight, and a dreadful battle must ensue. . . . How many have fallen we know not. . . . I shall tarry here till it is thought unsafe and then I have secured myself a retreat at your brother's, who had kindly offered me part of his house."[1]

On Tuesday, the guns had been silent for more than twenty-four hours, but authentic news was hard to get. "Ten thousand reports are passing, vague and uncertain as the wind." But Abigail had plucked up heart. Mourning the death of Dr. Warren, "those favorite lines of Collins continually sound in my ears — 'How sleep the brave — '"[2] She gave her feeling outlet by teaching the verses to Nabby and Johnny, who learned them with fervor, and in the truest sense, by heart.

Companies of colonial soldiers were now stationed at points

pointed for its unveiling. John Quincy Adams refused the invitation to be present, and spent the day solitary in his house writing in his diary: "What a day in the annals of mankind is Bunker Hill! What a day was the 17th of June, 1775; and what a burlesque upon them both is an oration upon them by Daniel Webster! . . . Daniel Webster is a heartless traitor to the cause of human freedom; John Tyler is a slave-monger. What have they to do with the Quincy granite pyramid on the brow of Bunker's Hill? . . . with the ideal association of the thundering cannon which I heard, and the smoke of burning Charlestown which I saw, on that awful day? . . ." This statement will surprise those whose chief impression of Daniel Webster is gathered from Stephen Vincent Benét's imaginative masterpiece of fantasy. J. Q. A. was at loggerheads with Webster on the question of slavery, Adams being an uncompromising abolitionist.

along the coast in anticipation of raids, for the British held the Boston and Charlestown peninsulas and might strike out against the mainland from either one. "We have two companies [of provincials] stationed in this town — one at Germantown, one at Squantum; in Weymouth one; in Hingham two, etc. I believe I shall remove your books this week to your brother's." Everyone whose home was near the shore was securing a retreat further inland. Colonel Quincy and his family would go to Deacon Holbrook's; Richard Cranch and Mary and their children to Major Bass's. But only in case of necessity.[3] Mr. and Mrs. Bowdoin, refugees already, decided to seek some less exposed haven, and called on Abigail to take ceremonious and affectionate farewell. "He wished he could have stayed at Braintree," she wrote, "but his lady was fearful."[4]

John Adams must not think that *his* lady was fearful. "We hear that the [British] troops destined for New York are all expected here: but we have got to that pass that a whole legion of them would not intimidate us! I think I am very brave upon the whole. If danger comes near my dwelling I suppose I shall shudder. We want powder, but with the blessing of heaven we fear them not!"[5]

Particulars of the battle were now coming in, and the Quincy-Cranch circle at Braintree, pooling information and sorting it out together, got a pretty clear picture of the event.

Dr. Warren, the last man out of the redoubt, was killed as he went, by a bullet through the head. The British won Bunker's Hill and the Charlestown peninsula. But they paid dear.

Oh, how the hearts at Weymouth and at Braintree kindled at the tale. "Ours" had now been matched in equal fight with the flower of the British Army, and their final withdrawal hardly bore the face of defeat. "Figure to yourself . . ." wrote Abigail eagerly — as if she had been an eyewitness — "the town in flames all around them, and the heat from the flames so intense as scarcely to be borne, — the day one of the hottest we have had this season, and the wind blowing the smoke in their faces — and then consider that we do not count sixty men lost! Every account agrees in fourteen or fifteen hundred slain upon their side."[6]

The final figures were nearer one thousand of the British killed, including seventy officers, against one hundred forty-five Americans killed, and three hundred wounded and prisoners.[7]

The overwhelming number of wounded and the difficulties of transportation completely upset whatever inadequate preparations had been made. "Our prisoners," wrote Abigail, "were all brought over to the Long Wharf, and there lay all night, without any care of their wounds or any resting place but the pavements until the next day." Then they were carried to the jail, "since when we hear they are civilly treated." The British wounded were not much better off. Abigail heard that "their wounded men die very fast, so that they have a report that the bullets were poisoned."

John Adams always bitterly blamed Dickinson, and the delay caused by the second petition, for the defeat at Bunker's Hill, and for the worst feature of it, the death of Dr. Joseph Warren, "a hero," he said passionately, "of more worth than all the town." Abigail's hurt was of like kind.

"Not all the havoc and devastation they have made has wounded me like the death of Warren."[8]

But if the British had taken to burning houses, Weymouth was not safe, Braintree might soon be in ashes. The redcoats might come roaring out along both Necks! * "I would not have you distressed about me!" wrote Abigail to her anxious, distraught husband. "Danger, they say, makes people valiant. I have felt distressed but not dismayed."

John Adams was kindled to admiration. "You are really brave, my dear! You are a heroine, and you have reason to be. For the worst that can happen can do you no harm."[9]

It was, however, cold comfort to a husband separated from his wife by four hundred miles to be convinced that she would, if necessary, meet a violent death with courage, and would thereafter go directly to heaven.

Abigail was invited to Cambridge to meet Washington and his

---

* Boston had only one neck, but the British were now also encamped in the Charlestown peninsula, which was joined to the mainland by the Charlestown Neck.

companions soon after their arrival. The enthusiasm the new general aroused in her was never after to be dimmed. "I was struck with General Washington," she wrote. "You had prepared me to entertain a favorable opinion of him, but I thought the half was not told me. Dignity with ease — the gentleman and the soldier — " Yes, she flew to poetry, to Dryden, to really describe him:

> "Mark his majestic fabric; he's a temple
> Sacred by birth, and built by hands divine;
> His soul's the deity that lodges there,
> Nor is the pile unworthy of the god."

And with all that, "modesty marks every line and feature of his face." [10]

As for General Lee, "he," said this surprising provincial lady, "looks like a careless, hardy veteran, and brought to my mind his namesake Charles XII of Sweden." It pleased Abigail that both gentlemen expressed their warm regard for her husband. Washington had not forgotten the debt he owed to John Adams, who had nominated him to lead the Continental Army. Lee was a queer man, with all his dogs. He made one of them climb on a chair and "shake hands" with Mrs. Adams. The lady preserved her patience. But the incident seemed to reveal a certain trivialness of mind which she could only hope would not injure Lee's conduct in battle.

All Abigail heard convinced her of Washington's supreme excellence for the command. "My brother has a captain's commission and is stationed at Cambridge," she wrote. Many of the young men of her neighborhood panted to be in the thick of it; not merely minutemen staying on the farm until called by local emergency, but to enlist with General Washington in the Continental Army. Her brother-in-law Elihu confided to Abigail his impatience at being only a local captain of minutemen.

"But why is that not enough for him?" said Mrs. Hall.* "Why can't he be content to stay here and mind his farm, and help take care of us? He gets excitement enough here! There's fighting

---

* The former Mrs. Adams senior, mother of Elihu, Peter, and John.

enough here! There was Grape Island. And there was the light-house raid. And there was the raid off the Moon with the whale-boats. Why does he want to go off to the army? No, I never will consent to it. Never."

"Your good mother is really violent against it," wrote Abigail to her husband. "I cannot persuade nor reason her into a consent. Neither he nor I dare let her know that he is trying for a place."

So Elihu, encouraged by his sister-in-law, went away without his mother's consent and got his captaincy in the army before the siege of Boston had begun.

It was a peculiar siege. The British had ships and could have got out by sea had there been any friendly place to go. But the coasts north and south bristled with armed men. Nor did their command of the sea bring them any supplies of fresh food, except fish. Yet the besiegers who were trying to starve them out were compelled at the same time to starve thousands of their friends, patriot Americans who were trapped in Boston with the British.* The plight of these besieged citizens roused Abigail's indignant pity; "that of the most abject slaves under the most cruel and despotic of tyrants." The British, however, behaved with moderation. Martial law was proclaimed, and a curfew was imposed.[11] But a ten o'clock curfew was no hardship. The British felt themselves on a live volcano, and lived in constant dread of conspiracy and of spies who were, indeed, all around them. "No man dared now to be seen talking to his friend in the street," [12] said the angry Abigail. "An order has been given that no person shall be seen to wipe his face with a white handkerchief. The reason I hear is that it is a signal of mutiny." She was pleased to think that the British reinforcements from New York would only increase the food shortage for the enemy. "Every additional man adds to their distress."

But the distress was not all on one side, nor was it to be confined to Boston. A more terrible and undiscriminating foe was about to ravage both sides alike, and range indifferently both city

---

* "There are about five thous-ᵈ Inhabitants still remaining in Town Amongst which is all the Selectmen who are not permitted to come out at all." Isaac Smith senior to Isaac junior, Smith-Carter Mss. June 1775.

and country. Uncle Isaac Smith got early news, and wrote concerning the hundreds of ill-tended, ill-fed wounded, crowded together in the fly-laden heat — "they begin to have the flux." [13]

Contagion made no bones at all about crossing the guarded Neck. On the tenth of August, Abigail wrote in haste to her husband: "Your brother Elihu lies very dangerously sick with a dysentery. He has been very bad for more than a week. His life is despaired of. We are all in great distress. Your [step] father is with him in great anguish . . . [Your brother] is sensible of his danger and is calmly resigned to the will of heaven."

Even as she wrote, the unexpected word reached her that her husband was on the road and almost home. Congress, unable to bear the humid heat of August in Philadelphia, had adjourned for a brief recess. Abigail's postscript was a tempestuous mixture of joy and grief. "The joy is overclouded and the day is darkened . . . the sympathy I feel for the loss of your brother cut off in the pride of life and the bloom of manhood." [14]

John Adams arrived in time to attend his brother's funeral. But neither he nor anyone else could hope to assuage the bitterness of his mother's grief. Unaware of it, her son's children were perhaps her greatest comfort. She could not mutter to Elihu's three babies, as she was tempted to do to his young widow: "What did I tell you? I told him so. I *told* him!"

John Adams, though he grieved for his brother and cherished every moment with Abigail and their children, yet had public cares heavy on his mind. He attended General Court at Watertown, he conferred with General Washington on the army's needs, and he talked with Ward, Lee, Putnam, Gates, and Mifflin. He looked about him at the growing order of the camp, the regular drilling. "Our Army," he said, with an odd mixture of thoughts, "will be the best military school in the Empire!" He noted exactly the shortage of tents, of shot, of powder, of sick supplies, and in particular of cannon. So, as fully informed as a man could be about matters civil and military at the front, John Adams set off again on the twenty-eighth of August for Philadelphia.

But even as he left home that day — John Hancock's wedding day — the pestilence arrived there. One of the men, Isaac, was unwell when the master left. His disorder soon showed itself to be a violent dysentery. "There was no resting-place in the house for his terrible groans." Two days later, Abigail herself was seized with the same illness "in a violent manner." But hers only lasted, fortunately, three days. The next victim was one of the maids — Susy. She was sent home to be nursed. "Our little Tommy was next, and he lies very ill now," wrote Abigail to her husband. Then another maidservant, Patty, was seized. "Our house is a hospital in every part." Still weak from her own illness, Abigail had to be about nursing the rest. All Braintree was stricken at once. "I can scarce find a well person to assist in looking after the sick." Neighbor after neighbor fell. Family after family had children dying or dead. "Mr. Wibird lies bad; Major Miller is dangerous, and Mr. Gay is not expected to live. We have been four Sundays without any meeting. So sickly and so mortal a time the oldest man does not remember.[15]

"As to politics," she declared impatiently, "I know nothing about them. The distresses of my family are so great that I have not thought of them. As to my own health, I mend but very slowly . . . hope it is only with my being fatigued with looking after Tommy, as he is unwilling any one but mamma should do for him. And if he was, I could not find anybody that is worth having." The mother's tender, constant care had its reward. Three-year-old Tommy, so near death, began to mend. His fever abated. His eyes lost their glassy look, and the warm cloths to his stomach assuaged his violent pains. His tense little body relaxed. He smiled tenderly on his faithful guardian. It had happened as he expected. Mamma had driven away his sickness. "But were you to look in on him," she wrote his father, "you would not know him. From a hearty, hale, corn-fed boy, he has become pale, lean and wan . . . entirely stripped of all the flesh he had save what remains for to keep his bones together. Two of the children, John and Charles, I have sent out of the house, finding it difficult to keep them out of the chamber. Nabby continues well." Of the remaining domestic or farm staff, "Jonathan is the only one who remains in the family who has not had a turn of the disorder."[16]

Thus does Providence show His power. Not many weeks

before Abigail had felt on familiar terms with Deity, hailing Him as a fellow ally, going off eagerly on the Fast Day in July to pray against the wicked British. "I really believe they are more afraid of the Americans' prayers than of their swords!" she had said complacently, getting into the chaise with Mary Cranch. The sisters had driven off together to Dedham to hear some pungent preaching and some really stirring prayers. "I could not bear," said Abigail, "to hear our inanimate old bachelor!" [17] And indeed Mr. Wibird was not the man for such a day.

But now Providence was less partial. Little Tommy had only just brought forth her humble prayers of thanks for his definite emergence from the dark valley, when a message summoned her to the Weymouth Parsonage. Her mother was stricken.

"Have pity upon me. Have pity upon me, O thou my beloved, for the hand of God presseth me sore. . . . How can I tell you (O my bursting heart!) that my dear mother has left me? This day, October 1st, about five o'clock, she left this world. . . . After sustaining sixteen days severe conflict nature fainted and she fell asleep. Blessed spirit where art thou? At times I am almost ready to faint under this severe and heavy stroke, separated from *thee* who used to be a comforter to me in affliction; but blessed be God, his ear is not heavy that He cannot hear, but He has bid us call upon Him in time of trouble.

"My poor father, like a firm believer and a good Christian, sets before his children the best examples of patience and submission. . . .

"Sickness and death are in almost every family in the province.

"Almighty God! restrain the pestilence. . . ." [18]

Her husband replied — "If I could write as well as you, my sorrow would be as eloquent as yours, but upon my soul I cannot.[19] I bewail more than I can express the loss of so much purity and unaffected piety and virtue to the world. I know of no better character left in it. . . . But I grieve for nobody more than my children. Her most amiable and discreet example, as well as her kind skill and care, I have ever relied upon in my own mind for the education of these little swarms. I am sure that my children are the better for the forming hand of their grandmother." [20]

But, in his earnest desire to comfort her, John did not forget his wife's impatient protest, in the midst of the epidemic, that she can give no thought to politics. "Your mother," he wrote, "had a clear and penetrating understanding and a profound judgment, as well as an honest, a friendly and a charitable heart. There is one thing, however, which you will forgive me if I hint to you. Let me ask you, rather, if you are not of my opinion? Were not her talents and virtues too much confined to private, social and domestic life?

"My opinion of the duties of religion and morality comprehends a very extensive connection with society at large and the great interests of the public. . . ."

A profound natural psychologist, John was well aware that the education of the children was not only his wife's chief duty at present there at home, but was the likeliest avenue out of her crushing sorrow. He referred to Newton and Locke, the intense importance of the earliest years, of habit-formation and the set of the will. "It should be your care and mine to elevate the minds of our children and exalt their courage; to accelerate and animate their industry and activity; to excite in them contempt of meanness, injustice and inhumanity, and an ambition to excel. . . . If we allow their minds to grovel and creep in infancy, they will grovel all their lives." [21]

But where's his wife? Where's his companion? Abigail is not only a mother. Her husband needs her too. And he tugs heartily at her attention. "Cheerfulness is not a sin in any times," he says. "I hope that you will resume your wonted cheerfulness and write again upon news and politics. . . ." [22] I have nothing now to write but repetitions of respect and affection. . . . Yours, yours, yours — J. A." [23]

She had not waited for the appeal, though no doubt she was glad to have it. It is fine to be needed. Her sorrow had had unrestrained vent through her pen — "I have written many things to you that I suppose I never could have talked" [24] — and now she is back at his side, again alive to the world around her at every pore. But she is maturer. Some of the naïveté of her black-and-white view of the world is gone. Among the news that now and then leaks out of tormented Boston, she remarks not only the distress of the inhabitants, which no language can paint, but "the soldiers [British] are obliged to do very hard duty," [25] keeping their packs with them everywhere for fear of sudden alarm.

If anyone had ventured to say to her at any time that there are two sides to every question she would probably have replied — yes, indeed, a right side and a wrong side. But she was learning to make allowance for honest error. "My heart," she replied, "is made tender by repeated affliction; it never was a hard heart." [26]

John Adams was pleased with Hancock's recent marriage to Abigail's cousin, Dorothy Quincy, which he had long taken for granted, and saw nothing wrong behind Dorothy's stately front. He wrote to Abigail that he wished *she* could come to Philadelphia — they would be as happy as John Hancock and his lady. "Two pair of colors belonging to the Seventh Regiment were brought here last night and hung up in Mrs. Hancock's chamber with great splendor and elegance. (That lady sends her compliments and good wishes.) Among a hundred men, almost, at this house, she lives and behaves with modesty, decency, dignity and discretion, I assure you. Her behaviour is easy and genteel. She avoids talking upon politics. In large and mixed companies she is totally silent, as a lady ought to be. But whether her eyes are so penetrating and her attention so quick to the words, looks, gestures, sentiments, etc., of the company as yours would be, saucy as you are this way, I won't say!" [27]

Abigail might laugh at this sketch of herself, but there was food for reflection there too. Not for the first time it was brought home to her that she had married a man with exacting standards. A woman must be interested in politics, informed, ready to discuss them with her husband in conversation — and in letters! — even to discuss them in small intimate groups, like the Quincy circle, when few if any strangers were present. On such occasions an intelligent woman might even have opinions of her own, and they would be respectfully listened to. Oh, nothing to complain of there! But — in a large, mixed company, no matter what the talk, no matter what her information and her thoughts — a woman must be totally silent, or forfeit the admiration of John Adams.

Abigail did not dispute the point, but she thought about it. She must have John's approval. And yet — ? Certainly the brilliant friend of her girlhood, Mercy Otis Warren, did not practise such extreme decorum! And however John might value the softness of a woman's manner, and deplore and hate anything that seemed to tend toward the dominating or the masculine, he had left his wife in a position where softness, perhaps, was not the chief quality needed. She was in sole charge of the farm, giving orders, shouldering responsibility, paying wages, hiring and dismissing; final court of appeal for everyone, directing everybody all day long. Her thoughts began to warm up, like a kettle on the fire, and a little bubble of discontent rose to the surface. "I wish I could have more of the assistance of my dearest friend. . . . In the twelve years we have been married I believe we have not lived together more than six.[28] But it is my lot. I hope in time to have the reputation of being as good a farmeress as my partner has of being a good statesman." [29]

John Adams, blandly unaware of inconsistency, replied with no idle gallantry — "It gives me concern to think of the many cares you must have upon your mind. Your reputation as a farmer, or anything else you undertake, I dare answer for. Your partner's character as a statesman is much more problematical!" [30]

As for their separation, it is at least a comfort to her that he minds it as much as she does. "I hope I shall be excused from coming to Philadelphia again, at least until other gentlemen have taken their turns. But I never will come here again without you, if I can persuade you to come with me. Whom God has joined together ought not to be put asunder so long with their own consent." [31]

There was not much hope of his coming home soon, however. "We have so much to do and it is so difficult to do it right." [32] John Adams was busy indeed. During his terms in Congress he served on more than ninety committees and was chairman of twenty-five. This is a record not approached by any other member. Just as in Boston, it was impossible, even for those who would gladly have avoided him, to do without his lucidity, his judgment, his energy, his honesty, his mass of accurate information, and his first-class brain.

Meanwhile the Provincial Congress in Massachusetts, convinced by the logic of circumstances that John Adams was right on the necessity of forming at least a pro tem government in the province, was beginning to make a definite move in that direction. They decided to reopen the law courts, under their own control, and appointed John Adams as Chief Justice. "I wish I knew what mighty things were fabricating," Abigail wrote. "If a form of government is to be established here [in Massachusetts] what one will be assumed." She foresaw all kinds of possible dissensions, ten thousand difficulties. The reins of government had been so long slackened, how could its restraints be voluntarily assumed? "If we separate from Britain," said this lawyer's wife, "what code of laws will be established?" And then again, "How shall we be governed so as to retain our liberties?" No government could be free which was not administrated by general stated laws. But who would frame the laws? Who would enforce them? People hated new ways, always wanted to go on as before, were jealous of new authority. Yes, "I feel anxious for the fate of our monarchy, or democracy, or whatever is to take place." [33] But that a new independent government must and would take place, John Adams's wife never doubted.

Economic questions were also to the fore. She suggested the need of a continental excise on spirits,* and of a practice of barter with the West Indies, an exchange of produce, "in order to keep among us our gold and silver." A silver dollar was now so rare that "our traders will give you a hundred pounds of paper for ninety of silver." [34]

Was this a woman who was to hold her tongue when politics were discussed in a mixed company?

From December 9th to February 8th, '76, John Adams was back at Braintree, summoned home by his appointment as Chief Justice of Massachusetts. The necessary organization of the law courts was already completely formulated in his mind, and he was at once charged with the duty of drawing up a proclamation to explain and start off the new judicial system. This proclamation

---

* Continental, to be fair to everyone; excise, so as to limit the consumption of spirits, as well as raise money.

was to be read at the opening of every court of justice, and at the town meeting in every town. The Council also recommended that "the several ministers of the gospel" throughout the colony — whose influence had been so fundamental in maintaining public order and morality during the "lawless" year — should read it to their congregations "immediately after divine service on the sabbath following their receipt of it."

He wrote it during the Christmas recess at home. It was like old times for his wife and family to have him there, driving his busy quill at his desk beside the roaring fire. His presence lifted all their hearts and quickened the vitality of the convalescent house. His warm, hearty approval and comfort shone round on them all; on pretty ten-year-old Nabby, praised for the good help she was to her mother — and also praised for her beginning Latin and French; on pale, thin little Tommy, petted into better appetite and higher spirits; on Johnny, whose letters were respectfully appreciated — "John writes like a hero, glowing with ardor for his country and burning with indignation against her enemies" — and on cheerful little Charles, who must not be forgotten.

But it was to his wife that John Adams's presence meant the most. She loved her children dearly, and spoke to John with pity of "unfruitful women." Yet, in these perilous times, she could understand what Bacon meant when he said that those who had children gave hostages to fortune. Certainly the childless "are freed from the anxiety every parent must feel for their rising offspring." [35]

The only anxiety she ever felt for her husband was in regard to his health or safety. Never once did she, like many other wives, feel anxious lest he should do or say the wrong thing, make mistakes, offend people, be foolish or boorish, or commit himself to a course of which her judgment disapproved. Her confidence in him was not a half-pretense, to boost him up; not the result of a theory of wifely duty, nor a submissive unintelligent ignorance of what he was about. It was a full, co-operative, entire agreement with the whole of his point of view, and an admiration of his methods and actions.

When Abigail brought in her sewing to the study fire and sat there in her ample wadded winter clothes and watched his flying pen, he worked twice as well. Reading his document to her, sensing its resonance against her mind, he wrote more clearly and vigorously than in solitude. Her questions clarified his thought. What is government really for? What aim should it have in view? Aye, he had often asked himself that question. Is it order? Is it security? Is it more than these? And from what source does government derive its authority? Not from the divine right of kings. Then where does power ultimately reside?

As they discussed and meditated in cosy, happy companionship in their snug retreat, the old year passed away and the year 1776 took its fateful place in the great procession of time. The January snow whirled outside the window, and hissed down the great chimney onto the leaping flames, while John Adams, in communion with the eager spirit of his wife, wrote down:

"*As the happiness of the people is the sole end of government, so the consent of the people is the only foundation of it.* . . .

"*It is a maxim that in every government there must exist somewhere a supreme, sovereign, absolute and uncontrollable power; the body of the people; and it never was, or can be, delegated to one man or a few.*" [36]

In February, on his way back to Philadelphia, John Adams purchased and sent to Abigail a pamphlet entitled *Common Sense*, by a recent adventurer from England, Tom Paine. It was written in defense of doctrines which, as John Adams remarked, would soon be the common faith. Said Tom Paine — "The design and end of government is freedom and security. In the early ages — mankind were equals in the order of creation. . . . Arms must decide the contest. The appeal was the choice of the king and the continent hath accepted the challenge."

Since the pamphlet was anonymous, and the publication of John Adams's two letters intercepted by the enemy a few months before had made him willy-nilly the first open protagonist of independence in the public press, popular rumor flew over the continent that John Adams was the author of *Common Sense*. "I could not have written anything in so manly and striking a style," said John Adams, with his usual modesty, "but I flatter myself I

should have made a more respectable figure as an architect, if I
had undertaken such a work! This writer seems to have very
inadequate ideas of what is necessary to be done in order to form
constitutions for single colonies as well as a great model of union
for the whole." [37]

Before returning to Philadelphia, John Adams more than once
visited the winter camp at Cambridge at Washington's request, to
confer with the Commander-in-Chief and to attend councils of
war. The question at issue was when and how to attack Boston.
The Continental Congress was urgent for it. John Hancock wrote
that he stood to lose as much as any man, but never mind about
smashing up his property, he was perfectly willing to have Boston
bombarded. What am I to bombard Boston with? was Washington's question to John Adams. Where was the artillery, the money,
the army? The American Army had then less than ten thousand
men; their cause was unformulated; their status uncertain; the support of Congress vague. But over their heads, above the snowy
roofs of Harvard College, Abigail saw a new flag flying. On January 1st, 1776, the flag had been hoisted for the first time, and its
brilliant color, its new, audacious message, caught the eye from
every quarter.*

*   *   *   *   *

It was March, 1776, and a Saturday night. "Hark! The house
this instant shakes with the roar of cannon!" But this time it is
"our" cannon — Washington was bombarding Boston. "It has been
said to-morrow and to-morrow for this month"; but now the time
has come, it is today, and General Washington, backed rather by
New England than by Congress, short of men, money, and supplies, has felt that inaction itself is a form of dry rot, and has
begun the attack.

* Thirteen alternate red and white stripes in the field, with the cross of
St. George and St. Andrew, red and white respectively, on a blue ground in
the corner, was the flag designed and used by the East India Company in
1704; was probably flying at the mast of the tea ships; and was hoisted at
Washington's camp at Cambridge in 1776. The number of the stripes at once
suggested the number of the colonies, and the star flag was evolved from
this base, the first one traditionally being arranged and sewn by Betsy
Ross of Philadelphia.

One of the young farm hands ran into the house for his gun. "Farewell, mistress! Orders are come for all the remaining militia to repair to the lines before Monday mid-night! I must go to my mother's and get ready!"

"No sleep for me to-night!" said Abigail. "Here, take some meat — your mother will give you parched corn . . . and take this blanket for your use in camp. Don't thank me, friend! You are taking your life with you!" The man saw her hands tremble as she made up the bundle. But her eyes were bright in the candle shine. Again and again a heavy cannonade made the dishes on the dresser dance, and the windows rattled as if a huge soft fist had struck the house a heavy blow. But how different to her was the sound of this cannon from the ominous thunder of those others at the start of Bunker Hill! "My hand and heart will tremble," wrote Abigail, as she poured out her immediate feelings to her husband at the close of the Sabbath day, but it was with a deep excitement. "The cannon continued firing, and my heart beat pace with them all night."

On Monday afternoon she and her children and household watched the mustered militia march away to Boston, every man carrying three days' provisions and a blanket if he could get it. "And now we have scarcely a man but our regular guards in Weymouth, Hingham, Braintree or Milton. Can you form an idea of our sensations?" [38] She and her children climbed Penns Hill and sat listening to "the amazing roar" of the twenty-four-pounders, and watched the bursting shells in the April dusk. It was terrible! It was sublime! Back to lie down in bed, but not to sleep. The cannonade, no longer intermittent, was an incessant roar. "I could no more sleep than if I had been in the engagement. How many of our dear countrymen must fall." Her pity reaches also to "the unhappy wretches" on the other side.

She endured two nights, with little or no sleep, and on Tuesday the battle still raged. "I sometimes think I cannot stand it. I wish myself out of hearing as I cannot assist them!"

But when, after a mysterious quiet on Wednesday, the militia all came marching back on Thursday and reported that they had taken Dorchester Hill, she was disappointed. Is that all? "I would

not have suffered all I have for two such hills!" She wrote to her
"dearest friend," passionately quoting Shakespeare. "There is a
tide in the affairs of men which taken at the flood . . ." Even
while she wrote the lines — Sunday evening, March 10th — her
ears were "again assaulted by the roar of cannon." Trembling with
excitement she hurried with Nabby and Johnny to their lookout
post on the hill.

Another week of this strain, till finally, at Saturday dawn, what
a sight there was to see! "Between seventy and eighty vessels of
various sizes lie in a row in fair sight of this place." They lie low
in the water. They are loaded to the gunwales. What can be the
meaning of this? They have been plundering the town! Impossible
that they could be evacuating it! She can't believe the rumors that
she hears when she returns to the house. But "some very important
crisis seems at hand." Next morning, Sunday, the news that seemed
impossible is confirmed. The enemy are in full flight. Boston is
free!

"From Penns Hill we have a view of the largest fleet ever seen
in America." You could count upwards of a hundred and seventy
ships. Their bare masts looked like a forest.[39] "They have not yet
come under sail. I cannot help suspecting some design which we
do not yet comprehend. No one knows where they are off to, but
the rumour is New York." As Abigail said, almost too astonished
to give way to rejoicing, it was only lifting the burden from one
shoulder to another perhaps less able to support it. Mewed up in
Boston, the British had been kept out of mischief. Now they were
escaping; to threaten another town. Yet is it not a victory? "To
what a contemptible situation are the troops of Britain reduced!"
She gazed at the white full-sailed ships skimming away before the
wind, and felt amazed that they should leave such a harbor, such
entrenchments, such fortifications, and the largest city in the colonies, "and that we should be in peaceable possession of a town
which we expected would cost a river of blood, without one drop
shed! . . . Every foot of ground which they obtain now they
must fight for, and may they purchase it at a Bunker Hill price!"[40]
Eleven hundred loyalist Tories who had taken refuge in Boston,
confident of the triumph of British arms, were struck with sudden

ruin. Many of them had been rich people; overnight they became paupers. It was not hard to picture their bewilderment and despair, "crowded in vessels which will scarce contain them," despatched to Halifax, the nearest British territory. "What will become of them there, God knows. The place is full already." *

It is a hard thing to be on the wrong side of any war, but worst of all to be on the wrong side of a revolution. John Adams wrote to his wife: "Mr. Hutchinson, Mr. Sewall and their associates are in great disgrace in England. Persons are ashamed to be seen to speak to them. They look despised and sunk." [41]

Abigail was eager to get in to Boston to see how it looked, but the news that there was an outbreak of smallpox in the city prevented her. A friend, however, went to her house in Queen Street to see what state it was in. It had been occupied by one of the doctors of a regiment and was "very dirty but no other damage had been done to it." Hancock's mansion too was safe, and the furniture unhurt. The town in general had been left in a better state than most people expected. The chief complaint was of "contempt thrown upon our places of worship" by using them as barracks and hospitals. There had been some vandalism in Boston, of which Sam Quincy's house and furniture was an outstanding example; and Abigail and her neighbors were shocked to see fragments of good furniture, thrown overboard from the ships, washed up on the shores at Weymouth and Braintree by the tide. But on the other hand, she was free to admit that some of the British officers had left behind rent money for the owners of houses they had occupied, and, actually, money to pay for any accidental damage. This was surprising evidence of "honor and justice." [42] And the haste of the evacuation and the shortage of ship space had caused immense stores to be left behind in the town which well might make up for a few repairs to meetinghouses: "Vast quantities of coal, which the inhabitants have been

---

* Abigail heard and reported the details of their plight: "They are much distressed for want of houses at Halifax; provisions scarce and dear. Some of them with six or eight children around them, sitting upon the rocks, crying, not knowing where to lay their heads."
Familiar Letters, p. 162.

cruelly denied through the winter, cannon and warlike stores in abundance, horse fodder," [43] and so on.

Washington made a triumphal entry into Boston on foot. The bells were rung, and prayers of thanksgiving offered. Harvard bestowed on General Washington an honorary degree of LL.D. And then the camp was struck, the army marched away from Cambridge to the southward "where they expect the seat of action to be," and Cambridge sobered itself to become again a scholastic town.

Abigail looked to the spring planting. An access of joy and energy flowed through her. "I feel very differently at the approach of spring from what I did a month ago," she wrote. "We knew not then whether we could plant or sow with safety, whether where we had tilled we could reap . . . or whether we should be driven from the sea-coast to seek shelter in the wilderness."

The refugees who had fled from shore and city were turning homeward like the birds.

What a weight had been lifted, how sweetened was the air! Just to move about freely again was a joy, talk to whom one pleased, go out to a party and come home at midnight or after, take a boat and go fishing without a permit — how the ordinary commonplaces of living sparkled as with a new dew. Every citizen, even the most stolid, experienced a little of the acute, sharp joy of convalescence or childhood, when nothing is commonplace, each thing is seen with clear eyes.

But Abigail, in all her joy and energy, did not forget that there might be another "Boston" soon. The long task was not finished; it had not properly begun. She wanted an official beginning, a bugle note to all the world. "I long to hear that you have declared an independency!"

"Your description of your own *gaieté de cœur* charms me," replied her husband. "Thanks be to God, you have just cause to rejoice. As to declarations of independency, be patient! Read our privateering laws [allowing privateers to prey upon British trade] and our commercial laws. What signifies a word? . . . Yet this is not independency, you know. What is? Why, government in every colony, a confederation among them all, and treaties with foreign nations to acknowledge us a sovereign state, and all that." [44]

So they wrote to each other in March and April, 1776.

In the spring of 1776 a sudden acceleration took place. A tide rose, a dam broke, and all John Adams had so long desired and worked for was accomplished. The three months, May, June, and July, 1776, were the grand climax of John Adams's life, no matter what greater public recognition the future had in store. And after them, John Adams might well write to Abigail and to his friend and former pupil, William Tudor — "I have had a pretty good trick at the helm. . . . Some of you younger folk [Tudor] must take your turn and let me go to sleep. When a few mighty matters are accomplished here I retreat like Cincinnatus to the plough and like Sir William Temple to his garden, and farewell politics!" [45]

Abigail heard this with pleasure but with skepticism.

The mighty matters were three interlocked steps which John Adams had continually urged as necessary to American success — that is, government in each colony, confederation of the colonial governments, and treaties with foreign nations. A statement or declaration of the causes of the revolt of the colonies was also a recognized necessity, although to John Adams it appeared largely a matter of form.

Three committees were formed — one to encourage formation of individual state governments, one for treaties, and one to draw up a declaration. John Adams was on the latter two of these.

"When I look back to the year 1761," he wrote Abigail, "and recollect the argument concerning writs of assistance in the superior court which I have hitherto considered as the commencement of this controversy between Great Britain and America, and run through the whole period from that time to this, and recollect the series of political events, the chain of causes and effects, I am surprised at the suddenness as well as greatness of this revolution." [46]

Abigail, reading this letter in Boston, was deeply aware of the ripe mellowness of his mood. The man who wrote was leagues ahead of the man who had been exasperated with Dickinson and his colleagues for their "silly" temporizing, their "piddling" behavior. In the hour of success, John Adams's imperiousness was softened, his impatience disciplined. In a religious mood, he saw a wisdom greater than man's in the delay, once so intolerable. It had cost dear, but had the Declaration of Independence been made sooner, even seven months ago, "we might before this have formed alliances with foreign states, have mastered Quebec and been in possession of Canada. On the other hand time has been given for the whole people maturely to consider the great question of independence, and to ripen their judgment, dissipate their fears . . . by discussing it in newspapers and pamphlets, by debating it in assemblies, conventions, committees of safety and inspection, town and country meetings, as well as in private conversations, so that the whole people, in every colony of the thirteen, have now adopted it as their own act. This will cement the union, and avoid those heats and convulsions which might have been occasioned by such a Declaration six months ago. . . . I am well aware of the toil and blood and treasure that it will cost us to maintain this Declaration and support and defend these States. Yet through all the gloom I can see the rays of ravishing light and glory.

"I must submit all my hopes and fears to an overruling Providence, in which, unfashionable as the faith may be, I firmly believe." [47]

Abigail Adams had gone to Boston on Saturday, July 12th, with all her children, to be inoculated for the smallpox. The inoculation was performed immediately on their arrival, but they were not considered infectious until some results appeared.* So Abigail was still at large on Thursday, July 18th, when the printed Declaration arrived in Boston. "After hearing a very good sermon," she wrote her husband, "I went with the multitude into King Street to hear the Proclamation for Independence read and proclaimed from the balcony of the State House. The troops appeared under arms . . . bells rang, privateers in the harbor fired — forts — batteries — can-

---

* All got on well but Charles, who after three inoculations "has to be sure taken the distemper in the natural way. Indeed this smallpox is no triggel." A. A., Aug. 20, '76; Thaxter MS. Charles was very ill indeed.

non. . . . The King's Arms were taken down from the State House and every vestige of him burnt in King Street. . . ." [48] It was a thrilling occasion. But even more impressive was the Sunday service a month later. "Last Sunday, after service, the Declaration of Independence was read from the pulpit by order of Council. Dr. Chauncy's address pleased me. The good man, after having read it, lifted his eyes and hands to heaven. 'God bless the United States of America, and let all the people say Amen.' " [49]

The work on the treaties was not in the limelight but it was no less vital. As John Adams had urged, the committee had been empowered by Congress to draw up a model for a treaty with France. But in this model treaty he saw clearly that the whole principle of the new United States' relationship with other countries, its commitments and responsibilities, would be laid down. And he knew in his own mind, and had publicly expressed, what that relationship should be. "We ought not," he had said in Congress back in September '75, "to enter into any alliance which should entangle us in any future wars in Europe. We ought to lay it down as a first principle and a maxim never to be forgotten, to maintain an entire neutrality in all future European wars. Therefore, in preparing treaties to be proposed to foreign powers, and in the instructions to be given to our ministers, we ought to confine ourselves strictly to a treaty of commerce. Such a treaty would be an ample compensation to France for all the aid we should want from her." The speech had created a great effect.

When the treaty came before Congress, it occasioned great surprise, because it did not offer complete alliance.

But John Adams saw that, for her own sake, France would jump at the chance of an alliance to free America. Yet he realized that if America were to engage in a European war she would become too subordinate and dependent on her ally: "We should be little better than puppets, danced on the wires of the cabinets of Europe, the sport of European intrigues and politics." His arguments prevailed, "the treaty passed without one particle of alliance, exclusive privilege or warranty," [50] and Adams saw the foreign policy of the new sovereign power shaped by his hand.

Well might Abigail, sharing intensely in the struggle from afar, write to her husband of her pride and joy that "a person so nearly connected with me has had the honor of being a principal actor in laying a foundation for our country's future greatness." [51]

His letters were her meat and drink. From her Uncle Isaac's house in Boston, where she was convalescing from smallpox, she wrote — "I have spent the three days past almost entirely with you. The weather has been stormy. I have had little company and I have amused myself in my closet, reading over the letters I have received from you since I have been here.

"I have possession of my aunt's chamber, in which, you know, is a very convenient, pretty closet, with a window which looks into her flower garden, and bookshelves . . . and a pretty little desk, where I write all my letters and keep my papers, unmolested by any one. I don't covet my neighbor's goods, but I should like to be the owner of such conveniences! I always had a fancy for a closet with a window which I could more particularly call my own." [52] But in case the expression of this modest wish should seem like a complaint, she hastened to assure her husband that their poverty does not rouse in her any discontent. She has a suit of homespun ready for him when he comes back, she has been busy making clothes for the children. Colonel Warren has borne witness to her husband that the farm is flourishing under her care. They have all they need, she does not hanker for riches or great position or a fashionable life like Cousin Dorothy Hancock's. If John could be at home with her, she would ask no more. No ambition of hers need ever distract him from the fascinating, exacting, unrewarding leadership which he has achieved in the poorly paid public affairs of a new and poor country. No, no. Let him indeed even give up the Massachusetts Chief Judgeship which brings in regular income but which will involve giving up more important tasks in the large world! "All my desire and all my ambition," she earnestly assures him, "is to be esteemed and loved by my partner, to join with him in the education and instruction of our little ones, to sit under our own vines in peace, liberty and safety."

*   *   *   *   *

The main tide of war had now swept away from Boston, but the seafaring men of Boston, Braintree, Weymouth, Hingham, Salem, and Marblehead were all taking to privateering, an exciting and rewarding sport. There would soon be no men left, Abigail said, half laughing. Women would have to work the farms, as well as direct them. "I am willing to do my part!" she told her husband. "I believe I could gather corn and husk it! But I should make a poor figure at digging potatoes!" [53]

On June 14th, 1777, the Stars and Stripes was adopted as the flag of the American Army — thirteen red and white stripes to mark the thirteen independent states, thirteen stars in the corner on a blue ground to mark "the new constellation" of the Union. The Union Jack was a foreign flag now, forever. But among the Americans who now joyfully celebrated the first anniversary of their freedom, there were some who were not free. There were still Negro slaves. Samuel Johnson, paid publicity agent of the British Government, had sourly commented in London that "the loudest yelps for liberty came from the slave-drivers of the south." And Abigail told her husband — "I have sometimes been ready to think that the passion for liberty cannot be equally strong in the breasts of those who have been accustomed to deprive their fellow-creatures of theirs." [54]

There were other thousands of American patriots who had un-granted rights to claim — the very rights which the Declaration held to be "unalienable." Well in advance, before any declarations had been irrevocably crystallized, Abigail Adams had clearly and audaciously pointed out this neglected multitude, of whom she was one, and had broken a lance for their liberty. "By the way," she wrote to her husband, in March 1776, "in the new code of laws which I suppose it will be necessary for you to make, I desire you would remember the ladies and be more generous and favor-able to them than your ancestors! Do not put such unlimited power into the hands of the husbands. Remember all men would be tyrants if they could. If particular care and attention is not paid to the ladies, we are determined to foment a rebellion, and will not hold ourselves bound by any laws in which we have no voice or representation.

"That your sex are naturally tyrannical is a truth so thoroughly established as to admit of no dispute, but such of you as wish to be happy give up the harsh title of master for the more tender and endearing one of friend. Why then not put it out of the power of the vicious and the lawless to use us with cruelty and indignity with impunity?"

But her masculine husband, clear-minded and generous though he was, found this simply funny. What next? "As to your extraordinary code of laws, I cannot but laugh! We have been told that our struggle has loosened the bonds of government everywhere — children and apprentices . . . schools and colleges . . . Indians, Negroes grow insolent. But your letter was the first intimation that another tribe, more numerous and powerful than all the rest, were grown discontented. This is rather too coarse a compliment, but you are so saucy I won't blot it out! Depend upon it, we know better than to repeal our masculine systems. Although they are in full force, you know they are little more than theory. We dare not exert our power in its full latitude. We are obliged to go fair and softly, and in practice you know we are the subjects. We have only the name of masters, and rather than give up this, which would completely subject us to the despotism of the petticoat, I hope General Washington and all our brave heroes would fight! . . . A fine story indeed! I begin to think the ministry as deep as they are wicked. After stirring up Tories . . . bigots . . . Canadians, Indians, Negroes, Hanoverians, Hessians, Russians . . . at last they have stimulated the women to demand new privileges and threaten to rebel!"

Abigail did not quarrel about it. He was thoroughly wrongheaded, but perhaps she expected what she got. She replied gaily and charmingly — concealing the iron hand of good sense in the velvet glove of her soft manners:

"I cannot say that I think you are very generous to the ladies; for whilst you are . . . emancipating all nations, you insist upon retaining an absolute power over your wives. But . . . we have it in our power not only to free ourselves but to subdue our masters, and without violence throw both your natural and legal authority at our feet —

"Charm by accepting, by submitting sway,
Yet have our humor most when we obey."

Such questions after all were purely academic to Mrs. John Adams. Except when challenged on the equality of the sexes, John Adams never failed to honor his wife as his equal.

One day she added a postscript — "I wish you would burn my letters!" He was deeply stirred. "Is there no way for two friendly souls to converse together although the bodies are four hundred miles off? Yes, by letter. But I want a better communication. I want to hear you think or see your thoughts. The conclusion of your letter makes my heart throb more than a cannonade would. You bid me burn your letters! But I must forget you first! [55]

"In one or two of your letters you remind me to think of you as I ought. Be assured there is not an hour of the day in which I don't think of you as I ought, that is, with tenderness, esteem and admiration." [56]

VII

John Adams Returns Home
"for Good"

ABIGAIL was leading two lives. She was active all day directing house and farm, but "It is true I never close my eyes at night till I have been to Philadelphia, and my first visit in the morning is there." [1]

Through John's eyes she watched history in the making. He had resigned the post of Chief Justice of Massachusetts — now that the courts were functioning another could do it as well — and had become President of the Board of War. He was in fact what might be called War Minister, and his responsibilities and labor were the greater because the government was immature and he and his board had all to make. Thomas Jefferson was his favorite fellow member on that board. "Jefferson in those days," he said later, "never failed to agree with me in everything of a political nature." [2] And though John Adams did not bother his wife with dry or technical details, he cleared his mind by discussing with her the basic principles.

"We have at last agreed upon a plan for forming a regular army," wrote the President of the Board to his wife. "We have offered twenty dollars and a hundred acres of land to every man who will enlist during the war" (that is, for the duration). [3] It was not a waste of his time to discuss such matters with her. Even Mr. Lovell sent Mrs. Adams "a map to show the present theatre of war." So she felt drawn close to her husband, still his full comrade and partner. "Is there," she said, "a dearer name than friend? If there is, teach it to me." [4]

*　　*　　*　　*　　*

Philadelphia was now in danger, from the armies of General Howe marching up from the south, whither they had gone by water from Boston. Adams's confidence in Washington, however, was complete. "Howe will make but a pitiful figure." And as to the possibility of Howe's taking Philadelphia, he tells Abigail cheerfully — "I almost wish he had Philadelphia, for then he could not get away. I really think it would be the best policy to retreat before him and let him into this snare, where his army must be ruined." [5]

Washington, after losing the Battle of the Brandywine on September 11th, 1777, pursued this very strategy. He abandoned Philadelphia to the British, thereby saving the military stores at Reading. Congress hastily left the city before the enemy's advance and reassembled finally at Yorktown, Pennsylvania. Howe complacently encamped at Germantown and prepared to make Philadelphia his winter quarters.

It was a low moment for the American cause. Friends all around Abigail thought the occupation of Philadelphia was a major defeat, the beginning of the end. Tories lifted up their heads. There were several to tell Mrs. Adams that she would never see her husband again. All communication would be cut off, he never would be able to return! Many prisoners, she knew, had already been shipped to England. If John Adams was taken, he would certainly suffer a like fate, and once in England his execution for high treason was certain. "It is a plan your enemies would rejoice to see," she wrote him guardedly, "and will effect if it lies in their power." But she refused them the satisfaction of frightening her. Her bright eyes would meet theirs disconcertingly, her color did not change. "I am not apt to be intimidated, you know. I have given as little heed to bugbear reports as possible. I have slept as soundly since my return * not withstanding all the ghosts and hobgoblins as ever I did in my life." Nor was she the only one to ride high the tides of rumor. Mary Cranch and the Quincy and Palmer women, and Mrs. Peter Adams, prim but loyal, and many another neighbor responded to her cheering leadership.

"We are in no wise dispirited here," she wrote. "If our men are

* From a visit to the Warrens at Plymouth.

all drawn off and we should be attacked, you would find a race of Amazons in America." And when Mr. Wibird came, "in the horrors," moaning that General Howe's taking of Philadelphia "would immediately negotiate a peace," she could not help replying warmly that "I did not believe it, and that if General Washington and his whole army should be cut off I hoped that an army of women would oppose him."

But when provocative visitors had gone, her mind contemplated clearly the reality of battle, and her heart recoiled. "Why is man called *humane* when he delights so much in blood and slaughter and devastation? Even civilised nations!" [6] . . . But nothing short of victory or defeat could now stop the war. And good news was drifting down from the northward that even as Washington and his Virginians were being beaten on the Brandywine, the New England troops under Gates and Herkimer were giving a dose of the same medicine to General Burgoyne.

The news of the final, complete capitulation of Burgoyne reached Boston before it reached Yorktown, and Abigail, on October 22nd, wrote joyfully: "I believe I may venture to congratulate my love upon the completion of his wishes with regard to Burgoyne! Tis reported to-day from many ways that he has with his whole army fallen into our hands." And three days later, on her wedding anniversary, she drove into Boston with daughter Nabby "to join to-morrow with my friends" in the services of thanksgiving for the victory. "The vaporing Burgoyne" and the rest of the prisoners were expected to be brought into Boston later in the week.

On the eleventh of November, believing that his trick at the helm was done, John Adams shrugged public burdens from his shoulders and became again, in his mind, a private citizen. "A slavery it has been to me," he wrote Abigail, "whatever the world may think." He would not have his wife send a servant or horse. "The expense is so enormous that I cannot bear the thought of it. I will crawl home upon my little pony and wait upon myself as well as I can." He even added, as he weighed his empty purse, "I think you'd better sell my horse." But as he mounted at last, and turned his way to the north, he was in chuckling good spirits. The bright fall weather was the best riding weather in the world. Cousin Sam, riding with him, was an excellent companion. And when, after ten or eleven days of travel, he arrived home to an exhilarating welcome at Braintree, he was in a contented mood.

Abigail, clinging to him that evening, said, "Ah, Jack — Jack — I have you home safe at last! But are you home to stay?" and he answered her with hearty reassurance.

"Indeed I am! From this moment I become a private gentleman, the respectful husband of Mrs. A. of B. and the affectionate father of her children — two characters which I've scarcely supported for these three years past, having done the duties of neither!" [7]

"You talk about three years?" said Abigail, half laughing but equally near tears. "It may be true the last three have been the worst. But look you, sir, we have been married now thirteen years, and scarcely half of that time — if you add everything up — have we spent together. And the children — they are missing you at just that impressionable time when they need their father most!" [8]

It was, in fact, delightful to see the children making friends again with their father. Nabby and Jack, twelve and ten, and responsible for their years; Charlie, irrepressibly jolly; and five-year-old Tommy, bound and determined to keep his end up, and assert his equality with Charlie. They were all handsome. They were all gifted.

John had frequently complained — "If I live much longer in banishment I shall scarcely know my own children.[9] I've often wanted to send each of my little pretty flock some present or other. . . . I've walked over the city twenty times and gaped at every shop like a countryman to find something, but could not. I wish, my dears, you would have written me what you wanted!" [10]

But he had brought gifts for them all. Now how rapidly he broke down barriers, established contact; with what respect he listened to their remarks! It was always better than Abigail had dreamed. The house hummed with his presence.

Abigail heard her husband assuring all his relatives, friends, and clients that he was home to stay. They must elect a new representative to Congress in his place. Mr. Adams must now attend to his wife and family, and — faith — his own income! Yes, he was open for law business! Cases poured in. An immense and lucrative practice was open to him.

"My heart is as light as a feather!" said Abigail, "and my spirits are dancing! We are starting a new life!"

"Ay, this is what I mean by domestic felicity!" said John. He drew her to the window, beside Dick Cranch, and looked out over the lion-colored winter fields. "I've had to leave this rural kind of life for too long, and reconcile myself to the smoke and noise of a city! [11] To give up my private peace for the vexation of worming out the deep intrigues of politicians! . . . I've panted for domestic life and the duties of the farm, like yours, brother Cranch! [12] And now we shall all four be together again, as in the old days — you and your Polly, and my bright-eyed mistress Nabby and me!"

Abigail's heart was almost more full of happiness than she could bear. How much more had *she* wanted to lay down her heavy burdens, to relinquish responsibility, to rest in the guidance and protection which she had always found in her husband, and in his warm, enveloping love. Instead of "solitary hours spent ruminating upon the past and anticipating the future," she could now share her hopes and fears with him.

Bar the door now against the world. Out with the candle. War may still rage, but we have "our private peace."

*   *   *   *   *

Abigail had three weeks of entire content. Then young Johnny, now weekly mail carrier between Boston and Braintree, rode home carrying a large packet from Congress, with portentous seals. Abigail's heart leapt into her mouth when she saw it.

A day and a night its presence threatened her while she waited for John to return from handling a lawsuit at Portsmouth, New Hampshire. He came home suddenly, forewarned by a returned Congress member, and lost not an instant in breaking the seals and sharing the contents with her.

"Ay — here it is! Mr. Deane is recalled from Paris. . . . I am appointed in his place. . . . Here, see, are new commissions to Franklin, Arthur Lee, and myself, as plenipotentiaries from the United States to the King of France . . . !"

They sat down together on the settle. Indeed her legs would no longer support her. Her trembling hand could hardly hold the letter he handed her. There was a roaring in her ears.

"The question is," said his strong voice from a great distance, "shall I accept the commission or return it to Congress?" [13]

One of the letters, that from her friend Elbridge Gerry, contained a direct appeal to her. "I hope to have the concurrence of your lady when I urge the necessity of your accepting your appointment. It is the earnest wish of Congress and every friend to America. . . . Chagrin and disappointment will result from a refusal." [14]

So '77 passed into '78 in a haze of preparations, farewells, visits, delays, and Abigail, numbed by activity in the daytime, tried to conceal from her husband the sleeplessness which threatened her nights.

On February 14th, 1778, the wind blew sharp around a lonely figure on Penns Hill. The American frigate *Boston* lay at anchor out in the sea lane. At about noon a rowboat could be seen to put out from Uncle Norton's beach and to make its tedious, rocking way, up and down on the waves, toward the ship. Well Mrs. Adams knew that, wrapped in heavy watch coats with their feet buried in straw in the boat bottom, her husband and son were the cause and burden of the boat's labor. One week before that day the American treaty with France had actually been signed in Paris. But as far as America was concerned that event was still concealed in the womb of the future, and John Adams's fate was leading him blindly forward, ostensibly to accomplish something that was already done. The dark spot of the boat was hard to see in the surf, and was soon out of sight; useless to stand and stare. Abigail, shivering, drew her cloak tighter and went down to the warm house.

Uncle Norton Quincy came in later to bring her all the details of the departure, and her husband's last note. "Johnny behaves like a man!" Over the teacups by the fire Norton described how Captain Tucker and a young midshipman, not so much older than Johnny, had arrived promptly from the beach, and a pleasant noon lunch they had had together as planned, before all walked

down to the water's edge. There the sailors launched the ship's
barge, and carried their passengers pickaback to it through the
surf. Johnny waved gallantly to the last, his round young cheeks
wet with spray. "Give my love to Mamma —" came back in the
wind. Yes, she had judged herself aright. She could not have borne
it had she been there on the shore, she could not have borne to
see them go.

Next day Abigail, searching distraction, snatched her quill and
wrote to her young cousin John Thaxter, now in Yorktown —
"Dear Sir — My hands and my heart have both been full, my
whole time has been taken up in prepareing my dearest Friend,
and Master John, for their voyage, and yesterday they embarked. . . .

"And now cannot you immagine me seated by my fireside bereft
of my better Half and added to that a Limb lopt off to heighten
the anguish . . . in vain have I summoned philosophy, come then
religion. . . .

"The world may talk of honor, but sure I am no consideration
weigh'd with me but the belief that the abilities and good integrity of your Friend might be more extensively usefull to his country in this department at this particular time than in any
other. . . .

"My desire was you know to have run all hazards and accompanied him, but I could not prevail upon him to consent — the
dangers from Enemies was so great . . . in case of capture my
sufferings would enhance his misery . . . these arguments prevailed upon me to give up the favorite wish of my heart. Master
John was very happy in his pappa's consent to accompany him,
but young as he is a mother's heart will feel a thousand fears and
anxieties. . . ." [15]

The decision to send Johnny had arisen out of a variety of considerations, in which the immediate problems of the boy's education, the responsibility of his extraordinary promise, and the need
of establishing his father's influence in his life, all played their
part. Against his youth were set the advantages of foreign travel,
the example of Benjamin Franklin's little grandson, Benjamin
Franklin Bache, already over in France, and the value and safe-

guard of his father's company. So the son went with the father.

The mother's heart, however, hardly woke up to its full burden, fears, and anxieties until Johnny was well away. The wife's feelings eclipsed the mother's. "Tender as maternal affection is, it was swallowed up in what I found a stronger." [16] "Whence shall I gather firmness of mind, bereft of the prop upon which it used to rest?" [17] she wrote her husband. The long, free-written letters which were her only relief were stored in ships which idled weeks in dock, sailed at last without warning — missing perhaps some last important packet by an hour — and driven by contrary winds, chased by privateers, as like as not finally gave up all their papers to the grim safekeeping of the sea. Her husband, on his side, wrote her frequent letters, but sodden and unread, one after the other, they drifted in the ocean with the seaweed as if he had but thrown them, like waste paper, overboard. For six months Abigail did not receive a line. Husband and son might have dropped over the edge of the world when they set off on that winter sea.

Meanwhile Abigail heard rumors that Franklin had been assassinated, that the *Boston* had been taken by British men-o'-war, that her husband was in the Tower, and if in the Tower most certainly condemned to death. These were not the kind of idle tales which could be flung off swiftly by the stout of heart. British frigates had been cruising on the coast for weeks watching for the *Boston*, and twice, early on in her voyage, she was sighted and chased and fought off her pursuers.

With official news of their landing in France her sensations of relief were only temporary. "I promised myself a negative kind of happiness whenever I cd hear of your safe arrival but alas," said Abigail, "I find myself some days more unhappy than I would ever wish an enemy to be, in vain do I strive to divert my attention, my heart, like a poor bird hunted from her nest, is still returning to the place of its affections." [18] And to John Thaxter she wrote — "No news from the far country — no letters, no vessels — heigh ho ten times in an hour." [19] Her usual active life went forward but not her heart. The summer set in hot and enervating, "the hottest summer I ever remember," and she was all the lonelier because she had put Nabby in school in Boston, where she boarded as her mother had done before her as guest of Uncle Isaac and Aunt Elizabeth.

In late August and early September war came their way again; "poor Boston is again distressed. . . . Howe's fleet is hovering about this coast 20 sail of them and I own my spirits not a little agitated. As I sit writing to you [John Thaxter], I hear the alarm guns fired. . . . More guns — I believe I shall not sleep very soundly to-night. You inquire after my dearest Friend. O sir, I know not how to curb my impatience . . . only twice have I heard . . . dated in April. I wish a thousand times I had gone with him." [20]

But Abigail knew she must not give way to this brooding misery. She taught Charlie — who was almost beyond her now, but no good school was handy — and she taught Tommy his horn-book, she directed house and farm, she pursued her usual social activities, she read, and with her account books of an evening she concentrated on how to circumvent the rising inflation. "A Regulating Bill is still kept off . . ." she wrote John Thaxter, "how does it go down with you? There is no reformation with regard to prices here, though money grows scarcer.[21] A hundred pounds lawful money is reduced to thirteen pounds six and eightpence." [22] The price of labor was steeply rising, "the most indifferent farmer is not to be procured under 10 or 12 pounds per month." She curtailed her simple style of living still further — only two maids now, and two industrious young fellows whom she engaged to work the farm on shares. "You know my situation and that a ridged economy is necessary for me if I am to preserve independancy. . . . I mean that I might always have it in my power to answer the first demand of a creditor, a dun was always my abhorrence."

But how deadly dull was this economy, this paring of pence. Was this the way for an Ambassador's wife to live? "My frugality will be termed meanness." But "to those who reflect upon me for not living any ways answerable to the character my partner sustains in publick life, I would make the same reply which one of Queen Elizabeth's ministers did to her, when upon visiting him she took notice of the meanness of his habitation, 'the house may it please your majesty is big enough for the man but you have made the man too big for the house.' " [23]

One sunny September morning a couple of chaises drove up and out stepped eight or nine French officers of the new-arrived fleet, come to fight in the American cause. Mrs. Adams's composure was unshaken — except, indeed, by delight. Tangible result of the new treaty, the French fleet had just come to Boston, after various minor encounters with the British in American waters, and the well-bred French officers hastened to pay their respects to the wife of the gentleman who was an American Envoy to France. Her little room was filled with them, their glittering uniforms, their fast, fluent speech, their Gallic grace. Some of them had already met her husband in Paris. The strain on Abigail's French was not severe. Monsieur Rivière, the leader of the party, spoke English well. And when the others politely withdrew, Monsieur Rivière accepted an invitation to dine and spend the day.

If these gentlemen, many of them of noble blood and born in great houses, were surprised at the setting from which an Ambassador to the Court of France had gone out, their perfect manners gave no sign. And in Mrs. Adams they found the ease of an equal. She spoke gracefully and with unmistakable sincerity of sharing her husband's joy "in finding the great interest of our country so generously espoused and nobly aided by so powerful a monarch." They discovered she had read Molière, and could discuss his plays in a lively way.[24]

"The gentlemen officers have made me several visits," Abigail wrote, "and I have dined twice on board . . . sumptuously entertained with every delicacy that this country produces," and a lot of foreign ones. The Count d'Estaing invited her and her family to a party on board the fleet with any friends she chose to bring, and sent his barge to fetch her. It was a gay feast, with music and dancing on deck for the young folks. Abigail immensely enjoyed all this attention, took most warmly to the French, and wished she had it in her power "to entertain every officer in the fleet." [25]

But none of this could really restore her morale. Six months

without any word from John, and then two or three letters
which rasped on her taut nerves as dry and cold, had filled her
with a bitterness of repressed reproach. Neither she nor John were
accustomed to repress themselves for long. In the reaction from
the excitement of Count d'Estaing's party, she seized her pen and
let down the sluices on her anxiety, her misery, and her sense of
neglect. Had her husband, her lover and friend, "changed hearts
with some frozen Laplander, or gone to a region which had
chilled every drop of his blood?" If he could not take the trouble to notice and acknowledge her letters with his own hand, perhaps he would direct his secretary —

She dared not finish the sarcasm. "My heart denies the justice
of the accusation . . . but my soul is wounded at a separation
from you and my fortitude is all dissolved in weakness when I
cast my thoughts across the Atlantick and view the distance, the
dangers and hazards which you have already past through . . .
the time of your absence unlimited, all, all conspire to cast a gloom
over my solitary hours. In vain do I strive to throw off in the
company of my friends some of the anxiety of my heart." And
that heart, she added, "so wounded by the idea of inattention
that the very name of my dearest Friend would draw tears from
me." [26]

Then a fresh batch of letters from John Adams arrived, crossing hers, saying that he had not received a line from her up to
June 6th, nor heard a word about her, directly or indirectly, since
his departure; but by no means reproaching her about it. Going
on cheerfully to tell her how delightful France was — "It is one
great garden." And the manners of the French had such politeness, elegance, and charm. "In short, stern and haughty republican as I am, I cannot help loving these people for their earnest
desire and assiduity to please." Religion and government needed
improvement, but that did not worry him. "I have well fixed
it in my mind as a principle that every nation has a right to
that religion and government which it chooses." The French
seemed content with theirs. He was greatly struck by the popularity of the young King and Queen, and Johnny was writing her
about the marvelous — and truth to tell, extravagant — illumina-

tions in Paris on the occasion of the birth of their first child, the little Princess Royal. "The nation is very happy," said John Adams, "to have discovered a way by which a dauphin may come to them next year or the year after." [27]

This direct contact with her husband's own spirit was the only antidote to Abigail's poison, and of a sudden she was healed. "Your letters of April 12th, June 3rd, and 16th, calmed my soul to peace," she hastened to write. "I cannot describe the effect they had upon me. Cheerfulness and tranquillity took place of grief and anxiety. I placed them next my heart and soothed myself to rest with the tender assurances of a heart all my own." [28]

But again a long silence sapped the letters of their power, the antidote wore off, the poison again worked in blood and nerves. Although John Thaxter rejoined her household as tutor, in return for his board and the use of the office (a little private law practice), he was not much company. Too quiet and too busy. The dismal and lonely winter shut Abigail up from her father, her sisters, her friends. And she gave way wholeheartedly to depression. "How lonely are my days, how solitary my nights." There was no one in the house with her at Christmas time but Charlie and Tommy and the two domestics. Even Nabby, now her mother's best companion, is away on a visit to the Warrens. "By the mountains of snow which surround me I could almost fancy myself in Greenland." It is bitter cold, the wind is blowing a hurricane, the roads are impassable. And Charlie, who has developed one of those poignantly sweet treble boy voices that make a boy's choir so like the imagined songs of angels — unearthly, ethereal — had learned to sing a Scotch song which went:

> His very foot has music in't
> As he comes up the stairs.

"How often," she wrote, "has my heart danced to the sound of that music." [29]

Yes, Charlie was certainly the one to see his mother's tears.

Perhaps afterwards she wished that those letters about the Laplander and so on had been among the many sunk; but no, by the usual perversity of circumstance, those were the very ones that got through. And her husband, cut to the quick, turned on her his thunder.

"The joy which the receipt of these packets afforded me," he wrote from Passy, "was damped by the symptoms of grief and complaint which appeared in the letters. For Heaven's sake, my dear, don't indulge a thought that it is possible for me to neglect or forget all that is dear to me in this world! If I were to tell you all the tenderness of my heart, I should do nothing but write to you. It is impossible for me to write as I did in America! It is not safe to write anything that one is not willing should go into all the newspapers of the world. . . . I have written to you not much less than fifty letters. I am astonished that you have received no more. But almost every vessel has been taken. . . . It would be an easy thing for me to ruin you and your children by an indiscreet letter, and what is more it would be easy to throw our country into convulsions. For God's sake never reproach me again with not writing, or with writing scrips. Your wounds are too deep. . . . Millions would not tempt me to write you as I used. There are spies upon every word I utter and every syllable I write. Be upon your guard. I must be upon mine, and I will." [30]

Abigail was shaken to her feet, and her tears were roughly dried for good and all. Between the lines, in half-writ, guarded sentences, she felt that her husband was grappling with large affairs and with hidden dangers of a different kind from those she had been troubled by. He was careful, too, not to send a letter that was all reproach. He knew the note to strike to bring back sunshine to her downcast face. "Your son," he wrote, "is the joy of my heart, without abating in the least degree my affection for the young rogue that did not seem as if he had a father, or for his brother and sister. Tell Abby her papa likes her the better for what she tells her brother — viz. 'that she don't talk much,' — because I know she thinks and feels the more." [31]

Abby was indeed feeling too much for her years, stifling back into her reserved little heart a terrible grief, a quite devastating loneliness. The separation from her favorite brother and close companion was a sort of death. To suffer so much, and to control her suffering, matured her early. And Johnny, out in the world

with no mother or substitute mother near, at a strict school at
Passy where he was taken out to dine by his father only at week
ends, continued to keep a stiff upper lip and behave like a man.
Both these elder children had somehow imbibed with their Latin
lessons — was it from their tutor John Thaxter? — some of the
Stoic philosophy, and both exemplified it to the end of their days.

Their mother was not of that school. But even at her most
depressed moments, Abigail was not entirely unworthy of her
dignified children and her robust husband! Just after a bitter out-
burst she would remark that she had decided to avoid instilling
into her children a narrow nationalism (this was after the French
visits, when the charm of other nations was to the fore). One
should look for merit wherever it was to be found. But oh, this
America, this New England. She looked out at the dazzling whiteness of the drifts, which hard frost had now made not a barrier
but a bridge. The music of sleigh bells rang out cheerfully in the
snapping air. "The sublimist winter I ever saw! The Bay has froze
so hard that people have walked, rode, and sledded over it to
Boston. . . . Difficult as the day is," exulted Abigail — "cruel as
the war has been — separated as I am — I would not be any other
than an American!" [32]

So she took up the daily burden — dull as her part of it often
seemed — the wearisome struggle to make ends meet. If her husband had been left at home to pursue his law business, instead of
being elevated to an expensive, precarious, ill-paid, and thankless
public office, she "need not have had a care of this kind." [33] Yet
farewell repining, carping, and complaint.

"It is true says one," she wrote to John Thaxter, "that mankind in general are a worthless and ungrateful set of beings for a
man to wear out himself in serving, but if we do not lay out ourselves in the service of mankind whom should we serve? Our own
insignificant selves? That would be sordid, indeed.

"Thus I hush all my murmurings by considering we are all
embarked upon the same bottom and if our country sinks we must
sink with it." [34]

*   *   *   *   *

Abigail was alone this time for eighteen months. On the second of August, 1779, the French frigate *Sensible* put in to Boston Harbor, and John Adams and his young son Johnny Q. disembarked. Abigail's precarious happiness was all the greater because her friends in Congress, especially Mr. Gerry and Mr. Lovell, who kept her informed, had told her there was every likelihood of her husband's being sent straight from Paris to Holland.

John Adams had come back of his own accord, in the absence of directions from Congress to do anything else. When letters had arrived confirming Franklin as Ambassador to Versailles, appointing Arthur Lee to Madrid, but containing no advices for John Adams, nor even mentioning him, he had said, with outward cheerfulness, that he was now no more than a private citizen, and as a private citizen he had but one duty — to go home as soon as possible and take care of his family. So here he was, and however they felt in Philadelphia about his return, here at Boston and Braintree it was unmixed joy.

John Adams was not sorry he had come back; nor was he sorry, as he told Abigail, that he had been to France. He understood now many things that he could not have understood had he not gone.

"I found plenty to do!" he said, "as I will tell you later! What do you think of Johnny? Has he not grown? Our company on board the *Sensible* was the new French Ambassador to the United States, the Chevalier de la Luzerne, and Monsieur Marbois, the Secretary. They were in raptures with our son! They used Johnny to teach them English! He gave them lessons every day. Ay, he was strict with them, too! They said he made them no compliments, he had '*point de grâce, point d'éloges.*' I would not do! They must have Master John! Luzerne was greatly struck with Johnny's precocity. 'He is master of his own language like a professor!' he said.[35] And of course Johnny speaks French now, not in my clumsy manner, but like a Frenchman!"

"And can you speak it?" cried Abigail.

"Well enough to make shift to conduct a conversation on any subject!" said John Adams. "Not well, but adequately. I can read

it, write it, listen to and understand it, and make myself understood. Dr. Franklin can do no more. Franklin's recommendations
for learning to speak French quickly were to take a mistress or
to go to the play! He took the first method, I the second. But
on the boat going over I had a phonetic Grammar, and I was constantly associating in France with friendly people who knew no
English. Coming back I read French history on the voyage, as
easily, almost, as my native tongue.[36] But to learn a foreign language in youth, to learn it idiomatically, is a great advantage, and
that's one thing we can give to our children!"

So thoughtful parents plan, and no doubt it was an advantage
for John Quincy Adams to learn French perfectly and to become
early polished in cosmopolitan manners. Yet the greatest advantages his parents gave him were unconscious ones, their own selves;
second, lack of wealth, and third a sister. Charles Lamb once said
of his sister that he didn't know what kind of wife such a reading
woman would make, but she certainly was an incomparable old
maid; so John Quincy might have said that he didn't know what
kind of wife fate had in store for him but he surely had had a
nonpareil of a sister.

The two eagerly resumed their old comradeship and the roses
came back to Abby's cheeks and the sparkle to her eyes. Those
months were one of the happy seasons of her life, and happiness
was to be with her rather a rare plant, seldom in full bloom.

Her mother's more ardent temperament needed happiness for
daily bread. And every hour now she tasted its good substance.

John Adams supplemented his abundant talk with his journal,
where, when he had gone to Philadelphia to make his report, or
when he sat writing in his office, she could go backwards in time
and see his life pass. He hid nothing from her.

"I lost many of your letters which are invaluable to me," he
said, "and you have lost a vast number of mine. But not a word
to you about politics because you are a woman!" He roared with
laughter at her face. "What an offence have I committed! A
woman! I shall soon make it up." He was serious. "I think women
better than men in general, but I know you can keep a secret as
well as any man whatever. But the world don't know this. There-

fore if I were to write my sentiments to you, and the letter should be caught and hitched into a newspaper, the world would say I was not to be trusted with a secret." [37]

"So I must be the loser!" said Abigail. "I've always thought that in separations the one left behind was the greatest sufferer." [38]

"God knows how much I suffer from want of writing to you!" he said. "It used to be a cordial to my spirits! But the falsest thing the English press said of me was that I am disgusted with the Parisians. The very opposite is true! I admire the Parisians. They are the happiest people in the world, I think, and the best inclined to make others so. If I had had your ladyship and our little folks over there in Paris with me, and no politics to plague me, I could have been the happiest being on earth!" [39]

John Adams had had to straighten out many errors in the Commissioners' handling of affairs in France but he had nothing but praise of the Treaty. And John Adams had a talent for praise.

"Ah, the excitement here was tremendous when the news of the signing of the Treaty with France arrived!" said Abigail. "It came on the first of May, and the soldiers in Valley Forge, after their hard, terrible winter, went wild with joy. The dogwood was in bloom, and was abundant there, and they picked it and put it in their hats and paraded. Surely for that treaty we owe Mr. Franklin much!"

"Yes," said John Adams, "but the treaty was inevitable. France wanted it, as I surmised, as much as we did. The victory of Gates over Burgoyne brought the treaty to a head, it was not a victory of diplomacy. The longer I stayed in France the more I was aware of the supreme importance to the French of their struggle with England. The Count de Vergennes — the foreign Minister — only hesitated to make alliance with us in our fight with England until he had good assurance that he was not linking France to a losing cause."

"I remember meeting Dr. Franklin when he was in Cambridge in November of '75," said Abigail. "I dined with him — I wrote you about it. How I admired him! I couldn't very well help it. I'd been brought up to venerate him from my infancy. I found him social though not talkative, and when he spoke, something useful dropped from his tongue. He was grave, yet pleasant and affable. You know I pride myself on reading faces, and I thought I could read in his the virtues of his heart — patriotism especially. A true patriot must be a religious man!" [40]

John Adams would not harm her innocence by denying it.

"There has been nothing in any of your letters, to me or any-one else," she went on, "to change this first impression. When you wrote to Cousin Sam that important letter about the system of American embassies which he showed to so many members of Congress, there was no criticism of Mr. Franklin in it. You said there that three commissioners to France were too many, there should be only one. And everyone supposed you meant Mr. Franklin to be the one."

"And so I did," said John Adams. "Before I wrote that letter I considered carefully what would be the consequences to — myself, for instance, — if my plan should be adopted. Dr. Franklin's repu-tation was so high in America, in France, and all over Europe, that he would undoubtedly — as he ought — be left alone at the Court of Versailles. Mr. Arthur Lee held two commissions, one to the Court of France and one to the Court of Spain. The one to Versailles should be annulled, but that would leave the one to Spain in force. I alone would be left without commission — be-cause Holland is not yet ready to receive a Minister! Well, I was glad enough to come home! I did expect Congress would arrange for my passage back however, and pay my expenses. That was my only disappointment!" [41]

"And now what?" said Abigail, between hope and fear.

"Now — when I've written my report for Congress — as they have no business for me in Europe, I must contrive to get some at home! Prepare yourself for removing to Boston, into the old house, for there you shall go, and there I will draw writs and deeds, and harangue juries and be happy!" [42]

Abigail had three months with John, bright pageant of sum-mer's end and early fall. Her husband sent in his report to Con-gress. It was no pettifogging report of details, nor a backbiting of the absent, but a statesmanlike survey of the whole European situation as it affected the new United States of America. And then he settled down in his pleasant office at Penns Hill to draft a constitution and a Bill of Rights for the State of Massachusetts.

Congress, in the meantime, disconcerted by John Adams's uncalled-for return, deeply impressed by his report, had at last decided for what office they needed him. They commissioned him to return to Europe as Minister Plenipotentiary with powers first to negotiate a peace with Great Britain and second to negotiate a treaty of commerce with Great Britain, Mr. Dana being appointed Secretary to both commissions.

John Adams took leave of his wife on November 13, 1779, rode to Boston with his nine-year-old son Charles, and went on board the *Sensible*. Johnny Q., now twelve, and Mr. Thaxter, and the manservant Joseph Stevens, had ridden ahead and were already on board; Thaxter was going in the post of private secretary to John Adams.

The decision to take Charles was a natural result of the proved success of taking Johnny. It seemed only fair. Why should Johnny have all the advantages? Abigail had made another passionate plea to go herself and take all the family — or perhaps to leave little Tommy with one of his aunts. But she had been crushed by overwhelming arguments: uncertainty of domicile, necessity of being foot-loose for emergency, the likelihood of quick return, the financial strain, and — to her, clinching — "my dear, a lady is an odious creature at sea!"

So, in the bright Sabbath hush of the next day, she sat at home in an agony of weeping. "My habitation, how disconsolate it looks! My table, I sit down to it but cannot swallow my food. . . . Were I sure you would not be gone, I could not withstand the temptation of coming to town, though my heart would suffer again the cruel torture of separation. Does your heart indeed forebode that we shall again be happy? My hopes and fears rise alternately. I cannot resign more than I do, unless life itself were called for. I had a faith and reliance that supported me before, but now my heart so misgives me that I cannot find that confidence which I wish for. My dear sons! Little do they know how many veins of their mother's heart bled when she parted from them. My delicate Charles! How will he endure the fatigue of the voyage? John is a hardy sailor, seasoned before, I do not feel so much for him. I will not wish myself with you because you say a lady cannot help being an odious creature at sea; and I will not wish myself in any situation that should make me so to you. God Almighty bless and protect my dearest friend." [43]

Fortunately, she had two other children, fourteen-year-old Nabby and seven-year-old Tommy, to distract her with their daily problems and charms. Nabby indeed needed comforting herself, but her reserve prevented the healing overflow of her stricken heart. It was just as well that they could not follow the voyage. Their dearest ones were crossing the stormy Atlantic in a leaky, overcrowded ship, "with perhaps four hundred men on board, who were scarcely able, with two large pumps going all the twenty-four hours, to keep water from filling the hold, in hourly danger, for twenty days together, of foundering at sea." [44]

Letters arrived in February, telling of safe landing. But the ship had limped into harbor at Ferrol, Spain, three or four hundred leagues from John Adams's destination, and the rest of the way must be covered by land. No joke, this, to cross the Pyrenees in the dead of winter, "bad roads, bad taverns, and very dear. I must get some kind of carriage for the children if possible," wrote her husband. "They are very well. Charles has sustained the voyage, and behaves as well as ever his brother did. He is much pleased with what he sees. Sammy Cooper, too." (Another youngster in Mr. Adams's care.) But Mr. Adams fervently confesses — "These young gentlemen give me a vast deal of trouble in this unexpected journey. What could we do if you and all the family were with me?" He was amazed at the spectacle of the poverty and wretchedness of Spain: poor people standing about barefoot in the frozen mud, no business, no traffic. "Nobody appears rich but the churches."

Later letters described the miseries of the journey: wretched taverns, cold, verminous, filled with smoke because there were no chimneys, dark because there were no windows; poor food and bad beds. A thousand times John Adams regretted bringing his sons. "I have undergone the greatest anxiety for the children. . . . I hope their travels will be of service to them but those at home are best off." [45] And though he suppressed any word of little Charles's miserable homesickness — which indeed the sweet-natured Charles did his best to keep under cover himself — John Adams let fly candidly with his own. "If I return again safe to America, I shall be happy the remainder of my days because I shall *stay at home*, and at home I must be to be happy." [46]

The party arrived in Paris at last on February 5th, 1780, and settled at the Hôtel de Valois. By the sixteenth, John Adams could write his wife — "The children are happy in their academy, of which I send you the plan enclosed."

And those at home? Abigail wrote — "I am rejoiced to hear my Charles behaves so well, but he always had the faculty of gaining hearts and is more mourned for in this neighborhood than I could have believed if I had not heard it. All your letters from Spain (overland route to France) I have traced and followed you on the maps through your peregrinations, it has been a pilgrimage indeed, and the care of the children! . . . I cannot wish to have shared with you, it would have been an additional burden to you."

But all the while, above the deep current of her warm emotional life, she was conducting practical affairs with the most composed efficiency. Congress, inexperienced in European expenses and short of cash, consistently underpaid its early ministers, and more than one, unsustained by a private fortune, was to return bankrupt. That John Adams escaped this fate was almost entirely due to the ability of his wife.

At the very start of his ambassadorship, expenses had exceeded income. Paris was dear. The unexpected journey through Spain had already made hay of the budget allotted by Congress. None the less, said John to his wife, "I must and will send you something for your use by every opportunity."

Abigail had already decided that she did not want money in face of the rising inflation, she wanted goods. Some she could apply directly to the family's needs, and others she could barter at advantageous rates for groceries, furnishings, and farm tools. Cousin Will handled all this business for her, either by direct exchange of his own merchandise or by bartering for her with others, all on a strictly commercial basis — except that young Will

Smith, though an admirable businessman, was also incurably generous, and was bound to make the most liberal terms.

Immediately on his arrival at Paris John Adams wrote Abigail that he had made arrangements for her with a French house of exporters so that she could order direct from them "anything you want by any vessel belonging to your uncle or M. J., or Mr. T., provided you don't exceed one hundred dollars by any one vessel. Mr. Gardoqui will readily send them and draw upon me for the money." As a beginning he had at once dispatched to her a first consignment of "necessaries for the family."

So Abigail became a businesswoman, and showed that she could do it well. She kept the farm running, her family well clothed and fed, domestic and other equipment and buildings in good repair, paid her bills and taxes and kept out of debt; yet touchingly and gracefully assured her absent husband that she was "lost without her pilot"!

Meditating on the mysterious closeness, the absorption of identity which she had experienced in married life, she wrote to John Thaxter about marriage. Her ostensible reason was to rally her young cousin about the possibility of losing his heart to some gay Parisian and to urge on him the claims of "some worthy girl in my own country — some fair American," for Thaxter had a heart "unhackneyed by gallantires — a *rara avis* in these days of modern refinement and Chesterfieldian politeness." She condemned getting married for worldly reasons without love, or indulging in sensuality outside of marriage — vice, she roundly calls it. She could make allowance for individuals, and neither she nor her husband, though they commented at times on Dr. Franklin's extramarital affairs and illegitimate children, ever passed judgment on him for it. Yet such a habit, she advises her young man, with eighteenth-century candor, "excludes all that refined and tender friendship, that sweet consent of souls, that harmony of minds congenial to each other, without which it is in vain to look for happiness in that indissoluble union which naught but death dissolves. The heart must be engaged to reap the genuine fruits of tenderness; contemptibly low must that commerce be in which the mind has no share. . . . Even the senses will be weakly affected where the heart does not participate." [47]

As she reflected on the fascinations of the French ladies, and their very free manners — her husband had described how they petted and caressed Dr. Franklin, and had jocosely commented that Franklin's seventy years made him enjoy privileges "that were much to be envied" — the thought crossed her mind as to whether her warm-blooded husband could remain "loyal" to her during such long separation, in face of such temptations. Visitors from France brought fresh anecdotes of Franklin "embracing and being embraced by" the dazzling fair. But no, she is sure of her husband as of herself. That is never one of her worries. "Mrs. Dana made me a visit. We talked as much as we pleased of our dear *absents*, compared notes, sympathised, and mingled no little pride that no country could boast two worthier hearts than *we* had *permitted* to go abroad — and then they were such honest souls too, and so entirely satisfied with their American dames that we had not an apprehension of their roving. We mean not however to defy the charms of the parisian ladies, but to admire the constancy and fidelity with which they are resisted." [48] And again — "Much must be allowed for forms and customs," she remarks easily. "I can even consent that they should practice their *forms* upon your Lordship considering your natural fondness for the practise whilst I hold possession of that I think they cannot rob me of — 'tis mine by a free gift, mine by exchange, mine by a long possession, mine by merit, and mine by every law human and divine." [49]

When election time came on Massachusetts, Abigail was heart and soul in the campaign. Richard Cranch was elected Representative from Braintree, by a unanimous vote; Dr. Tufts was chosen Senator. But in the state election, the votes went against her views, as indeed she had feared they would. She wanted Bowdoin for governor, but the showy John Hancock, with his clever political tricks and wider publicity, was elected by a large majority; "low, mean arts," said Abigail, in the fierceness of political contest, "I could tell you many, yet nothing that would surprise you, for you know every avenue of his vain heart!" [50] And now John may well remember her appeals about the position of women.

Well, "if I cannot be a Voter upon this occasion," she wrote with good-humored irony, "I will be a writer of votes. I can do something in that way!" And since he might think even this unwomanly, she turned it sharply back upon himself — "What a politician you have made me — ?" [51]

"What a fine affair it would be," wrote John Adams to his wife, "if we could flit across the Atlantic as they say the angels do from planet to planet! I would dart to Penns Hill and bring you over on my wings." [52]

At the end of 1782, John Adams sent his wife, by careful conveyance, the volumes of his private journal and the letter books containing copies of correspondence. "I dare say there is not a lady in America," he wrote, "treated with a more curious dish of politics than is contained in the enclosed papers. You may show them to discreet friends, but by no means let them go out of your hands or be copied. Preserve them in safety against accidents." [53]

John Adams had arrived in Paris armed with powers which made him the most important American Ambassador in the world. True, there were only three American Ambassadors; but one of the three was Benjamin Franklin. Until this time Franklin had been in reputation, influence, and prestige the leading American representative abroad. The most important negotiation afoot had been the Treaty with France. Now that was accomplished, and Franklin, though showered with praise, and given sole and full powers at the Court of Versailles, felt himself suddenly shorn of his glory and shifted from the center of the limelight. For another negotiation was now to be begun, the treaty with Britain, beside which the one with France would look pale. And in this great, this crucial diplomatic effort, Franklin found himself allotted, not merely not the leading part, but no part at all.

Franklin's shock and mortification, though intense, were slight, had he but known it, compared with the consternation of Gerard, Luzerne, and above all de Vergennes. The position of France in the world was precarious in the extreme. De Vergennes, the most skilled diplomat of his time, was treading on eggshells, a secret here, a secret there, this item balanced against that, in order to gain for France a day or two more of safety. The forces of revolution and bankruptcy were gathering underneath. A victory against England was, to the mind of de Vergennes, France's only hope. For this he had needed the United States as a tool against England, and for this he had bought the help of Spain with the secret promise of Gibraltar and of some of the American fisheries and wilderness boundaries. A premature peace between England and the United States would free British troops and ships for use in Europe. Mr. Adams was also empowered to make a treaty of commerce. De Vergennes did not want England to have a treaty on terms of trade reciprocity. He wanted, and was determined to have, French priority. And further, Mr. Adams was going to be stubborn about the fisheries and boundaries; and he knew what Mr. Adams would think about that prickly burr that was tickling up his sleeve, the question of Gibraltar.

He therefore blocked the diplomatic channels and refused to allow Adams to publicize his commission. Franklin, instead of helping Adams, was blinded to the real situation by jealousy of Adams and by the flattery of the French diplomats, and sided with de Vergennes, even to the extent of trying to provoke Congress of John Adams's recall. And John Adams immediately left Paris for Holland, July 1780. A Dutch loan would free America from uneasy dependence on France.

Arriving without any portfolio for Holland, he took up residence as a private gentleman, put his two sons in school, and proceeded to make social contacts — one introduction leading to another — with the leading bankers and statesmen of the country. "This country where I am," he wrote his wife, "is the greatest curiousity in the world. This nation is not known anywhere, not even by its neighbors. The Dutch language is spoken by none but themselves. Therefore they converse with nobody, and nobody converses with them!" [54]

Difference of language, however, never daunted John Adams. He had gone to France in the first place not knowing any French (though he had at the time protested his unsuitability on that score). And now he was in Holland not knowing any Dutch. Were there no interpreters? Why, certainly! His French at least (in which he was now fluent) could obtain them. "A man must have something in his head to say . . . he will never fail to find a way of communicating to good purpose." [55] He got on excellently. And there is no greater tribute to John Adams's social gifts and his power to make himself interesting than the two years he spent among the Dutch. He invented an entirely new form of diplomacy — the personal, gradual approach — promoting the cause of his new country first by explaining it and then by seeking to build up confidence in it. Some questions asked by an intelligent Dutch banker and statesman in the early stages of his visit gave Mr. Adams the idea to write and publish a series of articles in the Dutch papers about the causes of the American Revolution, and the resources of the United States, which just hit the spot.

John Adams did not expect to be in Holland very long, because Henry Laurens had been commissioned as American representative there and would presumably take over. But Laurens was captured by a British frigate on the voyage and somehow did not manage to throw his papers overboard. The capture gave the game away. Holland hastily denied all interest in the United States, and panic seized the Dutch merchants as to any American connections. It looked as if all Adams's work would be undone. But in the nick of time the inept British monarch goaded his slavish ministry into a declaration of war against Holland for her detected unfriendliness in being about to receive an American ambassador. In January John Adams received from Congress a commission appointing him, in Laurens's place, as Minister Plenipotentiary to the United Provinces of Holland, with power to negotiate a treaty of alliance whenever practicable. This was not only staggering power for one man to carry — in addition to his other unique powers to treat with Britain — but was in the nature of a vote of confidence in him, in answer to Franklin's and Vergennes's innuendoes against him. A letter and resolution of Congress in approbation of John Adams's work accompanied and underlined it, and Abigail, informed of both by her friends, wrote him her joy. She added her pleasure in noting that error of the wicked British. "The United Provinces are at last obliged to declare themselves! . . . Britain will rue the day that in breach of the Laws of Nations * she fell upon their defenseless dominions and drew upon her, as it is thought she must, the combined force of all the Neutral powers!" [56]

Congress was encouraged to take advantage of the anti-British feeling now evident in Russia and in December appointed Mr. Dana as Minister to St. Petersburg.

So Mr. Dana moved off to St. Petersburg, and though John Adams missed him he was fully in favor of the move. It was decided between them that it would be a good opportunity for young Johnny Q. to see more of the world, so Johnny, now fourteen, joined Mr. Dana's party. They made a very strenuous journey of fifty-one days to the Russian capital, via Leipsic and Berlin. After leaving Leipsic Dana pushed on day and night, and but for the frequent accidents which forced them to pause, Johnny might have died of exhaustion. In Berlin the carriage broke up entirely, and they had to stay nine days. They found St. Petersburg, said Dana, "the finest city I have seen in Europe," and since by this time they had seen most of them, that was no idle tribute. They settled down in the Hotel de Paris, and Johnny prepared to get on with his education. His mother heard of his adventure in due course, and wrote cheerfully, "I learn by Mr. Brush that Mr. Dana is gone to Petersburg with Master John — for this I am not sorry. Mr. Dana's care and attention shd well satisfy him — and Russia is an Empire I shd be very fond of his visiting." [57]

Johnny's departure left Charles alone. The flat, foggy air of Holland was unwholesome both to him and to his father, and the delicate boy was passionately homesick for his mother and the happy life at Penns Hill. John Adams found that the duties of a father, especially a tender and anxious father, did not fit well with the increasingly exacting duties of an ambassador. He was sorry to admit to himself that it had been a mistake to bring Charles at all.

---

* It is interesting to observe this idea of the "law of nations" and of the method of enforcing it, quite taken for granted in 1781, without any recognized body of international law. Abigail was talking of the Armed Neutrality Pact, initiated by Catherine of Russia, between the neutral northern powers of Europe to protect their shipping against interference by the British Navy on the high seas.

And he at last decided that the lesser of two evils was to send the boy home again. So to Charles's rapturous joy he was placed in care of Commodore Gillon and set sail for Boston. His mother heard of it indirectly, by the unwise publishing of a passenger list including the name of "a son of Mr. Adams," and by later word from Mr. Brush. Her restraint gave way and she reproached her husband — "Why did you not write me about it?" She became a prey to all the horror of suspense — "3 frigates of the enemy and a 50-ton ship the *Chatham* are cruising upon our coast for the vessels which are expected from Holland. I tremble if he should not speedily arrive. His homesickness must have been great indeed to induce the poor fellow to cross the Atlantick without Father or Mother." On the voyage there was trouble with Gillon, and the passengers — Charles and a friendly protector among them — were put off at Bilbao, and stranded there for many weeks. The distracted mother, with two such young sons adrift in the world, ceased to try to be brave, or to disguise her feelings from herself. The well-known dangers of the Boston winter coast, and the added peril of British frigates seeking a hostage, threatened the one; the unknown rigors of the far-off frozen city threatened the other. "Ah, my dear John! * Where are you? in so remote a part of the globe that I fear I shall not hear a syllable from you. Pray . . . send me his letters to you. Do you know that I have not had a line from him for a year and a half? Alas! my dear, I am much afflicted with a disorder called the *heartache*, nor can any remedy be found in America. It must be collected from Holland, Petersburg, and Bilboa." [58]

So she wrote and felt on December 9th, 1781, and not until January 19th did Charles safely arrive at last, and change some of her heartache into joy. By the middle of March she could write that Charles was in good health and "going to school" to a temporary tutor, getting on with his Latin, and happy in his return to his native land. But the problem of education was getting serious again. "I know not what to do with my children. We have no Grammar School in the town, nor have we had for 5 years." It

* A. A. is writing to her husband re her sons, and exclaims here re Johnny Q.

would be expensive to board them out, and besides "I know not how to think of their leaving home, I could not live in the house were it so deserted, if they are gone only for a day it is as silent as a tomb." [59]

Charles had brought with him, too, another worry and heartache for the one his coming relieved. He brought the story of a severe illness his father had had at The Hague. Abigail had often dreamed, when silences stretched long, of her husband lying ill, without her to tend him, too ill even to write to her. Now her fears were seen to be no more than the truth, and she felt she had been too little anxious rather than too much.

John Adams was well again months before she heard of his sickness, had spent most of the summer (1781) in exciting work, and was writing to her regularly and vigorously, if guardedly. But her husband's letters, most of them, did not reach her, and hers to him were long delayed. The state of war between England and Holland made the passage of mails still more precarious. In August, after dreaming of his return, she awoke to write — "the next month will complete a whole year since a single line from your hand has reached my longing eyes. Congress have no despatches from you since October." Almost as bad as her personal deprivation is the advantage such cutting off gives to his enemies. "I cannot protect you from the slanderous arrow that flieth in secret, a specimen of which you will find enclosed in a letter from Mr. Gerry. My indignation is too big for utterance. I will not comment upon this low, this dirty, this infamous, this diabolical piece of envy and malice!" [60]

Undisturbed by slander of which he did not hear, John Adams was getting on well with the Dutch. The loan was in sight when he was suddenly summoned to Paris by de Vergennes in July 1781. Now Mr. Adams heard for the first time of the peace treaty, or rather armistice, which de Vergennes and Franklin had been concocting behind his back.* They had now gone so far that they had got preliminary articles for registration ready for signature. But alas! John Adams had such powers that without *his* sig-

---

* As part of a suggested pact between France and England, to be arranged by a congress of powers at Vienna.

nature it would be invalid. They were forced to summon him and show it to him. But they hoped — especially de Vergennes — that haste would be in their favor. There was a time limit on the document. They reckoned on hurry to push it through. Surely, when Franklin was ready to sign, Mr. Adams would not dare — especially when flustered! — to take upon his shoulders the whole responsibility of continuing a bloody fight which could be called to a halt that very day; or as soon as the fastest sailing ships could carry the winged word!

But the worst of it was, Mr. Adams was not flustered. He did not even waste time in giving way to anger. He simply took the document and shut himself up alone with it to go over it closely with a lawyer's eye. He was a past master at the quick digesting of complicated arguments and phrases. Although he was taken completely by surprise, and had no background to go on but de Vergennes's scanty communication of the secret diplomacy of the past twelve months, Mr. Adams was ready with his answer in two days.

John Adams refused categorically to be a party to any agreement which allowed British forces to remain on American soil, and also declined to enter into any negotiation which treated the United States otherwise than as an equal sovereign power.

Vergennes's disappointment could only vent itself in fury. He sent a diplomatic insult to Mr. Adams, addressing him as the *agent* of the United States, instead of as the Minister empowered to negotiate a treaty of peace. And he let fly privately to Mr. Franklin, as to what wonders they could have accomplished together — and so nearly had! — but for this obstinate madman.

Mr. Adams at once packed up and returned to his task in Holland, having single-handed saved his country from disaster.

But the cold anger of Franklin was worse than the almost impersonal anger of the Frenchman. If John Adams was wrong, as Franklin was determined to believe, then he, Franklin — accustomed to think of himself for long years past as *the* American diplomat in Europe — had been completely thwarted by a stronger man. But if John Adams was right, he had been shown up for a fool. Either way, he was determined to ruin John Adams. Perhaps, as a professed philosopher, he did not confess it baldly to himself — though he was coolheaded and cynical enough to do so. But he acted as if it were true. And he passed on the feud to his son-in-law and grandson, the Baches, father and son, who were to have their innings in later years as poison pens in the press.

French diplomacy was having better luck in America. In the autumn of 1781, the first full-rank Secretary for Foreign Affairs was elected by Congress. The winner of the ballot was Robert Livingston. *"He is not ignorant,"* wrote Luzerne to Vergennes on November 1st, *"of the part I took in his election."* [61]

Despite the French activities, the worst John Adams's enemies could obtain against him was a modification of his powers. His commission to make a treaty of commerce was taken away, without explanation, and four colleagues were given him to help in negotiating a peace with Britain. They were John Jay, Franklin, Henry Laurens, and Jefferson. Of these gentlemen, Franklin, Laurens, and Jay were already abroad. Jefferson was prevented from sailing by private affairs. John Jay, now representing the United States in Spain, was regarded by Luzerne as the cream of the collection, a strong pro-French, pro-Franklin man. Gerard and Luzerne lobbied for him! But that was not John Jay's fault, nor did he know it.

Abigail was highly incensed by the new commission, and wrote her husband in October — "You will see with whom and what you are colleagued! Some you can have little hope of assistance from, considering their present situation" — Laurens a prisoner in the Tower, and Jefferson with his dying wife — "and some will have no inclination but to obstruct your measures." [62]

In vain John wrote her, in a mood of determined humility and philosophy — "It is more honorable than before and much more easy, I assure you it has been a great comfort to me. The measure is right. It is more respectful to the powers of Europe concerned, and more likely to give satisfaction in America." Abigail was too painfully conscious of the slanders, public and private, marshaled against her husband, the attempts to belittle his service, which were being promoted by the French agents in America as the inevitable crisis of the peace treaty approached. But Abigail took the slanders too personally, without knowing what lay behind them, and unconsciously she played straight into the hands of the enemy. She wrote her husband, Why not give up this thankless task? Retire, come home!

But no sooner was the letter out of her hands than she hastily followed it with a change of mood. Not really retire, though. No, she could not believe her husband would "retire unnoticed nameless to a rustick cottage. . . . I need not much examination of my heart to say I would not willingly consent to it." Not riches but service is her aim. "Ardently as I long for the return of my dearest friend, I cannot feel the least inclination to a peace but upon the most liberal foundation."

Her husband received her ups and downs — all out of date by the time he got them — calmly, though tenderly. He was himself in good heart as the summer of 1782 moved through to the fateful autumn. His spirits always rose before a fight. And this fight he was immensely ready for, armed at all points, knowing now intimately the policy of his opponents, and resting secure in the knowledge that no treaty could be made without his signature. So he gave himself unreservedly to pushing through the business in Holland, so as to have that in the bag before he moved on to Paris.

"I am going to dinner with a Duke and a Duchess and a number of Ambassadors and Senators in all the luxury of this luxurious world," he wrote his wife cheerfully from The Hague, "but how much more luxurious it would be to me to dine upon roast beef with Parson Smith, Dr. Tufts, or Norton Quincy! or upon rusticoat potatoes with Portia! . . . I hope to sign the Treaty [with Holland] this week or next, or the week after. All points are agreed on and nothing remains but to transcribe the copies." [63]

Done at last, with that notable achievement in his pocket, he traveled quickly to Paris to join the quorum of commissioners with Jay and Franklin. And as if she felt the mood of serenity and triumph in which her husband now, in that October, approached his major task, Abigail, in far-off Braintree, filled the night of their wedding anniversary (never forgotten) with a sober digestion of experience. Quarrel as she might with a fate which had cut her off "in the midst of my days from the only society I delighted in," yet she could rejoice too that the same supreme Being who "blessed us in each other, endowed my friend with powers and talents for the benefit of mankind," and gave him a willing mind to improve them for the service of his country. "You have obtained," she now realized, slanders or none, "honor and reputation at home and abroad. Oh, may not an inglorious peace wither the laurels you have won!" [64]

Abigail did not know that the treaty had been signed six weeks before she wrote these words but her satisfaction was complete when she learned the news. She wrote, "Peace! . . . The garb of the favorite of America is woven of an admirable texture, and proved the great skill, wisdom and abilities of the master workmen. It was not fabricated in the loom of France, nor are the materials English, but they are the product of our own American soil.

"May you, my dearest friend, return to your much-loved solitude with the pleasing reflection of having contributed to the happiness of millions." [65]

VIII

Abigail and Nabby in Europe

Now surely the time of separation was over.
"If you had known Mr. Adams would be away so long,"
asked one of those friends who so add to the joy of life, "would
you have consented to let him go?"

Abigail paused a moment to collect herself, then answered with
some of her husband's own fullness and emphasis. "If I had
known, Sir, that Mr. Adams would have been able to accomplish
what he has done, I would not only have submitted to the absence
I've already endured, but would if necessary, endure three years
more!" [1] (But God forbid, she inwardly groaned.) "You must be
proud, of course, of your husband's great honor and distinction,"
said the friend. "Oh, I can't refrain," confessed Mrs. Adams,
"from considering his honors as badges of my unhappiness." Yes,
she did not acquire indifference, nor reconcile herself to the habit
of absence.

"You write so wise, so like a minister of state," she complained
to him. And further — she aged thirty-eight, he forty-seven —
"The age of romance has long ago past but the affection of almost
infant years has matured and strengthened until it has become a
vital principle.[2] Should I draw you the picture of my heart . . .
the early possession you obtained there, and the absolute power
you have always maintained over it, leave not the smallest space
unoccupied. I look back to the early days of our acquaintance
and friendship; nor have the dreary years of absence in the smallest degree effaced from my mind the image of the dear, untitled
man to whom I gave my heart." [3]

John Adams was tired and cross and homesick. He sent in his
resignation as soon as the provisional articles were signed. He

was writing to all his friends about going home and had been trying to get away. With his extraordinary indifference to the record, so characteristic and so damaging, he chafed at remaining to put his name on the parchment of the Peace. The work is done. Why worry over a trifle? But the daily duty — just this more, and then just this — continued to hold him fast.

Mr. Dana was resigning from Petersburg, and wrote his friend that they would soon serve in Congress together. And John Adams wrote back — "I shall be happy to sit alongside of you upon one of those seats and rise up now and then and tell stories of our peregrinations and the robbers we met upon the highway!" [4]

So far was he from any ambition for further service in Europe that he wrote to Congress in praise of Mr. Jay and Mr. Dana, and "Would heartily recommend Mr. Jay for the now necessary and most important post of Minister to Great Britain."

Yes, there was no mistaking his desire. But as usual it was to his wife that he showed his heart fully. "Whether there should be peace or war, I shall come home in the summer. Our son is now on his journey from Petersburg through Sweden, Denmark and Germany . . . he shall come with me, and I pray we may all meet once more, you and I never to separate again. You may depend upon a good domestic husband for the remainder of my life. My children, I hope, will once at length discover that they have a father who is not unmindful of their welfare. They have too much reason to think themselves forgotten, although I know that an anxiety for their happiness has corroded me every day of my life. With a tenderness which words cannot express, I am yours forever. . . ." And again — "I am determined not to wait for an acceptance of my resignation, but to come home without it, provided it does not arrive within a reasonable time. Don't think therefore of coming to Europe. If you do we shall cross each other. . . . I shall certainly return home in the spring. . . . With or without leave, resignation accepted or not, home I will come." [5]

So in a passion of restlessness, Abigail awaited him. "One month of daily expectation is more tedious than a year of uncertainty." She filled her heart and her time with the affairs of her children.

Charlie and Tommy, thirteen and eleven, must begin to prepare for Harvard. She tried to put them in Andover, but it was full. That delightful sister Betsy, however, married to an impecunious parson, and having a boy and a girl of her own, was ready to open her roomy house at Haverhill to nephews who wished to tutor with her husband. And the Reverend Mr. Shaw was both a scholar and an excellent educator. This solved the school problem very satisfactorily. Charles and Tommy and their cousin Billy Cranch all went together. But though no care could be better than Aunt Shaw's, Charles was too delicate. His mother had to go from time to time and fetch him home to get stronger. And then he caught the measles epidemic in the heats of August — "it was very mortal in Boston — three hundred children buried since March." [6] A long holiday on the farm at Penns Hill put him on his feet again, and he resumed his studies in the fall, but Abigail was called to Haverhill early in November, for Tommy had rheumatic fever a second time. He lost the use of his limbs for a fortnight, with "fever and a stricture across his breast," but it was not so bad as his mother first feared.

They were eager attractive boys, earning praise from Mr. Shaw, encouraged to think of college life as not more than a year and a half away. Charles was determined to be ready at fifteen. "I have a thousand fears for my dear boys as they rise into life," their mother wrote their father. "The most critical period is the University. I hope before either of our children are prepared for college you will be able to return. I have hitherto been able to obtain their love, their confidence and obedience, but I feel unequal to the task of guiding them along." [7]

But Abigail's daughter's problems were not those of health or education, they were affairs of the heart. Mistress Nabby — second of the name — had a serious suitor. A dashing young lawyer, Royall Tyler, handsome, moneyed, well-connected, with elegant scarlet coat and a gift for poetry, had come to take up practice in Braintree, and instantly turned the heads of all the girls in the place except one. And to that one — accustomed as he was to easy conquest — he assiduously paid his court.

"Indeed my dear Sir, you would be proud of her," wrote her

mother. "She is not like her Mamma — she has a stateliness in her manners which some misunderstand as pride and haughtiness, but which is really only a too great reserve. She needs more affability, more of the charm of softness, but she has prudence and discretion beyond her years. In person she is tall, large and majestic. Her manners forbid intimacy. Indeed she is not like her Mamma. Had not her Mamma at her age too much sensibility to be very prudent? It however won a heart of as much sensibility — but how my pen runs — I never can write you a short letter." [8]

Mrs. Adams received the young man at first with some suspicion. Though charming and promising, he seemed too gay and dissipated, and Nabby, of course, was standoffish as a cover to her intense shyness. "Yet I see a growing attachment in him stimulated by that very reserve." [9] Indeed if Nabby had thought out a definite plan of fascination, she could not have done better. Her Palmer cousins at Germantown, where the young man lodged, were hardly on speaking terms, setting their caps at Tyler. And little eight-year-old Mary, Joe's daughter, was giving Royall Tyler a child's worship. He rode away from a very hothouse of adulation to the refreshing indifference of Miss Adams, who at seventeen had the grave dignity of a princess. He made more obvious headway with the mother, who looked on with sympathy and wrote vivid accounts to the absent father which might enlist his approval better than the young man could do for himself.

In the Christmas season when John Adams in Paris was resting on his oars after the accomplishment of the provisional treaty, Abigail wrote, "Let me draw you from the depths of politics to endearing family scenes. I don't know any young man whose natural disposition is more agreeable — his days are devoted to his office, his evenings of late to my fireside. His attachment is too obvious to escape notice. I do not think the lady wholly indifferent, yet her reserve and apparent coldness is such that I know he is in miserable doubt." [10] And in the spring she wrote confidently that yes, "I daily see that he will win the affections of your image, your superscription." And John Adams need not fear that the daughter had been attracted by the superficial charms of her suitor, "his dancing, singing and playing. He has given those things up since his residence in this town. The gay volatile youth appears to become the studious lawyer." [11] Falling in love would be good for Nabby, just what she needed; a little laughter, a little warmth. "Should she be caught by the tender passion sufficient to remove a little of her natural reserve and soften her form and manners, she will be a still more pleasing character." While Mr. Tyler, himself an eager reader of books, cherishing a secret ambition (very dismaying to John Adams when he sniffed it out) to be a writer of poems and plays, was developing his lady's taste in literature, Abigail, in obedience to John's anxious remonstrance, refused to encourage an engagement she would have allowed. But she wrote earnestly that "to extirpate the idea from the hearts and minds of either is not in my power, violent opposition never yet served a course of this nature. Whilst they believe me their best friend and see that their interest is near my heart, they submit to my prohibition, earnestly wishing for your return and for more prosperous days. What ought I to say? I feel too powerful a pleader within my own heart and too well recollect the love I bore to the object of my early affections."

But the father could not see his reserved daughter warming to life under the influence of a deep and slow passion. He did not think the match good enough and sent strong protests home across the sea. He had met Tyler in earlier days when Tyler was reading law with Mr. Dana and thought him a lightweight, a frivolous youth. Perhaps, living in a man's world, he had heard more details about Tyler's early dissipations. He reproached Abigail for falling for 'that young man's line, and urged that the affair be broken off for a while.

So Nabby was packed off to Boston. "What you wish has taken place, it is done with. Not that any of those qualities you justly dread have appeared in this gentleman since his residence in this town — I say this in justification of my having had a partiality in his favor. The world looked back to the days in which I knew him not." She added firmly that she had never heard any vices ascribed to him and though she agreed that a longer period of probation was necessary to establish a "contrary character," she wrote again, in June 1783,[12] that Tyler's business was increasing and that "if he has been the gay, thoughtless young fellow, he has at least practiced one year of reformation." He had even purchased a house, and that one of the best houses in the neighborhood. It was the Vassall House, vacated by its wealthy Tory owners during the Revolution, and in 1780 leased by the court to Richard Cranch. Now, 1783, the heir returned from exile and claimed her house under the terms of the new treaty,* obtained it, and put it up for sale. "Mr. Tyler has made the purchase," wrote Abigail. "There are 108 acres in the whole, 50 of which is fine woodland. The garden contains the best collection of fruit in town." [13]

Did not this look steady, look serious?

Mrs. Adams clearly suffered for both the young people. But far from being a stoic herself, she did not know a stoic when she saw one. Young Nabby's self-control was too perfect, had been practised too long. "I cannot affirm," wrote the mother, "that it is wholly eradicated from their minds but time will do it," she reassured her husband. He can count confidently on his daughter's filial affection. She will never marry anyone against his consent. "That she has a partiality I know and believe, but she has submitted her opinion, and relinquished the idea of a connection." But the young girl's awakened and hungry heart could not resign itself to complete banishment from the man who had become the very sun around which her little planet revolved. "It was her request that she might be permitted to see and treat the gentleman as an acquaintance whom she valued. 'Why,' said she, 'should I treat a gentleman who has done nothing to forfeit my esteem with neglect or contempt merely because the world have said he entertained a regard for me? If his foibles are to be treated with more severity than the vices of others, and I submit my judgment and opinion to the disapprobation of others in a point which so nearly concerns me, I wish to be left at liberty to act in other respects with becoming decency.' And she does," said her mother, rendering those bitter sentences to the father verbatim to let him judge

---

* The treaty with England specified that Tory refugees might reclaim their property under certain conditions.

for himself what repressed feeling lay behind them — "she does, and has conducted herself so as to meet the approbation of all her friends. She has conquered herself." [14]

Unfortunately, Abigail bolstered up her plea with a "poetick piece" of Tyler's which had moved her own heart. She was in haste to add, "You will tell me you do not want a poet, but if there is a mind otherways well furnished, you would have no objection to its being a mere amusement?" [15] But John Adams could not stomach marrying his daughter to an obscure country attorney of shady past who was so much of a popinjay as to commit the indiscretion of verse! It is to be feared that finally cooked Tyler's goose.

Yet both parents, great lovers as they were, would have given way to the young people's passion had it been on the girl's side more articulate, and on the young man's side had it stood the test of time. But the test the parents set was too severe. John Adams had courted his Abigail for four years — and not without preliminary opposition. But they had seen each other frequently throughout the time; they had comforted and sustained each other's affection with the small change of love. Tyler, a more inflammable character and much courted by women, was asked to stand, first discouragement, and then absence with the slenderest thread of hope. It is not surprising that he should have given way under the strain — and it is still not quite certain that he did. At first he stood up to it well, better than could possibly have been expected from a man of his type. His endurance is eloquent witness to the powerful fascination of Abby's grave, sincere beauty. In the autumn of '83 Abigail replied again to the anxious father's questions that "tho the connection is broken off and nothing particular has since passed, yet it is evident to me, as well as to the family where he lives, that his attachment is not lessened. He conducts prudently, and tho nothing is said upon the subject I do not imagine that he has given up the hope that in some future day he may obtain your approbation. Your daughter (tho fully obedient) — her sentiments she says are not to be changed but upon a conviction of his demerit, I most sincerely wish you was at home to judge for yourself, I shall never feel safe or happy until you are." [16]

That brings her to her own feelings. For more than a year past she has been entreating him at intervals to allow her to come to him — "but you must give me full assurance of your entire approbation of my request. I cannot accept a halfway invitation. Permit me, my dearest friend, to renew that companionship — my heart sighs for it, I cannot, oh I cannot be reconciled to living as I have done for three years past. . . . But I resolve with myself to do as you wish . . . waking or sleeping I am ever with you. If you do not consent, so much is my heart intent upon it that your refusal must be couched in very soft terms — and you must pledge yourself to return speedily to me." And so he did pledge himself, and so he hoped and intended, and she lost a good chance to go in June 1783 with her favorite cousin, young Will Smith, as escort. Will was then setting off in his turn on the grand tour but he sailed without her, taking only her letters, and she took her husband's word that Cousin Will would probably pass him on the high seas. Autumn would surely bring him who had been due in the spring. Often in her desperate restlessness she "wandered from room to room without a heart and soul at home, and felt myself deserted, unprotected, unassisted, uncounselled! . . . oh there is a moral evil in this separation!" [17]

When she took Nabby into Boston in December, for another long visit to Uncle Isaac and Aunt Elizabeth, Uncle Isaac came in, stamping the snow off his boots, and called from the hall that whom should he just meet in State Street but Mr. Dana, arrived that hour from shipboard. He was coming in to dine with them right now — "particularly on your account, my dear niece, when he heard you were here!" Abigail, stricken and speechless — Dana back and Adams not! — had to go to her room to weep passionately, so as not to give way to "childish emotion" when she greeted him.

No, Mr. Adams was absolutely necessary over there, Mr. Dana explained, to work on the new commission for the treaties of commerce with Mr. Franklin and Mr. Jefferson. Dana's vivid word pictures of her husband and son increased her longing but roused her pride. He at once delivered a letter from her husband informing her of his "determination to pass another winter abroad," and

Braintree and the Adamses' birthplaces

FROM A SKETCH BY ELIZA QUINCY

urging her to come to him with the least possible delay. She resolved irrevocably on the great adventure.

Difficulties loomed up mountain high. She must arrange for the care of her sons, the care of the farm and all the business that had been under her hands, must break the ties and the habits of a lifetime to take up a kind of life which she did not know about and did not want. "You invite me to you, you call me to follow you, the most earnest wish of my soul is to be with you — but you can scarcely form an idea of the conflict of my mind, it appears to me such an enterprise — the ocean so formidable — leaving my children and friends with the idea that perhaps I may never see them again, without my husband to console and comfort me under these apprehensions — indeed dear friend, there are hours when I feel unequal to the trial. If you were abroad in a private capacity I should not hesitate so much at coming to you. But a mere American as I am, unacquainted with the etiquette of courts, taught to say the thing I mean, and to wear my heart in my countenance, I am sure I should make an awkward figure; and it would mortify my pride if I should be thought to disgrace you." She thinks wistfully of her life "sequestered in this humble cottage, content with rural life and my domestic employment, in the midst of which I have sometimes smiled upon recollecting that I had the honor of being allied to an ambassador." Her longing for him cannot be denied, no monsters can keep her from him now, but, as she candidly says, "the difficulty is my fears and anxieties are present, my hopes and expectations distant!" [18]

But she went to work in her orderly, seemingly casual way. Her Uncle Isaac Smith and cousin Tufts would take care of her business. Sister Betsy Shaw would continue the care of her sons. One strong tie had been broken by the death of her father, Parson Smith, in September. He had often begged Abigail not to go abroad while he lived. Now he was gone, dying in great pain of a "stranguery" with Christian fortitude, surrounded by his three daughters, his son's dear wife, and two of his sons-in-law. Sons indeed they were to him, taking the place of his only son William, who had sunk by this time completely out of sight and touch with the family circle. William's children and patient wife were parceled out among the family. Abigail had had one, a loving little niece, living with her for some years.*

As well as a legacy from her father of half the Medford farm and some money, Abigail inherited a caretaker. The faithful and well-loved slave woman Phoebe was left her freedom in Parson Smith's will and a generous legacy of a hundred pounds a year for life. This made her a matrimonial catch, and she soon took a husband — "Mr. Abdee, whom you know." Abigail had the wedding at her house, and afterward it occurred to her that Phoebe and her husband would be the ideal caretakers of house and furniture in her absence. The Abdees accepted the trust with enthusiasm and simple pride. Mrs. Adams was certain of their care and faithfulness.

Then she needed servants for the journey. The death of Colonel Quincy in February 1784 put a good manservant out of a job, one John Briesler, who had originally been brought up as a bound boy in the family of General Palmer. Both families recommended him to their relative as "a virtuous, steady, frugal fellow, with a mind much above the vulgar, very handy and attentive." And so began a happy association of many years. For a maidservant she had a nice woman named Esther, who later became Briesler's wife.

At last the tedious arrangements were all made, the farewells, for years or forever, said. The sensitive and delicate Charles, still everybody's favorite, again lost his mother, and Mrs. John Adams, with her daughter and two servants, went on board the ship *Active* on the twentieth of June, 1784.

She had told her cousin Isaac, twenty years before, that she longed to see the world. Now her wish was to be granted, with fate's perverseness, at a time when she least desired it. At forty, she saw her children's childhood fast departing, and longed to have around her a united family for at least the holiday seasons of the last precious years.

"Patriotism in the female sex," she had written her husband a year ago, "is the most disinterested of all virtues — excluded from honors and from offices we cannot attach ourselves to the state

* She grew up to be happily married, in early teens.

or government from having held a place of eminence — even in the freest countrys our property is subject to the control and disposal of our partners, to whom the laws have given sovereign authority — deprived of a voice in legislation, obliged to submit to those laws which are imposed upon us, is it not sufficient to make us indifferent to the public welfare?"

Yet that strange passion was in her blood. For its sake she had submitted to a lot the most trying of any to her temperament. "Hope and fear have been the two ruling passions of a large portion of my life, and I have been bandied from one to the other like a tennis ball." [19] Above all she had mourned, "Life is too short to have the dearest of its enjoyments curtailed. The social feelings grow callous by disuse. The blossom falls and the fruit withers and decays. Could we live to the age of antediluvians we might better support this separation. Give me the man I love! I know I have a right to your whole heart, because my own never knew another lord." [20]

Well, that sacrifice at least is over. The dripping anchor is weighed, the sails belly out, dazzling, in the bright breeze. Soon they have left Boston Harbor, with its green fertile islands, they are out in the sea lane opposite Mount Wollaston. She strains her eyes to see the loved home of her childhood. Good-by, dear Braintree; good-by, old duties. As when she was a bride, she is leaving behind the lesser loves to give herself completely to her husband. But self-deception was never one of her gifts, and there is an agony that she can't hide — an eye or a limb lost in battle. Go forward to her new life gallantly as she may — "Who shall give me back time? Who shall compensate to me those years I cannot recall?" [21]

But, ah, what a hideous motion as the dancing ship meets the full roll of the Atlantic.

Mrs. Adams went precipitately below.

*   *   *   *   *

These were not the days of the fast clipper ships. The boat was a trader of about three hundred tons, with clumsy equipment and the usual large crew to work it. Heavy-laden as she was, she none the less bobbed like a cockleshell on even a moderate sea. The cargo was oil and potash. The oil leaked, the potash smoked and fermented. "All adds to the *flavor*." The passengers all succumbed to the rolling of the ship.

The ladies slept two by two in little cabins without windows, curtained off from the main cabin. Several of the gentlemen slept in the latter, and it was the lounge and dining room by day. For the first sixteen days Abigail Adams was unable to undress — or at any rate no more than New England "bundlers," as she said — owing partly to the prostration of seasickness and partly to her exposed situation. Her servants were as sick as herself, and she and her daughter were tenderly cared for by a sailor named Job. John Adams had been perfectly right — a lady was an odious creature at sea; and she was only too thankful he was not with her.

After that, however, she got her sea legs, struggled up to the deck — assisted by two of the gentlemen — to be bound into her chair and get some fresh air. After that her progress was rapid. Oil and potash could not be helped, but poor housekeeping could. Why put up with bad and irregular meals, dirty decks, and a slovenly steward ("be thankful the pen is not in the hands of Swift or Smollett," she wrote to Mary Cranch). Mrs. Adams "made a bustle among the waiters and demanded a cleaner abode. By this time Briesler was upon his feet, and as I found I might reign mistress on board without any offence, I soon exerted my authority with mops, brushes, infusions of vinegar, etc., and in a few hours you would have thought yourself in a different ship. Since when our abode is much more tolerable, and the gentlemen all thank me for my care." [22]

The captain, too, was grateful. He was, she thought, a good captain, an admirable seaman, kind and humane to his men. There was nothing cross or dictatorial in his manners, yet the men were all "as still and quiet as any private family." As for the passengers, there were six gentlemen and one lady, besides Mrs. Adams's party. The other lady was also named Mrs. Adams — no relation — a quiet, pretty woman, who politely shared her cabin with Esther so that mother and daughter could be together.

It was a good passage, averaging a hundred miles a day. The *Active* made it in thirty days. But it was tedious. "O dear variety! How pleasing to the human mind is change." Abigail Adams had books and needlework and her neighbors to entertain her, but her best amusement was writing. "Reading tires one; work I do sometimes, but when there is no writing there is less pleasure in working." But ah me, a ship is little better than a prison. "I cannot find such a fund of entertainment within myself as not to require outward subjects for my amusement. 'Tis a vast tract of ocean we have to traverse." She tried to remind herself that the ocean was a secret world of wonders, but the changeless round horizon brought yawns. One longed for "the varieties of landscape." Already she was secretly consoling herself with dreams of returning to her native land.

Yet rest and sea air wrought its magic in the blood. By July 20th, when they landed at Deal, her spirit of adventure was fully awake. She had learned all about the rigging. Her pen dripped with nautical terms. "We made land on the 18th," she wrote her sister Mary, "expected to put in at Portsmouth, but a sudden squall and fog prevented, we carry double-reefed topsails only, the captain couldn't leave the deck for forty-eight hours, but suppose there was no danger as we had plenty of sea-room." Then the fog lifted, they saw the cliffs of Dover through driving rain, and the ship anchored in the Downs "and the little town of Deal was before us." Some of the gentlemen, impatient to land, talked of going on shore in the pilot boat, which came out in the morning. There was a high surf, but Mrs. Adams, encouraged by the pilots, decided to go with them. Captain Lyde had told her so many dismal stories of coming up the Channel (another week's voyage), of the bad weather, cross tides, and colliers who took pleasure in running foul of other vessels, that Abigail was determined to land if she could. The ladies were wrapped up and lowered from the ship into the boat, "the whole ship's crew eager to assist us, the gentlemen attentive and kind as though we were all brothers and sisters. We have spent a month together and were as happy as the sea would permit us to be. We set off from the vessel, now mounting upon the top of a wave as high as a steeple, and then so low that the boat was not to be seen." One of the gentlemen, braced against the boat, held Mrs. Adams firm, and she had both her arms around him. The other ladies were held in the same manner. Every wave gave them a broadside, and finally a wave "landed us with the utmost force broadside upon the beach." The roar of the surf was terrifying, so "out we sprang as fast as possible, sinking every step into the sand and looking like a parcel of naiads just rising from the sea." But a warm inn was at hand, with rest, change of clothing, hot tea, every attention. And they engaged carriages for next day, and settled down there for the night; five gentlemen, three ladies, and assorted servants. All, in fact, but Mr. Green, the Scotchman, who set off at once for London. "Nobody mourned." [23]

But Mr. Green, the unpopular passenger, the pest and bore on board ship, had played a useful part in Mrs. Adams's education. He was the first full-blown specimen of a species she was to encounter more of, the snob. She could pin him down and examine him under the magnifying glass of ocean travel, the daily life in the large general cabin, or on the limited deck. "He was always enquiring, 'Who was such a general? What was his origin and rank in life?'" Mrs. Adams restrained herself, and only answered mildly that "merit, not birth or title," gave a man eminence in her country. But she finally roused herself, and to the delight of the rest of the company gave the gentleman his comeuppance once for all by saying in her gentle voice, with her royal Quincy manner, that "no doubt it was a mortification to the British nobility to find themselves so often conquered by mechanics and mere husbandmen, but that Americans esteemed it their glory to draw such characters not only into the field but into the Senate," and that she believed no one could deny that they had shone in both. That finished Mr. Green. "Such men," wrote Mrs. Adams to her sister, "have no music in their souls." [24]

At six in the morning the four post chaises were at the door. The party distributed themselves among them and drove away on the London road. Eighteen miles to Canterbury and breakfast, first stop. Mrs. Adams, looking out eagerly as they drove, exclaimed that the country was cultivated like a garden down to the very edge of the road, "and what surprised me was that very little was enclosed within fences. Hedge fences are almost the only kind you see. And the cows and sheep were very large, such as I never saw before." Canterbury proved to be a larger town than Boston. It seemed to contain a number of old Gothic cathedrals which looked to Mrs. Adams, gazing at their heavy stone, more like jails for criminals than places of worship, "as if," she said, "they thought devotion might be stolen." [25] The houses, too, had a "heavy" look with their thatched or tiled roofs.

But the inns filled her with praise. Such efficiency, such food, such service, "with your powdered waiters"; and a fresh carriage ready for you as soon as you had finished your meal. They dined at Chatham and then hurried on their way so as to cross Blackheath before dark. Stories of highwaymen flew about. A man could ride the lonely forests from Boston to Philadelphia and never meet a robber, or think of one, but the great moor was not safe after nightfall in civilized England. As the carriages (two now) drove along at a spanking pace they were passed by a lighter conveyance, a gentleman alone in a chaise. And not long after they came upon the empty chaise and a mail coach stationary upon the highway. An excited group of passengers were crying, "A robbery! a robbery!" The man in the chaise was the person robbed, and this in open day, with carriages constantly passing! Everyone in Abigail's party at once took pains to hide his money. Now every place they passed and every person they met was crying out "A robbery! a robbery!" Abigail Adams was surprised, "if the thing was so common, to see such a fuss." The robber was pursued and taken in about two miles, "and we saw the poor wretch, ghastly and horrible, brought along on foot, his horse ridden by the person who took him, who also had his pistol. He looked like a youth of twenty only attempted to lift his hat and looked despair." Mrs. Adams could not help pitying him, especially when she heard them telling him — "Ay! You have but a short time. The assize sits next month, and then my lad you swing." [26] Not that she thought the penalty too severe, it was the bad taste of the taunts. In *her* country they might hang thieves but they did it more kindly! She was already making the

inevitable contrast between *Our* country and this, with the scales
already loaded in "our" favor.

About eight o'clock in the evening Mrs. Adams and her
daughter and servants were set down at Lows Hotel in Covent
Garden. This was Mr. Adams's usual hotel, and here she learned
for certain that neither her husband nor her son was in London.
But the disappointment was not unexpected, and she was still
surrounded with friends. Dr. Clark and Mr. Spear, fellow passengers, took lodgings at the same inn, and when they learned
that her cousin Will Smith was in town, good-natured Mr. Spear
set out at once in search of him. He had, however, to call first
at the customhouse, and outside it Will Smith and young Storer
were lying in wait to catch new arrivals. Spotting an American *
descending from a coach, they pounced on him for news. As soon
as they heard of Abigail Adams's arrival they set off at a run, and
ran almost the full mile to her lodging. Now she had a real welcome. They told her that her son had waited for her in London
a full month, expecting her on another ship, but when that ship
came in with letters only, he returned to his father at The Hague.
Will Smith had had a letter from his father three days before,
informing him of Abigail Adams's passage on the *Active*. He had
forwarded it to The Hague at once, so that he hourly expected
either Mr. Adams or Master John.

Meanwhile, the two young men took affectionate care of
their cousins (Charles Storer was Grandmother Quincy's great-
nephew) † and next morning conducted Mrs. Adams and her
daughter to the lodgings they had already taken for them at
Osborne's in the Adelphi, "well-situated on the Thames. In sight
of the terrace is Westminster Bridge one way and Blackfriars the
other." This was where John Adams had stayed most recently, and
where John Quincy Adams had awaited her arrival for a month.
Abigail and Nabby had a handsome drawing room and a large
bedroom at their private disposal, and they had hardly settled in
and looked about them before they were overwhelmed with
visitors. The news of their arrival spread, and all the Americans

---

* How did they know he was an American? Well, it can still be done —
† Grandfather Quincy married Elizabeth Storer.

in town flocked to welcome them, Tories or not. Here was old acquaintance from the happy past; a breath of home. "I hardly know how to think myself out of my own country," said Abigail, "I see so many Americans about me." [27]

She had more invitations than she could accept — or wanted to. Young Will Smith and Charles Storer escorted her and Abby everywhere. London was rather like Boston, she thought, but when you started to drive about in it, you found its sprawling extent. It was a *monstrous* great city.

They took her to see Mr. Copley's pictures, where she saw his full-length portrait of her husband, "very large and a very good likeness." It was owned by Copley. They visited Mrs. Wright's Waxworks, and the Foundling Hospital on Sunday. ("Really glad I was that I could, after so long an absence, tread again the courts of the Most High.") The little orphans all in uniform looked very neat, a touching sight. The Magdalen Hospital, again a divine service; she began to think the English more serious and religious than she had thought they were. The Magdalens were behind a screen which saved them from being stared at. Mrs. Adams was even persuaded to go for a walk with young Storer; one could see the effect of the city so much better on foot. But his enthusiasm took her too far. Though "the walking is very easy here, the sides of the street being wholly of flat stones" (not like the Boston cobbles), four miles was too much. "I shall not get the better of it for a week," she laughed ruefully.

It was a glorious holiday, the only one Abigail Adams had had since her marriage. Nothing to do but enjoy every day, and something new every day to enjoy. Even the pageant of the streets held endless variety, and the items of dress, manners, and food. Abigail Adams was surprised to find all three on a lower standard than at home in Boston. Gentlemen seemed very plainly dressed, and the ladies "much less so than with us." "True you must put a hoop on, and have your hair dressed, but a common straw hat with only a ribbon upon the crown is thought sufficient to go into company." Muslins are the taste. Or if you were very fashionable, you might have a dress of the new calico, perhaps blue and white.

English ladies seemed to Abigail Adams to lack the stylish

trimness of American ladies, and their manners were "masculine," they despised the softness that was so attractive in females and went in for being "Amazons." She was told that American ladies in London were much admired by the gentlemen, and she confessed you couldn't wonder at it. Having taken up this very natural point of view, based on her first callers, any English lady who did not fit the pattern because she was agreeable and well turned out was classified as not typically English — "she looks like one of us." [28]

As to dinners — why, our country is extravagant, she must confess, compared to this. Smith and Storer regaled her with anecdotes to add to her scanty experience. You would not find at a gentleman's table more than two dishes of meat though invited several days beforehand. She got nothing but "a turbot, a soup, and a roast leg of lamb with cherry pie" at the Atkinsons' dinner party, but it was such a jolly time that she hardly noticed the frugal fare. She really enjoyed it more "than if a sumptuous feast had been set before me."

But the gardens — Kew and Hampton Court and Ranelagh — ah, there the English climate came into its own! They were beyond praise. In the height of summer they were a riot of flowers, a miracle of green. "To walk in some of these places you would think yourself in a land of enchantment."

Full days ensured fatigue, and fatigue should ensure sleep. She summoned the mental picture of the flowers to soothe her in the night watches.

She tried to keep her suspense under control by having worked out the earliest possible day for son or husband to return from The Hague. That would be Friday, July 30th. Abigail Adams and Nabby stayed home that day, refusing all engagements. They had not long to bear that unendurable tension. Briesler ran puffing in — "as if he were really interested in the matter."

"Ma'am, young Mr. Adams is come!"

"Where, where is he?"

"In the other house, Madam. He stopped to get his hair dressed." Considering the journey, and the requirements of powdered hair, he was well justified.

"Impatient enough I was. Yet, when he entered, I drew back. Was this just another fashionable caller? Not really believing my eyes till he cried out —

" 'Oh, my mamma, and my dear sister!'

"His appearance is that of a man, and in his countenance the most perfect good-humor." [29]

Because he was an easy and well-bred man, there was no constraint, no stiffness in his greeting. At once they were all talking together, trying to bridge the unbridgeable years. It was a big gap, from twelve to seventeen, with not even frequent letters to diminish spiritual distance. But if they could not renew the old contact, they could make a new one, and they made it fast. Fortunately for their happiness there was a kinship of mind between them. And the woman who was a loved and attractive companion to young Will Smith and Charles Storer could also be an attractive companion to young John Quincy Adams.

If Abigail offers one of the most striking examples in history of equal friendship between husband and wife she also presents an outstanding example of friendship between mother and son. As for Abigail Adams junior, John Quincy Adams was better loved by his sister than perhaps any man she ever met. She had not forgotten him, nor he her. "His sister he says he should have known in any part of the world." [30]

He carried messages and letters from his father, whose ardent impatience throbbed in the cold ink. "Your letter has made me the happiest man upon earth. I am twenty years younger than I was yesterday. It is a cruel mortification to me that I cannot go to meet you in London." He urged her to provide such clothes as she needed for herself and daughter — "do what is proper, let the expense be what it may." Above all she must not get overtired. "Every hour to me will be a day, but don't you hurry or disquiet yourself. Be careful of your health." After a few weeks in Holland with him while he winds things up, she will have to set out with him to France, but there are no seas between — a good road, a fine season. He eagerly planned short daily stages, and much sight-seeing on the way. "It is the first time in Europe I looked forward to a journey with pleasure." He looked forward with special delight to showing her Paris, and imagined her enjoyment of it, language and all. (John Adams still suffered the illusion that his wife knew French.) For his own part, he felt himself *made* for the world of Paris. He signed himself, "Yours with more ardor than ever, John Adams."

Yes, that was a letter to comfort and quiet secret heartache; full of meat for reading and rereading. Meanwhile, she had her son to get acquainted with all over again, to take care of her and plan for her, and make the preparations and the journey easy.

She saw at once that young John was executive. It would be ten days, he told her, before they could get off. He was commissioned by his father to buy a carriage and had various other duties to carry out. But the time would fly. They could fill the days with entertainment and sight-seeing.

Abigail Adams remarked that *she* did not feel twenty years younger, with a grown-up son on one hand and daughter upon the other, "and were I not your mother I would say a likelier pair you will seldom see in a summer's day!" Yet, though the brother and sister were like each other, it took time to get used to young John. "I look upon him scarce recognising that he belongs to me. Yet I should be very loth anyone else should lay claim to him." [31]

Will Smith sailed for home the day after John Quincy arrived, having admirably filled the interval for his cousins. He carried with him a large batch of letters, especially the shipboard diary which both Abigail Adams and Abby had kept, the one for Mary Cranch, the other for Mary's daughter, Abby's bosom friend Betsy — who had once been John Adams's baby goddaughter.

Well, first Holland and then France it had to be. But Abigail Adams looked forward a bit ruefully. "As you know, I am fond of sociability"; and how was she going to satisfy that "in a country the language of which I am a stranger to"?

They expected to get off for The Hague on August eighth. On the evening of the seventh, John Quincy took his sister to the theater for a last treat. Abigail chose to stay home alone, in preparation for the journey on the morrow. Suddenly the door opened, and there was her husband.

Sharp joy went through her like a sword. Never afterward

could she speak of that moment. She gave a vivid description of her reunion with her son, but she drew a veil, she could not help it, over her reunion with her husband. Ah, he could not hold himself on the continent of Europe, he could not wait for her to come to him. With a young man's ardor he had hurried to her side the very instant he could drag his business to a conclusion. How different now the morrow's journey looked! It turned into a kind of honeymoon.

So they were together again "after a separation of 4½ years, indeed ten years except for a few visits." [32]

Next day, as planned, the happy party set off together in the sturdy English carriage so well purchased by young John, the servants following in a hired chaise. But the destination had changed. Holland was no longer necessary. John Adams was taking them direct to Dover and Paris.

Abigail in France

ABIGAIL went to England prepared to criticize. She went to France prepared to praise. But there was shock after shock.

When they disembarked at Calais, after twelve hours of misery buffeting about in the narrow seas, the best inn was a wretched affair. And when their stout English carriage was ready to take them on by road, the French postilions presented themselves in rags and huge jack boots, with a harness for the horses of ropes and chains instead of the shining steel and leather of English harness. Seven clumsy cart horses took the place of the smart English team of four which had brought them to Dover. Seven horses were none too many for the state of the roads, which under the French system of peasant forced labor were as bad as could be. The landscape through which they lumbered along was depressing. "The villages," wrote young Abby, "are the most wretched of all the habitations of man,"[1] streets narrow and dirty, houses mean and mostly windowless, apparently made of some kind of clay and covered with thatch. Flocks of men, women, and children were at work in the fields, yet the forced serf labor had poor results in agriculture. Crops and animals appeared thin and poor, "nor have they ornamented their fields with the hedge," which made England so pretty.

The manners of postilions, innkeepers, and peasants were a match for the rest of the country. "The English have a sprightliness and alertness, but in the French there is a heaviness, dirtiness, and no elasticity."[2]

The honeycomb of irksome laws which had resulted in these conditions lay behind the scenes, invisible to the passing traveler's eye. But there were outthrusts of the system which became sharply apparent. "Custom house officers in almost every town demanded a search of your baggage, even though it consisted only of your own private clothes." [3] One found they could be bribed to leave the bags unopened, but it cluttered up movement, and made one long again for the free travel in England.

Even Paris was a disappointment at first. They paused there briefly before going on to Auteuil, and John Adams anxiously urged his obviously unimpressed wife to reserve judgment — she hadn't really *seen* Paris yet! "One thing I know," she said somewhat tartly, "and that is that I have *smelt* it! It is the very dirtiest place I ever saw." Apart from a few of the public buildings, she thought "Boston as superior to Paris as London is to Boston." [4]

John Adams had leased a house at Auteuil to which he had moved from Paris during a serious illness the year before, and there they went in August 1784. Auteuil was a pretty place, four miles from Paris and one from Passy. It was on the edge of the Bois de Boulogne. This forest, laid out in straight avenues, was ideal for long walks and drives, and John Adams kept them up vigorously.

The house was a stately one, with white stone columns and a beautiful garden. It was fully furnished in the French style, but so large that housekeeping was a heavy task. There were about fifty little rooms upstairs, so small, said Nabby, as to make inconvenient bedrooms. [5] The reception rooms downstairs were spacious, but the French taste was not altogether to their liking. "No carpets" gave a chilly look to the rooms. Some had floors of red tiles and others, including the great salon, had shining parquet floors. All were cleaned the same way — swept, waxed, and polished. Never scrubbed. "Water is an article very sparingly used in this place." [6] A man called a *frotteur* did the polishing, with brushes fixed to his feet, on which he did a kind of roller-skating, [7] very jauntily, with arms akimbo.

Mrs. Adams found that no servant would do any work out of what he considered his province, even if it meant hours of idleness, so that she was forced to keep eight and even then suffered for want of a ninth. But with the help of Briesler and Esther, she managed to keep even French servants up to the mark. And they turned out to be very human. When American Esther fell ill, French Pauline nursed her like a sister.

Pauline was the lady's maid. Yes, though one blushed to tell it, one had to have a lady's maid — to dress one's hair. This tedious elaborate hairdressing was an absolute necessity. A lady could go into company scantily washed, and with a dirty chemise and soiled ribbons, Mrs. Adams observed, but never with undressed hair! The very servants went to the coiffeur to have their hair dressed and powdered. So Abigail and young Abby shared a lady's maid. John Adams and his son, by the same necessity, shared a *valet de chambre*.

But the garden was her comfort and joy. There were five acres of it, "so sweetly arranged." [8] Near the house were beds laid out in the formal French fashion with a profusion of summer bloom. In the middle of the garden was a fountain with two small stone images. There were rows of orange trees in tubs, and spacious walks, and grape arbors terminating in green alcoves. Large china vases dripped with growing flowers, trees were clipped to form arbors where one could sit, and statues were placed about to decorate a grove. There was no end to the delights; even the vegetable garden, hidden by a neat fence and a surrounding row of orange trees, was a pleasure. You could see the garden from every room in the house. Now, in August, the long French windows stood open, and a delicious fragrance pervaded the house. "This is a beautiful climate, soft, serene and temperate."

* * * * *

As soon as Mrs. Adams had got her house in order, she began to go visiting, for it was the etiquette in France for the newcomer to call first. If she had had any illusions about her French she had lost them in the struggle with her servants. To them she must speak willy-nilly, "bad grammar and all!" [9] But it was a different matter with her social equals. "Not speaking the language lays me under embarrassment. To visit a lady merely to bow to her is painful" [10] — especially as the ladies were very voluble and Mrs. Adams loved conversation. She struggled with it. She read Voltaire, Racine, Molière, dictionary at elbow, to beguile the tedium while her hair was dressed. In reading French, and understanding it when spoken, she became proficient, but her ability in speaking lagged. However, almost any visits were better than none, and she felt forlorn when winter mud made intercourse with Paris more difficult. But for her garden, she would rather have lived in Paris — the gaiety of Paris gradually magnetized her — but John's health could not stand the smells and lack of hygiene in the city.

No barrier of language prevented her from admiring the cultivated grace of the French ladies. "There is an ease and softness in their manners that is not found in any other country perhaps in the world." And the gentlemen were a fine sight, wearing their swords and carrying their tiny *chapeaux de bras*. But there were some odd points in this society of the "haut monde." There were no general introductions at a party. People seemed to do as they pleased, stroll about the room, speak to this one and that. At dinner, instead of the American arrangement in which the ladies all sat on one side of the table and gentlemen on the other, the ladies and gentlemen were mixed, and you conversed with the one who sat next to you. "Conversation is never general as with us," said Abigail rashly. She was not acquainted with the French salon, where brilliant general conversation was dominated and guided by a woman, and what she heard of Madame de Staël did not move her to admiration. As far as she could make out, the lady had done what no wife should: dimmed the luster of her husband, and she well deserved the loss of his affection.

On a chilly evening, gentlemen tended to stand about round the hearth, and "it shuts out all the fire from the ladies. I know," said Abigail Adams feelingly, "I have suffered from it many times." A curious inconsiderateness amongst a nation "who really do deserve the appellation of polite." Ladies would sit all night playing cards for high stakes and would then receive company at noon in bed, their hair carefully dressed in high powdered coiffure, but otherwise in deshabille. These French ladies were obliged to put their daughters into convents to keep them out of bad home influence!

The Marquise de Lafayette, who spoke some English, became

her friend; and Mrs. Barclay, the American Consul's wife, and the lovely Mrs. Bingham. That lady's behavior was a bit scandalous by Boston standards but she was very handsome and so lovable one must forgive her. Come to that, Mrs. and Miss Adams were often at Passy visiting Franklin and his frequent companion, Madame Helvetius. She was a queer one: rich, a "grande dame" (or so Franklin said), but with wild manners, always shouting and flinging her arms round people. She was slovenly dressed, too — "a chemise made of tiffany over a blue lute-string, which looked as much upon the decay as her beauty," wrote Abigail dryly. "A small straw hat with a dirty gauze half-handkerchief round it, and a bit of dirtier gauze than ever my maids wore was bowed on behind." When her little dog (whom she was kissing almost as often as she kissed Franklin) wet the floor, she wiped it up with her chemise.

Abigail's best friend in France was the high-bred Marquise de Lafayette. The product of an old and fine aristocracy met the New England parson's daughter, and each found in the other a lack of affectation, a love of the real things of life, and that serene simplicity of behavior which is the cream of good manners.

When the American lady visited the Marquise, the pretty pageant of etiquette was laid aside. The Marquise received her in her bedroom, where they could chat over their knitting with Madame de Lafayette's mother and sister, while the two children, Virginia and George Washington, played around them. And when the Marquise came to see her American friend it was with the same pleasant informality — "As we were sitting round the fire the door opened and this lady entered with all the freedom of a familiar friend, how much more agreeable than any other manner possible."

Only once did Abigail Adams see the Paris mob, which, like a clumsy giant roused, was soon to take up the glittering toy of the court and break it in pieces. The occasion was the *Te Deum* in Notre-Dame for the birth of a second prince, who seemed to make the succession doubly secure. Madame de Lafayette invited

Mrs. Adams and her son and daughter to drive with her to the ceremony. Jefferson also drove with them. It was a bright April day, and Paris was at its best. A holiday had been proclaimed, and crowds were in the streets. "I believe I may say with truth there were millions of people," wrote Mrs. Adams. As the carriage forced its difficult way along her bright eyes noted another fact, surprising at the time and later full of significance, and sullen threat. "There were as many police as there were people."

The mob, apparently gay and good-humored that day, had peculiar rights, young John Quincy Adams told his mother. It could squeeze in to watch the King have his dinner when he held a routine *couvert-à-roi*. And when the Queen had a baby — well, take this very Duke of Normandy whose birth they were now celebrating; it was lucky for her, said sophisticated John Quincy, that she was taken ill only an hour before her delivery. "For a few minutes before she is delivered, the doors of the apartment are always opened and everybody that pleases is admitted to see the child come into the world, and if there had been time enough all Paris would have gone *pour accoucher la Reine*." Yes, the mob knew its rights, and let none of them grow rusty by disuse. They were the safety valves to its immense oppression. But the safety valves were too few and too small, and explosion was very near at hand.

* * * * *

If Mrs. Adams was tempted to think she had been transformed by fairy spells into a princess, she was quickly weaned from her enchantment by the familiar, grueling worry about money. Expenses were like weeds in a garden too large for the gardener. Watch and keep them down all she could, they would mount. "Mr. Jay went home because he could not support his family here with the whole salary. What then can be done, curtailed as it now is?" [11]

Congress had just docked five hundred dollars from Mr. Adams's pay. Well, Congress was hard up and in a spasm of frantic economy; but they docked without a due perspective on expenses of ministers abroad, and they did it to a man who had just almost killed himself by a hideous winter journey,* in ill-health, raising a large loan for them in Holland.

Mr. Adams alone among the ministers then abroad was without private means, and lack of funds seriously curtailed the natural social instincts of himself and his wife during their time in France. They had to reduce entertaining to a minimum when the dinners they did give cost them fifty or sixty guineas at a time. Yet, as Mrs. Adams said, "More is to be performed by way of negotiation many times at one of these entertainments than at twenty serious conversations." She called the policy of her government "penny wise and pound foolish." And the very man who was so forced to pinch was the man, as she justly observed, who had been the means "in great measure of procuring such extensive territories to his country and saved their fisheries."

The social obligations of rank multiplied. A dinner once a week was a necessary minimum. "As your uncle had been invited to dine at the tables of many of the foreign ministers it became necessary to return the civility." Fifteen or twenty persons was the average for these formal dinners. They had luster. The Swedish Ambassador, Baron de Staël, was a favorite from the first. He was tall and graceful, a very handsome man and much attracted by Miss Adams. He managed to talk to her in French and complimented her to her brother, saying that one could not find in France a complexion to equal hers. Blanchard, who flew the Channel in a balloon on a crisp January day, was fêted by everyone. He and his flight companion, Dr. Jefferies, had come on to Paris to enjoy their glory. After that letters from John and Abigail wishing that friends in America could join them no longer said "if I had wings," but "if I had a balloon to bring you." [12]

Every American who passed through Paris came out to pay his respects. Frenchmen, Spaniards, Hollanders might turn up with letters of introduction which must be honored. Dr. Franklin would drive over for dinner, though oftener to tea, with Madame Hel-

---

* For description, see John Adams's account in his journal, *Works*, I, pp. 408–412. The company and help of his son probably saved his life.

vetius * or Madame Hewston. Mr. Jefferson drifted in and out like one of the family.

The theater and the ballet had put their spells on Abigail. As for the opera ballet! "The first dance which I saw upon the stage shocked me. The dresses and beauty of the performers were enchanting; but no sooner did the dance commence than I felt my delicacy wounded and I was ashamed to be seen to look at them. Girls clothed in the thinnest silk and gauze, with their petticoats short, springing two feet from the floor, poising themselves in the air with their feet flying and as perfectly showing their garters and drawers as if no petticoats had been worn, was a sight altogether new to me." But shock passed into delight. "Their motions are as light as air, and as quick as lightning. They balance themselves to astonishment. No description can equal the reality. They are trained to it from early infancy at a royal academy instituted for this purpose. You will very often see little creatures not more than seven or eight years old, as undauntedly performing their parts as the eldest among them." [13]

Yet she admits moral objections, "the tendency of these things, the passions they must excite. . . ." And the girls, fairies in their fairy world, hadn't a chance in real life. "As soon as a girl sets her foot upon the floor of the opera, she is excommunicated by the Church, and denied burial in holy ground. She conceives nothing worse can happen to her. All restraint is thrown off and she delivers herself to the first who bids high enough for her."

Such girls are a danger to young men in a monogamous society. And a young man the dearest in the world to Abigail Adams was observing them with a lively eye. But off the stage they were invisible to John Quincy. He left no part of his heart in France.

* * * * *

John Quincy Adams was working hard at his Latin in preparation for Harvard. Yet he dreaded the wrench of parting again, and he foresaw clearly the irksomeness of tutelage. "After having been travelling for these seven years almost all over Europe, and

* The house of Madame Helvetius was at Auteuil. A. A. says "she is my near neighbor."

having been in the world and among company for three, to return to spend one or two years in the pale of a college, subjected to all the rules which I have so long been freed from: then to plunge into the dry and tedious study of the law for three years . . . it is really a prospect somewhat discouraging for a youth of my ambition. But still I am determined that so long as I shall be able to get my living in an honorable manner I will depend upon no one . . . which I shall never be able to do if I loiter away my precious time in Europe and shun going home until I am forced to it." He never regretted this iron decision. At the age of seventy-seven, looking backward at his youth, he wrote in his Journal — "It is almost surprising to me now that I escaped from the fascination of Europe's attractions. My return home from Auteuil decided the fate and fortunes of my after-life. It was my own choice and the most judicious I ever made."

His mother's influence had colored his thought. With that unswerving strength and objectivity which made her private wishes nothing against a son's or a husband's welfare, she had made him see things plain. "I feel very loth to part with my son," she wrote, "I shall miss him more than I can express, but I am convinced that it will be very much to his advantage to spend one year at Harvard. . . . He will find there companions and associates. Besides, America is the theatre for a young fellow who has any ambition to distinguish himself. So that if his father consents, I think it not unlikely that you will see him in the course of next summer." There is also the all-important American girl. The mother is looking forward to a suitable wife. It's only teasing, but . . . "Where is Miss Nancy Quincy? Well, I hope. We often laugh at your cousin John about her. He says her stature would be a great recommendation to him, as he is determined never to marry a tall woman, lest her height should give her a superiority over him. He is generally thought older than your cousin Nabby; and partly I believe because his company is with those much older than himself." [14]

John Quincy Adams had been driven by circumstances into an early maturity, but he had much of his father's warmth and of his mother's charm — "A great flow of spirits and quick passions." [15]

Yet with a more austere behavior than his father had been able to boast at his age, he was learning of woman from his mother and his sister. For exercise he took his sister to walk in the Bois. For amusement he took her to the opera and theater in Paris. No other young lady was in his eye.

Young Miss Adams, suffering from the dying love affair with the inconstant Tyler,* and from the anticipation of a new separation from her beloved brother, was said by French society to be handsome but *triste*. But Madame de Lafayette said no, not *triste* but *grave*. This comforted Nabby, who knew that by *triste* the French meant mopy.

In fact Miss Adams aroused a lot of admiration for her fine figure and clear, bright complexion, in which Jefferson liked to see the ready blushes come and go. And she naturally enjoyed admiration, Mr. Jefferson's particularly. Although Jefferson had followed the fashion in placing his own daughter in a convent school, which was very contrary to Boston standards, he was so dear to the whole Adams circle that he could do no wrong. When the Marquis de Lafayette arrived in January with the news of the death of one of the two younger daughters whom Jefferson had left behind in America, all the Adamses felt it like a death in the family. Jefferson's habitual depression sank into a low melancholy. Mrs. Adams's motherly cheer, and Miss Adams's grave and quiet solicitude, were very soothing.

Meanwhile, during the winter of '84–'85, John Adams remained the chief and, for weeks at a time, the only conductor of American diplomatic business with the French Court. Franklin's infirmities kept him immobile, and Jefferson was constantly ill. But the business was straightforward and uncomplicated.† Mr. Adams and de Vergennes, having long taken each other's measure, worked together harmoniously, and a serene content possessed John Adams's mind. Now, instead of solitary lodgings, he had a

---

* At least letters from the Cranch cousins so reported him, and his own letters were infrequent and unsatisfactory. Probably hers were more so.
† Chiefly regarding the Barbary pirates and the vexed questions of tribute to the Emperor of Morocco, to prevent piracy on the high seas. One of the chief uses of the British Navy had been to police the seas, but the war situation had kept it busy with French and American ships.

beautiful and well-ordered home to return to, warmed by the lively presence of his wife and of a son and daughter who gave him every satisfaction a father could have.

Yes, during those months at Auteuil the happiness of all of them was all but complete. As complete as mortals mostly know. A time to look back on as under a charm.

It rushed to a close. On May the fourth, 1785, letters arrived from America bearing a commission from Congress which appointed John Adams the first American Ambassador at the Court of St. James's. It was a climax neither unforeseen nor yet quite expected. Farewell then to Auteuil, and to all the foreign things and people which had become so familiar and even liked. Farewell to the cold mirrored rooms and the tiled floors; farewell to Pauline, now so well trained, and to the statues and the pet bird. "Delightful and blooming garden," sighed Abigail, "how much shall I regret your loss. The fishpond and the fountain are just put in order; the trees are in blossom, the flowers are coming on . . . and the forest-trees, several beautiful rows of which form arched bowers at the bottom of our garden! It will not be easy to find in the midst of a city so charming a scene." [16]

And she will miss her friend the Marquise. And there's Jefferson. Yes, almost most of all. "I shall really regret to leave Mr. Jefferson. He is one of the choice ones of the earth." [17] But emotion lost its breath and was drowned in a tidal wave of packing and preparations. "May 10th. My son takes his departure for America tomorrow morning, and we go next week to England." [18]

X

Ambassador's Wife in London

Yo will be well stared at!" said the Duke of Dorset, the friendly British Ambassador in France.

But their sanguine temperaments could already foresee compensations in their bed of thorns. Back they went from ill-kept France to well-kept England, from a sullen peasantry to a cheerful one, from customs barriers in every town to untrammeled movement — except indeed for thieves on lonely stretches of highway. Above all, rejoiced Abigail Adams, from a country in which talking was so difficult to "a country the language of which I shall be able to speak without an interpreter — or so much twisting and twirling of my tongue, and then pronouncing badly at last!" [1]

The drive up the Dover Road to London had a home-coming feeling, and it was in good spirits and good humor that they prepared themselves for the ordeal of presentation at court.

Foreign ministers, according to custom, were presented in a private audience with the King. Four days after arrival, therefore, on Wednesday, June 1st, John Adams, standing in the King's antechamber at St. James's Palace, found that Dorset's words had expressed an exact truth. The room was very full. His escort, the Foreign Secretary, Lord Carmarthen, had gone in to announce his arrival to the King, and the American, first official representative of the seceded colonies, became the inevitable center of haughty curiosity and attention. He stood it with sturdy dignity. But before he could feel uncomfortably embarrassed, the Ambassadors from Sweden and Holland came up together and engaged him in conversation. Some English noblemen whom he had met before joined the group. Thanks to these gentlemen, John

Adams went on into the King's closet warmed and eased. The moment could be freed for the great emotions which alone rightly belonged to it. The inhibitions of false shame, the frozen voice of shyness, the truculent self-assertion which is the visible top of the iceberg of self-distrust, were absent. John Adams was himself.

Now at last the Atlas of the American Revolution, whose powerful emotion, marshaled argument, and extraordinary command of language had literally lifted the members from their seats time and again in the revolution Congress, stood face to face, as symbol of his people, with the King who had for long been symbol of their oppression. John Adams's magnetic power, his dignity, his feeling, were turned full onto that one man, the King. No wonder that under that great electric discharge the King became greater than himself.

Mulling it over afterwards with Abigail, savoring the full flavor of that meeting, it seemed to John most amazing of all that the King had behaved so well.

John Adams addressed George III in words which he had carefully prepared. "The appointment of a Minister from the United States to your Majesty's Court will form an epoch in the history of England and America. I think myself more fortunate than all my fellow-subjects in having the distinguished honor to be the first to stand in your Majesty's royal presence in a diplomatic character. I shall esteem myself the happiest of men if I can be instrumental in recommending my country more and more to your Majesty's royal benevolence, and of restoring an entire esteem, confidence, and affection, or in better words, the old good-nature and the old good-humor, between people who, though separated by an ocean, and under different governments, have the same language, a similar religion, and kindred blood.[2] . . .

"The King listened to every word I said with dignity, but with obvious emotion," said John Adams, "I felt more than I could express. Whether it was my visible agitation that touched him, or whether it was the nature of the interview, I cannot say. But he was much affected. Presently he answered me with more tremor than I had spoken with, and said — 'Sir, the circumstances of this audience are so extraordinary, the language you

have just used is so extremely proper — your feelings so justly
adapted to the occasion, — that I must say I not only receive with
pleasure the assurance of the friendly disposition of the United
States, but that I am very glad the choice has fallen upon you
to be their minister. I wish you, Sir, to believe — and I wish it to
be understood in America — that I have done nothing in the late
contest but what I thought myself indispensably bound to do by
the duty which I owed to my people. I will be very frank with
you. I was the last to consent to the separation. But the separation
having been made, and having become inevitable, I have always
said, as I say now, that I would be the first to meet the friendship of the United States as an independent power. The moment
I see such sentiments and language as yours prevail, and a disposition to give this country the preference, that moment I shall
say — let the circumstances of language, religion and blood have
their natural and full effect.' These were the King's exact words
as nearly as I can remember them."

"He talks of blood and language," said Abigail, "but he's a
German. Did he speak with a thick German accent?"

"No. His pronunciation is as distinct as ever I heard. Emotion
made him speak slowly, and he hesitated some time between his
periods. I was no less moved than he. When he had done, we
waited to recollect ourselves. Then the King asked me if I came
last from France, and when I said I did then he put on a change
of manner and an air of familiarity and jest, and said — 'There's
an opinion among some people that you are not the most attached
of all your countrymen to the manners of France!' I didn't quite
like it!" said John Adams to Abigail. "Between ourselves, I
thought it an indiscretion. It was out of keeping with the dignity
of the rest. I was a little embarrassed. Trying to reply in a light
enough tone to match his, I none the less said, 'That opinion, Sir,
is not mistaken. I must avow to your Majesty that I have no attachment but to my own country.' The King replied as quick as
lightning, 'An honest man will never have any other!' " [3]

The King then murmured a word or two to the Secretary of
State, and bowed dismissal. Mr. Adams retreated backward according to etiquette, and went his way.

The Master of Ceremonies joined him as he issued from the door of the King's closet, and escorted him through the crowded apartments to his carriage, servants roaring out before them "like thunder," "Mr. Adams's servants! Mr. Adams's carriage!"

The great hour had come and gone, and was folded up into time past. But it had not been inauspicious.

Three days later John Adams very much enjoyed his first full day at court, at the King's Birthday Levee, June 4th. At that levee, it was the King's custom to speak first to the foreign ministers, and he had made himself not only pleasant but human. "My father observed," said Nabby, "that he had never heard anything like conversation at Court before. One of the Ambassadors who had attended at the French Court for thirty years said Monsieur the King's brother had asked every time he had been to Court, which was generally every Tuesday, 'Have you come from Paris to-day?' and no other question. But George III conversed a quarter of an hour with the Spanish Minister upon music, of which he said he was passionately fond, especially Handel's music. He respected the memory of Handel, for he owed to him the greatest happiness of his life, and observed that Handel had said of him when young, 'that young man will preserve my music.' " [4]

There was every reason to reflect with a certain deep satisfaction on the parting compliment of the Count de Vergennes when Mr. Adams took leave at Versailles — "It is a great thing to be the first ambassador from your country to the country you spring from! It is a mark!" [5]

On June 9th John Adams was presented in private audience to the Queen, and made her a noble speech, recommending to her attention "a rising empire and an infant virgin world. Another Europe, madam, is rising in America. . . . It will in future ages be the glory of these kingdoms to have peopled that country." He begged her indulgence to "a person who is indeed unqualified for courts and who owes his elevation to the distinguished honor of standing before your Majesty, not to any circumstances of illustrious birth, fortune or abilities, but merely to an ardent devotion to his native country, and some little industry and perseverance in her service." [6]

But the Queen of England was no Abigail Adams. Neither her mastery of the English language nor her mental equipment was equal to comprehending Mr. Adams's majestic periods. She replied with the formula she had learned by rote for all foreign ambassadors. "Sir, I thank you for your civility to me and my family, and I am glad to see you in this country." Then she "very politely" inquired whether he had got a house yet. John Adams might have replied that that was a matter he was leaving to his wife.

Two days later it was Abigail's turn to be stared at, not in private presentation, but when the Queen held a Circle. That happened on Thursdays. "Last Thursday Colonel Smith was presented at Court," she wrote her sister, "and tomorrow my ladyship and your niece make our compliments. There is no other presentation in Europe in which I shall feel so much as in this."

The Queen's Drawing-room really was a circle. The day Abigail went two hundred people, ladies and gentlemen, were arranged around the walls of a large reception room in St. James's Palace. There was no order of precedence, people stood as they came. At two o'clock a bugle announced the approach of royalty, and the King and Queen and their entourage entered the door. At the door they divided, the King and his gentlemen going round the room to the right, and the Queen and her ladies going round to the left. "Only think of the task!" said Abigail with sympathy, "the royal family have to go round to every person, and find small talk enough to speak to all of them!" She noticed that they very prudently spoke in a whisper, so that only the person next you can hear what is said. But the effect of this slow, whispering progress was anything but lively. Who spoke of the gaiety of courts? The only entertainment to be found was watching the main actors as they came round, and — if a court habitué — the comparative length and graciousness of their pauses. "The King is a personable man," said Abigail, although she did not like the effect of his red face and white eyebrows. George III was this year forty-seven years old, three years younger than John Adams.

Mrs. Adams came off very well. When the King got to her, Lord Onslow, the gentleman in waiting, presented her, saying simply, "Mrs. Adams." "Upon which I drew off my right-hand

glove, and his Majesty saluted my left cheek. He then asked me
if I had taken a walk to-day. I could have told His Majesty,"
remarked Mrs. Adams, "that I had been all the morning preparing to wait upon him; but I replied, 'No, Sire.' The answer
seemed to surprise the King, 'Why, don't you love walking?'
says he. I answered that I was rather indolent in that respect. He
then bowed and passed on." More than two hours after this it
came to her turn to be presented to the Queen. Standing in
silent tedium and increasing fatigue on aching feet, Mrs. Adams
had long exhausted every detail of the Queen's appearance. Her
dress was purple and silver. She resembled the King in having a
red face and light eyebrows, but "she is not well-shaped nor
handsome." Charlotte was in fact a dumpy figure, made worse
by excessive childbearing. She had at this time borne fourteen
of her ultimate nineteen children. Even royal portrait painters,
Benjamin West for one, trying their best to flatter, could not
disguise her wide froglike mouth, though they did refine her
pug nose out of knowledge. Perhaps there was something in
Mrs. Adams's appraising gaze which was uncourtier-like. Perhaps
Charlotte was uncomfortably conscious of being looked at as a
woman rather than a Queen. Or perhaps — product as she was of
an insignificant German court — her snobbishness resented having to receive among duchesses the daughter of a mere "dissenting parson." Whatever it was, the two women disliked each other
at sight. "The Queen was evidently embarrassed when I was presented to her. I had disagreeable feelings too. She however said,
'Mrs. Adams, have you got into your house? Pray how do you
like the situation?'"[7] As far as we know, her duty thus accomplished, the Queen never spoke to Mrs. Adams again.

"The drawing-room at St. James's!" exclaimed Mrs. Adams in
an exasperated moment. "Never again would I set my foot there
if the etiquette of my country did not require it! I know I am
looked down on with a sovereign pride. The smile of royalty is
bestowed as a mighty boon. As such, however, I cannot receive
it. I know it is due to my country, and I consider myself as com-
plimenting the power before which I appear as much as I am
complimented by being noticed by it."[8]

And at a later day, when England was in imminent danger of invasion by Napoleon, Mrs. Adams, though warmly for England, reflected that there would be one compensation in England's disaster. It would bring the Queen down to the dust. "Humiliation for Charlotte is no sorrow for me. She richly deserves her full portion for the contempt and scorn which she took pains to discover."

Others, however, were more pleasant. Mrs. Adams liked the Princesses. Even at the presentation circle, the Princess Royal and Princess Augusta, who followed behind their mother, dressed in black and silver, paused to speak to the attractive American ladies with real friendliness. The Princess Royal, who was probably tired to death herself — not only of that particular Circle but of the whole tiresome routine of her life — "looked compassionate, and asked me if I was not much fatigued, and observed that it was a very full Drawing-room." The Prince of Wales, seen at later Drawing-rooms, was admired by the American ladies as a handsome man, if, Mrs. Adams modified, he had not sacrificed so much to Bacchus! The Prince's manners were graceful and ingratiating, and he took pains to pay due attention to the foreign ministers and their appendages. But he did not think it his duty to speak to everyone in the room. He followed his pleasure. Nabby got fun out of the dullness of one Drawing-room watching the vain efforts of a lady near her, "Lady C," who made herself conspicuous by extreme anxiety to have her daughter spoken to by the Prince. It was no good. The Prince stood and conversed an hour next to her with the lovely and well-bred Lady Stourmont,* but walked away at last serenely blind to the existence of Miss C. Of such small poisoned darts were the tragedies of court life made. Abigail despised it from beginning to end. "I own I never felt myself in a more contemptible situation than when I stood four hours together for a gracious smile from majesty, a witness to the anxious solicitude of those around me for the same . . . I however had a more dignified honor for his Majesty *deigned to salute me*." [9]

The King's compliment was partly one to her appearance.

* Wife of Lord Stourmont.

Mrs. Adams in her wide-hooped white gown with lilac bows could bear being stared at. Her mirror had assured her of it. "My head is dressed for St. James's and it looks, in my opinion, very tasty." [10] But an independent and sympathetic witness was alongside, a young American, former aide to Washington, named Colonel William Smith (no relation). "Mrs. Adams and Miss were presented at Court this day and behaved to a charm," he wrote back to America. "Mr. Adams fully answers your and Mr. Jay's account of him. The ladies of his family do honor to this country. . . . I attended them to the Queen's Drawing-Room and free from partiality assert that they were fully equal to any there. As for the young lady — she is more than painters can express or youthful poets fancy when they love." [11]

*   *   *   *   *

Abigail Adams might have answered the Queen — probably did — that she had found a house, and that she did indeed like the situation of it. It was in Grosvenor Square, "one of the finest squares in London." At Auteuil they had the Bois; here they had Hyde Park — which they thought resembled Boston Common, only larger, with more trees about. It would be very nice and handy for walking or, preferably, driving. And when they drove farther afield, there were fresh delights. The flowery pageant of England in summer overwhelmed sight and scent. "All the villages that I have seen round London are just gardens!" [12] Not only was it beyond compare lovelier than France, but even America — even Braintree — had to take a back seat. "But give us time!"

Most of the gentry had retired to their country seats for the hot weather, and, fashionably speaking, London was now a desert. The King and Queen were at Kew, or Windsor, whence they came in to St. James's every fortnight for levees or Drawing-rooms. Most of these affairs were very thinly attended during the summer, but the King seemed unable to disentangle himself from the habit. Sometimes the royal family could be encountered riding in the Park with retinue — the King in his Windsor uniform of blue and gold, the Queen in black hat and cloak, the Princess

Royal, Princess Augusta, Princess Elizabeth, Princess Mary, Princess Sophia, all on horseback in white muslin polaineses and white chip hats with white feathers, all flowing, floating, blowing — surely their magical appearance expressed a temporary happiness!

But, however bravely they might ride by, back in the seclusion of their dull palace life they were not a happy family. Abigail was called on by the foreign ministers and their ladies, by the Countess of Effingham, one of the Queen's ladies, by Miss this and Lady that, and soon learned the current talk. The Prince of Wales was dissipated. Reckless extravagance. Debts. The King behaved harshly. And the Prince, even before he was twenty-one, had publicly appeared in the Opposition. The Prince said his father had hated him ever since he was seven years old.[18] The Princesses thought their mother hated them.

George III would have been shocked at the charge that he hated his son, or that he and the Queen were dominating their children, taking the life out of them. Why, he loved children, all and any children! And indeed it was a charming sight at the Children's Ball at Buckingham Palace to see the King fussing over his little guests — charmed with their dancing — warning them against chilling their little stomachs with cold drinks. . . .

Yes, it was not until the Prince was seven years old that he had noticed a horrid change in his father's feeling. Not until he grew up that he named it. Domestic miseries such as these soured Charlotte's expression and coarsened her manners to those whom she had no reason to conciliate. This Queen, knowing so well what pregnancy meant, could keep Mrs. Siddons standing to read a play, when far gone with child, until she fainted, sooner than allow an actress to be seated in her royal presence.

Mrs. Siddons was pregnant when Abigail first saw her act. This prevented her from "exerting that force of passion and energy of action which have rendered her so justly celebrated," but she had contrived her dress very neatly to disguise her situation, and "chose only those tragedies where little exertion was necessary such as Shakespeare's *Othello*." Although already the mother of several children, Mrs. Siddons did not look more than twenty-five.

Tall, commanding, majestic, she was supreme in tragedy. Her greatest part by public acclaim was Lady Macbeth. But Shakespeare, brought to overpowering life by the genius of Mrs. Siddons, was rather a dose. "Much of Shakespeare's language is so uncouth that it sounds rash," Abigail confided to her sisters. "He has beauties which are not equalled. But I should suppose that they might be rendered much more agreeable for the stage by alterations. I saw Mrs. Siddons a few evenings ago in *Macbeth*, a play, you recollect, full of horror. She supported her part with great propriety, but she is too great to be put in so detestable a character." [14] Abigail Adams preferred her as Matilda in *The Carmelite*, and looked forward to seeing her in "her most pathetic characters in *Venice Preserved* and *The Fatal Marriage.*"

The second of the great Handel Festivals instituted annually by the King took place soon after the Adamses' arrival in June, before the summer migration of society.

"The most powerful effect of music I ever experienced," said Mrs. Adams, "was at Westminster Abbey, the celebration of Handel's music . . . five days set apart for the different performances. I was at the piece called *The Messiah*. When it came to that part the Hallelujah, the whole audience rose and all the musicians, every person uncovered. : . . I could scarcely believe myself an inhabitant of earth. I was one continued shudder from the beginning to the end of the performance." [15]

*   *   *   *   *

With society again in full swing, Mrs. Adams found herself saddled with the difficult job of maintaining the dignity of the new American embassy on insufficient funds. And she succeeded in doing it. Her first dinner, a *sine qua non* to the Diplomatic Corps, was graced by a timely present from an American captain of a gigantic turtle, considered a great luxury, which provided an ample and thoroughly American repast. Mrs. Adams's standards of a good dinner were far from stingy. And her occasional at-home days, on the London pattern, were conducted with quiet elegance. Mrs. Adams, however, despised the London pattern.

Almost everybody held receiving days and routs, some on the

weekly at-home day, some by special invitation for an evening. "Card-tables were the chief occupation." It bored Abigail Adams. Rooms were so crowded that not half the company could sit at once. The only agreeable thing, she thought, was that you might go away when you chose without disturbing anybody. You might not start conversation with anyone, even if you met them three times a week, without being specially introduced. "Yet this," said Abigail, fresh from conversable France, "is called *society* and *polite life!*" [16]

"I was at a stupid rout at the Swedish Minister's last evening," she described to her sister, "got home about twelve. There were about two hundred persons. Three large rooms full of card-tables. The moment the ceremony of courtseying is past the lady of the house asks you, 'Pray, what is your game? Whist, cribbage, or commerce?' — and then to hunt a set! The lady and her daughter last evening were almost fatigued to death . . . toiling at pleasure for seven hours, in which time they scarcely sat down. I went with a determination not to play but could not get off. So I was set down to a table with three perfect strangers, and the lady against me stated the game at half-a-guinea apiece. I thought it full high; but I knew she designed to win so I said no more, but expected to lose. It happened otherwise however," said Mrs. Adams with dry satisfaction, "I won four games of her. Luck rather than skill, though I have usually been fortunate."

A ball at the French Ambassador's was more fun, more the kind of real gaiety Mrs. Adams would have liked to provide, though her good taste warned her that such display would have been out of key for the representatives of a new country — and a democracy at that — even if they could have afforded it. This Ambassador, Abigail observed, had twenty thousand guineas allowed him to furnish his house, and an annual salary of ten thousand more. With such resources he could attract the very cream of smart society. "The Prince of Wales came about eleven o'clock. Mrs. Fitzherbert was also present. She appears with him in all public parties, and he avows his marriage wherever he dares." The light from the lusters was more favorable to beauty than daylight, and the dresses were much prettier than the huge-hooped regulation court dress which took up such a lot of room in dancing. Here one small hoop was all, or even no hoops. And "the prettiest girls in England" looked like Dresden china shepherdesses come to life, hats and all. Abigail's prevailing color this time was sapphire blue, Nabby's was rose pink. But poor Nabby had the London cold, and couldn't have any fun, so her mother — who was enjoying herself immensely — had to take her away at one o'clock and miss supper.

Was Nabby's heart really broken by an inconstant lover? Would she return anon to Boston and marry him, and find him — God forbid — inconstant still? Stately and handsome, more like a princess than the King's dumpy daughters, she moved through the minuets and the country dances, indifferent to her partners and surroundings.

Seeing Mrs. Fitzherbert was the high point of the evening. "It seems this amorous Prince," Abigail Adams eagerly narrated to Mary, "has been for two years violently in love with a widow lady near forty years of age. As she is said to be a lady of virtuous character she avoided him . . . and finding that he could not bring her to his terms, it is said and believed, that he has married the lady. . . . She now appears with him at the opera, rides in his carriage with her servants behind it. He is three times a day at her house. . . . In the eye of heaven the marriage may be valid, but the law of the land annuls it, she can never be Queen or the children legitimate. . . . They say his toast is 'fat, fair and forty'!" [17]

The rumor of this secret marriage had just got about, and Abigail Adams, after a visit to court, noted gleefully, "The Royal family appeared much out of spirits yesterday . . . the nation are all in a ferment, though they hardly dare speak loud." [18]

When in April a new play, *The School for Scandal*, appeared at Covent Garden Theatre, Mrs. Adams remarked that "tho it is one of the best modern plays that has appeared upon the stage," the title was really almost too appropriate. "Scandal is the forte of this nation, and a school in which they have arrived at great experience, that and lying make the greater part of their daily publications, as their numerous Gazettes fully testify!" [19]

Mrs. Adams was not merely referring to society gossip but to the more dangerous and more personal scandal which daily attacked her husband and her country.

Underneath the glittering surface of society's correct behavior to the American Minister and his wife, strong anti-American currents were flowing. All the soreness of a proud country defeated was in them. More dangerous still was the determination of a certain section of the public not to accept the defeat. Both feelings were headed up and fanned on by the refugees from America — the Tories, as Abigail continued to call them — who had confidently expected to go home again in triumph. These people, who included old friends and connections like Jonathan Sewall, bitterly resented the creation of an American legation. They hoped the American Minister would not be received at court, or, if received, at least on some less honorable footing than that of a "real" foreign power. And the full honors accorded John Adams caused the refugees at once to "spit forth their venom," as Abigail made no bones about expressing it. The newssheets of an exceedingly scurrilous period continued to pour forth attack after attack. Mrs. Adams shared to the full her husband's difficulties, and understood them well.

Mr. Adams's task was twofold. One part of it was to obtain a treaty of commerce with Great Britain, in conjunction with Mr. Jefferson. The second, and more delicate negotiation, was to obtain the implementing of the peace treaty.

"The civil and polite reception given to the American Minister and his family from the Court does not ensure to America justice in other respects," Abigail wrote her Uncle Isaac.[20] And to her sister she explained clearly — "The immense debt, due from the mercantile part of America to this country sours this people beyond measure, and greatly distresses thousands who never were nor ever will be politicians — the manufacturers who supplied the merchants. I think our countrymen greatly to blame. . . . It makes the path very difficult for negotiation.[21] The Marquis of Carmarthen and Mr. Pitt appear to possess the most liberal ideas with respect to us of any part of the ministry."

Progress was extremely slow but not all their business was abortive. The Ambassador from Portugal was already a friend of

Mr. Adams, and had been closeted with him frequently to some purpose. Abigail wrote her son John Quincy, "Your sister has written you so many pages that I suppose she has not left me anything to write to you, but as I am very rarely honored with a sight of any of them I shall venture to inform you that Mr. Jefferson is here from Paris and that the Treaty with Portugal will be completed in a few days." [22]

After a stay of seven weeks, enjoyed in spite of his dislike for the court, Mr. Jefferson returned to Paris, to his house on the Champs-Elysées, his daughter in her aristocratic convent, his debt-ridden grandeur, and M. de Vergennes's insinuating "but."

Mrs. Adams was getting a good stiff training as a public character. Certainly she had read attacks on her husband before. There had been plenty in America, but then she herself had been living a retired and private life. She had not had to go to a party or royal drawing room or fashionable rout and know that everyone there had just read the paper that morning, and that the sizzling criticism was very likely present in the mind of her neighbor.

But if Grandmother Quincy's training had given her a fine start in social poise and correct behavior, and Boston society had provided good practice, her time in France had furnished a superlative finishing course.

Fulfilling her duties as ambassador's wife, Mrs. Adams presented several American ladies at court, among them the magnificent Mrs. Bingham, "and I own I felt not a little proud of her." She had got her dress in Paris, and her loveliness was really stunning. "The various whispers which I heard around me, and the pressing of the ladies to get a sight of her, must have added an atom to the old score, for [the Queen] could not but see how attractive she was. 'Is she an American, is she an American?' buzzed everywhere. 'You have,' said an English lord to me, 'one of the finest ladies to present that I ever saw.' " And again there was the lovely Miss Hamilton of Philadelphia, "an heiress, with sweet and modest manners." "The Emperor's Ambassador whispered your Pappa, 'Sir, your country produces exceeding fine women!' " [23]

Indeed, Mr. Jefferson's presentation was the only failure. One might compare English and French manners, as he did, to the disadvantage of the English. Yet, Abigail Adams confessed to Aunt Elizabeth, "on many accounts I like this Country best and have in my heart a greater fondness for it." [24] That is the statement of a happy and confident woman, one who found herself in command of the situation, neither uneasy nor at a loss. And she gave her husband, in Grosvenor Square as in Boston, the continual refreshment of a happy home.

Abigail's children were a great source of her happiness. The two eldest seemed perfection itself, and their uncommon devotion to each other was one of their charms. The brother and sister exchanged a regular journal of their thoughts and doings. John Quincy was absorbed in his readjustment to American ways in the simple household of Uncle and Aunt Shaw at Haverhill, where he was tutoring for Harvard under Uncle Shaw, and making reacquaintance with his brothers and cousins. Bent on doing a year's study in a few months, he had no time for his father's old pastime of gallanting the girls.

Nabby's many, many pages contained painfully intellectual comment on the passing scene, the ridiculous habits of courts, and the elaborate elegance of English country houses, her own activities of various kinds, the compliments of Mr. Jefferson; but hints of something else crept in more and more frequently between the lines.

The hour soon came when some subtle thawing in Miss Adams's manner gave Smith a welcome signal, he made some direct questions and received satisfactory answers. "I perceived all at once upon a day," wrote Abigail to her son, "a dejection dispelled, a brightness of countenance and a lightness of heart" in your sister, "and in the evening a gentleman asked permission to attend us to the theatre." The request was in itself a declaration of successful suit, and when they returned late, the Colonel placed in Mrs. Adams's hands, "with much emotion," a bunch of testimonials to himself as to character, courage, and so on, obtained from the generals under whom he had served — documents which the Colonel repeatedly relied on through life with naïve and unshaken faith to get him out of scrapes or to make his fortune. In

this case they were to be presented to John Adams in lieu of statements of income, real estate, and expectations.

The engagement was cheerfully accepted by both Mr. and Mrs.
Adams. After all, the chief thing was a daughter's happiness. And
she did seem happy. "I think she must feel a calmness and serenity
in her present connection which she never before experienced. I
am sure it has relieved my mind from a weight which has hung
heavy upon it for more than two years." [25]

Abigail Adams wrote to her son — "When I used to visit your
chamber at Auteuil and converse with you and mutually express
our anxiety with respect to future events, neither of us dreamt of
what has now taken place. You was then frequently witness to a
regard and attachment which repeated proofs of neglect, finally
dissolved. Instability of conduct first produced doubt and apprehension which in silence she suffered. Time and reflection dispelled
the mist and illusion and has united her to a gentleman of a very
different character. . . . And so, my dear son, your sister is
really and bona fide married, as fast as the Bishop and a Clerk could
tie them, in the ceremony of the Church of England with all its
absurdities about it — that through necessity," added the New
England parson's daughter acidly, "for you know that such is the
liberality of this enlightened country that the dissenting clergy
are not permitted to perform marriages!" [26]

It was a consolation to Mrs. Adams, however, that the ceremony
was performed by the Bishop of Asaph. This distinguished divine
had been an outspoken supporter of the cause of American independence, and had gone out of his way to welcome the American
Minister. He had introduced his wife and daughter to Mrs. Adams,
with the happiest results. "Truly well-bred," said Mrs. Adams,
measuring them by her yardstick of Grandma Quincy and the
Marquise, "a friendship and acquaintance which I should like to
cultivate." They wore well. Above all, the Bishop — whose very
office made him suspect to a New England nonconformist —"justly
deserves the character of a liberal man." [27] Such conclusions were
in themselves broadening to the mind.

But the disabilities which in England followed dissent from the

Established Church could not fail to rankle in Abigail's mind. "The dissenting clergy in this country," she had written to her Aunt Elizabeth, "appear a very different set of men from those which inhabit ours. They are cramped, condemned and degraded. They have not that independent appearance and that consciousness of their own worth which gives an air of dignity to the whole deportment. Dr. Price (for instance) notwithstanding his literary fame and his great abilities, appears like a man who has been browbeaten." [28]

So with all the mumbo jumbo — to Abigail's mind — of the Established Church, and the consoling dignity of the Bishop of Asaph, there took place a reversal of the system by which an Abigail Smith had become an Abigail Adams. Now an Abigail Adams became an Abigail Smith.

After a short honeymoon, Colonel and Mrs. William Stephen Smith set up housekeeping on Wimpole Street. Aunt Betsy Shaw, whose charm was of the heart and deepened with the years,* wrote her niece from Haverhill, "I would wish you, for your own comfort, to be a most obliging wife," and "Mr. Shaw joins me in wishing you 'health, long life, long youth, long pleasure, and a friend.' "

*   *   *   *   *

On April 30th, 1787, Abigail Adams, herself only forty-three years old, became a grandmother. Nabby's little son was christened William Steuben, after his father and his father's friend. The proud grandmother, wrote to her son John Quincy — "You became an Uncle on the end day of April. Your nephew has the brow of his grandpappa and the shape and form of his father. Colonel Smith set off for Lisbon (on a mission to Spain and Portugal) as soon as he thought it safe to leave your sister." And so excellently had Abigail entered into the relationship of mother-in-law that she unaffectedly added, "We felt his absence

---

* Presently, on the very day of the funeral of one husband, she was to be asked in marriage by another, in a country teeming with maiden aunts.

not a little, he was not only the sensible rational companion but the enlivener of all our scenes and the soul of our little parties." [29]

The marriage seemed in every way satisfactory. True, Nabby had never given William Smith the shy ardor she had offered Royall Tyler. But there are many natures in which, if that first love is thwarted, something in them is forever frozen. Nabby, cooled and tutored in self-possession by the time she met her husband, could never again give herself without reserve. But he took it for granted that she loved him to capacity, and that no woman could have loved him more. Her mother was pleased to see how she lived on his letters while he was abroad, and what good long lively affectionate letters they were. As they sat one warm day together in Hyde Park, the daughter said to the mother, "This is our first separation, and I pray it may be the last!" The baby filled up full the cup of joy, put the final lid on old sorrow.

Abigail Adams, enchanted with her first grandchild, found room in her heart that summer to adopt another. "I have had for a fortnight a little daughter of Mr. Jefferson's," she wrote in July, "who arrived here with a young Negro girl, her servant, from Virginia. Mr. Jefferson wrote me some months ago that he expected them, and desired me to receive them. I did so and was amply repaid for my trouble. A finer child of her age I never saw. So mature and understanding, so much sensibility, united, are rarely met with. I grew so fond of her, and she was so much attached to me, that when Mr. Jefferson sent for her, they were obliged to force the little creature away. She is but eight years old. She would sit sometimes and describe to me the parting with her aunt who brought her up and the love she had for her little cousins, till the tears would stream down her cheeks; and how I had been her friend and she loved me. Her papa would break her heart by making her go again. She clung round me so that I could not help shedding a tear at parting with her. She was the favorite of everyone in the house. I regret that such fine spirits must be spent in the walls of a convent. She is a beautiful girl, too." [30]

Abigail looked again at the date of her letter — July 16th. Why surely that must be Commencement Day. In Harvard Yard the gay crowds would be gathering. The Doctors would march in procession in their scarlet gowns, and the graduates, perhaps thirty of them, in their black gowns, carrying their mortarboards until the great moment when they were capped. John Quincy Adams would be one of them. His name would be read out in the assembly, as his father's had been before him. And like his father, he would deliver an oration. The mother's heart trembled. To see and hear her son on his great day was her right and his. Ah, these sep.rations were unnatural, not to be borne.

"God willing, once I set my foot on American ground," she wrote her son, "not all the embassies in Europe consolidated into one shall tempt me again to quit it. I do not wonder at your longing to return, and I have many inducements which you had not, — not one single one to remain here.

"My dear lads, you know that we shall return poor, but at the same time you know what have been the services your father has rendered his country . . . his honor and his integrity shall be your inheritance. If we can get you all through college the world is all before you and providence your guide." [31]

Well, John Quincy was through college, and all the concern he had caused his parents so far was that he worked too hard. His health suffered from his incessant drive. But he felt especially obligated not only to his parents, but to the college authorities, who in recognition of his father's public services refused to accept any fee for his tuition. He graduated Phi Beta Kappa. His oration was obtained by the newspapers and printed in the public press. And at the same time he had avoided the high-hat manners which his father and mother had rather dreaded for him. He was well-liked by his fellow students.

And now what next? That was a constant subject of discussion between John and Abigail.

John Adams had written to their cousin and agent, Cotton Tufts. "A year will soon be about, and what are we to do with John? What lawyer shall we desire to take him, in town or country? (expenses, etc.) Shall I come home and take all my boys into my own office? I was once thought to have a tolerable knack at making lawyers." [32]

Johnny wrote promptly to his father — "Should you return home next spring, and be yourself at leisure to instruct me, I would certainly prefer it to studying elsewhere. But if you are still detained in Europe, I should wish to live in some place where there might be society sufficient for relaxation at times, but not enough to encourage dissipation."

Yes, to go home in the spring was their other chief concern. In December, John Adams at last received permission from Congress to go home any time after February 24th. It was accompanied by a resolution of praise. "Resolved, that Congress entertain a high sense of the services which Mr. Adams has rendered to the United States in the various important trusts which they have from time to time committed to him; and that the thanks of Congress be presented to him for the patriotism, perseverance, integrity, and diligence with which he hath ably and faithfully served his country." [33]

Foreign Secretary John Jay's personal word of heartfelt sincerity was almost equally valued — "You have been in a situation that required much circumspection. I think you have acquitted yourself in a manner that does you honor." [34]

*   *   *   *   *

Coming in from his last conference at Whitehall, the February sleet sweeping along the square and making the bare trees in the center garden almost invisible from the windows, he said to his wife:

"Guess what Lord Carmarthen's parting words were, my dear!"

Abigail poured his tea, while he hitched his chair a little nearer to the glowing coal fire.

"Something noncommittal, cold and polite!" she guessed.

"Well, I thought I knew him," said John, "but he surprised even me. His Lordship thought it proper to express a wish *that this country had some sort of a treaty of commerce with the United States of America!*"

Abigail threw up her hands. "Is it possible?"

"So!" said John Adams. "I remained for the moment speechless, and he immediately very quickly said, 'I presume, Mr. Adams that the States will all immediately adopt the new Constitution. I have read it with pleasure. It is very well drawn up.' So all this oracular utterance was to signify to me what has all along been insinuated, that there is not as yet any national government, but that as soon as there shall be one, the British Court will treat with it." [35]

News of ratification by Delaware, Pennsylvania, and New Jersey had already reached England.

Abigail's public spirit was not dormant. Up to the last John Adams was pressing John Jay, even with exasperation, for formal letters of recall, never did obtain them (not Jay's fault), and for the want of them was forced to make a last-moment trip to Holland to take ceremonious leave in person, still acting as American Minister to the Dutch Court.

"What sins I've done that I must pay for by this winter journey I know not!" he grumbled.

But Mr. Jefferson welcomed his necessity, and urged on him a job of retrieving American credit from some more private difficulties created by an American agent. Bankruptcy was again threatening the new U. S. currency. And when her husband had gone, Abigail bethought herself why not get a new loan for the United States from Holland while he was about it? It was a good chance. No harm in trying. John Adams had already proved over and over again his unique skill in dealing with the Dutch financiers. She wrote to Thomas Jefferson in Paris urging her idea that John try to obtain a new loan for the United States from Holland, and asking his co-operation. He was convinced by her plea, and met John Adams at The Hague and they went together to Amsterdam.

John wrote thence to Abigail Adams — "Well, ma'am, you have put off your own journey! If you should meet souwesters on the coast of America and have your voyage prolonged three weeks by it, *remember it is all your own intrigue which has forced me to this loan.* I suppose you will boast of it as a great public service. . . . I think I shall be forced, to open an additional loan. At least, that is Mr. Jefferson's opinion." [36]

Money enough was obtained in this new loan to meet the United States debts and preserve credit for two years at least, till the new government should have time to collect revenue from taxes.

John Adams's farewell interview with the King of England was as friendly as their personal intercourse had always been. A bluff honesty and an honest patriotism were two qualities which John Adams and George III had in common. The official sentences interchanged, the King fell into chitchat about Mr. Adams's family — how many children were left behind in America, what were they doing, and what was the form of education in Massachusetts? Domestic details were always dear to the King's heart. It was no pretense. And if his friendly talk became at times a little garrulous, it was appreciated by his hearer. The King was at all times a great gentleman. The Queen, as Mrs. Adams would dryly comment in her private circle only, was never a great lady.

John Adams, bent on the courteous, made three attempts to do his official duty by the Queen, but she detested them both as proud colonial upstarts; he had overwhelmed her at their first meeting. "The Queen was indisposed." Yet such an excuse could always be valid with a lady forever in the family way.

As preparations to depart went briskly forward in Grosvenor Square, the English Parliament seemed to be making preparations for a war. But what war? With whom? "The world can find no enemy nor object." [37] Habit suggested France.

"In the general flame which threatens Europe," wrote Abigail Adams, "I hope and pray our own country may have wisdom sufficient to keep out of the fire. I am sure she has been sufficiently a burnt child." [38]

Mr. and Mrs. Adams embarked on April 20th, 1788, from Cowes for Boston. Colonel and Mrs. Smith embarked a few days later from Falmouth for New York, but they got home first.

This, Abigail's last voyage, was horrid. She missed her little grandson acutely — why couldn't they sail on the same vessel? "O what a relief would his sportive little pranks have been to me in the tedious hours! I took only a few books and a little sewing, all of which were exhausted in one week."

As for her servants, they kept her busy taking care of them. "Briesler has been much the sickest person on board ship. I expected him to have been half nurse, instead of which he has needed constant nursing." While as for Esther — "yesterday at five she had a daughter, a poor little starveling, but with special lungs. I had for the first time in my life to dress the little animal, who looked buried in its clothes. I hope and pray I may never again go to sea!" [39]

So ends ambassadorship.

But in her heart there is a deep contentment. She and her husband have been together, are still together, never more to be parted — he has sworn — by anything but Death. And the ship is turned homeward; every tossing, tedious day is one day nearer.

But nearer what, my dear? Does she realize how far away she has traveled in spirit from the narrow walls of her cottage? She rose easily to her high place. But how will she step down again? Will she not feel the jar?

Her husband, with worldly wisdom, tried to prepare her mind, in anxious tenderness and candor. But she reassured him.

"I have learned to know the world and its value. I have seen high life. I have witnessed the luxury and pomp of state, the power of riches and the influence of titles. Notwithstanding this I feel that I can return to my little cottage and be happier than here; and if we have not wealth, we have what is better — integrity." [40]

X I

America Again

A BIGAIL was not actually returning to her cottage. She was going to live in the Vassall House, the very house which might have been her daughter's married home. Royall Tyler had not fully completed the purchase when the news of Nabby's marriage to another set all his plans awry. So the Vassall House came again into the market, and John Adams instructed his agent, Dr. Tufts, to purchase it for him in the autumn of '87.

The Vassall House was the most impressive in Braintree after Colonel Quincy's, and its land was equally extensive. Abigail was pleased at the purchase, and plunged into house decorating at long distance with zest. "Painting both within and without I shd be glad to have completed as soon as possible in the spring, the East lower room to be painted what is called a French grey and as the furniture is red [the Louis XVth chairs, always called "the Lafayette chairs," bought and used at Auteuil, were upholstered in red damask], a paper conformable will look best. The chamber over it will have green furniture and may be in the same manner made uniform by a paper green and white."

The original John Vassall had been a sugar planter in the West Indies, and, permanently dazzled by the tropic sun, had wanted a dim house of soothing shadows. It was to seem at first sight to Mrs. Adams dark and cramped. "It feels like a wren's house!" [1] It was, however, a sturdy, well-built house, with a dignified entry and fine staircase, definitely a gentleman's mansion and not a farmer's cottage as Penns Hill had been. They set to work to think of a suitable name for it. John Adams's favorite was "Peacefield," and so he called it during his lifetime. But neighbors and subsequent generations simply called it the Adams Mansion.

The *Lucretia* made port on the anniversary of the battle of Bunker Hill. When John Quincy got word that the ship was in, he hurried from Newburyport to meet them. There was great competition for Abigail's loved presence.

The arrival home, so long dreamed of by Abigail, fulfilled her expectations in full measure; pressed down and running over. The bright New England air, the breezy joyousness of Boston with its steep streets and white-painted houses, the high honor of their welcome, and, more than all else, the eager warmth of friends and family. "The Governor * was for escorting us to Braintree in his coach-and-four, attended by his light horse; and even Braintree was for coming out to Milton Bridge to meet us, but this we could by no means assent to! Accordingly we quitted town privately, your Pappa one day and I the next," wrote Abigail to daughter Nabby on July 7th, "and we went to our worthy brother's where we remained until the next week, when our furniture came up."

The furniture came by water, was hastily lightered from the ship to the beach at Norton Quincy's farm, hauled by farm wagons to the mansion, and piled up anywhere. So there was litter and confusion all around the Vassall House when Abigail Adams arrived to survey her new home. When she got out of the chaise and had her first good look at the house, she sat down on the horse block and shed tears of disappointment. "We have come into a house not half repaired," she candidly complained to her daughter, "such a swarm of carpenters, masons, farmers, as have almost distracted me — "[2]

John Adams did not help matters by his eager attention to the outdoors and his determination to stock the farm. Says Abigail with rueful humor, "We have for my comfort six cows without a single convenience for a dairy. But you know there is no saying nay. (Sweetly do the birds sing!)" †

John Quincy Adams remained five weeks, gave his parents yeoman service in settling in, and had a wonderful time himself. It was the first glimpse he had caught of the kind of young manhood he might have had. But manhood had begun and those lost

* John Hancock.
† Summer 1788.

years of home life were part of the price John Quincy had to pay
for his exceptional education in foreign affairs.

Charles, aged eighteen, and Thomas, sixteen, were part of the
restored circle. Only Nabby was absent, away on Long Island with
her husband, and prevented by pregnancy from arduous travel.
She would certainly have come if she could for her brother's
twenty-first birthday. On July 11th John Quincy wrote in his
diary — "This day completes my twenty-first year. It emancipates
me from the yoke of parental authority, which I never felt, and
places me upon my own feet, which have not strength enough to
support me. I continue therefore in a state of dependence."

He had two more years to run of his three-year articles * with
Theophilus Parsons of Newburyport.

*   *   *   *   *

It had been twelve years since Abigail had been so near to all
her children. At least one child, if not two, and at the last three,
had been divided from her by a waste of waters. Nabby, who had
always been under her wing, was three hundred miles distant, and
approaching, far too soon after the first, the crisis of her second
childbed. Well, at least there was no sea to cross. John Adams
wrote his daughter, "Our anxiety for you has prevailed upon me to
make a great sacrifice, in consenting to your mother's journey to
Long Island." ³

On November 24th, 1788, Abigail wrote to Mary, "Mrs. Smith
safely abed before I reached her, she and my young grandson as
well as usual at this period." This second son was christened John
Adams. The young grandmother was delighted to see her other
grandson again, not yet two years old and already with a younger
brother to push him out of babyhood. "Master William is the very
image of his Mama at the same age, except that he has a greater
share of vivacity and sprightliness — the merest little trunchion that
you ever saw, very pleasant and good-humored." And she added,
toward the end of her visit, "The little boy grows finely, but I

---

* J.Q.A. was an "articled clerk" in the law office of Theophilus Parsons,
the regulation way of studying law until very recently, in both England and
America.

don't feel so fond of him yet as I do of William. Whether it is because he was born in our own house, or the first or the best tempered child I cannot determine." [4]

Nabby's married circumstances seemed all one could wish. Her husband and she had taken a house on Long Island at Jamaica, with a good garden and fifty acres of land. Mrs. Adams liked it. "I find this place a very retired one, rural and delightful. I am eleven miles from New York with a great ferry between." Colonel Smith's mother and numerous brothers and sisters were friendly and well-bred people, and seemed very fond of their new sister-in-law. One of them, Belinda, with the admired "softness of manner," was in charge in Nabby's house when Mrs. Adams arrived, taking care of her sister-in-law "with much ease and tender sisterly affection." And a lot of neighbors came to call, very genteel people, "but all of the ceremonious kind." Indeed, Nabby confided to her mother that that was the way in New York.

"When we arrived in this ntry," she said, plaintively, "I found myself in a land of st Not one I had any friendship for! I was visited in New Y fifty or sixty ladies. I returned their visits, and there the acquaintance ceases."

"What, no repeat calls? No invitations?" said her mother incredulously.

"Oh, yes, I've visited frequently with some," admitted Nabby, "but with no one shall I ever become intimate." She explained further — "There is no family where I can make a home and go with freedom and unreserve."

She saw her mother concerned on her behalf, and braced herself to be cheerful, or at least philosophical. "My home is satisfying!" she said. "It's enough for me. I have as much society as I wish in our own family." [5] That might have been true enough. There were six daughters in the family and four sons, not to mention many cousins.

Among the charming Smiths the fourth daughter, Sally, about seventeen, was graver than the rest. She was tall, had a fine figure and pretty face, "unaffected and artless, modest and composed. She wants only a little more animation to render her truly interesting." But Sally certainly made herself interesting to Mrs. Adams, for the latter goes out of her way to make excuses for her not being as lively as Belinda. "She has dignity, and that you know is inconsistent with a gay playful humor!" [6]

Little did Mrs. Adams suspect that she was favoring the good points in a future daughter-in-law.

When the time came for Mrs. Adams to make her wintry journey homeward, she carried in her heart some hidden causes of disquiet. They chased themselves round in a circle, like three blind mice. Bundled up in the stage, with her feet deep in straw, she brooded on them as the springless waggon bounced in a seasick manner over the ruts and stones of the Boston Post Road. One was that Nabby's second pregnancy had followed too close upon her first, and her strength was depleted in spite of her elastic youth. And one was that Nabby was lonely. Well, so are we all; but Nabby was lonelier than most. She had clung touchingly to her mother at parting, so reserved as she usually was.

"I wish I lived nearer you, Mama!"

"I wish so too, dear. But you will get used to it."

"No," Nabby had said, with the quiet conviction of experience. "I do not find that time lessens the painfulness of a separation!" [7]

And the last and greatest was something Abigail did not like to put into clear words to herself; not to call it dissatisfaction with her son-in-law. But why did not Colonel Smith take up an independent career?

When they had all been together in London, John and she had talked this over together, and John had there urged the young man to go on with his preliminary studies in the law; why not enter one of the Inns of Court and qualify himself for the bar? Mr. Adams had offered him time for study. But Colonel Smith had set the idea rather haughtily aside. Now John Adams had written and again ventured through his daughter to influence his son-in-law to a career of his own. "My desire would be to hear from him at the bar, which in my opinion is the most independent place on earth. A seeker of the public employment is the most unhappy of men. Mr. Smith's merit and services entitle him. . . . But I would not be dependent; I would have a resource. There can be none better than the bar." [8]

But nothing so humdrum was on the program of William Stephens Smith. He had a high opinion of his merits and capacities. He had hoped to be left behind as Minister Plenipotentiary to the Court of Great Britain. But since that had not materialized — though he had persuaded John Adams to suggest it, or at least to leave him as chargé d'affaires — well, something as good or better probably would. Had he not been aide to George Washington, who was certain to be President?

* * * * *

Washington for President was the phrase that was buzzing about wherever men met together. The new Constitution was about to be tested. The first Federal election was falling due and it was an apprehensive hour. The timbers of the ship of state had appeared all right in drydock, well and truly fashioned. But when launched on the great ocean of affairs, would she float?

The name of Washington gave assurance. To him as a person, rather than to an untried and not perfectly understood system, the ordinary people clung.

The machinery went into motion. The individual states appointed electors to the first Electoral College, and the Electoral College, numbering this time sixty-nine members from ten states,* met in February, 1789.

The Constitution required that the votes of the Electoral College should determine who should be the two Chief Executives. The largest number of votes should determine the President, the second largest number should automatically determine the Vice-President. The idea was that two men should be elected who would be equally capable of acting as the Chief Executive in case of accident to the first.

Washington received a unanimous vote, the only man in history whom everybody wanted for President. John Adams had no competitor for second place. His wife had said and thought that he was not popular — too outspoken to be popular. But what is it

---

* Rhode Island and North Carolina had not yet joined the Union by ratifying the Constitution and New York had trouble with her elections. They came in later.

to be popular? Certainly he was not, like Washington, worshiped as a demigod and a hero, but John Adams was universally trusted. Even his enemies believed in his integrity. And when it came to voting for the highest office in the state, this public trust might give a man a power rivaling that of the chief. This enormous confidence had many facets. Men relied on John Adams as a lawyer, as a framer of treaties and laws, as a dealer with foreign dynasties, and as a man who understood as well as anyone alive the principles which lay behind government itself.

Yet John Adams got only thirty-four out of the sixty-nine votes, the other thirty-five having been deliberately scattered among ten politically impossible candidates, no one of which got more than nine votes. This vote scattering, which reduced John Adams's majority in a humiliating degree, was due to the secret intrigue of Alexander Hamilton, who here showed the innate duplicity and love of pulling secret wires which became increasingly dangerous, and ended in his own complete disaster.

It was not that Hamilton did not want John Adams. He rather admired him, and believed that "to a sound understanding Mr. Adams joined an ardent love for the public good." But he wanted him in with as little power as possible. So he set to work to clip his majority. His plan was a clever one, deceiving many of John Adams's supporters. He sent riders despatch to the state elections to warn candidates that there was serious risk that John Adams would win the first place over Washington, or at least tie him, unless measures were taken to prevent it by casting away some of Mr. Adams's natural votes. "He had made an exact calculation on the subject — New Jersey were to throw away three votes and Connecticut two, and all would be well," as a Connecticut friend told John Adams. "So our electors threw away two votes where they were sure they would do no harm." [9] And Mr. Gerry bore independent witness that others of the "States which were not unanimous for you" had thrown away votes "apprehensive that this was a necessary step to prevent your election to the chair." [10] Without understanding Hamilton's real reason for the policy, John Adams perceived the fact and resented it.

Adams accepted his position with determination to pull his weight to make the new machinery of government work smoothly and fulfill the ideals which he had often expressed — "the formation of a national government which may bind us together." John Adams never nursed a grudge. And Hamilton had not at present any grudge against John Adams. His intrigue had been largely impersonal; and it had been successful. He was ready to welcome the Vice-President.

New York was to be first seat of the Federal government. Abigail was delighted at the prospect of living near her daughter. The date set for the launching of the new government was the first Wednesday in March, which happened to be March 4th. But to John's chagrin she could not set out with him. A farm cannot be suddenly left; someone must supervise the spring planting, the finishing of the new dairy, the mending of fences; someone must disband the numerous household, arrange the care of the house and farm for an indefinite time. There was Tom at Harvard, and Charles in a scrape. Not to mention Abigail's pet lark and puppy. At least John could get a house in New York ready for her. So they bid each other reluctant farewell, and John drove in the spring weather. Abigail heard afterwards of the reception he met on the road all the way along. Crowds turned out to greet him, "most affectionate and respectful." In one place they would present him with specimens of local manufactures, cloth, buttons; at another with the freedom of their city. Surprisingly enough at New York, stronghold of the antifederalists under Governor Clinton, both parties emulated each other in their testimonials of respect and affection to John Adams.[11]

The Vice-President's main duty was to preside over the meetings of the Senate. As soon as a quorum had arrived John Adams was solemnly inducted into this duty and, on April 21st, he assumed the chair he was to occupy for eight years. The heart of his speech of acceptance was an eloquent tribute to George Washington.

But as the profound emotions stirred up by the great day of Washington's inauguration sank down again to their place at the bottom of his heart, John Adams turned with reproach and loneliness and exasperation to the empty pillow at his side. Why could not Abigail be here to share them?

"My dearest Friend, — If you think it best, leave Thomas at college, but I pray you to come on with Charles, as soon as possible. As to the place, let my brother plough and plant as he will, as much as he will. He may send me my half of the butter, cheese, etc., here. As to money to bear your expenses, you must, if you can, borrow of some friend enough to bring you here. If you cannot borrow enough, you must sell horses, oxen, sheep, cows, any thing at any rate rather than not come on. If no one will take the place, leave it to the birds of the air and beasts of the field, but at all events break up that establishment and that household. . . ."

"Ah?" said Mrs. Adams. "Well, well. Sweetly do the birds sing!"

Leave the farm to the birds of the air and the beasts of the field, and depend on what in our old age? She could not escape the penalty of her foresight and her competence.

But her arrangements with Richard Cranch were almost completed. Impatience and thoroughness struggled within her as the days grew warmer, the flowers came out, the cows calved, the first crop of hay matured. . . . In high June with a great send-off from friends and relations, with her luggage and furniture, her son Charles to escort her and her young nieces,* and her maid Polly, she embarked on the packet, and set out for New York by water.

* Her brother's children, Matilda and Louisa.

XII

New York

THIS time Mrs. Adams traveled like a queen. Wherever the boat put in to take up goods or passengers, the news of her being on board flew about. At Providence, Rhode Island, where the packet docked for the night, Mrs. Adams went to an inn. Within an hour of her arrival, local notables and friends came calling on her, reproaching her for not sending them word, inviting her to dine or drive. Rhode Island was Antifederalist, but the people admired John Adams personally and no bitter party feeling had yet arisen. "Mr. Brown (a Quaker) sent his carriage and son to conduct me to his house which is one of the grandest I have seen in this country . . . magnificence and taste. Mrs. Brown met me at the door. . . . 'Friend, I am glad to see thee here.' The simplicity of her manners and dress with the openness of her countenance and the friendlyness of her behaviour charmed me beyond all the studied politeness of European manners. 22 persons to dine with me tho the notice was so short . . . elegant entertainment upon a service of plate. Towards evening I made a tour around the town, and drunk tea and spent the evening with Mr. and Mrs. Francis. . . . large company to be presented. About eleven I returned to my lodgings and next morning went on board the packet. . . ."

The exhilaration of these affairs was short, but of how long the miseries of the sea! The captain of the packet, who was also called Brown, had "very civilly taken his wife to attend upon me during my passage . . . but neither civility, attention nor politeness could remedy the sea-sickness or give me a fair wind or dispel the thunder-gusts. In short I resolved upon what I have frequently before, that I would never again embark upon the water, but this resolution I presume will be kept as my former ones have been. We were five days upon the water. Heat, want of rest, sea-sickness and terror, (for I had my share of that!) all contributed to fatigue me, and I felt upon my arrival quite tame and spiritless. Louisa was very sick, but behaved like a heroine. Matilda had her share, but when she was a little recovered she was the life of us all. Polly was half-dead. . . . Charles ate and slept without any inconvenience." [1]

The Captain was her willing slave, and on docking at New York he went himself to the Hall of Congress to announce her arrival. John Adams, of course, could not leave his place without automatically dismissing the Senate, but Sam Otis, her cousin by marriage, Secretary to the Congress, quit his taking of minutes, met her at the water's edge with a carriage, and drove her to Richmond Hill, the house John Adams had taken. There she found her daughter and Colonel Smith waiting to welcome her, "to my no small joy," with baby John, "grown out of knowledge." They had everything "so well arranged that beds and a few other articles seem only necessary toward keeping house with comfort, and I begin to think my furniture will be troublesome to me, while Mrs. Smith remains with me." Her "tame and spiritless" feelings soon vanished. It was noon of a bright June day. The house was lovely. It stood on rising ground. In front lay the "noble Hudson," on the left the city, screened by trees, on the right an open expanse of fields and pastures, and at the back a grove of trees and a flower garden enclosed with a hawthorn hedge. When John came home to dinner from the Senate, nothing seemed wanting to complete her joy, nothing except the riddance of those troublesome little heartaches below the threshold, about Nabby's being obviously expecting again, about Colonel Smith's lack of prospects, and about Charles's peccadilloes.

Charles had accompanied her to New York to start working in an office there, studying law. The trouble with Charles was that he was simply too charming, too fond of the popularity he came by so easily. He could not say no, could not turn the cold shoulder even on an undesirable companion. So he fell a prey to bad company. There were men at Harvard who drank too much, who played too high. Abigail knew of such, before her own sons went to college. But you didn't have to keep their company. John Quincy Adams did not, nor Will Cranch. She had written from England asking John Quincy to be sure to look after his younger brother. But Charles wasn't going to be bossed by Johnny. . . . Had there always been something a little soft about Charles? Soft here, obstinate there? So difficult to deal with, because he did not hold his shape. As long as he was with you, he seemed so sweetly reasonable, he went into the mold you made. But, away from you, the mold would not stay, and without the home pressure his shape altered, became — like his uncle, Abigail's lost brother. But his mother would not give up, she struggled valiantly.

Well, now she was to have Charles under her wing for a time, and she could see how pleased he was to see his sister again. Nabby and he made fast friends, and Charles was soon introduced to the lively bevy of young Miss Smiths on Long Island. Charles was repentant, reformed, bent on behaving circumspectly, and as always, bad or good, possessing the art of winning love and giving happiness. When he came in from his office day after day he greeted his mother with warm affection. He knew that the painful subject would never again be raised between them, unless by his own fault. Abigail had never been a nagging parent. That too she had learned from Grandma Quincy.

"Amongst the many good rules and maxims of my worthy Grandmother with whom I chiefly lived during the early period of my life, I recollect with pleasure that one of them was never to bring a painfull subject twice into recollection. If a poor culprit had transgressed she reprimanded with justice and dignity, but never lessened her authority by reproaches. The consequence was that love toward her and respect for her opinion prevented a repetition of the offence."[2] It was a good habit and good psychology, even if the perfect consequence did not always follow. There is no doubt that Charles to the end of his wasted life maintained a great love toward his mother and respect for her opinion, even

though it was to him a source of pain. But in the sunny house at
Richmond Hill they were a happy family group and all was set
fair.

Mrs. Adams must now assume her social duties and she took
them up with eager pleasure. "I took the earliest opportunity
(the morning after my arrival) to go and pay my respects to Mrs.
Washington. Mrs. Smith accompanied me. She received me with
great ease and politeness. She is plain in her dress, but that plain-
ness is the best of every article. She is in mourning. Her hair is
white, her teeth beautiful, her person rather short than otherways,
hardly so tall as myself, and if I was to speak sincerely I think she
is a much better figure! Her manners are modest and unassuming,
dignified and feminine, not the tincture of ha'ture about her.
His Majesty was ill and confined to his room. I had not the
pleasure of a presentation to him.

"Mrs. Washington is one of those unassuming characters which
create esteem. A most becoming pleasantness sits upon her countenance, and an unaffected deportment which renders her the
object of veneration and respect. With all these feelings and sensations I found myself much more deeply impressed than I ever
did before their Majesties of Britain." [3]

Apart from the President and his wife, Mrs. Adams, as the
newcomer, must of course receive callers, and they crowded upon
her. Before June ended, she had been called on by "the lady and
daughter of the Governor, Lady Temple, the Countess de
Brehin, Mrs. Knox, and twenty-five other ladies, many of the
Senators, all their ladies, all the foreign Ministers, and some of the
representatives." In all this whirl she longed for her competent
servants the Brieslers, who were following her and arrived a week
or two after. Briesler could take full charge of the domestic staff
and affairs, and Esther, among other things, could dress her
mistress's hair. New York took almost as much hairdressing as
Paris.

The Washingtons' cordiality manifested a wish for closer
friendship. Mrs. Washington promptly returned Mrs. Adams's call
and invited her back. And Washington, having missed her first
visit through illness, would not make that an excuse a second time

lest he should seem not sufficiently anxious to see her. "The fever which he had, terminated in an abscess, so that he cannot sit up. Upon my second visit to Mrs. Washington he sent for me into his chamber. He was laying upon a settee, and half raising himself up, begged me to excuse his receiving me in that posture, congratulated me upon my arrival in New York and asked me how I could relish the simple manners of America after having been accustomed to those of Europe." [4] Mrs. Adams replied that she esteemed the simple manners of her countrymen, but she had noticed many had some taste and fondness for luxury and the manners of Europe. It certainly never entered her head that Washington himself, still less that she and her husband, would ever be accused by their enemies of loving luxury.

Abigail had met Washington in Boston years before. The impression he made upon her then was not weakened, it was only deepened and amplified when she came to know him better. "Our august President is a singular example of modesty and diffidence. He has a dignity which forbids familiarity mixed with an easy affability which creates love and reverence." [5]

Weak from his fever and tortured by his abscess, the President crawled downstairs and had a bed put into his carriage and "rides out in the way with six horses in his carriage and four attendants. Mrs. Washington accompanies him. I requested him to make Richmond Hill his resting place, and the next day he did so, but he found walking up the stairs so difficult [Mrs. Adams's drawing room was on the second floor] that he has done it but once."

Indiscriminate calling, long continued, in such a society would soon leave everyone with no spare time, no peace. In self-defense it was necessary for leading hostesses to adopt the English plan of an "At Home" day, let Senator Maclay and his ilk carp as they might. "I have waited for Mrs. W. to begin," wrote Mrs. Adams, in August, "and she has fixed on every fryday 8 o'clock. I attended upon the last, with Mrs. Smith and Charles. I found it quite a crowded room. The form of reception is this — The servants announce, and Col. Humphries and Mr. Lear (the secretary) receives every lady at the door and hands her up to Mrs. Washington to whom she makes a most respectful courtsey and then is

seated without noticing any of the rest of the company. The
President then comes up and speaks to the lady, which he does
with a grace and dignity and ease that leaves Royal George far
behind him. . . . Ice-cream and lemonade . . . and the company
retire at their pleasure, performing the same ceremony when they
quit the room. Now on Monday evenings Mrs. Adams receives
company. That is, her rooms are lighted and put in order. Servants and Gentlemen and Ladies, as many as inclination, curiousity
or fashion tempts, come out to make their bow and curtzy, take
coffee and tea, chat half an hour or longer, and then return to
town again. On Tuesday the same ceremony is performed at Mrs.
Jay's." [6]

It was not too tedious. No one felt it necessary to go every time
to all the receptions. But dissipation? Heavens above! "I cannot
help smiling when I read the Boston press, that the President is
rumored amidst all the 'dissipations' of the city of New York. . . .
Not a single public amusement is there in the whole city, no, not
even a public walk, and as to dinners, there are six made in Boston
to one here. There are six Senators who have their ladies and
families with them, but they are in lodgings the chief of them,
and not in a situation to give dinners. . . . The weather is so warm
we can give only one dinner a week, 24 persons at a time." Mrs.
Adams, by August 9th, had got through the Senators and begun
with the House; though she couldn't find a cook who would not
get drunk. In the meantime, while she had already returned sixty
calls, the intense summer, the busy flies, no screens, no ice, played
their usual havoc.

"My family all sick, Mrs. Smith's two children with hooping-
cough, Charles with dysentery, Louisa and Polly with summer
complaint. . . . It is very sickly in the city." Yet she immediately
adds — "I am every day more and more pleased with this place.
Should they go to Philadelphia I do not know how I could possibly live through the violent heats."

Another rumor against Washington comes to her in the mail
from New England, and she hastens to his defense. "The President
uses no more state than is perfectly consistent with his station.
I do not love to see the news writers fib it so." And then John

Adams gets libeled for putting on dog, and she categorically contradicts it. "The Vice-President ten times to one goes to Senate in a one-horse chaise, and *levees* we have had none. The President only has his powdered lackies waiting at the door."

It is envy which gives rise to such rumors. And Abigail provided her sister with an answer to give to any envious neighbors.

"It has been my lot in life to spend a large portion of it in publick life, but I can truly say the pleasantest part of it was spent at the foot of Penns Hill in the humble cottage when my good man was a practitioner at the Bar, earnt his money during the week and at the end of it pourd it all into my lap to use or what could be spaired to lay by. Nobody then grudged us our living, and 25 years such practice would have given us a very different property from what we now possess." [7]

The relationship of President's wife and Vice-President's wife was new to history. The first two made it a very intimate one. Mrs. Washington, once the wealthy young widow Custis, inheritor of great estates, mistress of hundreds of slaves, and entirely a product and flower of the Southern culture, curiously enough found most congenial company in the New England lady. Mrs. Washington was a quiet woman, not lively-minded nor with much to talk about. She was not much of a reader, and the theater rather bewildered her. The pitfalls of her new position hedged her round. "I live a very dull life here, and know nothing that passes in the town . . . more like a state prisoner than anything else," she complained. The new friend fascinated her. She knew so much, she had seen so much, she knew reams of poetry by heart, she had such interesting opinions. Her presence enlivened any ladies' tea party, kept one entertained on the dullest of drives and calls. Mrs. Washington continually asked for her company, and she had what she wanted. "We live in a most friendly intercourse," wrote Mrs. Adams, "and Madam makes very few visits but those of ceremony when she does not request my ladyship to accompany her, and I have several appointments of that kind on hand now." [8]

While Mrs. Washington wrote to her niece that she was sending her a present of a watch and chain — "I hope it is such a one as will please you — it is of the newest fashion . . . such as Mrs. Adams the Vice-President's lady and those in the polite circle wares." [9]

In October, when Congress rose for recess, John Adams felt he must have a journey for relaxation, and was eager to see his new farm and how all that livestock was doing. So he determined on a short visit to Braintree. Abigail decided not to accompany him — too strenuous, and Nabby was still weak after the birth of her third son in September; and there was Charles, and her household. "The President sets out this week for a like excursion. He wd have had Mr. Adams accept a seat in his coach but he excused himself from motives of delicacy.

"We yesterday had a very pleasant party together," wrote Abigail to Mary. "The whole family of us dined with the President on Thursday, and he then proposed an excursion to Long Island by water to visit Princes Gardens, but as Mrs. W. does not love the water" (nor in fact did Mrs. A.) "we agreed that the gentlemen should go by water and the ladies should meet them at a half-way house and dine together, and yesterday we had a most beautiful day for the purpose. The President, Col. Smith, Major Jackson, Mr. Izard, etc., went on board the barge at 8 o'clock. At eleven the ladies, namely Mrs. W., Mrs. A., Mrs. Smith, Miss Custis" (Mrs. Washington's attendant granddaughter) "set out in Mrs. W.'s coach-and-six and met the gentlemen at Harlem, where we all dined together and returned in the same manner. Whilst the gentlemen are absent we propose seeing one another on terms of much sociability. Mrs. Washington is a most friendly good lady, always pleasant and easy." [10]

Although Mrs. Washington, at fifty-eight, was considered quite an old lady by everyone, and seemed so to Mrs. Adams at a lively forty-five, they were both grandmothers, and could find there an inexhaustible subject. "A grandchild," said Abigail, "is almost as near to your heart as your own children; my little boys delight me and I should feel quite melancholy without them. William came from his Grandmamma Smith an almost ruined child, but I have brought him to be a fine boy by now." [11]

It became the custom, on public occasions, for Mrs. Adams

to have her station "always at the right hand of Mrs. Washington." And if, when Mrs. Adams entered, someone else had taken that place and showed no signs of giving way, the "President never fails of seeing that it is relinquished for me." [12]

Even more than the heroes of antiquity such as David, Julius Caesar, Alexander, who all one day or other were moved by whims of vanity, selfishness, or eroticism, George Washington, having relinquished personal hope, fulfilled the classic ideal of the heroic. Common soldiers, fellow officers, aristocracy of the South, rough-cornered intelligentsia of Boston, merchants of New York, students of Harvard College, all were moved to hero worship. On the Eastern tour, made in October and November by advice of John Adams, he was greeted with wild enthusiasm, serenaded with "the Hero comes." "He was much gratified with the attention shown him," wrote Abigail to her son John Quincy, "I have it from his own mouth. Is it human nature to be otherways?" And she added her own heartfelt comment — "*He ought to be immortal, for who can ever fill his place?*" [13]

Indeed, Washington's tact and power were so great, it gave one pause. A close observer, valuing democratic government, almost trembled at it. Washington's very existence created an aristocracy, even if only of one individual. John Adams, who saw him at his daily work, felt him in a man's world, often discussed his opinion with Abigail, and it is his thoughts as well as hers that she expressed in the balanced judgment which constitutes one of the finest tributes to Washington: "This same President has so happy a faculty of appearing to accommodate and yet carrying his point that if he was not really one of the best intentioned men in the world he might be a very dangerous one. He is polite with dignity, affable without familiarity, distant without haughtiness, grave without austerity, modest, wise and good. These are traits in his character which peculiarly fit him for the exalted station he holds, and God grant that he may hold it with the same applause and universal satisfaction for many years, as it is my firm opinion that no other man could rule over this great people and consolidate them into one mighty Empire but he who is set over us." [14]

However, it could not be denied, the air around him was a little rare, a little chill. Dinner with the President was more formidable than festive. Mr. Maclay's vinegar hero worship cannot stand the strain. "At a little after four we went to the President's to dinner. President and Mrs., Vice-President and Mrs., Gov. and wife, Mr. Jay and wife, seven other guests and the President's two secretaries. The President and Mrs. Washington sat opposite each other in the middle of the table; the two secretaries one at each end. It was a great dinner and the best of the kind I ever was at. The room however was disagreeably warm. The middle of the table was garnished in the usual tasty way with small images, artificial flowers, etc. The dessert was first pies, then iced creams, jellies, etc., then water melon, musk melon and other fruit. It was the most solemn dinner I ever sat at. Not a health drunk; scarce a word said. When the cloth was taken away the President, filling a glass of wine, with great formality, drank to the health of every individual round the table. Everybody imitated him, charged glasses, and such a buzz of 'Health, sir!' and 'Health, madam,' and 'thank you, sir,' and 'thank you, madam,' never had I heard before. The ladies sat a good while, and the bottles passed about; but there was a dead silence almost. Mrs. Washington at last withdrew with the ladies. The President is a cold formal man. I often looked around the company to find the happiest faces. The President seemed to bear in his countenance a settled aspect of melancholy. No cheering ray of convivial sunshine broke through the cloudy gloom of settled seriousness. At every interval of eating or drinking he played on the table with a fork or knife like a drumstick." [15]

* * * * *

But tame-cat affairs in ladies' drawing rooms or the stately formalities of dining with the President were by no means Mrs. Adams's chief interest. Every morning at ten o'clock John Adams drove down to the Senate, and every afternoon he returned to four o'clock dinner — unless they were dining out — with a budget of news. Mrs. Adams could not say that *she* did not know what was going on in the town. A husband could be a wall between his wife and the world, like Mr. Washington, or he could be a channel like Mr. Adams. Pacing the gravel walk under the trees, sitting on the piazza and watching the innumerable boats flitting by like huge white butterflies on the Hudson, Mr. and Mrs. Adams zestfully shared each other's lives. And since his affairs went along in a great public tide, it was his life that they mostly shared. Going over the day in the Senate with her sharpened his perceptions, refreshed his memory, often — looking at a matter through her eyes — gave him a new insight.

There were twenty-two members in the Senate; seldom more than twenty in attendance. The government was experimental, feeling its way, forming itself as it went. Those in favor of giving it a good deal of power, the Federalists, were scarcely in a majority over those who favored restricting it (in favor of local States' rights) — the Antifederalists. Consequently on important points the presiding officer often had to give a casting vote. John Adams had to do so twenty times in the First Congress.

"If the United States had chosen for the V–P's chair a man wavering in his opinions," Abigail justly commented, "or one who sought the popular applause . . . this very constitution wd have had its death wound during the first six months of its existence. On several of the most trying occasions it has fallen to this dangerous Vice to give the casting vote for its life." [16]

In January, the well-informed Abigail wrote her sister, "The next question I presume that will occupy Congress will be the assumption of the State debts, and here I apprehend warm work and much opposition but I firmly believe it will terminate for the general good."

On February 20th, Abigail speaks of going to the House for the first time "to-morrow" to hear the debate, with Mrs. Dalton, Mrs. Jay, and Mrs. Cushing. "I hope," she says fervently, "some method will be adopted speedily for the relief of those who have so long been the sufferers by the instability of Government." [17]

The debate was a revelation in verbal fireworks. And so it continued day after day. John Adams reported that in the Senate — to which the public were not admitted — things were just as hot. The controversy had risen to a passionate height, and a dangerous deadlock had been reached, when Jefferson arrived in New York in March to join Washington's Cabinet as Foreign Secretary or Minister of State.

No one welcomed Mr. Jefferson more warmly or more sincerely than his old friends John and Abigail Adams. "Mr. Jefferson is here," wrote Mrs. Adams joyfully, "and adds much to the social circle." [18]

They had no idea that Mr. Jefferson was going to act as a catalyst to the situation, and that some very curious and poisonous crystals were to be formed as a result.

The bile and gall and sulphur and brimstone stirred up in people's blood and viscera by this hot political fight over assumption seemed to take form in actual fever. At all events, a great distraction from debates in Congress hit New York at the end of May, 1790, put many of the main actors out of commission, and almost cost the President his life. "The disorder termed the influenze has prevailed with much violence," wrote Abigail, "and in many places been very mortal, particularly upon Long Island. Not a creature has escaped in our family except its head, and I compounded to have a double dose myself. Hitherto he has escaped, not so the President. He has been in a most dangerous state, and for 2 or 3 days I assure you I was most unhappy."

It was not only on Washington's account that she worried. It seemed to her that the very union of the states and the permanency of the government depended upon Washington's life.

"Most assuredly I do not wish for the highest post! I never before realised what I might be call'd to."

As for her own household, her remedy for influenza did not encourage malingerers. "I keep a bottle of tartar emetic and administer it as soon as they complain." (She gave herself several "pukes.") [19]

After all that worry and sickness, personal and vicarious, Mrs. Washington and Mrs. Adams both felt the need of a holiday. Just to get complete change, to wash their hands of all domestic duties, and of the repercussions of politics on husbands. And it is evidence of their real affection for each other that they took it together. In June, "I last week accompanied Mrs. Washington to the Jersies

to visit the Falls of Passaic. We were absent three days and had a
very agreeable tour."

They returned from their holiday to an atmosphere of impending change, the pulling up of new-formed roots, the breaking of
ties. When Congress rose in August for the summer recess, it
would be the end of business in New York. The Washingtons
prepared to go to Mount Vernon for the recess, and Abigail
wrote, "I shall part with her, tho I hope only for a short time,
with much regret. No lady can be more deservedly beloved and
esteemed than she is and we have lived in habits of intimacy and
friendship." [20]

*   *   *   *   *

One of the last important acts of Congress at New York was
to sign a treaty with the Indians in July. Abigail was much interested in the Indian delegation. They lodged at an inn near Richmond Hill and she had never seen anything like them before.
"They are very fine looking men, placid countenance and fine
shape. Mr. Trumble says they are many of them perfect models.
. . . They are very fond of visiting us. We entertain them kindly
and they behave with much civility. Yesterday they signed the
Treaty and last night they had a great bonfire, dancing round it
like so many spirits, hopping, singing, yelling, and expressing their
pleasure in true savage style. These are the very first savages I
ever saw." [21]

Their chief, MacGillvery, dressed in the white man's fashion,
spoke English like a white man, and was not particularly dark-
skinned. "He is grave and solid, intelligent and much of a gentleman."

So the Indians went away content, and Mrs. Adams, whom
they had called "Mammea" (she professed herself at a loss to
know what that implied), turned her attention to preparations
for departure.

Charles was going to board with his sister. It was a wrench
to have to leave those two behind, Nabby in "unsatisfactory circumstances," Charles in — what? It was hard to explain her un-
easiness about Charles. He "is quite fat. He is very steady and

studious. There is no fault to be found with his conduct. He has
no company or companions but known and approved ones, nor
does he appear to wish for any other." [22] Indeed he seemed to
have made it a rule not to go into company except with his father
or his brother-in-law. Every morning for a year past he had
driven into the city with his father, and gone to his office as his
father went to the Senate. In the evening he had returned in the
same manner. It was a little too careful, too perfect, too circum-
spect. It wasn't, in fact, like Charles! The mother missed in him
something gay, resilient, and debonair. He was too sober, too self-
repressed, too eaten by inward shame and remorse and a desperate
determination to make amends. But what could one do? She had
urged all these things on him, and now she was distressed at
seeing them. "I sometimes think his application too intense, but
better so than too remiss." [23]

John Quincy's application was also too intense, but up to now
the only worry was on account of his stomach. John Q. had now
completed his three years' articles with Mr. Parsons, and in July
had been admitted to the Boston Bar. In August he moved into
Boston, opened his father's old office on Court Street. Instead of
showing pleasure at starting out in life, however, he seemed depressed. The prospect of a young barrister's tedious waiting for
briefs caused him to fret. His mother had tried to cheer him,
turning away from her Indians. "You must expect to advance
slowly at first . . . but it must be some dire misfortune or
calamity, if I judge not amiss, that will ever place you in the
shallows." [24]

What was behind all this chafing at dependence, this excessive
impatience to be making an income and standing on his own feet?
Was it what one would naturally suspect? Yes; indeed it was;
rumor brought her word, and Thomas confirmed it.

A lovely girl named Mary Frazier had captured John Q.'s heart
two years before in Newburyport. And at her touch the bright
young man came alive. The seasons flew; the melon parties, the
water parties, the picnics, the snow parties, the dances; the walking home after Meeting; the sitting on piazza steps in the dusk.
All the glorious iridescent days and nights of joy and pain. And

then, the dreaded end. Then, Boston. Sitting in the old office, hour after hour, among his father's books. Then the sudden first case, a hurry call, which he was sure he muffed — though Charles wrote him a most kind, encouraging, brotherly letter about it. The intolerable vista that swam before his sleepless eyes of years of this — his clothes, his food, his books, his rent, his pocket money, all provided for him by his parents; nothing, not a cent, not a crust of bread, of his own.

Abigail approached the delicate subject with a mother's nervousness. A nervous touch is always wrong. "Your Father sets out for Philadelphia to-morrow to see a house belonging to Mr. Hamilton, the uncle of my favorite Nancy" (whom she had presented at court). "Perhaps you may one day come and see her but you must get a great deal of money first, 'tis said this uncle has already wounded her by preventing a connection with a gentleman who was not great and noble and rich enough for him." She sets out ostensibly to comfort and reassure her son because he can't support himself yet. But what is it but to point up his lack of riches, his ineligibility, his necessarily prolonged dependence? "I will prophesy for you that you will be able by the close of one year to pay your own board, and if you do that it's as much as you ought to expect, and if you do not, why don't worry your face into wrinkles about it, we will help you all we can, and when you are better off than those who assist you, you shall help them again if they want it, so make yourself easy and keep free from entanglements of all kinds. Thomas says you are in love. So far as it will serve to make you more attentive to your person, — for you are a little inclined to be negligent, — so far it may be of service to you." [25]

Parents work against serious handicaps. Abigail had in some ways come off very well, notably well, in adjustment to a grown son. There were many directions in which she had approached him as an equal, even looked up to him. And a great many parents can never say as much. But, though she herself had married at twenty, perfectly convinced, at the time and ever since, that hers was a mature passion, she could not give her son credit for equal dignity and maturity at twenty-three.

With some irony and some bitterness he read her letter, missing none of its implications. Thwarted, miserable, and rebellious, he yet felt he had no case. She hardly needed to rub it in. But that fierce maternal anxiety that wants to guard the young from every pitfall, small and great — and how great a one could this be! — made her write again in November concerning rumors of his attentions which are passing her way. "Do you not know that the most cruel of situations to a young lady is to feel herself attach'd to a Gentleman when he can testify it in no other way than by his actions, I mean when his situation will not permit him to speak?" [26] The best of mothers can be diabolically clever when setting themselves to break off such an affair. That was precisely the line to take, the very one which kept John Quincy awake in anguish night after night, which was slowly impaling him on its inescapable point. He could not afford to marry unless his parents helped him. He could not bring himself to ask them to help him — more than they were doing, which was too much already — and if he should ask them, the warnings against too early marriage which had been so valid with his father, and which were repeated in his mother's letters, proved that they would refuse, or would at best do it unwillingly. No. There was no way out but one. The takings of his first year in Boston showed all too clearly what that way must be. And John Quincy Adams was not the man to hug illusion, and deny the logic of fact. He made a clean cut. He said good-by to Mary Frazier, for her own sake; he wrenched himself away from a false, an untenable situation; and he broke his heart. He was never the same man after.

So little did his mother understand his deep, repressed, mature suffering that when he paid them a visit in Philadelphia in the new year, feeling his way on this subject for the last time, her sympathetic concern was curiously beside the point. She wrote her sister that J. Q. A. was "depressed owing to want of business in his profession and the dismal prospect for practitioners of the law in Massachusetts. Being still dependent on his parents irks him. He appears to have lost much of his sprightliness and vivacity." Although these feelings are "proof of a good mind and sensible [sensitive] heart, I cd wish they did not oppress him so much. He wishes sometimes he had been bred a farmer, a merchant or anything by which he could earn his bread, but we all preach patience to him." [27]

So these good and excellent parents, with the best of intentions and great self-confidence, interfered with the first choice of both their elder children. In neither case had the choice been really intrinsically unsuitable; in neither had it been a mere passing fancy. But as Abigail herself would say, useless to look backward; let us look forward.

XIII

Philadelphia

FROM the autumn of 1800 the city of Philadelphia was the seat of government and the official home of John and Abigail Adams. These ten years brought for the Adamses growth and fulfillment in every respect except one — Abigail's health. The climate of Philadelphia, as she had foreseen, never suited her, and she was obliged to spend long periods away from it.

The house they first settled into was the Hamilton (no relation to Alexander) property, Bush Hill. It was a large brick house, well outside the city. There were no bushes left on the hill — the British troops had cut them all for firewood when using the house during Howe's occupation of Philadelphia. But it made a good sheep pasture and a shepherd and his flock came every day, to the delight of any resident grandchildren. There were open fields in front, and the views were rather beautiful, though "the country round has too much of the level to be my style," said Mrs. Adams, "and as to the river — the Schuylkill is no more like the Hudson than I to Hercules!" Behind the house was the usual shady grove with a spacious gravel walk winding through it, and this time (reminiscent of Auteuil) it was ornamented by a number of marble statues.

Everything promised well except that nothing was ready. The furniture arrived by water just at the same time as Mrs. Adams arrived by chaise — although she had traveled very slowly, not more than twenty miles a day. She drove up to the house, expecting to find everything got in order by the Brieslers, and there were the painters rushing about with wet brushes finishing up, and the rooms all empty, dank and chill not only with wet paint but with four years of disuse. But this time Mrs. Adams did not sit down and cry. This sort of thing was becoming quite a habit. So, murmuring that it was no more than she expected, she ordered fires in every room, and retired to the inn for the night.

At that, "the furniture must come in and we must inhabit it unfit as it was, for to go with 14 or 16 to lodgings was much beyond my revenue." Sickness naturally followed within a day or two. First niece Louisa was ill, then the maid Polly; then son Thomas, liable to rheumatism, was helpless for eighteen days, and "had to be carried from his bed to the settee, and fed like an infant," in spite of pukings and bleedings. "Dr. Rush has attended them, and I have found him a kind friend as well as physician."

Mrs. Adams had been very ill herself just before leaving New York, and while still convalescent had further taxed herself by helping to nurse Nabby's baby, who nearly died of inoculated smallpox. But she managed to get through the journey and the subsequent difficulties without a relapse, thanks to her resilient vitality.

Cordial Philadelphia, hearing of Mrs. Adams's arrival, could not wait, never thought of waiting; the quicker the warmer. Visits and calls of welcome "took place none the less every day from 12 to 3 o'clock in the midst of rooms heaped with Boxes trunks, cases, etc." Poor Abigail Adams lost weight. But all was done at last. And it was lovely to see old friends again. Mrs. Adams summed up early impressions in her journal letter to her sister — "Inhabitants most courteous, servants terrible." [1] (The new cook was put to bed drunk.)

And now the social whirl of Philadelphia, the gayest city in the United States, sucked her in. All those calls to return — invitations to tea and cards, to routs, pouring on her. "I will spend a very dissipated winter if I accept half!" she said to John. Mrs. Washington arrived — also to a house not ready — and invited them to dinner; and presently started her drawing room. Charles arrived for a long Christmas holiday, and escorted his mother to the drawing room — "the circle very brilliant. How could it be otherwise, when the dazzling Mrs. Bingham and her beautiful sisters were there, the Misses Allen and the Misses Chew — in short a constellation of beauties?" [2] Mrs. Bingham with her Paris gowns was evidently the arbiter of fashion, and under her leadership the society of Philadelphia scintillated. The visiting Duke de La Rochefoucauld himself admitted, "I have seen balls where the splendor of the room, and richness of the dresses, did not suffer by comparison with Europe." And the beauty of the ladies he thought surpassing. "It would be no exaggeration to say that in the numerous assemblies of Philadelphia it would be impossible to meet a plain woman." This enormous butterfly of compliment inevitably carried a sting in the tail. "The young men for the most part seem to belong to another species."

Philadelphia boasted a theater, and a box was provided by the actors for the President and Vice-President. Abigail was delighted. "It did not equal the French theatre, but the house was very neat and prettily fitted up." She saw *The School for Scandal* played by American actors, and enjoyed it, but missed "the divine Farren." [3] Curiously enough, too, she missed the English weather. "The climate of Old England for me! People do not grow old half so fast there. Two-thirds of the year here we must either freeze or melt. The weather now is winter in all respects." She looked out of her windows on the sun-glittered surface of the January whiteness and turned away blinking. "Such a plain of snow as puts out my eyes!" [4]

Never has she been such a prisoner of weather. The two-mile drive to town was over an unpaved road of miry clay. In open weather "you must wallow to the city," the mud up the horses' knees. If dry or frozen, "the holes and the roughnesses are intolerable."

Not only weather kept her tied down that winter. Thomas, just after entering Mr. Ingersoll's office in Philadelphia as an articled clerk to study the family trade of law, had a sharp return of rheumatic fever, and was ill for two months. His mother nursed him tenderly. For the first four weeks he was again entirely helpless. And he was greatly depressed. Charles's coming was as good as medicine for him. Charles "cheered his spirits." That was Charles's great and universal gift.

Tom, just out of Harvard and now taking his turn as the son at home, had not particularly wanted to study law. His mother, with her prosperous merchant relatives, rather wished Tom could have gone into merchandise, "as I am sure he has more of a turn for an active life." Yet after all, as she said to Mary, "Let us look into our national legislature. Scarcely a man there makes any figure in debate who has not been bred to the law." And though the accents of John Adams are plain in the remark, she made it with full conviction. She has herself glanced over the men of note in the legislature — all of whom came from time to time to her table or her drawing room — and George Washington was the only notable exception.

Tom found it heavy going at first, however. And his health made it all the harder. His mother was certainly no mollycoddle. "Tom is not strong yet," she remarked, when he was back at work again after his illness. "I fear an attendance upon two offices through the day and studying through the evening at home is not calculated to mend it. But it is a maxim here that he who dies with studying dies in a good cause, and may go to another world much better calculated to improve his talents than if he had died a blockhead. Well, knowledge is a fine thing, and Mother Eve thought so; but she smarted so severely for hers that most of her daughters have been afraid of it since!" [5]

"Come, now!" said John Adams, "you are always complaining that women are not better educated — that fathers give their boys all the advantages!"

"Yes, education," said Abigail, musing. "Nothing's more important, yet how incalculable it is! Here I've had little grandson John more under my eye than ever I had my own children, and yet — look at the naughty things that he will sometimes say and do! Where does he learn them? . . . That reminds me I must write to Nabby and recommend her Dr. Watts' *Moral Songs for Children*. They can learn them as easy as they can learn 'Jack and Jill' and 'Little Jack Horner,' that John can now say so glib. One must keep in mind the great importance of instilling precepts of morality early into their minds. I'm sometimes led to think that human nature is a very perverse thing, and much more given to evil than to good." [6]

Her son-in-law, for instance, she sadly reflected, was not evil but he surely was perverse. Abigail had hardly taken leave of her daughter and got to Philadelphia and settled in Bush Hill before the Colonel had up and sailed for England, just like that. What a time to go, anyway, early in December, with all the winter before you! The worst possible sailing weather. "His going was sudden and unexpected to us, but some private family debts which were due in England to his Father's estate was one motive, and some prospects of assisting his family by his voyage was a still further motive. I do not know why he has been so poorly provided for in the distribution of offices. The President has always said that he was sensible to his merit and meant to provide for him, but has not yet seen the way open to it. She, poor Girl, is call'd to quite a different trial from any she has before experienced, for tho' the Colonel was once before absent she was in her Father's house (in London). Now she writes that she feels as if unprotected, as if alone in the wide world. One of his brothers and sisters remain with her during the Col's absence. I have Johnny here with me, and a fine boy he is and the enlivener of the whole family." [7]

When Congress reopened in October 1791, Philadelphia hostesses presently became aware that they could not comfortably invite Mr. Hamilton and Mr. Jefferson to the same party. This perhaps was especially evident to Mrs. Adams, whose husband was a close personal friend of Mr. Jefferson, and a political ally of Mr. Hamilton. This latter alliance was the effect of John Adams's long contact abroad with the problems of commerce and credit, and his reluctant approval of Hamilton's schemes for national finance. Funding the public debt, assumption of the states' debts, creation of a Bank of America, and a system of revenue from taxation and excise, the four main points, each in turn aroused a storm. The Vice-President was not a member of the Cabinet. As presiding officer of the Senate he had no opportunity to debate. His splendid talents as debater and orator were all wasted. But he could exercise influence. He was not a man given to sit silent in groups of his peers who were discussing hot subjects as the wine bottle passed around the table. This influence was steadily exercised, in Senate and out, for the measures of Hamilton. And Jefferson could not bear it.

In April 1792, Abigail wrote to her sister — "The Southern members are determined if possible to ruin the Secretary of the Treasury, destroy all his well-built systems if possible, and give a fatal stab to the funding system. The V. President they have permitted to sleep in peace this winter. . . . The Secretary of State and even the President have not escaped. I firmly believe if I live ten years longer I shall see a division of the Southern and Northern states, unless more candor and less intrigue — shd prevail." [8]

The climate of Philadelphia had roused the dormant tendency to rheumatic fever which Abigail had had as a child, and which reappeared as inflammatory rheumatism. Remedies were not soothing. Blisters were applied to her wrists. Her daughter came from New York to nurse her, but in the midst of it was fetched away by her husband. Then Betsy Smith, on a visit to Mary Otis, took charge, and wrote to her sister-in-law, Will's wife — "I am now with Mrs. Adams, she has been very ill and confined to her room for seven weeks, but is now better and intends leaving here by the middle of next month. I shall very much regret the loss of her society from which is to be derived both pleasure and improvement. She has few superiors and not many equals. Whoever knows must esteem her, for she adorns every situation with peculiar dignity." [9]

The last thing Mrs. Adams noticed as she got into her chaise in Philadelphia for the journey to Braintree was the new coinage. "The coin is not permitted to wear the stamp of the President," she remarks, "because it would savor too much of royalty." [10]

The first thing she noticed on arrival — after the lovely greeting of delicate sweet scents and opal colors — was that her home place had changed its name. The long, straggling township, which for many years past had recognized a North Precinct and a South Precinct, had at last agreed on division into two "towns." The South Precinct retained the name of Braintree; but the North Precinct, in which the Adams Mansion stood, had taken the name of Quincy, after its most distinguished resident of old time, Abigail's grandfather.

Abigail, basking in this honor to her grandfather, found Boston ringing with praises of her son. Jefferson had recently sponsored the American printing of Tom Paine's new book, *The Rights of Man*. He had meant to do it secretly, as he promoted Freneau, but, bad luck, his signed letter to Paine appeared on the title page of the first Philadelphia edition. This book seemed to George Washington and John Adams and others of their way of thinking to be urging the American Revolution along the downward path of the French, to the overthrow of stable government. The President and the government party were therefore greatly satisfied when a series of articles signed "Publicola" began to appear in the Boston press which most ably answered the specious arguments of Tom Paine.

Jefferson at first thought they were written by John Adams — in England that was confidently stated to be so — but Madison perspicaciously pointed out to Jefferson that Publicola had an easier, less ponderous style. Publicola was, in fact, John Quincy Adams. Thus, by his own initiative, John Quincy unconsciously laid the foundation stone of his future career. For the articles gave Washington just what he needed, when he needed it.

John Adams sat down in a glow of fatherly pride to write to his absent wife with that warm appreciation of others and humble opinion of himself which he felt in his heart — "They get all that's good from their mother! Family and all! Look at Abigail's letters, for instance! Why, they were fit to print themselves, every one.

"You apologize for the length of your letters," he wrote, "and I ought to excuse the shortness and emptyness of mine. Yours give me more entertainment than all the speeches I hear. There are more good thoughts, fine strokes, and mother wit in them than I hear in the whole week. . . . And I rejoice that one of my children, at least, has an abundance of not only mother wit but his mother's wit. It is one of the most amiable and striking traits in his composition! . . . If the rogue has any family pride, it is all derived from the same source. His Pa renounces and abjures every trace of it!"

Abigail was left behind at Quincy when John Adams went back to Philadelphia after the second Presidential election. Washington again carried a unanimous vote which gave him first place. Although the Vice-President was not voted for as such, it was an understood thing that any rival candidates voted for by the Electoral College in 1793 were put up against John Adams, Washington being quite unassailable. Clinton of New York, a prominent stand-pat Anti, was the man campaigned for by the Antifederalists, and for the first time party strife and political methods, including lies and misrepresentations, were seen in full blast. Abigail was much disgusted. The influence of the "Jacobins" was very patent, and their democracy cry most irritating. John Adams got in, with seventy-seven votes against Clinton's fifty, but —

"Few old countries have exhibited more intrigue and falsehood than the Anti-federal party has done in the late election," wrote Abigail to her daughter. "The cry of rights of man, liberty and equality were popular themes. Their object was to represent the Vice-President as inimical to them, and as a man whose object was to introduce a government of King, Lords and Commons and a hereditary nobility. They made unfair extracts from his writings. . . . They said in Virginia that he has recommended to Congress to make a son of George III King of America!" Another line of attack was to say "that he was opposed to the President. This Washington himself contradicted."

But though her feelings as a wife were hurt, she was fair enough and keen enough to realize that all this row and rumpus was not directed personally against John Adams. It was really against Hamilton. "They despaired of destroying Hamilton unless they could remove the present Vice-President and place in his stead an enemy of Hamilton. Their object was to destroy his funding system and destroy the government." [11]

In fact the opposition was hard put to it to find a popular cry to use against two such men as George Washington and John Adams. If it had been Hamilton — why, he was wide open to attack. His affairs with women alone would have been a godsend for innuendo. But Hamilton was not up for election. Washington and Adams were in every important way above reproach. Both commanded unshakable public confidence. Yet the opposition had a case — as an opposition always has — if it could only put it into terms that would appeal to the mass. It was very clever to raise the cry of monarchy. Although it is hard to believe that any thinking man could possibly have taken it literally, it none the less put into picturesque and concrete form a dangerous tendency which did exist.

"Since the last election the President has been openly abused in the *National Gazette*," wrote Abigail, hardly able to believe it. But there were the sheets in front of her, sent on to her by her husband. "— abused for his levees as an ape of royalty; Mrs. Washington abused for her drawing-rooms; their celebration of birthdays sneered at; himself insulted because he has not come forward and exerted his influence in favor of a further compensation to the army. They even tell him that a greater misfortune cannot befall a people than for their President to have no competitor; that it infuses into him a supercilious spirit, renders him self-important, and creates an idea that one man only is competent to govern. They compare him to a hyena and a crocodile; charge him with duplicity and deception. The President has not been accustomed to such language and his feelings will be wounded I presume!" [12]

John Adams, spending the summer at Quincy with Abigail, learned of the fearful yellow fever epidemic in Philadelphia which had almost depopulated the city and was more certain than ever that city was an unwholesome place for her. When he returned to his duties in the fall he left her behind, though he missed her desperately. He was not the only one who missed her. Mrs. Washington had sent her love, and Mrs. Knox and Mrs. Bingham — many of the ladies, and even of the men! Mr. Jefferson for one. Another male admirer had said that Mrs. Adams was needed in Philadelphia, that she ought to be Autocratrix of the United States! In Abigail's absence from the Washingtons' levees, Mrs. Knox often took her place at Mrs. Washington's right hand. But it was not the same. A life-giving element was gone.

There were times when John Adams could hardly bear it. "I for my part," he wrote to her, "am wearied to death with ennui. Obliged to be punctual by my habits, confined to my seat as in a prison, to see nothing done, hear nothing said, and to say and do nothing. O that my rocks were within a mile or two, and my habitation and pretty little wife above all. Ah, I fear some fault unknown has brought upon me such punishments, to be separated both when we were too young and when we are too old." [13]

Mrs. Adams saw her house taking shape pleasantly according to her plans; her garden planted, the roses she had brought from the garden at Auteuil weathering the winters well, her dairy coming on, and butter going regularly by sea to her husband in Philadelphia. There was pleasant social intercourse with friends and neighbors, and above all it was heart-warming to have her eldest son coming out for week ends from Boston. A quiet, restful, healthful life, yet one fully occupied.

England, at war with the Jacobin party in control of France, and trying to restore the House of Bourbon, was attempting to apply the weapon of blockade. This involved interference on the high seas with neutral vessels bound for French ports, and American ships thus interfered with were in a mood to resent it. The situation was on a hair trigger, and Washington, after consulting privately with John Adams, decided to send a special envoy to England to arrange the treaty of commerce which somehow still waited completion.

"He made me a very friendly visit yesterday," wrote John Adams to Abigail, "which I returned to-day, and had two hours' conversation with him alone in his cabinet. The conversation, which was extremely interesting, and equally affectionate, I cannot explain even by a hint. But his earnest desire to do right, his deliberate and comprehensive view of our affairs with all the world, appeared in a very respectable and amiable light." [14]

Washington could not spare John Adams to go to England — in fact the Constitution would hardly allow it; if Washington died suddenly the government, so new and raw, would fall apart without the sturdy Vice-President to summon public confidence and go ahead without a break. The next best choice as envoy, on account of both gifts and experience, was John Jay. He was Chief Justice, but he at once made the self-sacrifice of resigning that post at Washington's request, in order to accept the thankless and difficult errand. Before his appointment could be ratified by Congress, a (Jefferson-Madison) bill had passed the House, pushed on by Madison, prohibiting the admission of any commodities from

Great Britain until the grievances complained of by American seamen should be redressed.

This bill came up before the Senate and was debated, and the Senate was equally divided on it, thirteen to thirteen. If it had passed, Jay's mission would have been abortive, no use his going, war with England would have been inevitable. But Vice-President John Adams had the casting vote. He alone conspicuously stood between the country and the disaster of then falling into Jefferson's plan (though Adams did not know it as Jefferson's). John Adams exercised his casting vote, and the measure was thrown out.

Yet such dramatic emergencies did not console John Adams for the paralysis of his great powers which the speakership of the Senate entailed. With his oratory all banked up within him, he had to listen to the inept and feeble speeches of others on subjects near his heart. With his incisive skill in debate, he had to see others missing points and letting their opponents get away with victory when they, at his hands, would have been utterly demolished. He could give the casting vote, yes; but had he been able to speak from the floor, the question probably never would have got to such a close call. It was a sort of daily purgatory.

He wrote to his wife — "My country has in its wisdom contrived for me the most insignificant office that ever the mind of man contrived or his imagination conceived."

John Jay went to England and came back a year later * with a treaty of commerce. Abigail said — "It is well the Senate only have the discussion of it, if it was to go to the House for ratification and was a Treaty from the Kingdom of Heaven proclaiming peace on Earth and Good Will to Men there would not be wanting Characters to defame and abuse it!" However, even in the Senate, Jay's Treaty was considered so unfavorable that it was difficult to get the two-thirds vote necessary to ratify it.

Abigail, who, wherever she was, always heard from husband or son or cousin or admiring male the inside story of whatever was going on — knew of French secret service money circulating in America against the Jay Treaty. "Hireling orators and printers . . . Bache's paper and the noted *Chronicle* have become the infamous vehicles of insolent and perfidious defamation. . . . Flood-

* March 1795.

gates of scurrility and abuse upon the President and Mr. Jay."
Particularly Washington. She can only compare it with the ostra-
cism the ancient Greeks inflicted on their best. " — these observa-
tions will occur to everyone who read the attacks upon one of the
Fairest Characters who ever gave fame to a Nation." [15]

The discovery of a secret correspondence between the French
envoy Fauchet and Edmund Randolph, who had succeeded Jefferson as Secretary of State, gave a severe setback to the Jacobin
Antis. Randolph retired in disgrace. Congress rallied in indignation
to the support of the government and passed the Jay Treaty.

"In the course of a few weeks," wrote Abigail to her son John
Quincy, "the table of Congress was covered with petitions from
all parts of the Union requesting them to make the necessary ap-
propriations to carry the Treaty into effect, that the faith and
honor of the United States might be preserved, even those who
did not like the treaty united in this wish, considering the faith
of the nation pledged.

"The triumph of the friends of government in Boston was such
as to astonish the Anarchists, for a Town Meeting was call'd by
them to oppose a memorial from the merchants in favor of the
treaty, when behold they were out-voted by an hundred to one.

"All through the towns and villages the voice was, we will support the Government, we will not have war. Even the little village
of Quincy," added Abigail Adams modestly, "presented more than
a hundred petitions." [16] And no doubt Mrs. Adams had done her
part in getting them.

John Adams's influence, backed by his years abroad, was strong
behind the scenes — closeted for long, intimate hours with Jay;
dining with the new Secretary of State Pickering; dining with the
President. He wrote to Abigail — then visiting Nabby in New
York — and warned her to be careful what she said in that milieu.
There was much he would like to tell her — "but mum-mum-
mum." When they got together for the summer at Quincy, she
would hear it all.

Abigail had been horrified and moved at the guillotining of
Marie Antoinette, and at the cruelties of the Reign of Terror now
setting in. She suffered for her friends the Lafayettes, now suspect
and in danger as aristocrats. But her point of view was like Wash-

ington's. She wanted everyone to let France alone. "I wish most ardently that every arm extended against that unhappy country might be withdrawn, and they left to themselves to form whatever constitution they choose; and whether it is republican or monarchical is not of any consequence to us provided it is a regular government of some form or other which may secure the faith of treaties." [17]

Mrs. Adams sympathized with Washington's unending troubles, in such excessive variety, in the Cabinet and out of it. Threat of war abroad need not be added to by rebellion and treachery at home. Why could not people settle down quietly and let the government they had themselves created get along with governing? The French people had had something to complain of, she had seen it for herself. It was not surprising they had lost their tempers. But "even in one of the freest and happiest governments in the world, restless spirits will aim at disturbing it." [18]

Colonel Smith had come back unexpectedly at the height of Abigail's illness in February '92 and carried his wife and children off with him to England. They remained a year, then back they came again, in time for Nabby to give birth to another baby, this time a little girl. Everyone was delighted, and the new Caroline grew up to be everybody's favorite. She had the charm and lovableness of her Uncle Charles without his weaknesses. As for Colonel Smith, he was suddenly rolling in money. Successful speculations in land, the sale of large tracts of upstate New York to some English nobleman, had apparently made him a millionaire. He bought a coach and six like General Washington's. He began to build a huge and elaborate house in New York which he named Mount Vernon. But even from the beginning it was looked at askance by the canny descendants of the Dutch patroons, and the common people called it "Smith's Folly." All this display was another kind of torture to Nabby's grave and sensitive spirit. However, at first Mr. and Mrs. Adams were rather impressed. They had been accustomed to excuse their son-in-law's restlessness by saying to their friends — "The Colonel is very active!" Now — "I wish my boys had a little more of his activity!" said John Adams.[19]

XIV

John Adams Becomes President

H E did not wish that long. A most important event took place
in the Adams family in the spring of 1794. Washington appointed a resident Minister to Holland, and the Minister he chose
was the young Boston lawyer, John Quincy Adams. This was the
reward for Publicola and other spirited articles in the Boston press
— articles which, like his father's before him, were not aimed at
stirring up the passions of the uneducated mob but at appealing to
the reason of the intelligent. They had done good service to President Washington, and they showed a mind of uncommon caliber.
Washington had only waited for a suitable task to present itself to
make use of both.

John Quincy, receiving the startling summons, saw the door of
opportunity opening, not where he had been vainly looking for it,
in the street door of his office, but in a dark corner where he had
assumed a blank wall. He might well curse himself for his too great
reasonableness in the matter of marriage. Life was not logical. In
trying to safeguard against bad chance, one forgot to allow for
good.

After a visit to Quincy to talk things over with his mother and
his father — just returned from Congress in Philadelphia — he
must wind up his business. Then the stage for Providence, and the
packet to New York, and on by stage again to Philadelphia
to receive his instructions, and study the situation awhile in the
State Department (reading there, chiefly, the six folio volumes of
his father's masterly correspondence when Minister to Holland
himself). He returned to Quincy for final farewells, and embarked
from Boston on September 17th, just as he had done as a boy. He
took his brother Tom with him as secretary. His mother was glad

for Thomas to have some experience abroad — the only member of the family who had not had any.

In October John Quincy Adams was in London, bearer of urgent dispatches for John Jay. He received Jay's advice as to how to conduct himself in Holland, conferred with him on the draft of the Treaty, and enjoyed a little relaxation showing his brother Tom about London.

Now that Abigail's son was American Ambassador at The Hague, there began one of the most remarkable correspondences between mother and son ever penned. "I wrote to my mother and to the Secretary of State," became a frequent entry in John Quincy's journal. Comment on scenes, persons, books, politics, international problems, and the philosophy of life passed freely between the gifted man in the early flower of his manhood and the lady at Quincy. No need for this mother to beg this son to write. He wrote because he wanted to. And though he had for her a large amount of that particular affection which is known as filial, he often called her "friend." The letters are more such as would pass from friend to friend. He valued her mind. He felt a sauce in her personal comments, quite her own. Her news and information from home were better than he could get from any newspaper, and from most dispatches; her keen, critical interest in his affairs at the Dutch Court were not just maternal. She enlarged his horizon and sharpened his wits. She kept him interested and warmed. And her thoughts were a woman's thoughts. She was, above all else, a fully completed woman, and as such she showed him all the time a slightly different world.

As for her, she appreciated to the full, with none of a parent's patronage, the different world which this intelligent man, her son, so freely showed to her. "Your letters," she told him, "always possess one good quality beyond many others, they have an intrinsic value which age does not impair." [1]

And now John Quincy was very much upset by hearing from his mother the surprising news that his brother Charles was married! The bride was impeccable, Sally Smith, one of the Colonel's charming sisters. But here was Charles beginning the practice of law in New York, no better off than John Quincy had been in

Boston; just as dependent on the help of parents; a bride with no more money in her own right than lovely Mary Frazier; and Charles was the younger brother! The elder brother suffered a burning sense of injustice, and did not conceal it.

The pen which was writing able reports of public affairs with such "valuable information and political foresight" that President Washington prophesied to his father that the writer would ere long be found "at the head of the Diplomatic Corps" dipped into a little personal gall. John Quincy informed his mother that the strangling of a first love often induced a premature state of frigidity, which he was conscious was beginning within himself. A cold ambition would replace the natural warm impulses of the heart. . . .

Abigail wrote back as best she could. "It was natural, my dear son, for you to make the reflections you did upon your Father's wish, & at the same time learning that your Brother was united to the choice of his Heart, I do not wonder that it awakens the dormant feelings of your soul & uncovers the fire which tho smothered gleam'd up again upon the recollection of the sacrifice you had made. . . . Sincere Friendships are more generally form'd at an early age when the Heart is tender soft & unsuspicious before we have been jostled by the tumults of life & put out of humour & conceit of the world or the paltry competitions of Ambition & avarice freeze up the generous current of the soul. But it must be longer than I hope you will remain single before you reach that frigid state, therefore do not despair of one day feeling a similar regard for a kindred soul yet in reserve for you.

"Your Brother Charles writes me that he is very happy. Sally is an amiable virtuous girl, with every disposition to make him a good wife & it will be his fault if he is not in future what he now is . . . happy, his business increasing and like to do well. When I was in New York I had much conversation with her, & tho I advised them to continue longer single, I did not wish to shake their determination to be for none other." [2]

But a few weeks later she is acknowledging some cloaks sent from London which John Quincy Adams had got "a young lady of great taste" to choose for him.

"Oh," says his mother, "I perceive some fair one has . . . taught you to admire! Youth & beauty have penetrated through your fancied apathy. . . . As you tell me that the enthusiasm of youth has subsided, I will presume that reason & judgment have taken its place."

She hears of the repeated sickness of poor Thomas. "He must return home when you take to yourself this lady whom you still leave in the clouds to me. Yes, you plainly tell me in your last letter that you are betrothed, but you leave me to the wide field of conjecture where to fix. My own imagination has carried me to the family of Mr. Johnson as I have before related to you. I approve of the young lady's discretion in sending you to the Hague without her, and shd learn to accumulate some solid property before you take upon you the charge of a family." [3]

In thus getting hastily engaged and announcing it to his parents, without giving the lady's name, John Quincy relieved his feelings by violently asserting his independence, and remarked that he was "old enough to get married." His mother insists on pretending not to read the bitterness, refusing to show hurt, maintaining a calm sensible tone which must have been galling to her son. "You are certainly old enough," she says mildly. "Your father was married nine days younger than you now are."

But what she can't tell him is the reason behind Charles's marriage. All is not well with Charles. He needs an anchor. The responsibility of a wife and home of his own may be his salvation. No great career will be placed in jeopardy by Charles's early marriage. All one can hope for there, she has sadly learned, is that the liquor habit may be controlled and a decent respectability maintained. What lies before Charles is no steep climb up the slopes of fame but a dreadful possibility of disaster. It is Sally to the rescue. Signals are set for quiet in the laboratory while the experiment proceeds.

With Charles safely married to Sally, and apparently steadied and happy, and John Quincy consoling himself with Louisa Johnson, a suitable American girl, Abigail gave way in this spring of 1796 to a halcyon interval. "If Envy owes me a grudge now is her time whilst I am in the peaceful enjoyment of domestic quiet free

from the anxious cares which are always attendant upon the most
elevated stations." [4]

The possibility of the most elevated station loomed. Washington had firmly announced his intention to retire at the end of his
term. As it affected John Quincy, this looked to Abigail like an
inevitable signal for her son's withdrawal to private life, whichever
way the new election turned. But Washington did not leave this
subject to embarrass his successor. His last act at the close of Congress was to appoint John Quincy Adams Minister to Portugal.

When Abigail heard presently that both the brothers had regretfully decided that Tom's health forbade his further service abroad
and that he was making plans to come home, she had a change of
heart. It would never do for John Quincy to go to a place like
Portugal with no one to keep him company or do for him! She
wrote hurriedly — he must not misunderstand her about Louisa.
She is in favor of the marriage! In fact — "I think you ought not
to go to Portugal alone. Your brother means to return to us, you
whose chief delight is in domestic life must feel yourself in a
desert without a companion. I advise you to marry the lady before
you go to Portugal, give my love to her and tell her I consider her
already as my daughter, and as she made England delightful to
you I hope she will every other country." [5]

For a young man engaged to be married and thus encouraged,
John Quincy Adams closed the year 1796 in his diary at The
Hague with a rather singular entry — "The situation of two objects the nearest to my heart, my country and my father, press
continually upon my reflections. They engross every thought and
almost every power, every faculty."

The ship bearing the mail arrived at last. It was the eldest son
of the President of the United States who called, at nine o'clock
of a summer morning, at Mr. Johnson's house on Tower Hill and
became part of a wedding cortege to the Church of All Hallows,
Barking. There he was married to Louisa Catherine Johnson, the
second daughter of Mr. and Mrs. Joshua Johnson, in the presence
of her family and one or two friends, Tom Adams acting as best
man. The slanting sun made colored patches on the dim stone, and
touched the bride's bright golden hair where her blue-ribboned

hat turned up at the side. The snowy powder of the groom made his eyes look the darker. The hum of London's traffic rattled outside, the cries of the cockney street hawkers were musically audible, coming and going, heard and not heard, as the two young Americans plighted their troth. Their low voices echoed among the ancient shadows as he vowed to love and cherish, she to love, honor, and obey, until death do us part. Then — for neither of them came to this marriage in a romantic mood, each knew the other had parted with the unrecapturable first ardor before they met — they filled in the day prosaically with a drive to "Tilney House, one of the splendid country seats for which this country is distinguished."

The day was July 26th, 1797. And sober as it was, it was a fortunate day. Louisa Adams's soft yielding grace and charming face concealed unexpected resources of strength and intelligence. In a mood of self-revelation years later she wrote — "I set out in life with the most elevated notions of honor and principle; ere I had entered it fully my hopes were blasted, and my ideas of mankind, that is all the favorable ones, almost, were suddenly chilled, and I was very near forming the horrid and erroneous opinion that no such thing as virtue existed. This was a dreadful doctrine at the age of little more than twenty." She was in this mood of heartbreak and disillusionment when she first met John Quincy, whom she married at twenty-two.

Abigail had foreseen that her husband would be elected to the Presidency, though not without a struggle. In November 1796 she had written her son — "No man can expect a unanimous choice; there were such a combination of circumstances united in Washington as no age or country have produced." And she sadly reflects, "It requires courage and firmness, wisdom and temperance, patience and forbearance to stand in such a conspicuous, such an elevated station."

But however clearly one might foresee a tussle, and however accurately one might list the qualities requisite for one who would aspire to be President, the dust and confusion of the arena were something else again. It was all the worse because it was the very first time there had been a contested Presidential election. No one

John Quincy Adams

FROM A PORTRAIT BY JOHN SINGLETON COPLEY
MUSEUM OF FINE ARTS, BOSTON

had before seen a Presidential campaign. Abigail described it to her son as she saw it.

"All the arts of the Jacobins are in practice, united with the pride of the Old Dominion and foreign influence. . . . The democratic Societies circulating Hand Bills containing libels on Mr. Adams, attacking him as attached to monarchy and titles." (They were even stuck on gateposts, doors of houses and posts, which she considers "a right Gallic measure.") "The *Chronical* [Bache's paper] has been teeming for this month past on the old story of Monarchy and Aristocracy, quoting detached sentences and ringing all the Changes and Chimes."

However, John Adams and his supporters did not let libels pass in complete silence, nor were they without any counteroffensive. As Abigail remarked, they too were "not without something of the joy of battle. . . . They have dropped all candidates by the Vice-President and Mr. Jefferson, who on the other side has his principles and practices thoroughly dissected. . . . You will readily suppose that a fiery ordeal is preparing."

The two friends were now in open fight. But to John Adams it was purely a political fight. It should not affect private friendship. He did not blame Jefferson for the mud-slinging campaign in the papers against himself. He blamed Bache and such small fry. Jefferson was above all that. So when the returns were in, and John Adams was at the top of the poll with seventy-one votes, Jefferson second with sixty-eight, a position which automatically gave Jefferson the post of Vice-President, John Adams concurred in his wife's opinion as expressed to her son; Abigail wrote: "I consider the Vice-Presidency as a conciliatory union of the States, and on that account a fortunate event. I have always entertained friendship for Mr. Jefferson, from a personal knowledge and long acquaintance with him; tho I cannot altogether accord with him in politics I believe him to be a man of strict honor and of rare integrity of heart." She added, a little puzzled as she reflected on it, but unsuspicious, "The most reprehensible part of his conduct was countenancing that Frenner [Freneau] when he was continually libelling the government." [6]

To have the opposing candidate for President elected to the

Vice-Presidency was a difficult circumstance. However, John Adams prepared himself to meet the future in a composed, confident, and tolerant mood.

The first action he had to take was, on February 8th, to announce to the Senate, as their presiding officer, the results of the election. His wife, in far-off Quincy, looking out of her window on the sunny winter day, shared with him the greatness of the moment, and met it with him in loftiness of spirit. Not pride but prayer filled her heart.

She wrote to him — "You have this day to declare yourself head of a nation. 'And now, O Lord my God, Thou hast made Thy servant ruler over the people. Give unto him an understanding heart, that he may know how to go out and come in before this great people; that he may discern between good and bad. For who is able to judge this thy so great a people?' were the words of a royal sovereign; and not less applicable to him who is invested with the chief magistracy of a nation, though he wear not a crown, nor the robes of royalty. My thoughts and meditations are with you, though personally absent; and my petitions to Heaven are that 'the things which make for peace may not be hidden from your eyes. . . .' " [7]

A week later John Adams formally laid down his job of presiding over the Senate, with a parting address; tribute to eight years of "perfect and uninterrupted harmony" with Washington, "without envy in the one or jealousy in the other," and "on the other hand, have never had the smallest misunderstanding with any member of the Senate." He thanked them that in sharp difference of opinion there had been no resentment of the casting votes but that he had received "uniform politeness and respect from every quarter of the house."

Then he drove home to Quincy for a few days — he liked journeys, they rested his active mind — saw his Abigail, shared his experiences and thoughts with her; sat in quiet by the bedside of his dying mother, whose life had been slowly ebbing for many months; and went back to Philadelphia alone for his inauguration. He had hoped to take his wife with him, but his mother's condition forbade it.

So Abigail was not there to see her husband at his moment of greatest triumph, the public peak and summit of his career, the climax which could never, humanly speaking, be surpassed. She did not hear the fanfare, the cheers of the great crowd, nor the thrilling chiming of the bells. She did not share the hush which fell over the assembly at the solemn taking of the oath; nor the emotion stirred in the House by the noble, rolling periods in the inaugural address of one of the greatest orators of his time.*

Nor did Abigail see the sight which had never been seen before, nor has ever been seen again, of a departing President assisting in the inaugural ceremonies of another.

From some points of view it might seem a lack of tact for Washington to be present on this occasion. Public farewells and floods of adulation had swept the country at the recent celebration of his birthday on February 22nd. To reappear at Mr. Adams's inauguration was to invite a repetition of that emotion, to blend a powerful element of sadness at the obvious end of an era with the joyful welcome due to the new elected leader. But Washington set such considerations aside for others which seemed more important. He wanted to show personal friendship and honor to Mr. Adams. He wanted also to show that he was behind the new administration, and give it publicly any prestige which his support might gain for it.

John Adams wrote from his heart to his wife the next day, with great simplicity — "Your dearest friend never had a more trying day than yesterday. A solemn scene it was indeed; and it was made more affecting to me by the presence of the General, whose countenance was as serene and unclouded as the day. He seemed to me to enjoy a triumph over me. Methought I heard him say — 'Ay, I am fairly out, and you fairly in! See which of us will be happiest.' †

* Mason, the treaty publisher, said he had never heard such a speech in public in his life.

† Bache's farewell to Washington when he retired, March 1797: "If ever there was a period for rejoicing, this is the moment — every heart in unison with the freedom and happiness of the people ought to beat high with exultation that the name of *Washington* from this day ceases to give a currency to political iniquity and to legalise corruption."

"When the ceremony was over he came and made me a call and cordially congratulated me, and wished my administration might be happy, successful and honorable.

"In the chamber of the House of Representatives was a multitude as great as the space could contain, and I believe scarcely a dry eye but Washington's. The sight of the sun setting full-orbed, and another rising, though less splendid, was a novelty." [8]

But Abigail was not there. The letter came to her where she was tied to the tedious duties of a sickroom, easing the lingering final hours of an aged woman. And her eyes rained to read it.

But when she was free at last to go to join her husband, to assume her place as First Lady of the United States, it was with a sober mind. Death came in April, and struck twice. In a single week, the death of John Adams's mother, eighty-eight years old, and Abigail's niece Mary Cranch, aged twenty-one, gathered the same group of relatives for funeral rites. "I have asked was all this necessary to wean me from the world?" mourned Abigail. "Was there danger of my fixing too strong an attachment upon it . . . forget that here I have no abiding place? . . . I have received your letters of April 16th and 19th. I want no courting to come. I am ready and willing to follow my husband wherever he chooses; but the hand of Heaven has arrested me. . . . I prepare to set out on the morrow." [9]

X V

When Yellow Leaves ...

As she got into the chaise, however, her attention was very
much upon the world and the immediate part she and her
husband were to play there. Among the letters which she could
reread to entertain her on the long journey there was one which
gave her a glimpse of the arena and of her champion's readiness at
all points.

"John Adams must be an intrepid," he wrote, "to encounter the
open assaults of French, and the secret plots of England, in concert
with all his treacherous friends and open enemies in his own country. Yet, I assure you, he never felt more serene in his life!" [1]

But her own heart trembled. As the chaise jogged southward at
a steady pace over the best road in America, the Boston Post Road,
traveling through forest and moorland with frequent glimpses of
the sea, Abigail took out her pen and inkhorn and wrote to her
sister. She quoted Shakespeare —

> "Is Heaven tremendous in its frowns? Most sure
> And in its favors formidable too . . .

"Such appears to me the situation in which I am placed, enviable
no doubt in the eyes of some, but never envyd or coveted by me."
Brooding on it she looked out of the window, and her gardener's
eye caught sight of something. She dipped into the ink briskly. "I
forget to mention to Mr. Porter to attend to the first caterpillar
webb and take them off as soon as they appear," she wrote with
restored cheerfulness. "Pray send me word! I see they are begin
ning along the road." [2]

She paused a day or two in New York and its environs to visit
her daughter Mrs. Smith and her son Charles and his wife and

baby. May was well in when "on Wednesday morning, about 25 miles from Philadelphia I was met by my friend, who claiming his own, I quitted my own carriage and took my seat by his side. We rode on to Bristol where I had previously engaged a dinner, and there upon the banks of the Delaware we spent the day, getting into the city at sunset." [3]

Abigail was fifty-three and John was sixty-two. They had reached an age when, in the average marriage, mutual interest is at a low ebb. The lover period is long past, the mutual care of young or growing children is finished, the man's widening interests have few points of contact with the narrowing field of the domestic woman. But seldom had Mr. and Mrs. Adams had a better day than this. His heart, when apart from her, yearned for her continually. When he was with her his mind sought after hers. And she brought to him at all times quick response, eager interest, grave judgment, and apt comment. Above all, never did she exacerbate his irritation or add to his fret, either by fanning the flame of his resentment, however just, or by opposing him with disagreement. Each was to each still the favorite, the wanted companion. John Adams, President of the United States, had just summoned a special first session of Congress to hear his report of the French Directory's bad treatment of the American envoys, and what he proposed to do about it. Issues of peace and war loomed on the horizon, and the weighty responsibility that rested on him was the heavier because it was new. But he took a day off to drive to meet his wife and honeymoon with her among the peach and dogwood blossoms on the banks of the Delaware.

They talked about France; and about Mr. Jefferson and Mr. Hamilton; and about daughter Mrs. Smith, and son Charles.

"I found Mrs. Smith and her children in good health," reported Abigail, "but Mrs. Smith grows very fleshy! However, being older and more moulded into the form of a woman, she doesn't look so burdened. The Colonel had been gone for a fortnight up to his new lands, leaving her solitary and forlorn indeed, but for the youngsters. This house they now have at East Chester is miles from the nearest neighbor! It's a poor, wild place, but they must retrench! That gambling in land has got hold of him. Buying one property and selling another, losing so much here, gaining so much there, huge sums passing — his accounts get very confusing. Nabby hardly knows how they stand. My thoughts about their prospects took away all my appetite. I could not discuss them with her. I saw her heart too full. Such is the madness of speculation and extravagance. *She* is not to blame in the least!"

"No. To her no blame is due," said John. He knew remonstrance with his son-in-law was useless. But yet the man had good abilities and some excellent qualities. If he would just get himself a sound steady job. . . . The cardinal's song whistled in poignant sweetness above their silence. John threw some fretful pebbles into the Delaware. Splash. Splash. "Well, how was Charles getting on?"

"Charles seems well-settled in New York. He lives prettily but frugally. He has a lovely babe and a discreet woman I think for his wife." Abigail could not help adding, "Quite different from many of the family!" [4]

"I will tell you a secret," said her husband, "knowing that you are one of the few women who can keep one! Your son John Quincy is going to be sent, if Congress agrees, to Berlin instead of Portugal. The political situation now demands that we have a minister there, one has been asked for, and Portugal must wait."

The sun lowered from the meridian too quickly, the holiday was too soon over. Yet it did not much matter. They were not to part. They got into the chaise and drove together through the flowery afternoon into the sunset city.

The house they were now in was the same one on Market Street which had been occupied by Washington. A larger house had been especially built as a Presidential mansion on Ninth and Market, and was just ready, but Adams refused it. The financial strain would be too great on a President who wanted to live on his salary. Washington had been in command of great private wealth, but even he had used little ostentation. The most showy item had been his cream-colored coach with the painted panels, drawn by six horses with postilions and outriders.

Relations between Mr. Jefferson and Mr. Adams, as Mr. Adams assumed office, were friendly. Mr. Jefferson made a graceful opening speech when he took his seat in the Senate as Presiding Officer, saying that "the high functions of the first office had been justly confided" to Mr. Adams. And Mr. Adams privately asked Mr. Jefferson whether he would consider placing his experience of France at the service of the government and accepting appointment on a new French Commission which Mr. Adams proposed sending to try to untangle the deadlock over there. Mr. Jefferson, however, refused this service very decidedly, not only for himself but for Mr. Madison or for any of his party.

June saw the routine of Presidential life for Mr. and Mrs. Adams fully under way. John felt the harness of office already easy on his shoulders, and as always when Abigail was with him, his eagerness was tempered by a steady serenity.

Abigail had made up her mind to "bear her honors meekly." In fact the road up had been so gradual, so natural in all its steps from the obscure parsonage of her birth, that there was no shock of transition. From the days when Grandmother Quincy had taught her lady's manners, and Grandfather Quincy had taught her public spirit, she had been unconsciously preparing for this station, the highest for a woman in all the world. The hand of destiny that had shaped her put her now into the place, and she fitted in exactly.

Not many months had passed before an observer could say of her, "She is very much respected by everybody. Notwithstanding she comes from the Eastward many acknowledge her to be superior to her sex." [5]

Abigail wrote her sister Mary an account of her day. "I keep up my old habit of rising at an early hour. If I did not I should have little command of my time. At 5 I rise. From that time till 8 I have a few leisure hours. At 8 I breakfast, after which till 11 I attend to my family arrangements. At that hour I dress for the day. From 12 until 2 I receive company, sometimes until 3. We dine at that hour unless on company days, which are Tuesdays and Thursdays. After dinner I usually ride out until 7. I begin to feel a little more at home, and less anxiety about the ceremonious part of my duty, tho by not having a drawing-room for the summer I am obliged every day to devote two hours for the purpose of seeing company."

The chief trial of that summer for Abigail was the keeping of the Fourth of July as established by Washington. "We must then have all the gentlemen of the city, the Governor and officers and companies, all of whom the late President used to treat with cake, punch and wine. . . . As we are here we cannot avoid the trouble nor the expense. I have been informed the day used to cost the late President 500 dollars. . . . More than 200 wt of cake and 2 quarter casks of wine besides spirit. You will not wonder that I dread it, or think President Washington to blame for introducing the custom if he could have avoided it. Congress never were present on that day,* so that I shall have a hundred and fifty of them in addition. . . . Long tables are set in the house and yard." [6]

To make it worse — this trying to live up to a standard set by a wealthier man and yet keep within one's income — Bache's paper started its long-continued personal abuse of President Adams by an attack on his salary. This made Abigail very angry. "The President's salary is $14,000 — the same granted to President Washington without half its value. . . ." [7]

Congress rose late in July, to avoid the "season of the pestilence," now annually looked for. The members scattered. Jefferson went to Monticello, and John and Abigail went back to refreshing Quincy.

On the way up to Boston through New York, they paused to pick up their grandsons, to take them away from the squalor and loneliness of Colonel Smith's farm at East Chester. They were put to school at an Academy in Atkinson, to board in the family of Aunt Peabody (sister Betsy, formerly Aunt Shaw). This was a fine chance for young William and John, now ten and nine. "It will be the making of them, the father's misfortunes will prove the salvation of the children, as their grandfather sometimes observed to me." [8]

Returning in October, Mr. and Mrs. Adams went round by East Chester to get Nabby and her baby girl, who were going to spend the winter with them in Philadelphia. They were held up at East Chester by news of the raging epidemic of yellow fever.

* Always before absent for the summer recess. The critical situation with France kept Congress in session this year until after the Fourth.

Congress had to extend its recess an extra month on account of it. "The deadly disease . . . but for the fleeing of the inhabitants to the number of thirty thousand, wd have made as great ravages as in the year 1793. The frost only puts a stop to it." [9]

During the month of enforced holiday at Nabby's farm, Abigail received a packet of letters from her sons abroad. John Quincy Adams, to his parents' astonishment, was grumbling heartily at having to go to Berlin. His disgruntlement gave his mother "real pain." She confided to him to console him, "If Washington had been in office I can tell you where you wd have been employed — as one of the Envoys to France. This was the desire and opinion of all the Ministers." [10]

As for Thomas, he was not keen about Berlin either. He dreaded making that winter journey, to such a climate, with his rheumatism. But go he must, he could not leave his beloved brother in the lurch. He implored his mother to start things moving to send out a substitute. Nothing else would release him. But he was greatly taken with his new sister-in-law. He reported that Louisa was beautiful and intelligent, would be a true helpmeet for her husband, and that "she loves him as she ought."

He added, "He is very happy and doubtless will remain so, for the young lady has much sweetness of temper. . . . She is indeed a most lovely woman, and in my opinion worthy in every respect of the man for whom she has with so much apparent cheerfulness renounced father and mother, kindred and country, to unite her destinies with his." [11]

Abigail knew that Tom's standards as to what was fit for his brother were exacting indeed. She was impressed. "This," she ruminated, "is a great deal for Thomas to say."

Relations with France steadily deteriorated and on March 5th, 1798, Abigail wrote to Will Smith, "I see not but war is inevitable. This morning for the first time dispatches have arrived from our Envoys. The latest is of January 8th, informing that they had not been received nor was there the least probability that they should be. . . . The French papers are full of abuse against them. In one they call Mr. Pinckney 'a Wretch sold to England.' Every deception is made use of to exasperate the publick mind against Amer-

ica and to prepare them for hostilities. Every paper being under
the despotism of the Directory not a line can be published to
undeceive them." [12]

This passage is evidence of how completely Abigail was in her
husband's secret counsels. The dispatches, though they inspired
John Adams's address to Congress in March, were not published
to Congress and the nation until April 5th. But his wife had read
them on the day of their arrival.

Bache's press never knew that but the uncommonly close relationship between the President and his wife was plain to the
naked eye, and the Jacobin newspapers were already sneering at
Darby and Joan. (Who were "Darby and Joan," Abigail wanted
to know. She could not place the reference. Oh well — she philo-
sophically decided to take it as a compliment!) [13]

John Adams's March message contained a paragraph, written
in by himself, permitting merchantmen to arm. Jefferson, fastening on this single gesture of self-defense, called this dignified and
temperate document "*an insane message.*" Hamilton set in motion
through a member of the House a demand for the dispatches to
be read in full. A resolution was adopted, and the President with
some satisfaction released them. He had only hesitated for fear
of the safety of the envoys.

The publication of the dispatches caused an uproar throughout
the United States. Jefferson's national pride was deeply touched.
He saw that he had been misled, and had misled others. There was
an almost universal demand for war with France to avenge this
insolence. John Adams rode on a tremendous tide of national
popularity. Addresses poured in on him, praising his stand. Young
men formed volunteer corps, drilled; marched two and two —
eleven hundred of them — wearing the black cockade, through
the streets of Philadelphia to offer the President their loyal services. A song, "Hail, Columbia," was made up to the music of the
"President's March" (composed for Washington) and was sung
to the President in theaters and other public places. Mrs. Adams
was saluted and cheered in the streets.[14]

"In short, we are now wonderfully popular except with Bache
and Co who in his paper calls the President" (a hale and vigorous

man of sixty-three) " 'old, querilous, bald, blind, crippled, tooth-
less Adams!' "

In fact, Bache's peculiar brand of personal invective, often point-
less, obviously false, but forever harping, did for that very reason
in the end get under people's skins. He observed Mrs. Adams in
the theater, for instance, moved to very natural tears by an immense ovation to the President with the "new song," and sneered
at it in his paper the next day. No one likes to be caught crying,
still less to have it rudely publicized. Mrs. Adams lost her temper.
A wife's pain lies behind the bitter tone, unlike her own, at "the
vile incendiaries who keep up in Bache's paper the most daring
and base, violent and calumniating abuse. . . . But nothing will
have an effect until Congress pass a Sedition Bill, which I presume
they will do before they rise. Not a paper from Bache's press
issues nor from Adams Chronical but what might have been prosecuted as libels upon the President and Congress." [15]

And on May 26th, in a calmer mood, she repeats her opinion
more firmly. "I wish the laws of our country were competent to
punish the stirrer up of sedition, the writer or printer of loose
and unfounded calumny. This would contribute as much to the
peace and harmony of our country as any measure, and in times
like the present a more careful and attentive watch ought to be
kept over foreigners. This will be done in future if the Alien Bill
passes without being curtailed and clipt until it is made useless."

The Alien and Sedition Bills were passed in the summer session
of 1798, as in times of war fever such measures always have been,
to be repealed when the national temperature returns to normal.
Whether or not John Adams really approved them, at least he
signed them. What his wife thought, we see.

But it is only fair to say that the bills were passed under John
Adams in the heat of immediate expectation of war, and they
were repealed under Jefferson in the calmness of the peace which
had been maintained singlehanded — one might almost say force-
fully created — by John Adams.

The expectation of war was so serious that in July Abigail
wrote, "The commander-in-chief of our Armies raised and to be
raised is the great, the immortal Washington. . . . 'His name is a

host, and the knowledge that he lives a bulwark.' His commission
. . . on 4th July is a new edition of our Declaration of Independence."

Meanwhile national indignation was intensified by the return of
John Marshall in June, with first-hand accounts of his ignominious
treatment by the French. One of the most dignified and able men
in the United States, a rising leader in the Federal party, and a
brilliant lawyer, his character and appearance gave sharper point
to his story, for in his person his government had been belittled.
The fact that Gerry (an Antifederalist or Democrat) was being
received politely made things no better.

Deeply stirred, Mr. Adams sent another message to Congress
in June, in which he included this pungent sentence:

*"I will never send another minister to France without assurances
that he will be received, respected, and honored as the representative of a great, free, powerful and independent nation."*

It was known now that Bache and his like had powerful back-
ing. The year had taught John Adams that there was a deep gulf
between himself and Thomas Jefferson. Their friendship could
have survived disagreement, but it could not survive distrust. It
was no longer possible for them to talk to one another. The ex-
ternals of politeness and quick avoidance were all that could be
endured if by chance or necessity they met. John Adams was
incapable of pretense.

"How different," Abigail bursts out, "is the situation of the
President from that of Washington! The Vice-President never
combined with a party against him and his administration, he
never intrigued with foreign ministers or foreign courts against
his own government and country! He never made Bache his companion and counsellor, on the contrary he aided and strengthened
every measure in support of the Executive and went hand in hand
with him." [16]

It stung all the more because she had liked and trusted Jefferson so much, as had John Adams also. These two great men were
bound together with a strong chain of mutual work, aims, interests, experiences, memories . . . yes, mutual admiration and respect. They could not move apart without pain.

Who could ever have convinced John Adams that in 1783, on his appointment to the Peace Commission, Jefferson had written of his "friend," "He has a sound head on substantial points and I think he has integrity. . . . His dislike of all parties and all men, by balancing his prejudices, may give the same fair play to his reason as would a general benevolence of temper." [17]

And yet four years later, after close association with Adams in Europe, Jefferson wrote, in spite of himself, "He is so amiable that I pronounce you will love him if ever you become acquainted with him."

These things at least John Adams never knew. No cynicism cut, as it might have done, at the very roots of his friendship. As far as he ever knew, all that was bad began with the rise of the Antifederal or Democrat-Jacobin party, and with Jefferson's leadership of the same.

Now the Jacobins appeared guilty of real sedition, in any language. Abigail wrote fiercely to Cousin Will (who had lost several of his ships to French privateers), "I believe it impossible for honesty and truth to reside in the breast of a Jacobin. . . . Talleyrand is in close communication with his friend Bache. . . . He was furnished with Talleyrand's letter. . . . Bache sent out his handbills on Saturday by the thousand." [18] Bache and another printer, Burke, who had recently been driven out of Boston for sedition, presently went too far. Each published statements "in the most positive language that the letters sent to Congress by the President as from Mr. Gerry were altogether a forgery. Bache . . . was arrested * in consequence as Burke will be. . . . Yet the Bill to punish sedition sent down from the Senate will be hard fought in the House, and will have the old French faction opposed to it." [19]

Abigail Adams had enjoyed France in her way and in her briefer

---

* Benjamin Franklin Bache was arrested on June 26th, 1798, on charge of libeling the President and Executive, and released on parole. It is interesting to see the change of tone in the *Aurora* after Bache's arrest. On June 28th one reads, "France already possesses the most valuable commercial parts of Europe. Let the British navy be removed and her empire is complete. The moment France has the ocean under her control she will dictate to us, as she does to the small powers of Europe, all the regulations of trade."

time almost as much as Mr. Jefferson had done in his. But her contacts had been almost entirely with the aristocracy, and of a kind which merely showed the social charm which whitened a decadent and heartless regime. The beginnings of the French Revolution had none the less roused her sympathy. An oppressed people were claiming the inalienable right to life, liberty, and the pursuit of happiness, which every American theoretically believed to be the right of all mankind.

But the Reign of Terror and the execution in particular of Marie Antoinette had filled her with horror. The rise of Napoleon to the leadership of the armies, and the change from a defensive war to protect France from invading armies which sought to restore the Bourbon dynasty to an offensive aggressive war designed to spread the doctrines of revolution everywhere in the world — that was as intolerable and horrifying to her as to the King of England himself.

Abigail reflected a feeling very general in the United States in 1798 when she wrote to Cousin Will in March and June — "France! — so unprincipled, so depraved, so bloodthirsty, so tyrannical a power never before existed. There are no established laws or customs or treaties which they regard, all barriers are broken down and levelled to their necessities and ambition, the people are no more in their estimation than mites upon a cheese.

". . . the astonishing success of the French in overturning every country into which they have carried their arms . . . gives new stimulus to their greedy ambition of becoming masters of the world. England alone appears capable of making a stand against them! Ireland appears to be in a state of actual rebellion. Martial law is proclaimed [there] and rendered necessary by the fermented state of the country. It appears to me that England is the only barrier remaining between France and America and that their attempts upon us will be measured by their success or defeat upon her." [20] Change the name of a single country, and Abigail Adams's letters to William Smith of Boston in March and June, 1798, could be lifted almost entire to the years 1939–1941.

The conversation of her intimate circle emphasized the aggressive intentions of the French toward the United States. Cousin

Will and other merchants were suffering heavy losses at sea. Sam Otis came in one day with another tale to tell, of perhaps even heavier import. *Invasion?* "Indeed, yes. I fear the French have opened their plan," he said, "by taking possession of Louisiana, whence they have easy access to Georgia and the other southern states. In this or some other way they will, in my opinion, compel us to war." [21]

"Indeed we are all but at war," said Abigail, her dark eyes glowing. "Intercourse with France forbidden, the Treaties declared void and no longer obligatory — navy building, and three frigates already at sea — a capture made! [22] All we need is a declaration of war. And — though the President must not hear me say this! — one undoubtedly would have been made — *ought* to have been made — but for Mr. Gerry's unaccountable stay in France! What can he be doing?"

"The President certainly appointed Mr. Gerry against the opinion of many of his friends," said Sam Otis. "Gerry's behaviour is an unpleasant surprise — most improper!"

"That vile intriguer Talleyrand has trapped him!" said Abigail, flashing. "But who would have thought it? I should have supposed him the most wary. Like the serpent he has charmed him! But what a fine answer was made to 'X. Y. Z.' by Mr. Charles Pinckney! *'Millions for defence but not a cent for tribute'* — this is the toast from Georgia to Maine!" [23]

Hamilton saw everything coming his way. Washington had been juggled into making him second-in-command of the new-formed army. General Knox, with experience both in battle and in the War Department during the Revolution, had been the far more suitable nomination of John Adams, but the President yielded to Washington.

A worse hurt, a very sharp one, was in connection with his son-in-law. Colonel Smith was by profession a soldier, and here was a chance for professional soldiers.

The President accordingly proposed Colonel Smith on his list of officers as Adjutant General, and it was approved by Washington. The nominations then had to be confirmed by the Senate. Taking advantage of his confidential knowledge of the list of

Washington's recommendations, Secretary of State Pickering hurried from the President's study to the Senate House to work up feeling against Colonel Smith. He also wrote a letter to Hamilton on the subject. He put, in fact, the machinery of the Hamilton party in motion against Colonel Smith, before the President's list reached the floor. The betrayal was high-lighted by the fact that the Senate confirmed all the nominations except that of the President's son-in-law. Confirmation of the nominations was looked upon as more or less perfunctory, and the personal insult was marked.

"It was the last day of the session," wrote Abigail to Cousin Will, "& there were many secret springs at work, some were made the tools of they knew not whom . . . others glad to do anything which they thought would wound the President. . . . I cannot however say but what much of the unpopularity in which Colonel Smith is placed is owing to his own folly & indiscretion which has ever been condemned by the Pres. and by me as fully as by others. Yet as an officer he was beloved . . . I think it will wound and hurt the Col. more than anything he ever met with." [24]

Sam Otis, as a member of the family, felt it too. "I had the mortification to hear Col. Smith negatived on Thursday by the Senate. . . . The poor fellow has now no prospect." [25]

But this incident gave John Adams a great light. He detected leakage. When Congress rose, immediately after the Smith incident, in the third week in July, members scattered hastily to escape the yellow fever, and Mr. and Mrs. Adams, with their household, drove up to Quincy.

Abigail Adams's Last Winter in Philadelphia

Two mosquitoes now took their place upon the national stage. Both were natives of Philadelphia. They have remained anonymous and unsuspected until the present day, but the combined searchlights of history and science have spied them out, and fidgeting bashfully they take their bow. The first bit Mrs. Adams on or about July 25th, perhaps at the very moment when she was getting into the coach to leave the city. It set the germs of malaria in her blood. The second, working later in the summer with hosts of its sisters spreading yellow fever about the town, bit Franklin Bache, the printer, Franklin's grandson, and silenced him forever.

Neither Mrs. Adams nor Mr. Bache even noticed or thought of the familiar short-lived irritation of the bite as the origin of their ills. Mrs. Adams found explanation enough in the weather and the travel. "The season of my journey was the hottest I ever knew." [1] She reached Quincy at last, in her husband's anxious care, and for eleven weeks she was confined to her chamber and expected to die. "A bilious disease and an intermitting fever" made her days and nights miserable. Even after she was up and about again, restored to life, the fever still hung on in a low, recurring way, right into November, "depressing my spirits and depriving me of my sleep in a manner which I never before experienced." [2]

She longed for frost, the blessed, healthy frost. And indeed the first frost, by killing off all the mosquitoes, did check plagues of malaria and yellow fever like magic. No one knew why, but they observed the fact, and drew the conclusion that cold itself was healthy.

Abigail's mosquito kept her from going to Philadelphia again until November 1799. But the hideous ravages of yellow fever in the late summers of '98 and '99 compelled long recesses for Congress. In '99 Abigail told John Quincy Adams, "Your father spent six months at Quincy in as much tranquillity as the public business of his station would permit."

Throughout the whole of this period from the summer of '98 to the fall of '99, in Quincy, in Philadelphia, and in the final climax at Trenton, John Adams was engaged in a singular struggle with the members of his cabinet. Or rather not so much with the members of his cabinet as with the unseen foe behind them, for whom they were the cat's-paws and stalking horses.

When Mr. and Mrs. Adams drove away from Philadelphia in the heavy choking dust that hot July, Mrs. Adams expected — and so did everybody else — that once Mr. Gerry got safely home, the administration next session would make a declaration of war against France.

But Mr. Adams had something else that he wanted to think about in the quiet. Colonel Smith's rejection was like a tiny leak in a dike. A torrent of ideas poured after. He looked backward. During the tussle over the generalship, something had gone on that he did not understand. Washington was away off at Mount Vernon, out of sight, out of touch, dimmed to the mental vision by distance, like a man muffled in a cloak. John Adams, recommending Knox, had stretched out a confident hand toward the muffled figure, sure of a reciprocal handclasp, as of old — and had met beneath the folds of the cloak the blow of a mailed fist. It was not Washington. What was it?

The answer became clear, carrying many implications in its train. It was Hamilton.

What then was Hamilton working for, if this accumulating evidence was correct and he was exercising secret dominance in the Cabinet through Pickering, and — yes — through McHenry? He was working indubitably for war.

Abigail, who saw so much with those bright eyes of hers, who heard so many crosscurrents of talk, had struck out one of her illuminating sentences when Hamilton had been made a general.

"I am surprised," she said, "at the want of knowledge of human nature! That man would in my opinion become a second Buonaparty if he was possessed of equal power!" [8]

That surely was the clue. Hamilton wanted to become a second Bonaparte. Therefore everything suggested by his henchmen, Pickering and McHenry, became suspect. John Adams's candid nature did not even yet suspect the extent of the treachery of those two, and he never suspected Wolcott — in some ways the arch traitor — at all.*

There might have to be war — it looked very much that way. But if so, it should be in spite of Hamilton's pressure, not because of it.

In the quiet of Quincy, going about his farm tasks, sitting beside the sickbed of his wife, John Adams gathered his soul. In the presence of the threat of death and sorrow, human affairs took on a different proportion. It was easy to see that in whatever difficulties lay before him as President of a disloyal cabinet he could steer his way correctly if he maintained clearness, steadiness, integrity. Did not allow personal resentment to cloud his vision, nor obstinacy to distort his just opinion.

The urge toward war on every side was tremendous. Even Abigail had shared it. Surely if she had been President of the United States instead of her husband, war would have been declared before Congress rose. How touched she had been by the young men. The youth of all the great cities from eighteen to twenty-three offering themselves; the students of Harvard sending in an address which she had learned by heart, so noble, so Roman, she thought it.

"We solemnly offer the unarrested ardor and unimpaired energies of our youth to the services of our country, our lives are our only property and we were not the sons of those who seal'd our

* It is quite touching to see him giving the suave Wolcott a justiceship for life as a parting present in 1800, when Wolcott had just been providing Hamilton with copies of papers from the State Department to provide ammunition for Hamilton's great attempt to blast John Adams's reputation. And Wolcott was touched at last by the man's simple greatness, and shedding tears of gratitude (and secret remorse) promised to be grateful as he ought. His reform was negative, and too late, but it was something.

liberties with their blood if we wd not defend with those lives
that soil which now affords a peaceful grave to the mouldering
bones of our forefathers."

And as for her ardent pro-Britishness, Hamilton himself could
not do better! The French thought they would invade England,
did they? Ha, let 'em just try! "They will find that they have
not Italians and Dutchmen to deal with." [4]

But now all her fire was quenched in sickness. She lay with a
different, pathetic charm, her cheeks flushed almost with her girlhood bright complexion, her eyes large with fever, holding her
husband's hand, being read to in his sonorous voice — Shakespeare
and Milton and sister Peabody's [5] letters, who "knew as well as
ever Shakspeare did every avenue to the heart." If left alone too
long she grew depressed. She, who had taken care of everyone,
now had everyone taking care of her. And it endeared her to
them all the more. Husband, nieces, friends, domestics, they took
their willing turns. Her pet birds and puppies were brought in to
amuse her. In her low state the tears were all too ready if she
brooded long: about Nabby and her difficulties; about parents and
friends long dead; and about Charles. In the nighttime, about
Charles.

Charles was going downhill. And it was not all his fault. Charles
was unlucky. He had fallen into complicated financial difficulties,
all of which he did not confess to his mother until the end of this
year. But in June, a friend and connection, Dr. Welch, with whom
all of the family had from time to time invested money, went suddenly bankrupt. He and Charles were in charge of the small re-
mittance which John Quincy Adams squeezed out of his meager
salary, with an eye to the future when he should return home
out of a job. Abigail got early word of Dr. Welch's failure, and
wrote at once to Charles to stop making any remittances to him
on John Quincy's account, but got no reply. "Indeed, my dear
son," she wrote John Quincy, "I am not without fears that you
will lose all you have been so prudently and carefully saving."

Charles's stubborn silence had painful reasons. In fact, Charles
was the worst person in the world to bear financial trouble, and
when remorse and mortification at mishandling his brother's funds

was added, it drove him into just the course bound to increase his distresses. Luck at cards could turn a man's fortunes overnight. Liquor could help a too sensitive heart to forget a misery it could not endure.

In November, the distressed mother, frail from her long sickness, wrote to one son about the other. "In several of your late letters," she said to John Quincy, "you have mentioned a subject which has been a source of distress to me for a long time; it is hard upon you. . . . I have written again upon the subject and expostulated in such terms as must procure an explanation and reply. I will write you whatever I can collect, but the poor child is unhappy, I am sure; he is not at peace with himself; and his conduct does not meet my wishes. He has an amiable wife, prudent and discreet, who has every wish and disposition to render *Home* the most delightful spot; two lovely children — I hope my letters will in time have their effect, I have discharged my duty I hope faithfully, but my dying bed was embittered (as I then thought it) with distress for the only child whose conduct ever gave me pain." [6]

In December Charles braced himself at last to the painful task of coming clean with what he had done with that part of his brother's money that had not sunk with Dr. Welch. He wrote explaining that to save Colonel Smith from immediate confinement for debt, he had exchanged John Quincy Adams's mortgage for a note drawn by Colonel Smith's young brother Justice, but the fall of the price of land had prevented him from paying the interest. "Justice Smith lives upon his lands and has a large tract in possession, but what he owes I know not. Charles you know never had the power of resistance. I dare say his own property has gone the same way. Charles said, 'I have not enjoyed one moment's comfort for upwards of two years on this account, my sleep has been disturbed and my waking hours embittered.' "

Justice Smith, it might be said, was a most attractive character, a genial bachelor, on whose large frontier tracts up in the Lebanon Valley of New York State Colonel Smith took refuge after his final ruin by his rash part in the Miranda expedition to South America in 1806.

Colonel Smith's foolishness was always getting him into trouble, his sweetness and good faith were always involving other persons to get him out. This time he unfortunately involved Charles Adams, whose sweetness and good faith certainly were not less than his own, but whose sensitiveness was painfully greater. The family disapproval on this matter — and they could not help it — added one more weight to Charles's sinking self-respect. A weight all the heavier because he knew how much they loved him.

*   *   *   *   *

Troops were drilling, camps were forming.

Colonel Smith by this time had a modest commission and was happy, doing wonders at camp. Preparations were going forward as if war were imminent. But the international crisis held off, marking time, while the President of the United States waited the return of the fully informed envoy, Mr. Gerry.

On October 1st, Mr. Gerry arrived, coming straight to Quincy to make his peace with the President. John and Abigail welcomed him, and heard his detailed reasons for staying. Sufficient or not, at least he now had definite news to give. Talleyrand desired to begin a new negotiation.

War was an essential part of Hamilton's plan and ambition. The cabal set themselves to prepare a form of words for the President's adoption at the opening of Congress which, holding him rigidly to his former statement that he would never again send an envoy uncertain of full reception, would leave no loophole of retreat, no alternative but war. Hamilton called a council of leaders and composed a careful draft.

Late in November, 1798, John Adams arrived at Philadelphia for Congress — ignorant of this council and its project. He called his Cabinet, examined their draft, and calmly rewrote the key sentences. With this revised speech he opened Congress. "Vigorous preparations for war would be continued since those alone will give us an equal treaty . . . further negotiations would depend upon evidence of return of good faith in France."

The more Hamilton's policy was resisted, the more he had to

declare that policy in order to fight for it. Moreover, John Adams now had evidence that not only was Hamilton dictating policy to members of the Cabinet, but far worse — there was a definite leakage of private information from the Cabinet to Hamilton. However, as he had said when he first entered on his stormy Presidency, he had never felt more serene. His inward compass pointed steadily to the north. The change in French policy was continually borne witness to by William Vans Murray, the American Minister to Holland. Encouraged by Mr. Adams, that excellent diplomat had incited the Dutch to make an offer of mediation, in order that a regular channel might be opened between the French and the American Government. On January 21st a French message reached the President. It declared that "the disposition of the French to reconciliation had been already unmistakeably made known at Philadelphia — it was the responsibility of the United States if they persisted in misconstruing or repulsing it." [7] This was followed in a few weeks by a letter from Talleyrand himself through the same channel, in which the experienced French diplomat introduced the very form of words which John Adams had used in his speech to Congress as his condition for sending an envoy to France.

On receiving Talleyrand's letter, so full and complete, John Adams determined on action. Useless to consult his Cabinet again — to do so was to invite not only obstruction but leakage. He must exercise the hitherto unused prerogatives granted by the Constitution to the President of the United States. On February 18th, 1799, the members of the Senate, not one of which knew what was coming, received a message from the President enclosing Talleyrand's letter, and announcing the President's appointment of William Vans Murray as special envoy of the United States to France. Always provided further unequivocal assurances of his right reception should be given the United States Government by the French.

This announcement was equally astounding to all parties. Jefferson averred that John Adams had held back Talleyrand's letter for months to jack up the war party, and only produced it now and made this nomination in order to get the mission rejected by the Senate! (It is hard to believe that Jefferson could really think that outright John Adams was capable of such a devious policy. Mr. Jefferson was always being tripped up by his own subtlety.) Hamilton's party felt the ground ripped out from under them.

Mr. Adams met protests by joining two other delegates with Mr. Murray on the Commission. He nominated Chief Justice Oliver Ellsworth and Patrick Henry. Hamilton warned his adherents they must submit. The Senate ratified. Now Hamilton and his faithful henchmen in the Cabinet settled down to a silent policy of stultifying delay.

John Adams wrote to his wife — "I have instituted a new mission, which is kept in the dark, but when it comes to be understood it will be approved. O, how they lament Mrs. Adams's absence! She is a good counsellor! If she had been here, Murray would never have been named nor his mission instituted! This ought to gratify your vanity enough to cure you!" [8]

And again he expresses the inward quiet, the sense of proportion, engendered in him by the profound experiences of the summer. Party strife is in abeyance (in his heart). Ambition has no more to ask. "I have no idea that I shall be chosen President a second time; though this is not to be talked of. The business of the office is so oppressive that I shall hardly support it two years longer. . . . I do not remember that I was ever vindictive in my life, though I have often been very wroth. I am not very angry now, nor much vexed or fretted. The mission came across the views of many, and stirred the passions of more. This I knew was unavoidable. The reasons which determined me are too long to be written. . . .

"Your sickness last summer, fall and winter has been to me the severest trial I ever endured.

"Not that I am at this moment without other trials, enough for one man." [9]

The Hamiltonians might well regret the absence of Mrs. Adams! As her health grew stronger, her old mood of Hurrah for Britain, 'ware Jefferson and the wicked French, returned. Nelson was her hero.

"Great Britain is fighting for all the other powers!" [10] she said to Cousin Will.

"Government of States and Kingdoms, tho' God knows badly enough managed, I am willing should be solely administered by the lords of the creation. I should only contend for Domestic government, and think that best administered by the female." [11]

John was taking care of France. Her mind was more concerned with her sons. Thomas got back from Berlin in February. He went straight to Philadelphia, to give dispatches and report to the President and Secretary of State, but in a week or two he came to Quincy to his mother. "His father needs him," she wrote eagerly to John Quincy, "he wants that comfort and relief, encompassed as he is with public cares and perplexities as well as a share of private anxiety for the health of your Mother, which is still feeble." Tom's visit in the early spring was like a tonic. It was health-giving happiness just when she needed it. After all, she had four children. Why should her mind brood so incessantly over the one? . . . But like the shepherd in the story, so it did. The lost one took more of her thoughts than any other. Tom left Quincy in April to return to Philadelphia, where he had taken lodgings and an office to set up as a lawyer. There was nothing wrong with Tom except his delicate health. But Charles . . . "Your brother Charles is — what shall I say that will not pain us both? Wd to God that I might kill the fatted calf and put upon him the robe of rejoicing. He has formed good resolutions, cd he keep them how it would rejoice us all. But the heart, the principles must co-operate. How sharper than a serpent's tooth it is to have a graceless child, may you, my dear son, never experience. Blessed be God, I have those in whom I can rejoice." [12]

She tried to dissuade Thomas from settling in Philadelphia. "The dreaded Yellow Fever must drive him annually from it . . . unless some measures are speedily discovered to stop its progress. It becomes every year more destructive and horrible. There is no doubt of its being still in the city, though the winter checks its baneful influence. New York and Boston both suffered the last season. Much pains is taken to investigate the causes, I hope the researches may prove successful, and God grant the remedy may be found." [13]

Congress rose early, to escape the hot weather and the plague, the ravages of the previous summer ('93 and '98 were the two worst epidemics known to history) being vivid in their minds. Husband and son joined Abigail at Quincy. In the long, hot peace of July, filled with the hum of insects and the sound of the everlasting surf, refreshing to an exile's ears, dispatches arrived with Talleyrand's reply. It bore a categorical acceptance of John Adams's terms, which itself was assurance of a disposition to peace. John Adams sat down in his study, with the scent of the roses of Auteuil blowing in through the windows, and wrote to Colonel Pickering. He directed immediate action, the prompt preparation of the commission papers and departure of the envoys. But Pickering delayed.

Late in August the raging yellow fever in Philadelphia compelled the moving of the government offices to Trenton. The very day they settled in, August 26th, Pickering received a private letter from Mr. Murray that another revolution had happened in the Directory, and Talleyrand himself was out. There were rumors of returning the French Jacobins to power. This was a stroke of luck for the Cabinet cabal. On consultation, it was resolved to send Mr. Adams the correctly prepared papers for the envoys — to show the work done — but to enclose a remonstrance against the Commission's going at this time. John Adams examined the papers, acquiesced in a short period of delay, set the latter part of October as its term, and promised to be himself in Trenton by October 15th. Hamilton came to Newark, to be within call.

John Adams arrived in Trenton on October 10th, rather unwell with a cold taken on the journey, but filled with that deep calm engendered in him by a sense of crisis, and fortified by the healthy quiet months at Quincy with his wife. He met the members of the Cabinet politely, yet one * of them soon perceived a difference in his treatment of them. Mr. Hamilton was soon on the spot too, to support his henchmen strongly in the background. All awaited

* Adam's only appointee so far, the new Secretary of the Navy.

the moment for a trial of strength. They expected a violent altercation. In such a scene, Mr. Adams could easily be provoked to put himself in the wrong — or so they conjectured. News from Europe, of British and Russian successes, made Hamilton believe the Bourbons were almost as good as back on the throne of France. A treaty made with any section of the revolutionists would be no treaty! They talked with passion. Mr. Adams watched their vehemence, and wrote a letter to his wife of calm surprise. He read their motives clearly. He saw it was not delay, it was final defeat of the mission they were after.

On the evening of October 15th he summoned the Cabinet to a meeting. They came, all armed for battle. But things did not go as they expected. He laid before them the draft of instructions to the Commission which had been sent to him at Quincy, and requested their advice on some technical points. The draft was discussed, amended, finally approved unanimously. But time was passing, it was eleven o'clock; too late to start a new discussion. The President stated no new propositions, and after a thoughtful pause it seemed good manners to go. The Cabinet members took their leave, suppressing yawns, feeling vaguely flat and punctured, but expecting to be summoned in the morning for the real showdown.

Instead, before breakfast in the morning two of them — the Secretary of State and the Secretary of the Navy — received a laconic order from the President, in writing, that the instructions finally agreed on for the Commissioners should be at once made out, and the frigate *United States* should be put in readiness for their use, and the Commission should set sail for France on or before the first of the coming month.

So the President used to the full the powers of his office as no one had supposed he would dare to do. So he defeated the schemes of Hamilton, who had the mind and will of a dictator, and who saw himself left without a generalship and without an army. So — accused by Jefferson of warmongering — John Adams by his single will carried America to peace. The averted war would have been as popular with the country at large as it would have been disastrous. John Adams lost some popular support, earned at one stroke the undying jealousy of Jefferson and the malicious hatred of Hamilton, and launched the United States on an era of peace and prosperity, for which his successor in office, who had only to reap the harvest, got most of the credit.

The Commission * sailed on November 5th. Napoleon Bonaparte was now in power.

They were received with all honor by Napoleon, a clear-sighted statesman who regarded war with America as preposterous. He concluded with them a peace which has remained unbroken to this day.

All John Adams cared was that that great end was accomplished; far greater than party strife or party victory.

And if tombstones were being designed, what John Adams wanted on his was just one line — "Here lies John Adams, who took upon himself the responsibility of peace with France."

* * * * *

The winter of 1799 was the last winter the Government was to spend in Philadelphia. When Congress rose in the spring for the hot season — the fever season — it would be farewell. They would reassemble in the fall in the new headquarters so long building on the banks of the Potomac.

Abigail enjoyed that winter. Her health was good, she was able to be with her husband and perform her social duties as First Lady; and two of her children were with her. Tom, who was a great comfort, and Nabby, with that darling little Caroline who "had soft and tender manners and yet was as lively as a bird." Colonel Smith had a commission as Lieutenant Colonel and was in camp with his regiment in the Jerseys. Poor Nabby, when peace was declared in the spring of 1800, her first thought was that her husband was out of a job again.

The President and his wife, though both had a great deal of natural dignity, put on no ostentation. The routine of drawing

* Chief Justice Ellsworth and Governor Davie of North Carolina. The first appointees, John Marshall and Patrick Henry, were unable to serve. The head of the Commission, William Vans Murray, was of course already abroad, in Holland, and had only a short overland journey to meet the others in Paris.

rooms, levees, and dinners was much as in Washington's time, but something had happened to thaw the etiquette. Talk flowed freely. John Adams, said a youth who knew him, "had not the smallest chip of an ice-berg in his composition." [14] While Mrs. Adams "continues the same pleasant attentive person as at Quincy." [15]

The last drawing room took place on May 2nd. But, for many weeks before, social festivity had been overshadowed, bright scarves and trimmings of the fashionable transparent muslins gave way to black and white. "I wish someone would persuade them that muslin is not suitable for winter dress!" Mrs. Adams had sighed. It was a French fashion, too. But mourning was a dismal change. And the reason for it sank through to the heart. George Washington was dead.

He died in the dead of winter at the close of the year. He had only had three years to enjoy his retirement, to call himself Farmer Washington; and the latter part of those had been disturbed by his technical generalship of the new-forming army.

Abigail's sister's son, William Shaw, rode to Mount Vernon with the official letter of condolence from the President and Congress to Mrs. Washington, and the official request to bury Washington's body in a national monument perhaps at the new city. He came back with Mrs. Washington's reply, and with details of the last illness.

"It was due to the General's eagerness to get on with some improvements on his farm that he caught his death," he told his aunt and uncle as they sat together in a firelit family circle in mutual sorrow.

"I can understand that," said John Adams. "But what in winter? In December?"

"He had in contemplation a gravel walk on the banks of the Potomac," said Shaw. "Between the walk and the river there was to be a fish-pond. Some trees were to be cut down, and others preserved. On Friday — the day before he died — he spent some time by the side of the river marking the trees. There came a fall of snow, but he still continued till his neck and hair were covered with snow. He spent the evening with Mrs. Washington, reading the newspapers, which came by the mail of that evening; went to bed as usual about nine o'clock — waked up in the night — found himself extremely unwell, but would not allow Mrs. Washington to get up or the servant to be waked. In the morning he was worse. Dr. Craik of Alexandria was sent for. He saw it was serious, and asked for more help. Two consulting physicians were called in, but all would not avail. On Saturday evening he died. Mrs. Washington was in the room but he took no particular leave of anyone." [16]

There was a silence, while all thought of the peacefulness of the end, the meaning of the loss. And the older ones were busy with memories.

"He was writing a history of the Revolution, I understood?" said Tom.

"No," said his cousin. "But he left a minute journal of his daily life — at least his public life! — which will contain material for a history. This Journal, and his library of 1500 volumes, and Mount Vernon with 4000 acres of land he has left to his nephew the Judge, after Mrs. Washington has had them for life. All his negroes, are to be made free on Mrs. Washington's decease." [17]

"May I read her letter?" said Mrs. Adams. And she wept upon it. Later she wrote to Hannah Smith — "You will have seen and admired Mrs. Washington's answer to the letter of the President, so expressive, so dignified, so pathetic. Yet there are persons who will not allow her the merit of having penned it. I know the contrary. Not only her last letter to me, but many others which upon different occasions I have received from her show her to be not only a good, a virtuous, a religious woman, but of a dignified mind."

No one certainly was a better judge of that than Abigail Adams.

The Presidential election was coming on apace. Mr. Adams had no organized party behind him, as did Jefferson and Hamilton. His mind did not run on those lines. He did no campaigning, spending the summer quietly at Quincy organizing his new Cabinet — now for the first time all his own appointees — and attending to current business. The election was not even run on a straight party issue, owing to the queer three-cornered turn given to it by Hamilton. And yet John Adams came near getting in for a second term. The defection of South Carolina was the chief and final weight which loaded the scale against the Federalists.

The defection of South Carolina and other waverers was due less to loss of confidence in Mr. Adams than to the extraordinary split in the Federal ranks made by Hamilton's complicated intrigues. Mr. Hamilton suffered from thwarted ambition; and the person who had thwarted his ambition (quite impersonally) was John Adams. Therefore he did not want John Adams to be President. But the only hope for his ambitions was the victory of the Federalist party. Jefferson was his personal enemy. He could not tolerate Jefferson as President.

Hamilton had the mortification not only of ruining himself but of seeing his two most hated enemies, Jefferson and Aaron Burr, tied for first place with seventy-three votes apiece. The House of Representatives appointed Jefferson, with Burr as Vice-President.

Braintree's answer to Hamilton's malignant attack was to give John Adams a big public birthday celebration on October 19th, to toast and praise him. People came in from Weymouth and Hingham and Boston. There were fireworks in the clear autumn evening over the sea. Abigail had already left, to break her journey to the new Capital, Washington, with a visit in New York with Nabby. But she read of it in the Boston newspapers with joy and comfort. In fact, she was so proud of it that she became quite stiff and Biblical with pride.

"It was truly gratifying to find in a world of calumny and falsehood that a prophet cd meet with honor in his own native soil." [18]

XVII

Retirement to Quincy

A BIGAIL needed something to be proud of. She needed to gather up all the good things she could and press them like fragrant healing herbs against that bruise in her mind which was the thought of Charles. When her fevers came on now, the doctor bled her and she was quickly well. But Shakespeare knew too much when he adjured the wise physician, "Say, canst thou minister to a mind diseased? Pluck from the memory a rooted sorrow?" What had she done that was so wrong with Charles? Or was it her fault, when John Quincy, surely brought up much the same — and Nabby and Tom, too — had turned out so well? "Seeing you a wise and virtuous man," she wrote to John in September 1800, "is a cordial to my heart and mitigates in some measure the weight of sorrow which weighs it down from another source by one from which I have not a hope of change, habits are so rooted, the temper so soured, the whole man so changed that ruin and destruction have swallowed him up and his affairs are become desperate. Sally and her infant daughter are gone to her mother, Susan [the other little girl] I brought home with me — all is lost — poor, poor, unhappy wretched man — all remonstrances have been lost upon him. God knows what is to become of him. His Father has renounced him — but I will not.

"Your sister and her little girl have passed the summer with me. The Colonel has been appointed Supervisor and inspector of the port of New York since the disbandment of the Army. As he has suffered in the school of adversity I hope he will consider and make a proper estimate of life." [1]

But the Colonel, no more than Charles, could make a proper estimate of life. With Charles the disease of alcoholism had fastened on his being, as on the being of his mother's brother before him. Moral suasion tormented but could not cure. The Colonel on the other hand was afflicted with an incurable ailment of another kind, a romantic megalomania, which always saw himself four times as large as life, performing an admired part on a stage. A little Hamilton, a pocket Napoleon, even an imitation Washington. So he would make a big splash with money when he had it, and then run into debt, to the ruin of his friends. Just the man to be caught by Miranda,* as he was a few years later. But Jefferson too was caught — even Napoleon said of Miranda, "He has fire in his heart." And Jefferson, resentful at the Colonel's public statement implicating him, when on trial in 1806, and trying to subpoena his Secretary of State, exercised one of those gestures of petty spite which marred his career, and removed the little man from his little post at the Port of New York. So he and John Adams's delicate daughter (Jefferson's once admired young friend) had to go live in the wilderness, on the farm broken out by Justice Smith in the Colonel's frontier land in upstate New York, and wring from that rough life as much comfort as they could.

John Adams had written his son-in-law in December 1798 — "I will be plain with you. Your pride and ostentation, which I have seen with inexpressible grief for many years, have excited among your neighbors so much envy and resentment that if they have to allege against you for any instance of dishonorable conduct, as it is pretended they have, you may depend upon it, it will never be forgiven or forgotten." [2]

But something more bitterly deserving the name of grief than Colonel Smith's efforts to assume greatness awaited Abigail in New York. She found her son Charles deserted and alone in the last stages of sickness and squalor. And the news of his death followed her to Washington three weeks after her arrival there. Her letters to her sister and to her son John Quincy in December, from Washington, D. C., give vivid detail of the end of his

---

* A Spaniard infected with the Napoleon virus who conceived a project of alliance between England and America for the conquest of the entire South American continent.

sad days. "Weep with me over the grave of a poor unhappy child who cannot now add another pang to those which have pierced my heart for several years past. Cut off in the midst of his days, his years are numbered and finished. . . .

"I knew not that he was sick. When I arrived at New York on my way to this city [Washington] I went to see him. He had been ill a week. But you may judge my feelings when I saw that his case was desperate. He was at lodgings. Your sister, who had spent the summer with me, returned to New York when I did. She removed him immediately to her home and every kind care and sisterly attention was shown him. The removal of him was all the release, all the consolation I could derive. I came to this city with a heavy heart in daily expectation of his death, which took place on the first of December.

"His constitution was so shaken that his disease was rapid. His sufferings were severe, his patience under them was great. Food has not been his sustenance, yet he did not look like an intemperate man. He was bloated, but not red. He was no man's enemy but his own. He was beloved in spite of his error, and all spoke with grief and sorrow of his habits.

"He appeared most tender and affectionate. His mind was constantly running upon doing justice and making reparation. Early principles, though stifled, now discovered themselves; and Mercy I hope was extended to him. The tender remembrance of what he once was rises before me. Think of him, my son, with the compassion of a brother." [3]

All this was on Abigail's heart during the journey, with the added pang that she could not wait with her dying son, for her public duties inexorably claimed her.

The execution of L'Enfant's beautiful designs for the city of Washington — the first American city to be designed from the start on a great basic plan — had been constantly held up for lack of funds from an unimaginative Congress. But the ten years allotted to Philadelphia were up, and the seat of government must be moved, ready or not. So it moved.

On November 21st, 1800, Abigail sat down in the unfinished

President's House,* in the smallest room she could find, by the
biggest fire she could get, and took up her eager pen to tell her
sister all about her adventures on the journey, and what she had
come to.

"I arrived in this city on Sunday (the 16th ult.). Having lost
my way in the woods on Saturday in going from Baltimore, we
took the road to Frederick and got nine miles out of our road.
You find nothing but a forest and woods on the way, for 16 or
18 miles not a village. Here and there a thatched cottage without
a single pane of glass, inhabited by Blacks. My intention was to
have reached Washington on Saturday.

"Last winter there was a Gentleman and Lady in Phila. by the
Name of Snowden. . . . They visited me and were invited to
dine . . . but did not as they left the city . . . they . . . live on
the road to this place 21 miles distant. I was advised at Baltimore
to make their House my stage for the night, the only Inn at
which I could put up being 36 miles ride from Baltimore . . . but
I, who have never been accustomed to quarter myself and servants upon private houses, could not think of it, particularly as I
expected the chariot and 5 more Horses with two servants to meet
me. I set out early intending to make my 36 miles if possible: no
travelling however but by day-light. We took a direction as we
supposed right, but in the first turn went wrong, and were wandering more than two hours in the woods in different paths, holding down and breaking boughs of trees which we would not pass,
until we met a solitary black fellow with a horse and cart. We
inquired of him our way, and he kindly offered to conduct us,
which he did two miles, and then gave us such a clue as led us out
to the post road and the Inn where we got some dinner. Soon
after we left it we met the chariot, then 30 miles from Washington, and 20 from our destination. We rode as fast as the roads
would allow of, but the sun was near set when we came in sight
of the Major's. I halted, but could not get the courage to go to
his House with ten Horses and nine persons. I therefore ordered
the coach man to proceed, and we drove rapidly on. We had got
about a mile when we were stopped by the Major in full speed,

* Not yet called the White House.

who had learnt that I was comeing on, and had kept watch for me, with his Horse at the door, as he was at a distance from the road. In the kindest and politest manner he urged my return to his House, represented the danger of the road, and the impossibility of my being accommodated at any Inn I cd reach. A mere hovel was all I shd find. I pled my numbers. That was no objection. He cd accommodate double the number. There was no saying nay, and I returned to a large Handsome, Elegant House, where I was received with my Family with what we might term true English Hospitality, friendship without ostentation, and kindness without painfull ceremony. Mrs. Snowden is a charming woman of about 45. She has a lovely daughter of 16, and one of 6, a son whom I had seen often in Philadelphia and who had several times dined with us. I need not add that they are all true federal characters. Every attention possible was shown me and the next morning I took my departure, having shared in the common bounty of Major Snowden's hospitality for which he is universally celebrated.

"I arrived about one o'clock at this place known by the name of 'the city,' and the Name is all that you can call so! As I expected to find it a new country, with Houses scattered over a space of ten miles, and trees and stumps in plenty, with a castle of a House, so I found it.

"The President's House is in a beautiful situation in front of which is the Potomac with a view of Alexandria. The country round is romantic but a wild wilderness at present.

"But surrounded with forests can you believe that wood is not to be had, because people cannot be found to cut and cart it! Breisler entered into a contract with a man to supply him with wood . . . but a few cords only has he been able to get. We have had some very cold weather and we feel it keenly. This House is twice as large as our meeting House. I believe the great Hall is as Bigg. I am sure 'tis twice as long. Cut your coat according to your cloth. But this House is built for ages to come. The establishment necessary is a task which cannot be born by the present sallery. Nobody can form an idea of it but those who come into it. . . . Not one room or chamber is finished of the whole. It is habitable by fires in every part, thirteen of which we are obliged to keep daily, or sleep in wet and damp places. To assist us in this great castle, and render less attendance necessary, bells are wholly wanting, not one single one being hung through the whole house, and promises are all you can obtain. This is so great an inconvenience that I know not what to do! . . .

"The ladies from Georgetown and in the 'city' have many of them visited me. Yesterday I returned fifteen visits — but such a place as Georgetown! I felt all that Mrs. Cranch described when she was a resident there. It is the very dirtyest Hole I ever saw for a place of any trade or respectability of inhabitants. It is only one mile from me, but a quagmire after every rain. Here we are obliged to send daily for marketing. The capitol is near two miles from us. As to roads, we shall make them by the frequent passing before winter! But I am determined to be satisfied and content, to say nothing of inconvenience, etc. That must be a worse place than even George Town that I could not reside in for three months! If they will put me up some bells and let me have wood enough to keep fires, I design to be pleased. We have not the least fence-yard or other convenience without, and the great unfinished audience-room I make a drying-room of, to hang the clothes in. The principal stairs are not up, and will not be this winter." But as the forlorn picture of the unfinished house takes shape, and the smell of the wet plaster is in our nostrils, she hastens to ameliorate it. "Look, there are six chambers made comfortable. And two lower rooms, one for a common parlor, and one for a levee room. And upstairs there is the oval room, which is designed for the drawing-room, and has the crimson furniture in it. It is a very handsome room now; but when completed it will be beautiful."

Now, she warns her correspondent, "Keep all this to yourself, and when asked how I like it, say that I wrote you the situation is beautiful, which is true!"

She had a nephew to welcome her, the attractive Will Cranch who had gone through Harvard with John Quincy Adams. There are other dear friends too, one especially — not too far off, though a difficult drive in present weather. "Since I sat down to write I have been called down to a servant from Mount Vernon, with a billet from Major Custis, and a haunch of venison, with Mrs. Washington's love, inviting me to Mount Vernon, where health permitting, I will go before I leave this place."

"Before I leave this place." It won't be long now before she has to lay down the rank of First Lady, and become again merely Mrs. John Adams of Quincy. This "castle" will before long be made comfortable. It will not be for her, but for a long succession of other ladies unknown who will queen it here, who will have bells and fires, and a drying-yard, whose husbands will be rich enough to support the place in style. Even the great "audience-chamber," the East Room, will be in glittering use. Yes, but we want to preserve our simple democracy, thought Mrs. Adams. We don't want an aristocracy of wealth. . . .

She could not foresee that Jefferson and Monroe would both die bankrupt through trying to keep up style in their great office on inadequate pay and lavish use of private funds.

Well, Aunt Tufts had not been altogether wrong when she had said that Abigail, off to Philadelphia to assume her duties four years ago, was going to "splendid misery." And she hadn't been altogether right, either. It had, on the whole, been tremendous fun.

But now, the sooner over the better. Her heart was heavy with her private sorrow. She longed for the simple duties, the healing quiet and orderly beauty of Quincy.

". . . if my future peace and tranquillity were all that I considered, a release from public life wd be the most desirable event of it. I feel perfectly tranquil upon the subject, hoping and trusting that the Being in whose Hands are the Hearts of all Men will guide and direct our national counsels for the peace and prosperity of this great people.

". . . we are all at present well, tho the news papers very kindly gave the President the Ague and fever. I am rejoiced that it was only in the paper that he had it."

When Mr. Jefferson assumed the Presidency, he was to make an experiment of new "American" manners: no levees, no drawing rooms, no order of precedence; dinners for fourteen guests at a round table, self-service through a hatch in the wall; careless personal dress, down-at-heel slippers. It was good and enlivening to break up the old patterns and try to make some new ones. But Mr. Jefferson could not have done it in New York or Philadelphia. Mere pressure of numbers would have driven him to order and organization, tedious and stiff as they may be, as it drove Washington and Adams. When Mrs. Adams tried to live one summer in Philadelphia without drawing rooms, in order to save everyone exertion, she had to work overtime receiving callers all day long. The emptiness of Washington — a handful of houses in a muddy wilderness carved out of the dense forest — was what made Jefferson's go-as-you-please ways temporarily possible. And ladies were scarce. Congressmen were forced to live in boardinghouses, and many left their wives at home.

Such ladies as were extant, however, besieged Mrs. Adams to start her drawing rooms, and she did. In January 1801 the first New Year reception was held in the President's House. Many candles and roaring fires did their best to make a festive air. The President and his wife received their guests in the beautiful oval room, with their red furniture from Auteuil, and gave Washington its first sensation of being a society. Foreign ministers wore their orders, gentlemen their snowy powder, their bags and swords. Ladies decorated the scene with their elaborate dresses. Washington, D. C., took a definite step from looking like a trading outpost to looking like the capital of a great nation. But it still had a very long way to go.

John Adams had not anticipated subjecting his wife to the rigorous life of the frontier when he brought her to Washington. He was alarmed when he saw what she would have to put up with, and he dared risk it no further when he saw her attacks of rheumatism return. The severe lesson of the near loss of her in the summer of '98 had left its mark. February was a bad season to travel, but worse yet to remain in a house so poorly heated. He packed her off to Quincy.

To Thomas, she had written earlier her final salutation to public life — "I feel not any resentment against those who are coming into power, and only wish the future administration of the government may be as productive of the peace, prosperity and happiness of the nation as the two former ones have been.

"I leave to time the unfolding of a drama. I leave to posterity to reflect upon the times past; and I leave them characters to contemplate." [4]

*   *   *   *   *

"I have commenced my operations of dairy-woman," said Abigail joyfully in May. "Tell Nabby she might see me, at five o'clock in the morning skimming my milk! And in July, you will find your father in his fields attending to his haymakers"; she demands

> Who that has reason and his smell
> would not among roses and jasmine dwell? [5]

A letter from John Quincy, concerned at a remark, in her last letter from Washington, that they would have to economize, offered earnestly to help them, and gave them exquisite pleasure. "Your father and I were both much affected with the filial and affectionate tender of what, thank God, we have not any occasion for! You know our habits . . . many curtailments necessary, and have made them, but we have many comforts and enjoyments; and we can adopt the words of Shakespeare — 'Hath not old custom made this life more sweet?' " [6]

In September, when the apples were ripe, John Quincy Adams came home from Berlin. First he took his wife direct to her parents at Washington,* and with her the little boy, George Washington Adams, who had been safely born, after one or two miscarriages had made hopes of a family faint. Then John Quincy left his wife in Washington for a week, and himself hurried to Quincy. His mother's joy was full.

When Louisa came on to them at last, they loved her. She and her husband's dear friend and sister Nabby (there to welcome her brother) became fast friends. John Quincy opened again the old law office in Boston, remaining there until, in 1803, he was elected to the Senate over the head of his father's old enemy, the traitor-

* Mr. Johnson had been given a post in connection with the Post Office organization.

ous politician Pickering. To be beaten by a younger man was bad enough; to be beaten by John Adams's son was unspeakable. So when Pickering got into the Senate a little later he laid himself out for John Quincy Adams. And such was the cabal against the latter that he found it better, to get any measure across, to have it proposed by someone other than himself. These were embittering experiences for a man new to the political arena. But that is another story.

Abigail shared an extraordinary amount of her son's life and thought. When he came out to Quincy from Boston of a Sunday, she "picked a political bone" with her old verve and more than her old wisdom. She eagerly watched his career when he went to Washington, and rejoiced in his wife, who was such a charming hostess in that forlorn spot. But she did not need to know, her son rightly thought, all that got under a man's skin.

There was one bitter stab, however, dealt by Jefferson's hand, which rankled like a poisoned thorn in Abigail's mind. The Judge of the District Court of Massachusetts had immediately appointed John Quincy Adams one of the new commissioners in bankruptcy, a job which would ensure him a sound income. But John Quincy Adams had held the post for only a short time when a new ruling, giving these appointments directly into the control of the President of the United States, came into force, and Jefferson instantly crossed from the list the name of John Quincy Adams. It was the only name the President deleted, and it was a marked gesture. Despite this, the next year young Mr. Adams was elected to the Senate. Jefferson, at any rate, had done his best to slap him down.

The thorn was accidentally probed out of its festering position in the mother's heart by the only possible surgery — free and frank expression — in an exchange of letters between herself and President Jefferson in 1804.

The occasion was the death in early womanhood of Jefferson's daughter Mary,* whom Abigail Adams had so dearly loved. And after hesitation, she wrote him a letter in which her desire to offer comfort could not conceal the wounds of old friendship. *"Quincy,*

* Mrs. Francis Eppes. The elder sister, Martha, who had wanted to be a nun, was Mrs. Randolph.

May 20th, 1804. Sir, Had you been no other than the private inhabitant of Monticello, I should, ere this time, have addressed you with that sympathy which a recent event has awakened in my bosom; powerful feelings of my heart burst through the restraint, and called upon me to shed the tear of sorrow over the [death] of your beloved and deserving daughter, which I most sincerely mourn.

"The attachment which I formed for her, when you committed her to my care upon her arrival in a foreign land, has remained with me to this hour; and the account of her death, which I read in a late paper, recalled to my recollection the tender scene of her separation from me, when she clung around my neck and wet my bosom with her tears, saying, 'Oh! now I have learned to love you, why will they take me from you?'

"It has been some time since I conceived that any event in this life could call forth feelings of mutual sympathy. But I know how closely entwined around a parent's heart are those cords and when snapped asunder, how agonising the pangs! I have tasted of the bitter cup. That you may derive comfort and consolation from that only source calculated to heal the wounded heart, a firm belief in the being, perfections and attributes of God, is the sincere and ardent wish of her, who once took pleasure in subscribing herself your friend.⁷ Abigail Adams."

Jefferson's own heart carried festering wounds. Her candor released his, as her loving sympathy reached his fatherly grief. He replied — *"Washington, June 13th, 1804.* Dear Madam — The affectionate sentiments towards my dear departed daughter . . . have recalled your kindnesses to her. . . . They had made an indelible impression on her mind, and to the last, on our meetings after long separations, whether I had heard lately of you, and how you did, were among the earliest of her inquiries.

"I . . . am thankful for the occasion furnished me of expressing my regret that circumstances should have arisen which have seemed to draw a line of separation between us. The friendship with which you honored me has ever been valued, and fully reciprocated; and although events have been passing which might be trying to some minds, I never believed yours to be of that kind, nor felt that my own was. Neither my estimate of your character, nor the esteem founded in that, has ever been lessened for a single moment. . . .

"Mr. Adams friendship and mine began at an earlier date. It accompanied us through long and important scenes. The different conclusions we had drawn from our political reading and reflections were not permitted to lessen personal esteem . . . conscious they were the result of honest conviction.

"Like differences of opinion existing among our fellow citizens attached them to one or the other of us, and produced a rivalship in their minds which did not exist in ours. We never stood in each other's way; for if either had been withdrawn . . . his favorers would not have gone over to the other but would have sought for some one of the homogeneous opinions. This consideration was sufficient to keep down all jealousy between us and to guard our friendship from any disturbance by sentiments of rivalship; and I can say with truth that one act of Mr. Adams' life and one only, ever gave me a moment's personal displeasure. I did consider his last appointments to office as personally unkind. They were from among my most ardent political enemies, from which no faithful co-operation could ever be expected; and laid me under the embarrassment of acting through men whose views were to defeat mine, or to encounter the odium of putting others in their places. It seems but common justice to leave a successor free to act by instruments of his own choice.

"If my respect for him did not permit me to ascribe the whole blame to the influence of others, it left something for friendship to forgive, and after brooding over it for some time, and not always resisting the expression of it, I forgave it cordially, and returned to the same state of esteem and respect for him which had so long subsisted. Having come into life a little later than Mr. Adams, his career has preceded mine, as mine is followed by some other; and it will probably be closed at the same distance after him which time originally placed between us. I maintain for him, and shall carry into private life, an uniform and high measure of respect and good will, and for yourself a sincere attachment.

"I have thus, my dear madam, opened myself to you without

reserve, which I have long wished an opportunity of doing; and without knowing how it will be received, I feel relief from being unbosomed.

". . . though connected with political events, it has been viewed by me most strongly in its unfortunate bearings on my private friendships. The injury these have sustained has been a heavy price for what has never given me equal pleasure." [8]

This gave Abigail a wide opening, a challenge even, to defend the appointments her husband had made in the last few months of his Presidency. She well knew the appointment of John Marshall as Chief Justice of the Supreme Court had been deeply resented by Jefferson and, she thought, most unreasonably so. At all events, the slander of "the midnight appointments" could be scotched — a slander which had made it seem as if John Adams had sat up late on the last night of his Presidency in Washington making appointments definitely and on purpose to wound and thwart the incoming President. She replied:

"Your letter of June 13th, came duly to hand. If it had contained no other sentiments and opinions than those which my letter of condolence could have excited, and which are expressed in the first page of your reply, our correspondence would have terminated here. But you have been pleased to enter upon some subjects which call for a reply. . . .

" 'One act of Mr. Adams's life, and *one* only (you repeat) ever gave me a moment's personal displeasure. I did consider his last appointments to office as personally unkind; they were from my most ardent political enemies.'

"As this act, I am certain, was not intended to give any personal pain or offence, I think it a duty to explain it, so far as I then knew his views and designs. The Constitution empowers the President to fill up offices as they become vacant. It was in the exercise of this power, that appointments were made, and characters selected, whom Mr. Adams considered as men faithful to the constitution, and where he personally knew them, such as were capable of fulfilling their duty to their country. This was done equally by General Washington in the last days of his administration, so that not an office remained vacant for his successor to fill upon his coming into office. No offence was given by it and no personal unkindness thought of.

"But the different political opinions, which have so unhappily divided our country, must have given rise to the idea that personal unkindness was intended. You will please to recollect, Sir, that at the time these appointments were made, there was not any certainty that the Presidency would devolve upon you,* which is another circumstance to prove that no personal unkindness was intended. . . . I know it was his opinion that if the Presidency devolved upon you, except in the appointment of Secretaries,† no material change ‡ would be made. I perfectly agree with you in opinion that these cabinet members should be men in whom the President can repose confidence, possessing opinions and sentiments corresponding with his own; or if differing with him, that they ought rather to resign their offices than to cabal against measures which he may consider essential to the honor, safety and peace of the country. Neither ought they to unite with any bold and daringly ambitious character to overrule the Cabinet or to betray the secrets of it to friends or enemies.§ The two gentlemen who held the offices of secretaries, when you became President, were not of this character. They were persons appointed by your predecessor nearly two years previous to his retirement. They had cordially cooperated with him, and were gentlemen who enjoyed the public confidence. Possessing, however, different political sentiments from those which you were known to have embraced, it was expected that they would, as they did, resign.

"I have never felt any enmity towards you, Sir, for being elected President of the United States. But the instruments made use of and the means which were practised to effect a change have my utter abhorrence and detestation, for they were the blackest calumny and the foulest falsehoods. . . . I can truly say, that at the time of election, I considered your pretensions much superior

---

* The House of Representatives not having yet given their decision between the tied candidates.
† The Cabinet.
‡ Change in policy.
§ Showing here her full information as to the Hamilton cabal in her husband's Cabinet.

to his who shared an equal vote with you. . . . I must rely upon the friendship you still profess to entertain for me, (and I am conscious I have done nothing to forfeit it) to excuse the freedom of this discussion, to which you have led with an unreserve, which has taken off the shackles I should, otherwise, have found myself embarrassed with. And now, Sir, I will freely disclose to you what has severed the bonds of former friendship, and placed you in a light very different from what some viewed you in.

"One of the first acts of your administration was to liberate a wretch, who was suffering the just punishment of his crimes for publishing the basest libel, the lowest and vilest slander which malice could invent or calumny exhibit, against the character and reputation of your predecessor; of him, for whom you professed a friendship and esteem. . . . The remission of Callender's fine was a public approbation of his conduct. . . .

"Until I read Callender's seventh letter containing your compliment to him as a writer and your reward of fifty dollars, I could not be made to believe that such measures could have been resorted to, to stab the fair fame and upright intentions of one who, to use your own language, 'was acting from an honest conviction in his own mind that he was right.' This, Sir, I considered as a personal injury; this was the sword that cut asunder the Gordian knot, which could not be untied by all the efforts of party spirit, by rivalry, by jealousy, or any other malignant fiend.

"There is one other act of your administration which I considered as personally unkind, and which your own mind will easily suggest to you; but as it neither affected character nor reputation, I forbear to state it.

"This letter is written in confidence. Faithful are the wounds of a friend. Often have I wished to have seen a different course pursued by you. . . ." [9]

Jefferson found himself hit too shrewdly. He had to reply, to clear himself to his inward self, as well as to Mrs. Adams. His answer is one of the best examples of his specious, twisted thought, his need to always have it both ways — to be a man of stainless, chivalric honor and to be a secret slanderer at the same time. He had, he said, "to rectify certain facts which seem not to have been presented to you under their true aspect. As early as 1796 I was told in Philadelphia that Callendar, the author of the *Political Progress of Britain,* was in that city, a fugitive from persecution for having written that book, and in distress. I had read and approved the book: I considered him as a man of genius, unjustly persecuted. . . . I expressed my readiness to contribute to his relief. . . . It was a considerable time after that I contributed to his relief, and afterwards repeated the contribution. Himself I did not see till long after, nor ever more than two or three times. When he first began to write, he told some useful truths in his coarse way; but nobody sooner disapproved of his writing than I did, or wished more that he would be silent. My charities to him were no more meant as encouragements to his scurrilities than those I give to the beggar at my door are meant as rewards for the vices of his life.

"With respect to the calumnies and falsehoods which writers and printers at large published against Mr. Adams, I was as far from stooping to any concern of approbation of them as Mr. Adams was respecting those of Porcupine, Femmo or Mussell, who published volumes against me for every sentence vended by their opponents against Mr. Adams. . . . I knew myself incapable of that base warfare, and believed him to be so.

". . . whatever I may have thought of the acts of the administration of that day, I have ever borne testimony to Mr. Adams's personal worth; nor was it ever impeached in my presence without a just vindication of it on my part. I never supposed that any person who knew either of us could believe that either of us meddled in that dirty work.

"But another fact is that I 'liberated a wretch who was suffering for a libel against Mr. Adams.' I do not know who was the particular wretch alluded to; but I discharged every person under punishment or prosecution under the sedition law, because I considered, and now consider, that law to be a nullity, as absolute and as palpable as if Congress had ordered us to fall down and worship a golden image; and that it was as much my duty to arrest its execution in every stage as it would have been my duty to rescue from the fiery furnace. . . . It was done in every instance, without asking what the offenders had done, or against whom they had offended."

He then became very high-flown about his motives and the tenor of his character, appealed to the country, posterity, and that Being, and so on, and continued:

"You observe there has been one other act of my administration personally unkind, and suppose that it will readily suggest itself to me. I declare on my honor, Madam, I have not the least conception what act was alluded to. I never did a single one with an unkind intention. My sole object in this letter being to place before your attention that the acts imputed to me are either such as are falsely imputed or as might flow from good as well as bad motives, I shall make no other addition than the assurance of my continued wishes for the health and happiness of yourself and Mr. Adams." [10]

Abigail does not let him get away with this. She states her case without mincing matters:

"Candor requires of me a reply. Your statement respecting Callendar, and your motives for liberating him, wear a different aspect as explained by you, from the impression which the act had made, not only upon my mind, but upon the minds of all those whom I have ever heard speak upon the subject. With regard to the law under which he was punished, different persons entertain different opinions respecting it. It lies not with me to determine its validity or constitutionality. That devolved upon the Supreme Judges of the nation. . . . If a Chief Magistrate can by his will annul it, where is the difference between a republican and a despotic government?

". . . If there is no check to be resorted to in the laws of the land, and no reparation to be made to the injured, will not man become the Judge and avenger of his own wrongs, and, as in a late instance,* the sword and pistol decide the contest? . . . Party spirit is blind, malevolent, uncandid, ungenerous, unjust and unforgiving. It is equally so under federal as under democratic banners. . . . Upon both sides are characters who possess honest views and act from honorable motives; characters who abhor

* The duel between Aaron Burr and Hamilton, in which Hamilton was shot dead.

calumny and evil speaking, and who will never descend to newspaper reviling. You have done Mr. Adams justice in believing him incapable of such conduct. He has never written a line in any newspaper to which his signature has not been affixed since he was first elected President of the United States.

"You exculpate yourself from any intentional act of unkindness towards any one. I will, however, freely state that which I considered as such. Soon after my eldest son's return from Europe, he was appointed by the District Judge to an office in which no political concerns entered. Personally known to you, and possessing all the qualifications, you yourself being judge, which you had designed for office, as soon as Congress gave the appointments to the President, you removed him. This looked so particularly pointed, that some of your best friends in Boston at that time expressed their regret that you had done so. I must do him the justice to say that I never heard an expression from him of censure or disrespect towards you in consequence of it.

"I have written to you with a freedom which only former friendship would warrant; and to which I would gladly return, could all causes but mere difference of opinion be removed . . . desirous of seeing my children and grandchildren heirs to that freedom and independence which you and your predecessor united your efforts to obtain." [11]

Jefferson's reply to this broadside was very remarkable. Candor was the last and least of its ingredients. He was driven to the conclusion — painful but surprising — that Mrs. Adams was citing "the removal of your eldest son from some office to which the judges had appointed him. I conclude then he must have been a commissioner of bankruptcy. But I declare to you on my honor that this is the first knowledge I have ever had that he was so.

"It may be thought, perhaps, that I ought to have inquired who were such before I appointed others. But it is to be observed that the former law permitted the judges to name commissioners occasionally, only for every case as it arose, and not to make them permanent officers. Nobody therefore being in office there could be no removal. The judges, you well know, have been considered as highly federal; and it was noted that they confined their nominations exclusively to federalists.

"The Legislature, dissatisfied, with this, transferred the nomination to the President, and made the office permanent. The very object in passing the law was that he should correct, not confirm, what was deemed the partiality of the judges. I thought it therefore proper to inquire not whom they had employed but whom I ought to appoint to fulfill the intentions of the law. In making these appointments I put in a proportion of federalists. . . . Had I known that your son had acted, it would have been a real pleasure to me to have preferred him to some who were named in Boston in what was deemed the same line of politics. To this I should have been led by my knowledge of his integrity, as well as my sincere disposition towards yourself and Mr. Adams."

He reverted to the easier case of Callender, and tries to lift that awkward subject from the particular to the general. He was in fact out against the Sedition Law itself. "You seem to think it devolved on the judges to decide on the validity of the sedition law. But nothing in the Constitution has given them a right to decide for the Executive, more than to the Executive to decide for them. Both magistrates are equally independent in the sphere of action assigned to them. The judges, believing the law constitutional, had a right to pass a sentence of fine and imprisonment. . . . But the executive, believing the law to be unconstitutional, were bound to remit the execution of it. . . . That instrument (The Constitution) meant that its co-ordinate branches should be checks on each other. But the opinion which gives to the judges the right to decide what laws are constitutional and what not . . . would make the judiciary a despotic branch."

And he winds up with a good smoke screen on the freedom of the press, the similar aims of the two political parties, and his own impeccable loftiness of character. His longing for real loftiness, his right conception of the generous and the fine, are self-confessed.

"While we deny that Congress have a right to control the freedom of the press, we have ever asserted the right of the States, and their exclusive right, to do so. . . . In general the State laws appear to have made the presses responsible for slander as far as is consistent with its useful freedom. In those States where they do not admit even the truth of allegations to protect the printer, they have gone too far.

"The candor manifested in your letter and which I ever believed you to possess has alone inspired the desire of calling to your attention those circumstances of fact and motive by which I claim to be judged. I hope you will see these intrusions on your time to be, what they really are, proofs of my great respect for you.

"Both of our political parties, at least the honest part of them, agree conscientiously in the same object — the public good; but they differ essentially in what they deem the means of promoting that good. . . . One fears most the ignorance of the people; the other the selfishness of rulers independent of them. Which is right, time and experience will prove. We think that one side of this experiment has been long enough tried and proved not to promote the good of the many; and that the other has not been fairly and sufficiently tried. Our opponents think the reverse. With whichever opinion the body of the nation concurs, that must prevail.

"My anxieties on this subject will never carry me beyond the use of fair and honorable means, of truth and reason; nor . . . however alienated my affections from a single friend who did not first withdraw himself." [12]

Abigail was not a lawyer's wife for nothing. She points out his begging of the question concerning John Quincy Adams, with equal firmness, candor, and courtesy, corrects him as to the powers of the Executive with regard to the law, and politely closes the correspondence.

"When I first addressed you, I little thought of entering into a correspondence with you upon subjects of a political nature. I will not regret it, as it has led to some elucidations, and brought on some explanations, which place in a more favorable light occurrences which had wounded me.

"Having once entertained for you a respect and esteem . . . I could not suffer different political opinions to obliterate them from my mind. . . . It was not until circumstances concurred to place you in the light of a rewarder and encourager of a libeller, whom you could not but detest and despise, that I withdrew the esteem I had long entertained for you. Nor can you wonder, Sir, that I should consider as a personal unkindness, the instances I have mentioned. I am pleased to find that which respected my son altogether unfounded. He was, as you conjecture, appointed a Commissioner of Bankruptcy, together with Judge Dawes, and continued to serve in it with perfect satisfaction to all parties, (at least I never heard the contrary) until superseded by the appointment of others. The idea suggested that no one was in office, and consequently no removal could take place, I cannot consider in any other light than what the gentlemen of the law would term a quibble, — as such I pass it. Judge Dawes was continued or reappointed, which placed Mr. Adams in a more conspicuous light as the object of personal resentment. Nor could I, upon this occasion, refrain calling to mind the last visit you made me at Washington, when in the course of conversation you assured me, that if it should lay in your power at any time to serve me or my family, nothing would give you more pleasure. With respect to the office, it was a small object, but the disposition of the remover was considered by me as the barbed arrow. This, however, by your declaration, is withdrawn from my mind. With the public it will remain.

"I will not any further intrude upon your time; but close this correspondence by my wishes that you may be directed to that path which may terminate in the prosperity and happiness of the people over whom you are placed, by administering the government with justice and impartiality." [13]

This correspondence had been carried on without her husband's knowledge. A month later she handed him the whole — seven letters in all, three of Mr. Jefferson's and four of hers. Her astonished husband read it with care, and laid it away with no comment but this — "Quincy, Nov. 19th, 1804. The whole of this correspondence was begun and conducted without my knowledge or suspicion. Last evening and this morning, at the desire of Mrs. Adams, I read the whole. I have no remarks to make upon it, at this time and in this place." [14]

It was probably a relief to Mr. Jefferson that Mrs. Adams

claimed a woman's last word, and saved him the embarrassment of further reply. Protestation of sincere friendship and of high dispassionate behavior against the evidence of facts wears thin. Five years passed, and Mr. Jefferson had another chance to prove his noble words by action. The Court of Russia sent a request for an Ambassador from the United States. What candidate was more obviously, patently, glaringly suitable than John Quincy Adams? Even that he belonged to the other party, Federalist-Republican, could hardly count against him, since he was notoriously far from being a party man. He had offended the Federalist party the year before by putting his weight on the side of Jefferson and the Democrats in the struggle over the embargo. But Mr. Jefferson none the less did not appoint John Quincy Adams. Mr. Jefferson nominated instead an obscure gentleman by the name of Mr. Short. What Mr. Short's qualifications were to represent America in Russia are lost in the mist of history. Before his name could be confirmed, Mr. Jefferson's second term as President ended in the new elections which placed Mr. Madison in the President's office. When Congress opened in the spring of 1809, Mr. Madison dutifully presented Mr. Jefferson's nominee for the important diplomatic mission to St. Petersburg, and the Senate promptly voted it down, saying candidly that they did not object to the mission but to the man. It was Mr. Madison who then presented hastily (and successfully) the name of John Quincy Adams.

Does one hear Mr. Jefferson's thwarted second self busily muttering in an undertone, excusing himself to Abigail, "Had I known that your son would have acted, it would have been a real pleasure to me to have preferred him! To this I should have been led by my knowledge of his integrity," and he might have added — "my knowledge of his exceptional experience and education, qualifying him so uniquely for this especial post, as none knows better than myself?" But no. Jefferson's deep-lying jealousy of John Adams went too far down into his subconscious for his intelligence to overcome it. He could not bring his will to give preferment and opportunity to John Adams's son.

Yet the avenue opened by Abigail between her husband and his former friend was still unclosed. Weeds and poison ivy perhaps made a thick tangle over its untrodden path, but a way had been cut through the timber of misunderstanding. It would not be hard to stroll down that avenue someday — if one did not have to go all the way, if one were sure of being met at the halfway mark. With one part of his divided heart, Jefferson longed to take those steps, to feel again the sturdy warmth of the warmest friend he had ever known.

In 1812, Dr. Benjamin Rush, friend of both men, negotiated with each one, to bring about a reconciliation. John Adams, guiltless of underhand action and unsuspicious of any, bore no grudge. To Rush's overtures he said, "His administration and mine are passed away into the dark backwards. I have always loved him as a friend." [15] Jefferson told Rush he had forgotten all the bitterness he once felt. So John Adams, in his hearty go-all-the-way-if-need-to manner, then wrote to Jefferson a simple letter sending him some specimens of homespun.

Jefferson was deeply moved. "A letter from you . . . carries me back to the time when we were fellow-laborers in the same cause, struggling for what is most valuable to man, his right of self-government." He dramatically threw to the winds what he chose to assume to be the old bone of contention: "As for France and England," said Jefferson largely, "the one is a den of robbers, the other of pirates." He passed quickly to domestic and personal detail of daily habits and family. "I salute you with unchanged affection and respect. . . ." [16] So the correspondence began.

Adams wrote oftener than Jefferson, saying with his habitual generosity, "Never mind if I write four letters to your one, your one is worth more than four of mine."

So the old friendship, nipped for a while by the frosts of party, put forth a green shoot. Adams was seventy-seven in 1812, Jefferson sixty-nine. The two elderly men found pleasure in exploring each other's minds, not along the dangerously divergent lines of politics, but in the wide field o   history of mankind, and of the theories and philosophies that lie behind all government and all human life. Not many could discuss these things as they could. It was a recreation, a distraction, an entertainment in their declining years. John Adams gave himself to it with all good faith;

Jefferson, as usual, with reservation. Following the mysterious adjuration of Abigail's "Ancient Author," "let not thy right hand know what thy left hand doeth," Thomas Jefferson, writing to John Adams with his right hand in candid friendship, concealed from that right hand what he was about, so to speak, with the left — writing a memoir, an autobiography, which with specious half-truths, loaded witness, unverified assertions, was preparing after his death to wound John Adams's reputation with a wound only short of mortal.

But their ghosts are not uneasy. They are indifferent now. America has taken them both to her bosom. Both of them ministered to her greatness, both fertilized her living growth with their own vitality. Both were needed. A great country is nourished by more than one or two great men. In the story of America, the separate genius of each — yes, and their titan struggle, too — has its right and necessary place. It is part of the democratic method, in which we still believe. But the lying and deception, the false witness, is no right part of that, and its results were evil and lasting. The division of South and North which led at last to the war between the states had its roots in this early distrust. And we have not seen the finish.

The immediate results left their mark on the austere, upright, sensitive spirit of John Quincy Adams. But he shared with his mother only his success, his work, and his uncompromising reasoning, not his suffering. Leave her in peace!

XVIII

Hath Not Old Custom Made This Life More Sweet?

Y ES, peace. That was the chief pattern of her days, her years. The seasons were their lovely frame, the sea and the bees and birds their constant soothing music. John was with her; never more would they separate until the great parting came which no man can avoid. The present was all-sufficient, and in the future there was nothing to strive for, except to make it as much like the present as possible.

Rural social life gave variety to their pleasant monotony: the Saturday Fish-Club of eight families, the visits of Mary and Richard Cranch — now Judge Cranch — of one or another of John's brothers, of Quincy cousins, and Smiths. Thomas is married and has come to live near by in the old homestead at Penns Hill. There is always a little "Chinese chatterer" darting about from one family to another, enjoying the "daffies" and the "puppy children" with Grandmamma.

Mrs. Adams in her silks and laces is a bit awe-inspiring to the little daughters of Josiah Quincy 3rd when they come to Sunday dinner, but she is a most engaging grandparent, and a busy supervisor of dairy and baking on weekdays. And John Adams, jovial and easy, makes the table lively, carving the liberal roast after a course of corn-meal pudding has clogged the too sharp appetite.

A little storm began blowing up on the international sky in 1808. The immediate cause was the impressment of seamen, the old grievance. Abigail's pro-British mood, fanned by Napoleon, is past. The British are now "insolent and haughty."

John Quincy Adams, to his father's indignation, backed Jefferson's embargo.* How strange. But John Quincy explained it carefully to his mother, earnestly anxious for her approval. And his mother in turn explained it to his sister Nabby. Well, his motives, anyway, were above reproach. And Abigail was proud of his complete independence of judgment, his strength to hold his own. He and Louisa now have three sons — John Adams and Charles Francis, as well as little George.

John Quincy Adams's career was moving on and up. When in 1809 he was made Minister to Russia by President Madison at half an hour's notice, Abigail's heart stopped for a second, beat on heavily. John Quincy noted in his journal, "I received yesterday a letter from my mother which would have melted the heart of a Stoic." She never expected to see him again in this life. But it was the price one must pay for greatness, for public service. Separation. Exile. She has paid it over and over again. It was a comfort to her to have his two little sons, George and John, left behind in her care.

In the autumn of 1811 Judge Richard Cranch died. Mary too lay dying. They told her of her husband's death. She said, "He has only stepped behind the scene; I shall know where to find him."

Abigail through her tears wrote it all to their absent son, her favorite nephew, Will Cranch, in Washington.

"I hope, my dear nephew, while I live, that you will consider me as a parent, although I can never supply her place to you." [1]

The loss of Richard and Mary was the worst break possible in their circle. Abigail's earliest childhood memories clung to Mary, her youth and maturity had found in her sister her best and closest friend. The bond between John Adams and Dick Cranch had drawn the sisters ever closer.

It did not seem so very long ago that two young men rode together to the Weymouth Parsonage in the bright October weather. And now it was a funeral cortege which ruffled the golden leaves, the years had all gone by, and that close quadruple relationship was ended. Almost fifty years of unbroken sweetness. "Such

* Trying to force redress of American grievances by trade pressure instead of war.

friends grow not thick on every bough." But like a fine piece of music, there was a triumph in the sorrow.

Thanksgiving Day, 1812, again at war with Britain. Abigail made a typical note — "In our own way, and with tempers suited to the occasion, we gave thanks. . . . We were in health. We had good news from a far country. We had food and raiment, and we still enjoyed liberty, and our rulers were men of our own election and removable by the people.

"Your uncle and aunt with their three children [Mr. and Mrs. Thomas Boylston Adams and Abigail, six, Elizabeth, four, and Thomas B., three], your Aunt Smith [brother William's widow, resident with Abigail Adams], George and John Adams with our own family, made the joyful group."

Letters are handed over the garden wall, from horsemen, carriages, sleighs. . . . The currents of the world flow in through the veins of the Adams breed.

In 1813 Nabby came home to die. Her husband in Congress now, representing his faraway outpost,* herself fatally ill with cancer and knowing it — she never told! — she "had the courage and resolution to have a bed placed in a carriage, and after a journey of fifteen days and three hundred miles she arrived in her father's house, attended by her dutiful children and her affectionate sister-in-law. . . . Emaciated, worn with pain, still she appeared delighted to embrace her parents, and feel herself surrounded with all that love, respect, and affection could afford." Immediately the best medical aid and advice was obtained, but opium was the only palliative, the only relief she could obtain.[2] She died three weeks after her arrival, on Sunday morning, August 30th, 1813. The Colonel hurried from Washington to see her, and got there just in time. She had all her wishes fulfilled except her desire to see her son. Her eldest son, William Steuben (who had missed his senior year at Harvard to go on the Miranda adventure, but had graduated later from Columbia), was away in Petersburg with his uncle, John Quincy Adams.

"My only source of satisfaction," wrote the grief-stricken Abigail Adams to John Quincy, whom she knew would so sorely feel

* Lebanon Valley, New York.

his sister's loss, "and it is a never-failing one, is my firm persuasion that everything — and our oversights and mistakes among the rest, — are parts of the great plan." [8]

Eighteen-fourteen flared up with the burning of the President's house, Capitol, and Library of Congress in Washington by the British, in that queer sporadic war in which Boston and Baltimore alike expected siege. "Useless," wrote John Quincy grimly, "to discuss now the policy, the justice or the necessity of our late war with Great Britain."

But Abigail was looking at the arson. "Modern Goths and vandals! All Europe blush at the deed. . . . The city a wilderness thinly inhabited . . . the great part of the population slaves! We have heard that private property was respected, but a general destruction of the public."

No one regretted that rash act more sincerely than the British home government, who were negotiating a peace treaty with John Quincy Adams when it occurred. Few English people were aware of it. All America resented it.

And now there is a ship of the Navy called the *John Adams*. Honor is given "the President," as all the neighbors called him, at all times and places. The lane before the house is called the President's Lane, and the rise is the President's Hill.*

Eighteen-sixteen rolled up, bearing with it a last sorrow for Abigail's loving heart. Her cousin Will Smith died in April. A warm and generous character, the finest type of openhanded, square-dealing American merchant.

"My friend and relative," Abigail mourned, "who from his earliest years I have loved as a brother, whose father's house in youth was a home to me, as my father's was to him. Although it can be but a short time before I shall follow him, I feel a limb lop'd from the body." [4]

But there was also in store a last joy. John Quincy Adams, eight years abroad, Ambassador to the Court of Russia, and then negotiator of the Peace Treaty and Ambassador to the Court of Great Britain (like his father before him), was coming home.

---

* Not to be confused with Penns Hill (much more of a hill) at the other farm, a mile or two down the village.

On the bright day of August 18th, 1817, "about ten this morning a carriage and four were seen coming down the hill." Yes, it was John Quincy Adams, a mature man, a polished diplomat, her little son of the Bunker Hill morning — coming home. "I ran to the door." His sons, George and John * and Charles, poured out of the carriage — "John, who with his former ardor was round my neck in a moment. George followed half crazy, crying out 'O Grandmother, O Grandmother'; Charles more shy. . . ." [5]

"The inexpressible happiness," said John Quincy Adams, "of that moment." All the family gathered from far and near. Within half an hour "my Uncle Peter Adams. . . . My son John went immediately to my brother's house, and he — Tom — came with his wife to dinner. . . . My brother's five children came immediately after. . . ." [6]

That was a Thanksgiving Day indeed, out of season, or with a whole season of its own. A day worth living for through a long life. Abigail looked round on her husband, her two excellent sons, her grandchildren, and her great-grandchildren. John Quincy Adams had just accepted appointment from President Monroe as Secretary of State. The August sunshine poured down upon the hot road; the great trees gave friendly shade; the house was now dignified and ample. Plenty and comfort, freedom, and love, and not an enemy ship on all the sea.

Now, Lord, lettest thou thy servant depart in peace, for mine eyes have seen thy salvation.

Abigail's room was the west bedroom, sunny and warm. Here her little grandson, Charles Francis, watched on a summer's day "the yellow and green brilliancy of the garden beneath the windows," and in the autumn he saw the yellowing leaves of the maples making an extra sunshine. Over the north wall, the oak beams, hardened by time to the consistency of iron, showed the adze marks of the hewing when they were green wood. Around the fireplace were the picture tiles brought home by John Quincy

---

* Their father had sent for his sons when his removal to England from Russia made it possible to have them with him, and their grandmother had parted with them regretfully in May 1814.

Adams in 1801, when he returned from Berlin and gave them to his mother.

Here is Abigail's armchair, which she used all day when rheumatism occasionally lamed her, and in the increasing lethargy of her last slow illness. And here is John Adams's high-backed armchair where he sat to be with her. Never tired of her company. Always wanting her most and best.

There Abigail was remembered by her grandchildren and her great-grandchildren, sitting enthroned with her little dog Satan beside her, talking in her lively way to visitors * who sat on the long sofa near by.

Here in the fourpost bed, on October 28th, 1818, of typhoid fever, she died. Yes, as she lay and dreamed into a sleep, with that dear hand to hold to to the last, it had been a long way to come. Much farther than she had fancied when she left the Weymouth Parsonage on that autumn day, October too, fifty-four years ago. The road had taken her through war and pestilence, over great oceans, into foreign places, it had given her scorn and honor, but much more honor; it had given her pain and joy, but much more joy. And most of all, she had found upon it a comradeship rare on earth.

Her husband survived her by eight years, dying in the second year of their eldest son's Presidency, and on the fiftieth anniversary of the Revolution, July 4th, 1826. Thomas Jefferson died the same day.

Let Abigail Adams's son, John Quincy Adams, speak her epitaph.

"Last Wednesday, the 28th of October, between eleven and one o'clock of that day, my mother, beloved and lamented more than language can express, yielded up her pure and gentle spirit to its Creator. She was born on the 11th of November, 1744, and had completed within less than a month of her seventy-fourth year. Had she lived to the age of the Patriarchs, every day of her life would have been filled with clouds of goodness and of love. There is not a virtue that can abide in the female heart but it was the ornament of hers. She had been fifty-four years the delight of my

* One of the last of whom was Daniel Webster.

father's heart, the sweetener of all his toils, the comforter of all his sorrows, the sharer and heightener of all his joys. It was but the last time when I saw my father that he told me, with an ejaculation of gratitude to the Giver of every good and every perfect gift, that in all the vicissitudes of his fortunes, through all the good report and evil report of the world, in all his struggles and in all his sorrows, the affectionate participation and cheering encouragement of his wife had been his never-failing support, without which he was sure he should never have lived through them. She was the daughter of William Smith, minister at Weymouth, and of Elizabeth Quincy, his wife. Oh, God! may I die the death of the righteous, and may my last end be like hers!"

Notes

CHAPTER I

1. *Works of John Adams* (8 vols.), ed. Charles Francis Adams, Boston, 1856, II, p. 88.
2. *Ibid.*, p. 48.
3. *Ibid.*, p. 45.
4. *Ibid.*, p. 78. John Adams's letter to Sam Quincy shown to Jonathan Sewall, and Sewall writes to J. A. to ask his friendship and correspondence.
5. *Ibid.*, p. 70.
6. *Ibid.*, p. 133 *n.*
7. *Ibid.*, p. 145.
8. *Ibid.*, p. 145.
9. Adams MS. "Mis Nabby Smith, Weymouth. These. In favor Dr. Tufts. from John Adams, Braintree. Feb. 14th, 1763."
10. *Ibid.*, April 20. "Miss Nabby Smith ('Diana') to Mr. John Adams, Braintree. Aug. 11th, 1763."
11. *Ibid.*, April 1764. The *Dictionary of American Biography* incorrectly states that it was Dr. Joseph Warren who inoculated John Adams. John Adams's letters to his betrothed make it clear that his physician was Dr. Perkins. There is no evidence in these early letters that Dr. Warren was taking part in this anti-smallpox campaign or was an acquaintance — no mention of him at all.
12. *Ibid.*, April 1764.
13. *Ibid.*, April 1764.
14. *Ibid.* Abigail was inoculated in 1776 as we shall see. Parson Smith himself suffered a late conversion, and June 3, 1778, his diary notes: "Was inoculated by Dr. Wales in the 72nd year of my age at Col. Quincy's. Tarried at the Col. 3 weeks wanting a day."
15. *Ibid.*, April 1764.
16. *Ibid.*, April 1764.
17. *Ibid.*, April 1764.

18. *Ibid.*, April 30, 1764. This Diana-Lysander business was a popular
    convention of the period, and implied no more affectation than
    our Buddy and Ginger type of nickname today.
19. *Ibid.*, April–May 1764.
20. *Ibid.*, April–May 1764.
21. *Ibid.* Spring and summer, 1764.
22. *Ibid.* Spring and summer, 1764.

CHAPTER II

1. *Samuel Adams*, James K. Hosmer, Boston, 1893; and *History of
   the United States* (6 vols.), George Bancroft, Boston, 1876, III,
   p. 420.
2. *Memoir of the Life of Josiah Quincy*, by his son. Boston, 1874.
   (Entry of August 28, 1765.)
3. *Works*, II, p. 53.
4. *Ibid.*, III, p. 465.
5. *Ibid.*, III, p. 467.
6. *Ibid.*, III, p. 467.
7. *Ibid.*, Sam Adams had had a similar duty the year before, May
   1764. See Bancroft, III, p. 418.
8. *Ibid.*, II, p. 154.
9. *Ibid.*, II, p. 157.
10. *Ibid.*, p. 157.
11. *Ibid.*, p. 158 *n.*
12. *Ibid.*, p. 163.
13. December 25, 1765. On December 29 they "dined at Weymouth,
    at Father Smith's." See *Works*, II, pp. 165, 167.
14. *Works*, II, p. 170.
15. *Ibid.*, p. 168.
16. *Ibid.*, p. 179.
17. *Ibid.*, p. 179.
18. Adams MS. From an undated love letter between 1761 and 1764.
19. *Works*, II, p. 195.
20. *Ibid.*, p. 197.
21. *Ibid.*, p. 197.
22. *Ibid.*, p. 203.
23. *Ibid.*, p. 198.
24. *Ibid.*, p. 199.
25. Adams MS. November 1766.
26. *Works*, II, p. 201.

CHAPTER III

1. *Correspondence of William Pitt, Earl of Chatham* (4 vols.), edited by W. S. Taylor and J. H. Pringle. London, 1838–1840, III, p. 153.

2. *Memoirs & Writings of Franklin*, Parsons, London, 1793, II, p. 371.

3. *Letters of Mrs. Adams*, ed. Charles Francis Adams, Boston, 1848, p. 9.

4. *Works*, II, pp. 210, 212. 1768.

5. *Ibid.*, p. 214.

6. *Ibid.*, p. 238.

7. *The History of the Rise, Progress and Establishment of America* (3 vols.), William Gordon, New York, 1789, I, p. 247.

8. *Ibid.*, p. 247.

9. *A History of Boston, the Metropolis of Massachusetts, from its Origin to the Present Period*, 2nd ed., A. Bowen, Boston, 1828, p. 254.

10. *Works*, II, p. 215.

11. *Ibid.*, pp. 227–228.

12. *Ibid.*, p. 227.

13. *Ibid.*, p. 230.

CHAPTER IV

1. *Works*, II, pp. 230–231. 1770.

2. *Works*, I, p. 110.

3. *Ibid.*, II, p. 232.

4. *Ibid.*, p. 232.

5. *Ibid.*, p. 233.

6. *Ibid.*, p. 233. 1770.

7. *Ibid.*, p. 243.

8. *Ibid.*, p. 255. 1771.

9. *Ibid.*, p. 255.

10. *Ibid.*, p. 269.

11. *Ibid.*, p. 269.

12. Smith-Carter MS. April 3, 1772.

13. *Works*, II, p. 299.

14. *Ibid.*, p. 304.

15. *Ibid.*, p. 302.

16. *Ibid.*, p. 306.

17. *Ibid.*, p. 314.
18. *Ibid.*, p. 308.
19. *Ibid.*, p. 310.
20. *Letters of Mrs. Adams*, p. 21.
21. *Works*, II, p. 312.
22. *Letters of Mrs. Adams*, p. 12.
23. *Works*, II, p. 312.
24. *Letters of Mrs. Adams*, p. 12.
25. Bancroft, IV, p. 266.
26. *Ibid.*, IV, p. 266.
27. *John Hancock His Book*, ed. Abram English Brown, Boston, 1898, p. 179.
28. *Letters of Mrs. Adams*, p. 10. 1773.
29. Hancock, p. 180. Letter of John Andrews, eyewitness.
30. *Ibid.*, p. 180.
31. *The History of the Province of Massachusetts Bay* (3 vols.), Hutchinson, London, 1828, III, p. 438.
32. Hancock, p. 180.
33. *Works*, II, p. 334 *n.*
34. Hutchinson, III, p. 438.
35. *Works*, II, p. 324. They decided against proclamation. Hutchinson says, "So many of the actors and abettors were universally known that a proclamation for discovery would have been ridiculed." Hutchinson, III, p. 438.
36. Hancock, p. 179.
37. *Works*, II, p. 337.
38. *Ibid.*, p. 326. February 1774.

CHAPTER V

1. *Familiar Letters of John Adams and His Wife Abigail Adams during the Revolution*, ed. Charles Francis Adams, p. 2.
2. *Works*, II, p. 331. 1774.
3. *Familiar Letters*, p. 12.
4. *Ibid.*, p. 21.
5. *Works*, II, p. 338.
6. *Ibid.*, II, p. 338.
7. Adams MS. June 1774.
8. *Familiar Letters*, p. 28.
9. Adams MS. June 30, 1774.

10. *Ibid.*, July 7, 1774.
11. *Works*, II, p. 340.
12. *Familiar Letters*, p. 5.
13. *Works*, II, p. 338.
14. *Familiar Letters*, p. 26.
15. *Ibid.*, p. 33.
16. *Familiar Letters*, p. 35.
17. *Ibid.*, p. 35.
18. *Ibid.*, p. 35.
19. *Ibid.*, p. 34.
20. *Ibid.*, p. 51.
21. *Ibid.*, pp. 33-34.
22. *Ibid.*, p. 41. September 24, 1774. Abigail Adams dates this letter bitterly from "Boston Garrison."
23. *Ibid.*, pp. 41-42.
24. Smith-Carter MS. March 29, 1773. Thomas Smith of South Carolina to Isaac Smith of Boston.
25. *Ibid.*, March 29, 1773.
26. *Familiar Letters*, p. 40.
27. Adams MS.
28. *Works*, II, p. 319.
29. *Letters from a Farmer in Pennsylvania to the Inhabitants of the British Colonies*, John Dickinson, Boston, 1768.
30. *Familiar Letters*, p. 49, and Adams MS. September 14, 1774.
31. Adams MS. September 16, 1774.
32. *Familiar Letters*, p. 59.
33. *Works*, II, pp. 405-406.
34. *Ibid.*, p. 406.
35. *Familiar Letters*, p. 52.
36. *Ibid.*, p. 56.
37. *Ibid.*, pp. 56-57, 69.
38. *Ibid.*, pp. 55-57.
39. *Ibid.*, pp. 60-62.
40. *Ibid.*, pp. 63, 64. June 15, 1775.

CHAPTER VI

1. *Familiar Letters*, pp. 67-68.
2. *Ibid.*, p. 68.
3. *Ibid.*, p. 69.

4. *Ibid.*, p. 73.
5. *Ibid.*, p. 69.
6. *Ibid.*, p. 71.
7. Bancroft, IV, p. 612.
8. *Familiar Letters*, p. 74.
9. *Ibid.*, p. 77.
10. *Ibid.*, pp. 78–79.
11. *Ibid.*, p. 73.
12. *Ibid.*, p. 80.
13. Smith-Carter MS. June 30, 1775.
14. *Familiar Letters*, p. 94.
15. *Ibid.*, p. 95.
16. *Familiar Letters*, p. 97.
17. *Ibid.*, p. 89.
18. *Ibid.*, p. 102.
19. *Ibid.*, p. 117.
20. *Ibid.*, p. 109.
21. *Ibid.*, p. 119.
22. *Ibid.*, p. 117.
23. *Ibid.*, p. 110.
24. *Ibid.*, p. 115.
25. *Ibid.*, p. 112.
26. *Ibid.*, p. 115.
27. *Ibid.*, pp. 121–122.
28. *Ibid.*, pp. 114–115.
29. *Ibid.*, p. 152.
30. *Ibid.*, p. 165.
31. *Ibid.*, p. 127.
32. *Ibid.*, p. 110.
33. *Ibid.*, p. 126.
34. *Ibid.*, p. 130.
35. *Ibid.*, pp. 128–129.
36. *Works*, I, p. 193.
37. *Familiar Letters*, p. 146.
38. *Ibid.*, pp. 137–138.
39. *Ibid.*, p. 142.
40. *Ibid.*, p. 144.
41. *Ibid.*, p. 145.
42. *Ibid.*, p. 149.
43. Smith-Carter MS. Letter of Andrew Eliot, Boston, to Mr. Isaac Smith, London, April 9, 1776.

44. *Familiar Letters*, pp. 149–155.
45. Tudor MS. June 1776.
46. *Familiar Letters*, p. 191.
47. *Ibid.*, pp. 192–193.
48. *Ibid.*, pp. 204. 1776.
49. *Ibid.*, p. 212. August 14, 1776.
50. *Works*, II, pp. 505–506, 516–517.
51. *Familiar Letters*, p. 201. July 1776.
52. *Ibid.*, p. 221. August 1776. Uncle Isaac and Aunt Elizabeth Smith were still at Salem.
53. *Ibid.*, p. 230. October 1776.
54. *Ibid.*, p. 148.
55. *Ibid.*, p. 166.
56. *Ibid.*, p. 175.

CHAPTER VII

1. *Familiar Letters*, p. 309.
2. *Works*, III, pp. 68, 82–83.
3. *Ibid.*, p. 83.
4. *Familiar Letters*, p. 228. September 22, 1776.
5. *Ibid.*, p. 301.
6. *Ibid.*, pp. 309–312.
7. *Ibid.*, p. 273.
8. *Ibid.*, p. 288.
9. *Ibid.*, p. 321.
10. *Ibid.*, p. 159.
11. *Ibid.*, p. 165.
12. *Ibid.*, p. 281.
13. *Works*, III, pp. 90–91.
14. *Ibid.*, I, p. 276.
15. Thaxter MS. Letter of A. A. to John Thaxter, February 15, 1778.
16. *Familiar Letters*, p. 328.
17. Adams MS. July 1778.
18. Adams MS. 1778.
19. Thaxter MS. July 23, 1778.
20. *Ibid.*, September, 1778.
21. *Ibid.*, April 9, 1778.
22. *Ibid.*, September 2, 1778.
23. *Ibid.*, April 1778.
24. *Familiar Letters*, p. 339.

25. *Ibid.*, p. 342.
26. Adams MS. November 1778.
27. *Ibid.*, p. 350.
28. Adams MS. Autumn 1778.
29. *Familiar Letters*, p. 351.
30. *Ibid.*, December 1778, February 1779, pp. 347, 358–357.
31. *Ibid.*, p. 348.
32. Thaxter MS. September 1778.
33. *Ibid.* September 1778.
34. *Ibid.* September 1778.
35. *Works*, III, p. 214.
36. *Ibid.*, pp. 211–213, 216, 223, 226.
37. *Familiar Letters*, p. 355.
38. Thaxter MS. March 2, 1780.
39. *Familiar Letters*, pp. 354–455.
40. *Ibid.*, p. 122.
41. *Works*, III, p. 162.
42. *Familiar Letters*, p. 356.
43. *Ibid.*, pp. 368–369.
44. *Works*, I, p. 412.
45. *Familiar Letters*, pp. 370, 374, and *Works*, III, pp. 231, 240.
46. *Ibid.*, pp. 376–377.
47. Thaxter MS. July 21, 1780.
48. Adams MS. September 1780.
49. *Familiar Letters*, p. 375.
50. Adams MS. July 1780.
51. *Ibid.*, September 1780.
52. *Familiar Letters*, p. 398.
53. *Ibid.*, p. 412.
54. *Ibid.*, p. 386. September 1780.
55. *Works*, VIII, p. 39.
56. Adams MS. January 1781.
57. *Ibid.*, September 20, 1781.
58. *Letters of Mrs. Adams*, p. 129. December 9, 1781. "Bilboa" was
    the old spelling for Bilbao, the capital of Biscay province in
    Spain.
59. Adams MS. March and April 1782.
60. *Ibid.*, August 1781.
61. *Ibid.*
62. Adams MS. October 21, 1781.

63. *Familiar Letters*, pp. 404–405. 1782.
64. *Ibid.*, p. 406.
65. *Letters of Mrs. Adams*, p. 139.

CHAPTER VIII

1. *Letters of Mrs. Adams*, pp. 133, 137.
2. Adams MS. April 10, 1782.
3. *Letters of Mrs. Adams*, p. 137.
4. *Works*, VIII, p. 57.
5. *Familiar Letters*, pp. 410, 412, 413.
6. Adams MS. August 1783.
7. *Ibid.*, November 1783.
8. *Ibid.*, October 8, 1782.
9. *Ibid.*, October 1782.
10. Adams MS. December 1782.
11. *Ibid.*, April 7, 1783.
12. *Ibid.*, June 1783.
13. *Ibid.*, December 27, 1783.
14. *Ibid.*, April 28, 1783.
15. *Ibid.*, April 28, 1783.
16. *Ibid.*, June 20, 1783.
17. *Ibid.*, August 5, 1782.
18. *Ibid.*, August 1782.
19. Adams MS. July 21, 1783.
20. Letters, pp. 135–136.
21. *Familiar Letters*, p. 406.
22. *Letters of Mrs. Adams*, pp. 161–170.
23. *Ibid.*, p. 170.
24. *Ibid.*, p. 167.
25. *Ibid.*, p. 171.
26. *Ibid.*, p. 172.
27. *Ibid.*, p. 173.
28. *Ibid.*, pp. 174–184.
29. *Ibid.*, p. 185.
30. *Ibid.*, p. 185.
31. *Ibid.*, p. 186.
32. *Works*, III, p. 389. (John Adams's Diary, August 7, 1784.)

CHAPTER IX

1. *Journal and Correspondence of Miss Adams*, edited by her daughter, New York, 1841.
2. *Ibid.*, p. 10.
3. *Ibid.*, p. 11.
4. *Letters of Mrs. Adams*, p. 198.
5. *Journal and Correspondence of Miss Adams*, p. 14.
6. *Letters of Mrs. Adams*, p. 195.
7. *Ibid.*, p. 189. Of course Mrs. Adams had never seen roller skating. She said "dancing like a Merry Andrew."
8. *Ibid.*, p. 195.
9. *Ibid.*, p. 193.
10. *Ibid.*, pp. 203, 211.
11. *Ibid.*, p. 192.
12. *Ibid.*, p. 211.
13. *Ibid.*, p. 234.
14. *Ibid.*, p. 231.
15. Abigail Adams, 1783. The Adams MS.
16. *Letters of Mrs. Adams*, p. 242.
17. Adams MS.
18. *Ibid.*, May 10, 1785.

CHAPTER X

1. *Letters of Mrs. Adams*, p. 243.
2. *Works*, VIII, pp. 255–259. Letter to Jay.
3. *Ibid.*
4. *Journal and Correspondence of Miss Adams*, p. 79.
5. *Works*, III, p. 391.
6. *Works*, VIII, p. 265.
7. *Letters of Mrs. Adams*, pp. 257, 270.
8. *Ibid.*, p. 270.
9. *Ibid.*, p. 260.
10. *Ibid.*, p. 255.
11. Letters of Col. Wm. Smith to Baron Steuben and to Rufus King.
12. *Letters of Mrs. Adams*, p. 264, September 2, 1785.

13. *Memoirs of the Life and Reign of King George III*, J. Heneage Jesse, London, 1867, II, p. 495 ff.
14. *Letters of Mrs. Adams*, pp. 275–276.
15. *Ibid.*, p. 266.
16. *Ibid.*
17. Adams MS. April 1785.
18. *Ibid.*
19. *Ibid.*, April 24, 1786.
20. Smith-Carter MS. June 1783.
21. *Letters of Mrs. Adams*, p. 275.
22. Adams MS. 1786.
23. *Ibid.*, February 16, 1786. Letter of John Quincy Adams.
24. Smith-Carter MS. August 1785.
25. Adams MS. Spring 1786. Abigail Adams to John Quincy Adams.
26. *Ibid.*, June 13, 1786.
27. *Ibid.*
28. Smith-Carter MS. August 29, 1785. Letter to Uncle Isaac and Aunt Elizabeth.
29. Adams MS. May 1787.
30. *Letters of Mrs. Adams*, p. 328, July 1787.
31. Adams MS. 1787.
32. *Ibid.*, June 2, 1787.
33. *Works*, VIII, p. 466.
34. *Ibid.*, p. 310.
35. *Ibid.*, pp. 475–476.
36. Adams MS. February 1788.
37. *Works*, VIII, p. 458.
38. *Letters of Mrs. Adams*, p. 343.
39. Adams MS. April and May 1788.
40. *Letters of Mrs. Adams*, p. 319.

CHAPTER XI

1. Adams MS.
2. Adams MS.
3. *Ibid.*, November 10, 1788.
4. Cranch MS. Jamaica, Long Island. November 24, 1788.
5. Bobbé, pp. 202–203.
6. Cranch MS. December 15, 1788.
7. Bobbé, p. 200.

8. *Ibid.*, p. 204.
9. *Ibid.*, p. 484. Gerry to John Adams.
10. Tudor MS. Letter from John Adams to William Tudor, May 3, 1789.
11. Adams MS. May 1789.

CHAPTER XII

1. Cranch MS. June 1789.
2. Adams MS. Letter to John Quincy Adams, December 1790.
3. Cranch MS. June 1789.
4. *Ibid.*, July 12, 1789.
5. *Ibid.*, July 12, 1789.
6. *Ibid.*, July 1789.
7. *Ibid.*, Summer 1789.
8. Adams MS. Letter to John Quincy Adams, November 1789.
9. Frank M. Etting Autograph Collection, *Washingtonia.* October 22, 1789.
10. Cranch MS. October 1789.
11. *Ibid.*, August 1789.
12. *Ibid.*, January 1790.
13. Adams MS. November 22, 1789.
14. Cranch MS. January 5, 1790.
15. *Journal of William Maclay*, William Maclay, New York, 1890, pp. 138, 177, 206.
16. Cranch MS. Autumn 1789.
17. *Ibid.*, March 1790.
18. *Ibid.*, March 1790.
19. *Ibid.*, New York, 1790.
20. *Ibid.*, Summer 1790.
21. *Ibid.*, July 4, 1790.
22. *Ibid.*, January 5, 1790.
23. *Ibid.*, January 5, 1790.
24. Adams MS. August 1790.
25. *Ibid.*, New York, September 1790.
26. *Ibid.*, November 1790.
27. Cranch MS. March 12, 1791.

1. Cranch MS. September 1790.
2. *Ibid.*, December 26, 1790,

3. *Letters of Mrs. Adams*, p. 352.
4. *Ibid.*, p. 353.
5. *Ibid.*, p. 358.
6. *Ibid.*, p. 356.
7. Cranch MS. December 12, 1790, January 1791.
8. *Ibid.*, April 1792.
9. Smith-Carter MS.
10. *Ibid.*, March 1792.
11. *Letters of Mrs. Adams*, pp. 360–361.
12. *Ibid.*, p. 361.
13. Adams MS. Fall 1793.
14. *Works*, I, p. 462. January 9, 1794.
15. Adams MS. November 1795.
16. *Ibid.*, 1796.
17. Cranch MS.
18. *Ibid.*
19. Adams MS. February 1793.

CHAPTER XIV

1. Adams MS. February 1798.
2. *Ibid.*, May 1796.
3. *Ibid.*, Spring 1796.
4. *Ibid.*, Spring 1796.
5. *Ibid.*, Spring 1796.
6. *Ibid.*, February 1797.
7. *Letters of Mrs. Adams*, p. 374.
8. Adams MS. March 5, 1797.
9. *Letters of Mrs. Adams*, p. 377.

CHAPTER XV

1. *Works*, I, p. 494.
2. Cranch MS. April 1797.
3. *Ibid.*, May 5, 1797, and later.
4. *Ibid.*, May 1797.
5. Smith-Carter MS. Mrs. Sam Otis to Mrs. Wm. Smith, March 30, 1798.
6. Cranch MS. June 23, 1797.
7. *Ibid.*, June 1797.

8. Adams MS. November 3, 1797.
9. *Ibid.*, Abigail Adams to John Quincy Adams, November 23, 1797, Philadelphia.
10. *Ibid.*, November 3, 1797.
11. Cranch MS. October 31, 1797.
12. Smith-Carter MS. March 5, 1798.
13. Cranch MS. December 1797.
14. *Ibid.*, April 26 and 28, and May 7, 1798.
15. *Ibid.*, April 26, 1798.
16. Smith-Carter MS.
17. *Autobiography of Thomas Jefferson*, ed. Paul L. Ford, New York, 1914, III, pp. 309–310.
18. Smith-Carter MS. June 19, 1798.
19. *Ibid.*, July 1798.
20. *Ibid.*, March and June 1798.
21. *Ibid.*, Letter from Sam Otis, April 3, 1798.
22. Adams MS. Letter to John Quincy Adams, July 14, 1798. Also, "Capt. Decatur has captured a 12 gun French privateer and brought her into this port." July 20, 1798.
23. *Ibid.*, July 14, 1798. Letter to John Quincy Adams.
24. Smith-Carter MS. July 1798.
25. *Ibid.*, Sam Otis to W. S. July 21, 1798.

CHAPTER XVI

1. Adams MS. July 1798.
2. *Ibid.*, Letter to John Quincy Adams.
3. Smith-Carter MS. July 1798.
4. Adams MS. April 1798.
5. *Ibid.*, July 14, 1798. Abigail's youngest sister, Betsey.
6. *Ibid.*, 1798.
7. *Works*, I, p. 541.
8. *Ibid.*, p. 547.
9. *Ibid.*, p. 545.
10. Smith-Carter MS. January 2, 1799.
11. Adams MS. 1796.
12. *Ibid.*, June 12, 1799. To John Quincy Adams.
13. *Ibid.*, February 1799.
14. *Figures of the Past*, Josiah Quincy, Roberts Brothers, Boston, 1892.

15. Smith-Carter MS. April 30, 1800. Hannah Smith.
16. Smith-Townsend MS. Letter of William Shaw to William Smith, January 1800.
17. *Ibid.*, January 1800.
18. *Ibid.*, March 1800.

CHAPTER XVII

1. Adams MS.
2. Bobbé, p. 238.
3. Cranch MS. December 8, 1800, and Adams MS. Letters to John Quincy Adams, January 29 and May 30, 1801.
4. *Letters of Mrs. Adams*, p. 380.
5. *Ibid.*, p. 386.
6. Adams MS. May 30, 1801.
7. *Letters of Mrs. Adams*, pp. 389–390.
8. *Jefferson's Letters*, pp. 143–144.
9. *Letters of Mrs. Adams*, pp. 390–394.
10. *Jefferson's Letters*, pp. 147–149.
11. *Letters*, pp. 394–396.
12. *Jefferson's Letters*, pp. 150–151. September 11, 1804.
13. *Letters of Mrs. Adams*, pp. 396–398.
14. *Ibid.*, p. 398.
15. *Jefferson*, Saul K. Padover, New York, 1942, p. 367.
16. *Ibid.*, p. 367.

CHAPTER XVIII

1. *Letters of Mrs. Adams*, p. 408.
2. Adams MS. August 1813.
3. *Ibid.*, July 1813.
4. Smith-Carter MS. August 7, 1816.
5. Adams MS. Letter from Abigail Adams to Harriet Welch, August 18, 1817.
6. *Ibid.* John Quincy Adams's MS. Diary, August 18, 1817.

A Comment on Sources

Two valuable collections of Abigail Adams Letters have been published (and edited) by her grandson, Charles Francis Adams, and have long been known to the public. The Smith-Carter, the Smith-Townsend, and the de Windt manuscript collections, in the care of the Massachusetts Historical Society in Boston, furnish others, as well as valuable correspondence of many family connections.

In addition to these, and the printed *Diary*, letters, and public papers of John Adams, I have been privileged to use three new sources of material, hitherto untapped.

The first and most important of these is the great collection known as the Adams Manuscript, privately owned by the Adams family.

The second is the recently discovered Adams collection of several hundred letters, including some two hundred written by Abigail Adams to her favorite sister, Mary Cranch, during the twelve years of John Adams's Vice-Presidency and Presidency. This collection is owned by the American Antiquarian Society, and I am gratefully indebted to them for their generous treatment. To avoid confusion with the Adams Manuscript and Adams letters referred to by me, I have referred to this as the Cranch MS.

The third is the Thaxter manuscript, a small collection of (twenty-five) letters written by Abigail Adams to John Thaxter, a young cousin who was a law pupil of John Adams, and who was for a time tutor to the Adams children, and went abroad as John Adams's secretary when he went to negotiate the peace. This interesting group of letters has been recently acquired by the Boston Public Library.

John Adams was often a center of controversy. His wife was always on his side. Though this in itself is a tribute to him, there is a risk in it to one who wishes to practice fair play.

I have taken pains to let Mr. Adams's outstanding opponents — Mr. Hutchinson, Dr. Franklin, Mr. Hamilton, and Mr. Jefferson — state their own case, and have read such histories, autobiographies, diaries, or letters as they may have left behind, with, I hope, an open mind.

In the pages of this book, when they speak, they at least speak for themselves.

AND ON FORM

George M. Trevelyan has said, "The poetry of History does not consist of imagination roaming at large, but of imagination pursuing the fact and fastening upon it." But in using imagination as a hunting dog or as a tool, how avoid the pitfalls of that horrid hybrid, "fictionized biography"?

My own method is to feel free to express the abstract by the concrete (a girl is feeling shy, then let her go through the motions of a shy girl) and to express "indirect speech" reported in a letter or journal by "direct speech" in dramatic form. But I do not feel free to make up an emotion which I am not *certain* was experienced by my subject, or to make up anything supposedly said or thought (no matter how appropriate).

Every sentence of dialogue in these pages attributed to any historical character is taken with little or no change from an authentic written source.

J. P. W.

Principal Manuscript Sources

The Adams Manuscript — in care of the trustees of the Adams Trust, Mr. Charles Francis Adams and Mr. Henry Adams.

The Cranch Manuscript (the Adams Letters) — owned by the American Antiquarian Society.

The Thaxter Manuscript — owned by the Boston Public Library.

The Smith-Townsend Manuscript collection — owned by the Massachusetts Historical Society.

The Smith-Carter Manuscript collection — owned by the Massachusetts Historical Society.

The de Windt Manuscript collection — owned by the Massachusetts Historical Society.

The Manuscript Diary of Parson Smith — owned by the Massachusetts Historical Society.

The Sparkes Manuscript — owned by the Houghton Library, Harvard University.

The Tudor Manuscript — owned by the Massachusetts Historical Society.

Principal Books and Publications
Read and Consulted

Adams, *Familiar Letters of John Adams and His Wife Abigail Adams during the Revolution.* Edited by Charles Francis Adams. Boston, 1876.

Adams, *Journal and Correspondence of Miss Adams.* Edited by her daughter. New York, 1841.

Adams, *Letters of Mrs. Adams the Wife of John Adams.* Edited by Charles Francis Adams. Boston, 1848.

Adams, *The Works of John Adams.* Edited by Charles Francis Adams (8 vols.). Boston, 1856.

Adams, Charles Francis, *Three Episodes of Massachusetts History* (2 vols.). Boston, 1893.

Adams, Henry, *History of the United States.* (9 vols.). New York, 1903. I–IV.

Adams, James Truslow, *The Living Jefferson.* Boston, 1936.

Adams, John Quincy, *The Diary of John Quincy Adams 1794–1845.* Edited by Allan Nevins. New York, 1929.

Adams, John Quincy and Charles Francis, *Life of John Adams* (2 vols.). Philadelphia, 1871.

Bancroft, George, *History of the United States* (6 vols.). Boston, 1876.

Beard, Charles A. and Mary R., *A Basic History of the United States.* New York, 1944.

Bobbé, Dorothie, *Mr. and Mrs. John Quincy Adams.* New York, 1930.

Bolton, Charles Knowles, *The Private Soldier under Washington.* New York, 1902.

Boston under Military Rule (1768–1769). A Journal of the Times compiled by Oliver Morton Dickerson. Boston.

Bowen, A., *A History of Boston, the Metropolis of Massachusetts, from its Origin to the Present Period,* 2nd ed. Boston, 1828.

Bowers, Claude G., *Jefferson in Power.* Boston, 1936.

—— *The Young Jefferson.* Boston, 1945.

Bridenbaugh, Carl, *Cities in the Wilderness*. New York, 1938.

Burney, *Journal of Fanny Burney*. See d'Arblay.

Correspondence of William Pitt, Earl of Chatham (4 vols.). Edited by W. S. Taylor and J. H. Pringle. London, 1838–1840.

Craik & Macfarlane, *The Pictorial History of England* (8 vols.). London, 1849.

Dickinson, John, *Letters from a Farmer in Pennsylvania to the Inhabitants of the British Colonies*. Boston, 1768.

D'Arblay, *Diary and Letters of Madame D'Arblay* (7 vols.). Edited by her niece. London, 1842.

Fitzgerald, Percy, *The Good Queen Charlotte*. London, 1899.

Franklin, Benjamin, *The Autobiography of Benjamin Franklin*. New York, 1939.

—— *Memoirs and Writings of Benjamin Franklin*. Parsons, London, 1793.

Gordon, William, *The History of the Rise, Progress and Establishment of Independence of the United States of America* (3 vols.). New York, 1789.

Hancock, *John Hancock His Book*. Edited by Abram English Brown. Boston, 1898.

Hicks, Frederick C., *The Flag of the United States*. Washington, 1926.

Hosmer, James K., *Life of Thomas Hutchinson*. Boston, 1896.

—— *Samuel Adams*. Boston, 1893.

Hutchinson, *The History of the Province of Massachusetts Bay* (3 vols.). London, 1828.

Jefferson, Thomas, *Autobiography of Thomas Jefferson*. Edited by Paul L. Ford. New York, 1914.

—— *Life and Selected Writings of Thomas Jefferson*. Edited by Adrienne Koch and William Peden. New York, 1944.

Jesse, J. Heneage, *Memoirs of the Life and Reign of King George III*. London, 1867.

Maclay, William, *Journal of William Maclay*. New York, 1890.

Miller, John C., *Origins of the American Revolution*. Boston, 1943.

Monaghan, Frank, *John Jay, Defender of Liberty*. New York, 1935.

Morse, John T., *Benjamin Franklin*. Boston, 1896.

Muzzey, David Saville, *Thomas Jefferson*. New York, 1918.

Padover, Saul K., *Jefferson*. New York, 1942.

Pattee, William S., *History of Old Braintree and Quincy*. 1878.

Pellew, George, *John Jay*. Edited by John T. Morse. Boston, 1890.

Prussing, Eugene E., *George Washington in Love and Otherwise*. Chicago, 1925.

Quincy, *Memoir of the Life of Josiah Quincy*. By his son. Boston, 1874.

Quincy, Josiah, *Figures of the Past*. Roberts Brothers, Boston, 1892.

Roof, Katharine Metcalf, *Colonel William Smith and Lady*. Boston, 1929.

Sparkes, Jared, *The Life and Treason of Benedict Arnold*. Boston, 1839.

Statesman and Friend, Correspondence of John Adams with Benjamin Waterhouse. Edited by Worthington Chauncey Ford. Boston, 1927.

Sumner, William Graham, *Alexander Hamilton*. New York, 1890.

Tudor, William, *Life of James Otis*. Boston, 1823.

Tyler, Mary Palmer, *Grandmother Tyler's Book*. Edited by Frederick Tupper and Helen Tyler Brown. New York, 1925.

Van Doren, Carl, *Benjamin Franklin*. New York, 1938.

Warren, Charles, *Adams Letters 1743–1814* (2 vols.). Massachusetts Historical Society, 1917.

—— *Odd Byways in American History*. Cambridge, 1942.

Wharton, Anne Hollingsworth, *Martha Washington*. New York, 1897.

Whitlock, Brand, *LaFayette* (2 vols.). New York, 1929.

Wilson, Daniel M., *Colonel John Quincy*. 1908.

—— *Three Hundred Years of Quincy*. Boston, 1926.

—— *Where American Independence was Born*. Boston, 1902.

Index

Index